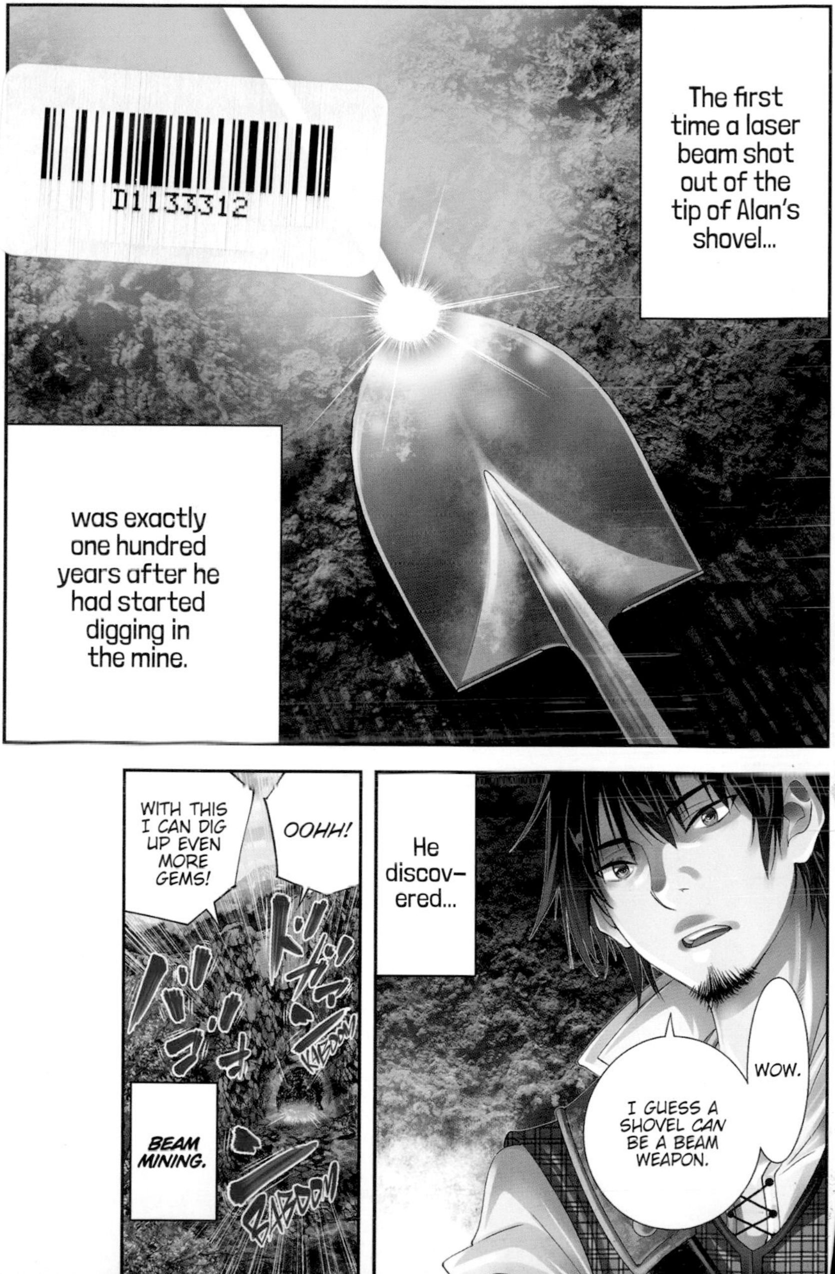
The first time a laser beam shot out of the tip of Alan's shovel...
was exactly one hundred years after he had started digging in the mine.
He discovered...
WOW.
I GUESS A SHOVEL CAN BE A BEAM WEAPON.
OOHH!
WITH THIS I CAN DIG UP EVEN MORE GEMS!
KABOOM
BEAM MINING.
BABOOM

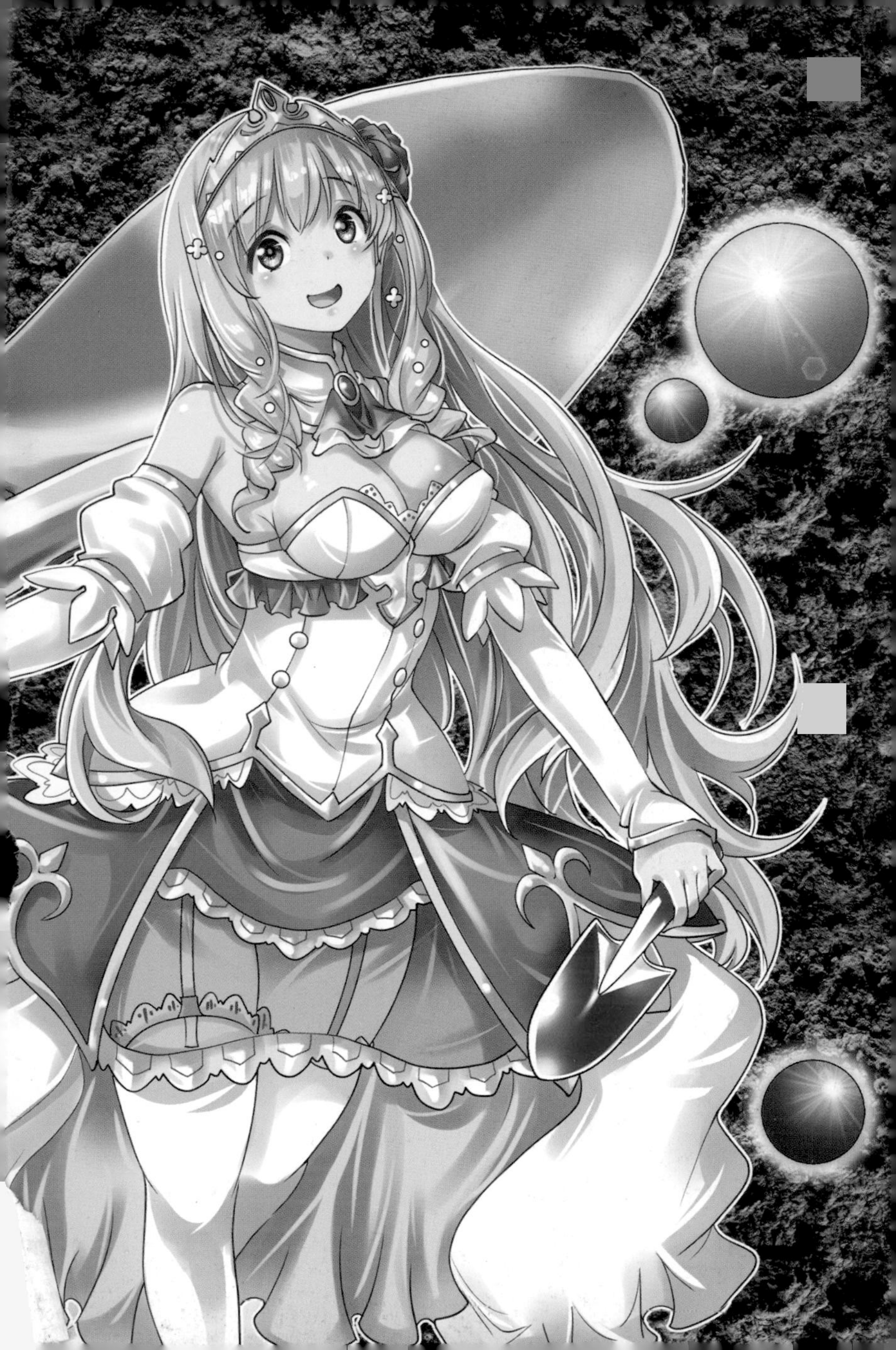

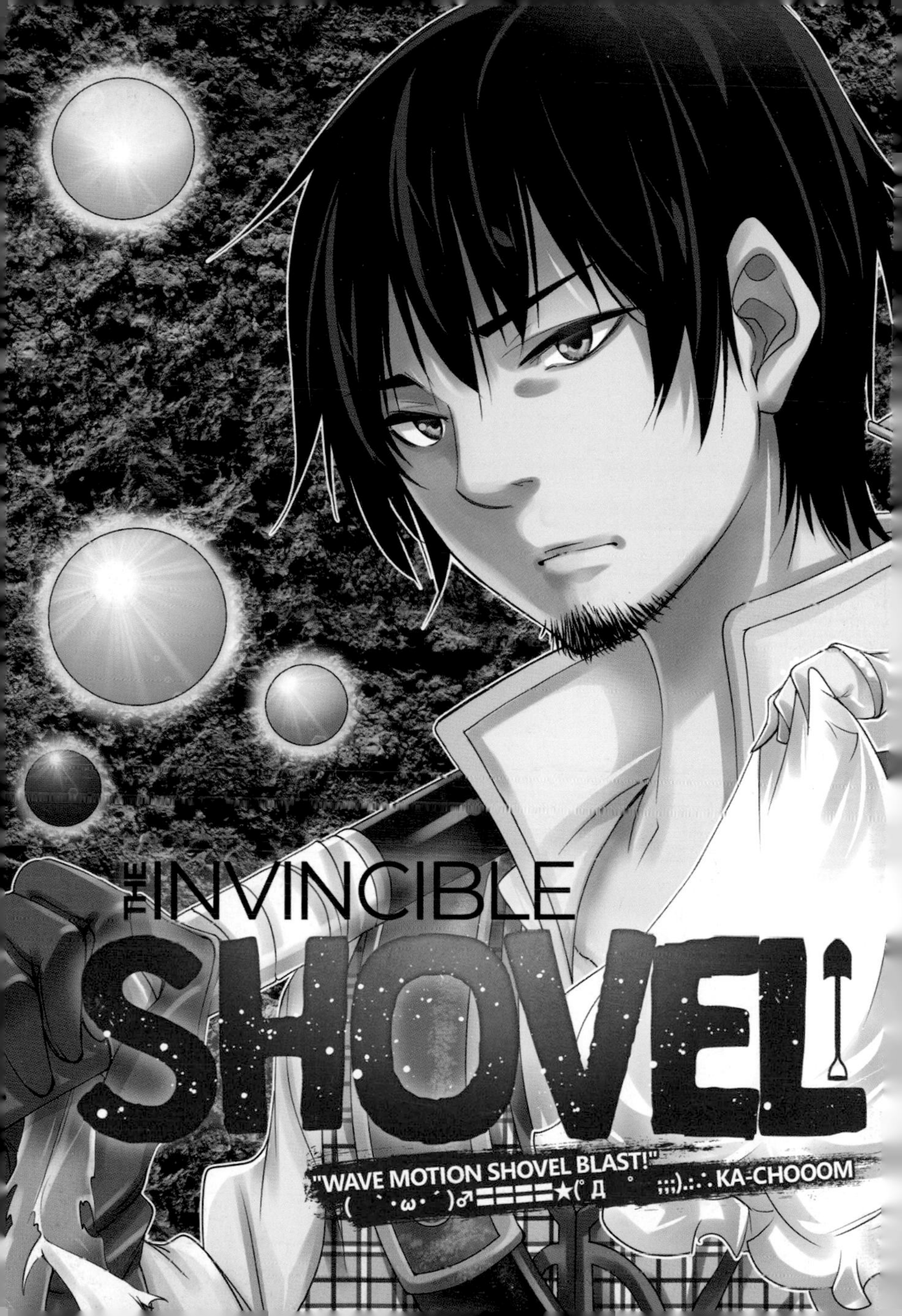
THE INVINCIBLE SHOVEL
"WAVE MOTION SHOVEL BLAST!"
(`・ω・´)♂=====★(゜Д ゜ ;;;).:∴ KA-CHOOOM

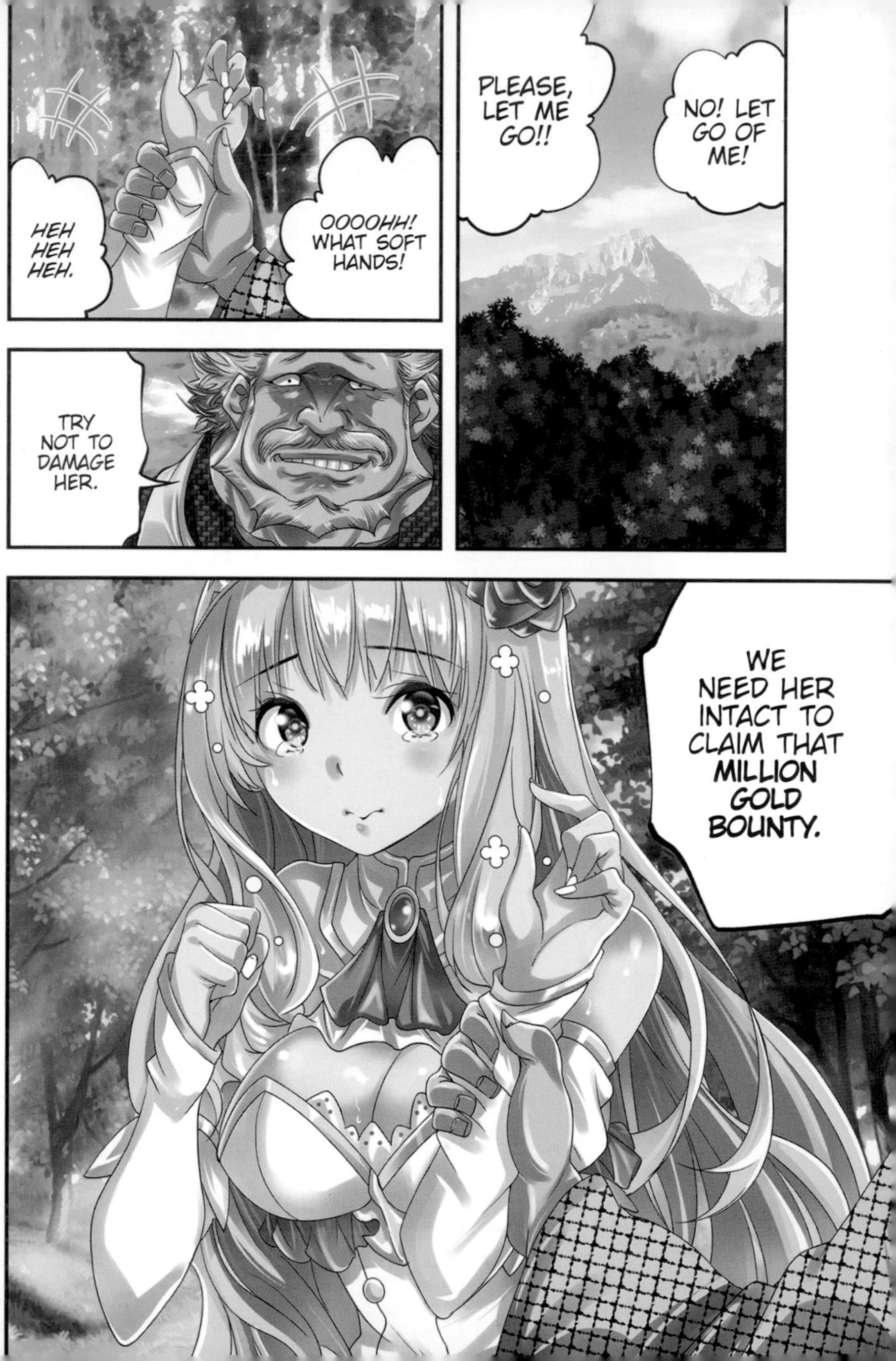
NO! LET GO OF ME!
PLEASE, LET ME GO!!
OOOOHH! WHAT SOFT HANDS!
HEH HEH HEH.
TRY NOT TO DAMAGE HER.
WE NEED HER INTACT TO CLAIM THAT **MILLION GOLD BOUNTY.**

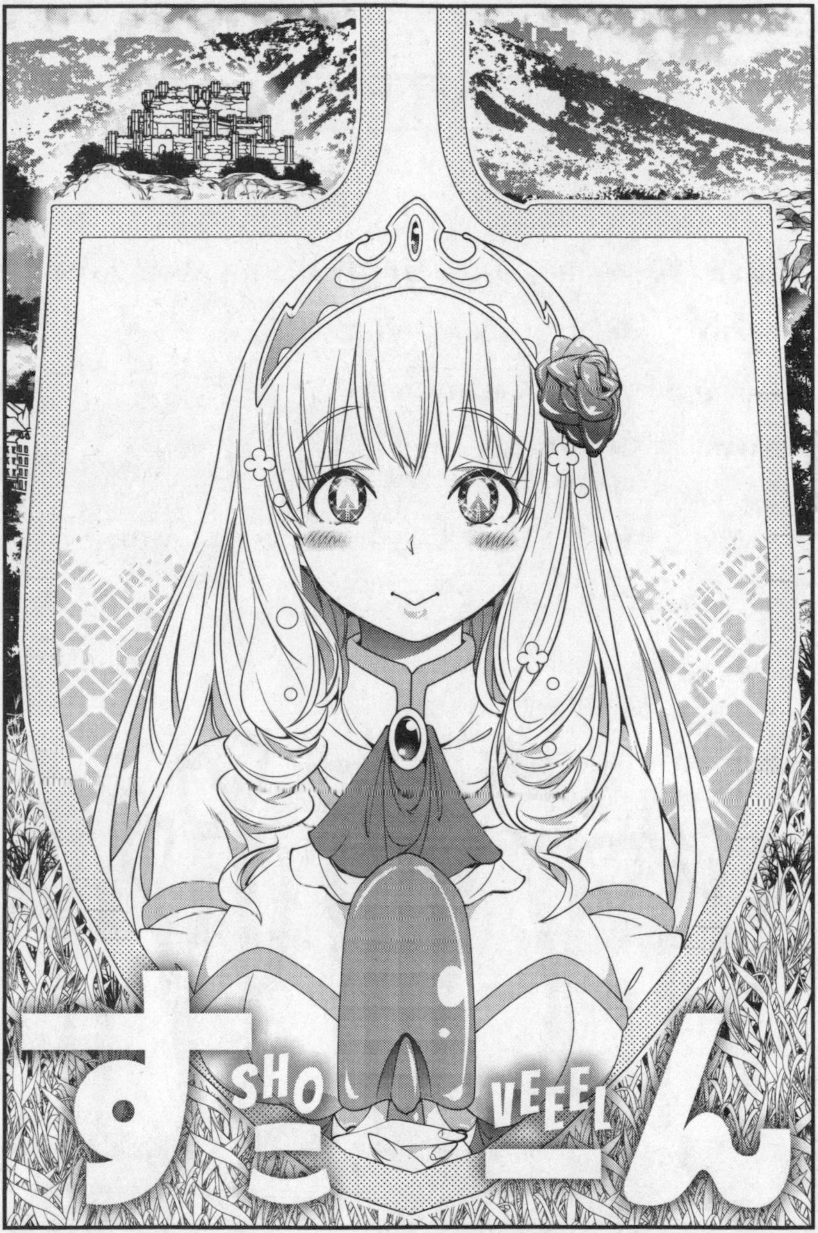
すこーん
SHOVEEEL

CONTENTS

DESIGN: YUUKO MUCADEYA + HIDEYUKI UEKUSA (MUSICAGO GRAPHICS)

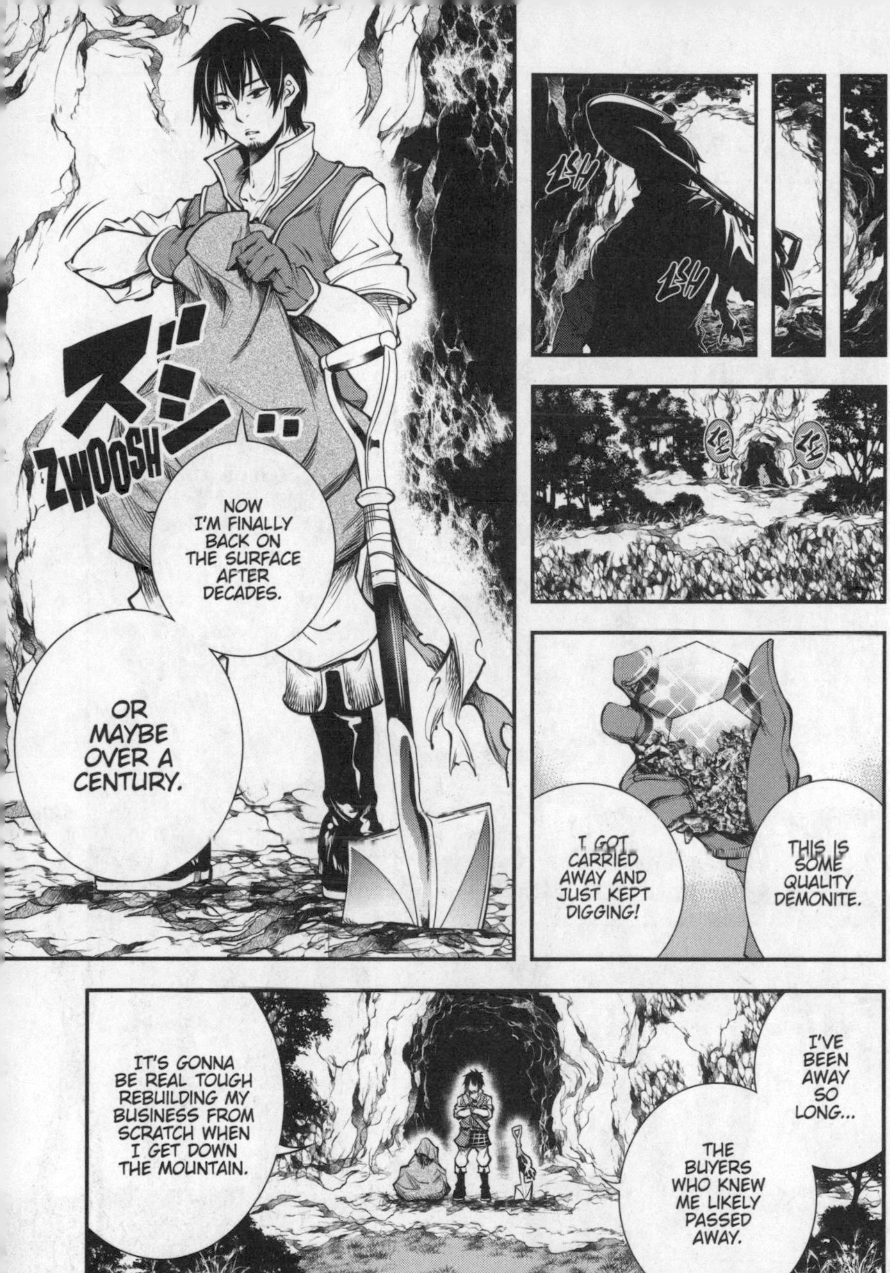
ZSH
ZSH
ZSH
ZSH
THIS IS SOME QUALITY DEMONITE.
I GOT CARRIED AWAY AND JUST KEPT DIGGING!
ズシーン..
ZWOOSH
NOW I'M FINALLY BACK ON THE SURFACE AFTER DECADES.
OR MAYBE OVER A CENTURY.
I'VE BEEN AWAY SO LONG...
THE BUYERS WHO KNEW ME LIKELY PASSED AWAY.
IT'S GONNA BE REAL TOUGH REBUILDING MY BUSINESS FROM SCRATCH WHEN I GET DOWN THE MOUNTAIN.

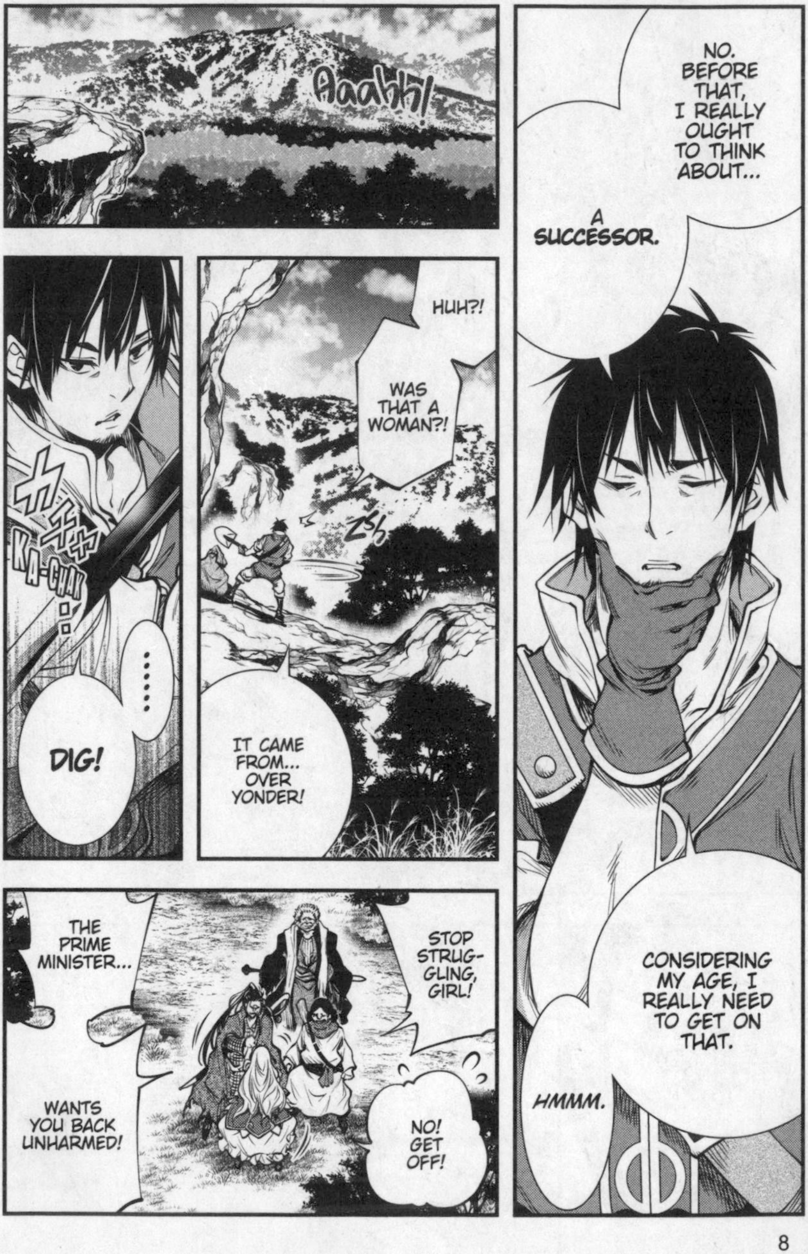
NO. BEFORE THAT, I REALLY OUGHT TO THINK ABOUT...
A SUCCESSOR.
CONSIDERING MY AGE, I REALLY NEED TO GET ON THAT.
HMMM.
Aaahh!
HUH?!
WAS THAT A WOMAN?!
IT CAME FROM... OVER YONDER!
KA-CHAK
......
DIG!
STOP STRUG-GLING, GIRL!
NO! GET OFF!
THE PRIME MINISTER...
WANTS YOU BACK UNHARMED!

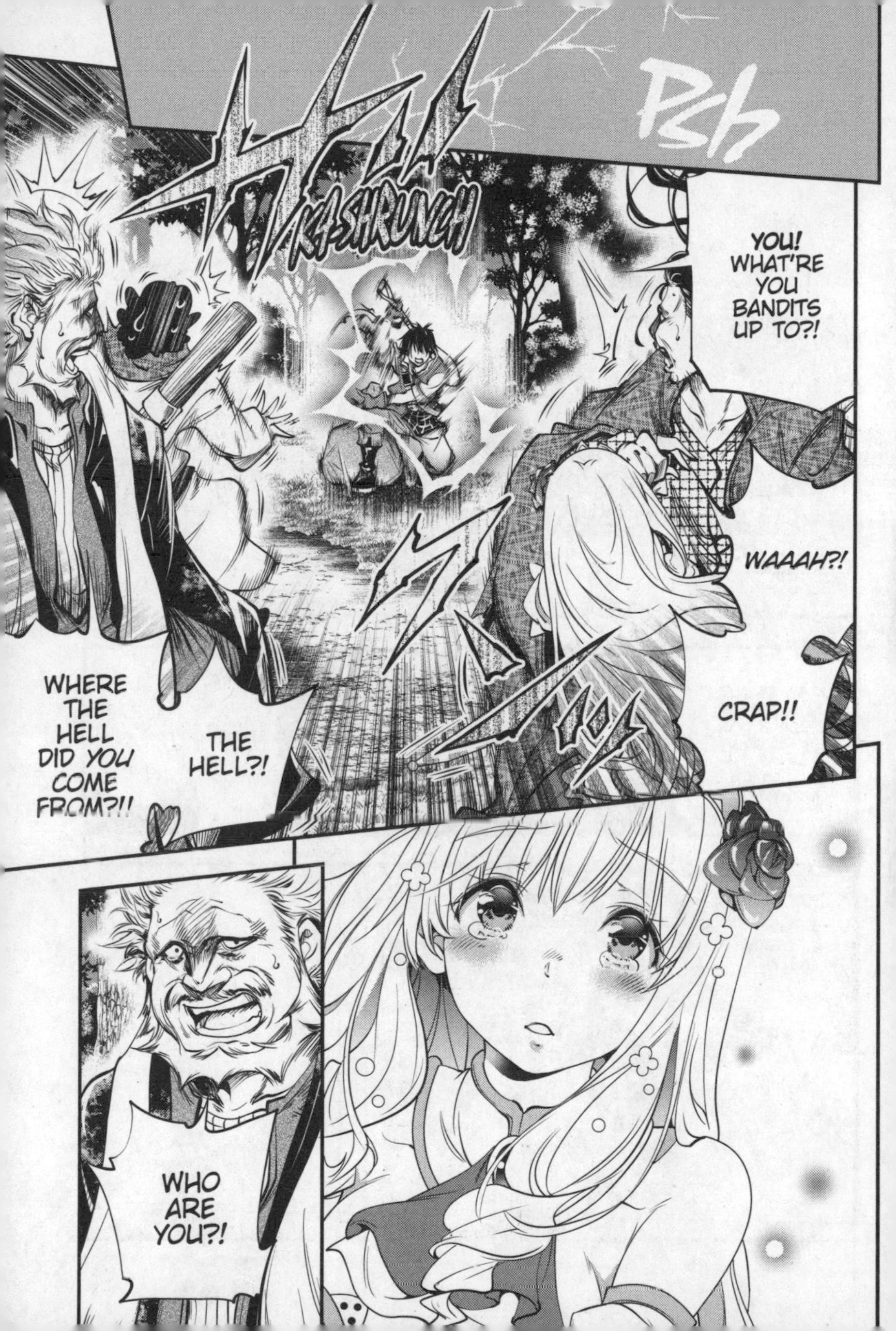
Psh
KASHRUNCH
YOU! WHAT'RE YOU BANDITS UP TO?!
WAAAH?!
CRAP!!
THE HELL?!
WHERE THE HELL DID YOU COME FROM?!!
WHO ARE YOU?!

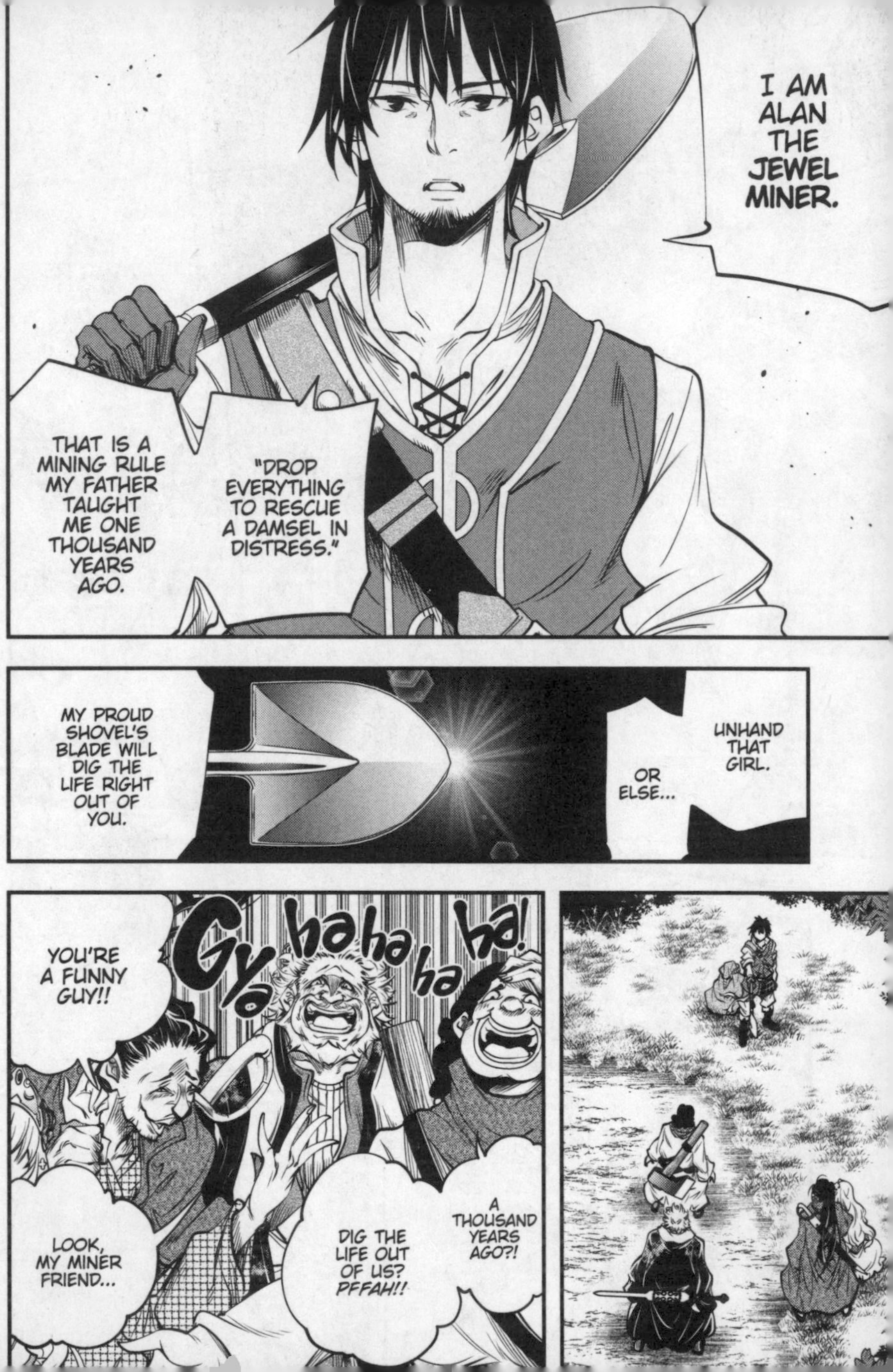
I AM ALAN THE JEWEL MINER.
"DROP EVERYTHING TO RESCUE A DAMSEL IN DISTRESS."
THAT IS A MINING RULE MY FATHER TAUGHT ME ONE THOUSAND YEARS AGO.
UNHAND THAT GIRL.
OR ELSE...
MY PROUD SHOVEL'S BLADE WILL DIG THE LIFE RIGHT OUT OF YOU.
Gya ha ha ha ha!
YOU'RE A FUNNY GUY!!
A THOUSAND YEARS AGO?!
DIG THE LIFE OUT OF US? PFFAH!!
LOOK, MY MINER FRIEND...

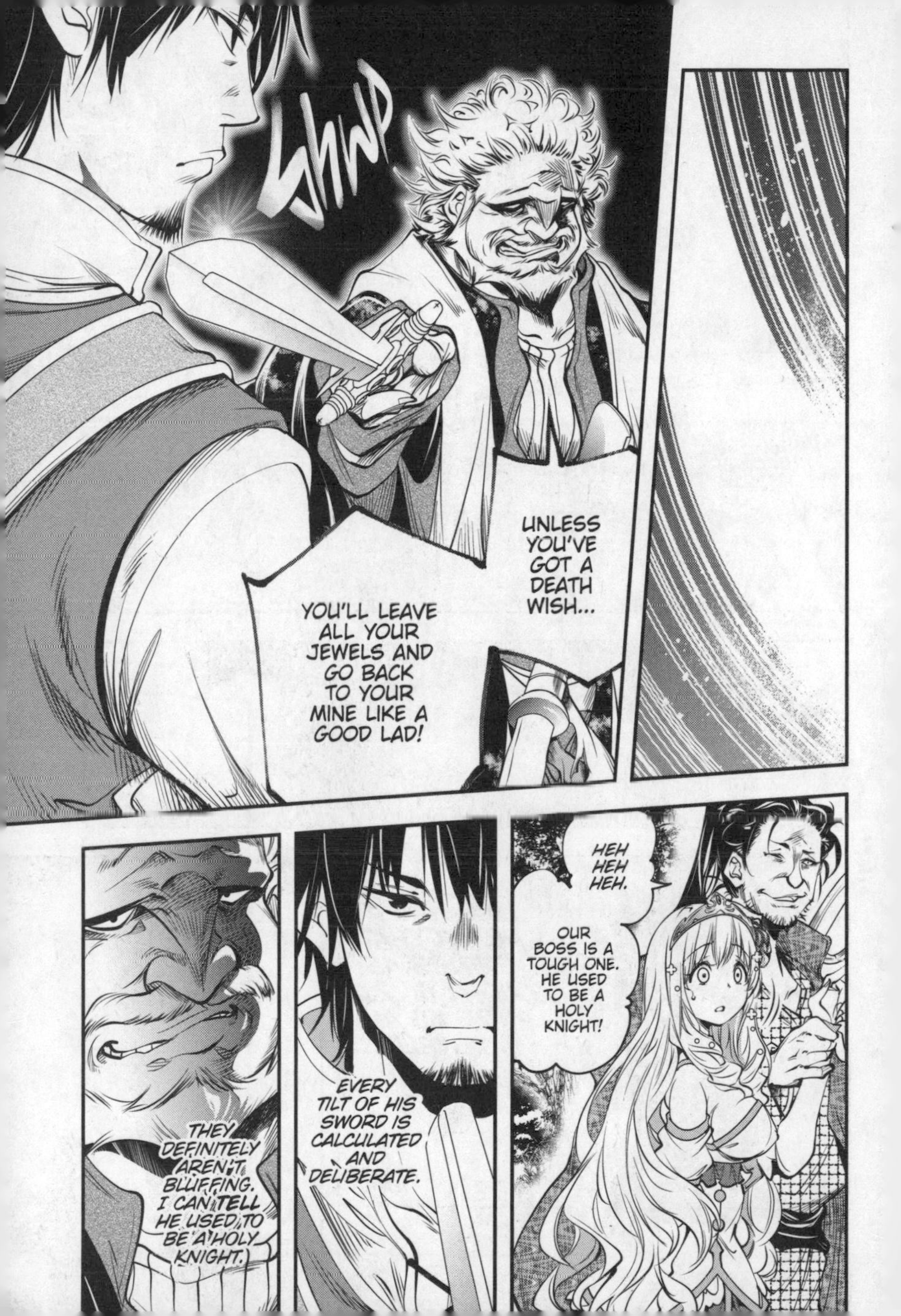
SHWP
UNLESS YOU'VE GOT A DEATH WISH...
YOU'LL LEAVE ALL YOUR JEWELS AND GO BACK TO YOUR MINE LIKE A GOOD LAD!
HEH HEH HEH.
OUR BOSS IS A TOUGH ONE. HE USED TO BE A HOLY KNIGHT!
EVERY TILT OF HIS SWORD IS CALCULATED AND DELIBERATE.
THEY DEFINITELY AREN'T BLUFFING. I CAN TELL HE USED TO BE A HOLY KNIGHT.

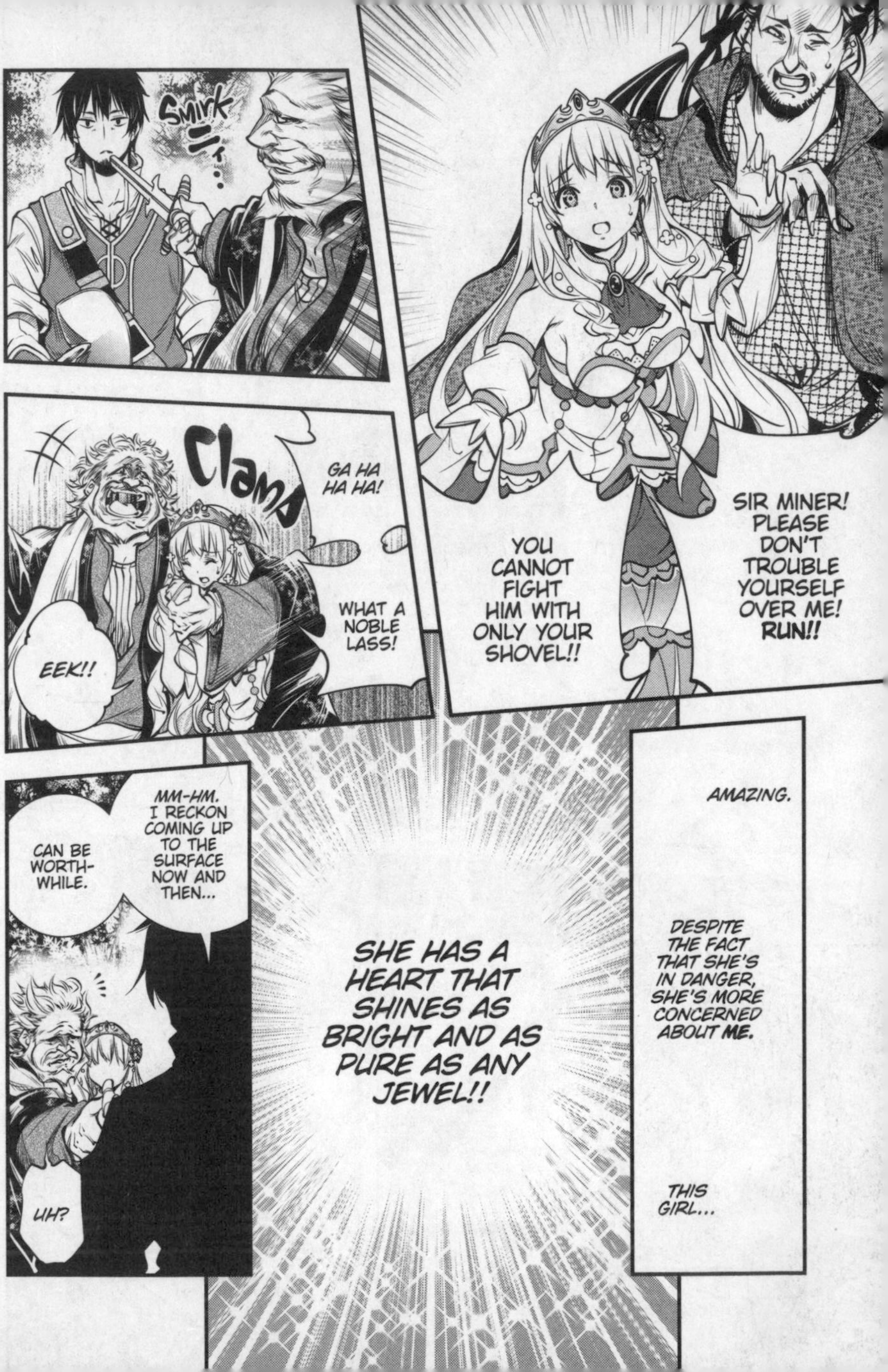
SIR MINER! PLEASE DON'T TROUBLE YOURSELF OVER ME! RUN!!
YOU CANNOT FIGHT HIM WITH ONLY YOUR SHOVEL!!
Smirk
ニィ…
Clamp
GA HA HA HA!
WHAT A NOBLE LASS!
EEK!!
AMAZING.
DESPITE THE FACT THAT SHE'S IN DANGER, SHE'S MORE CONCERNED ABOUT ME.
THIS GIRL...
SHE HAS A HEART THAT SHINES AS BRIGHT AND AS PURE AS ANY JEWEL!!
MM-HM. I RECKON COMING UP TO THE SURFACE NOW AND THEN...
CAN BE WORTH-WHILE.
UH?

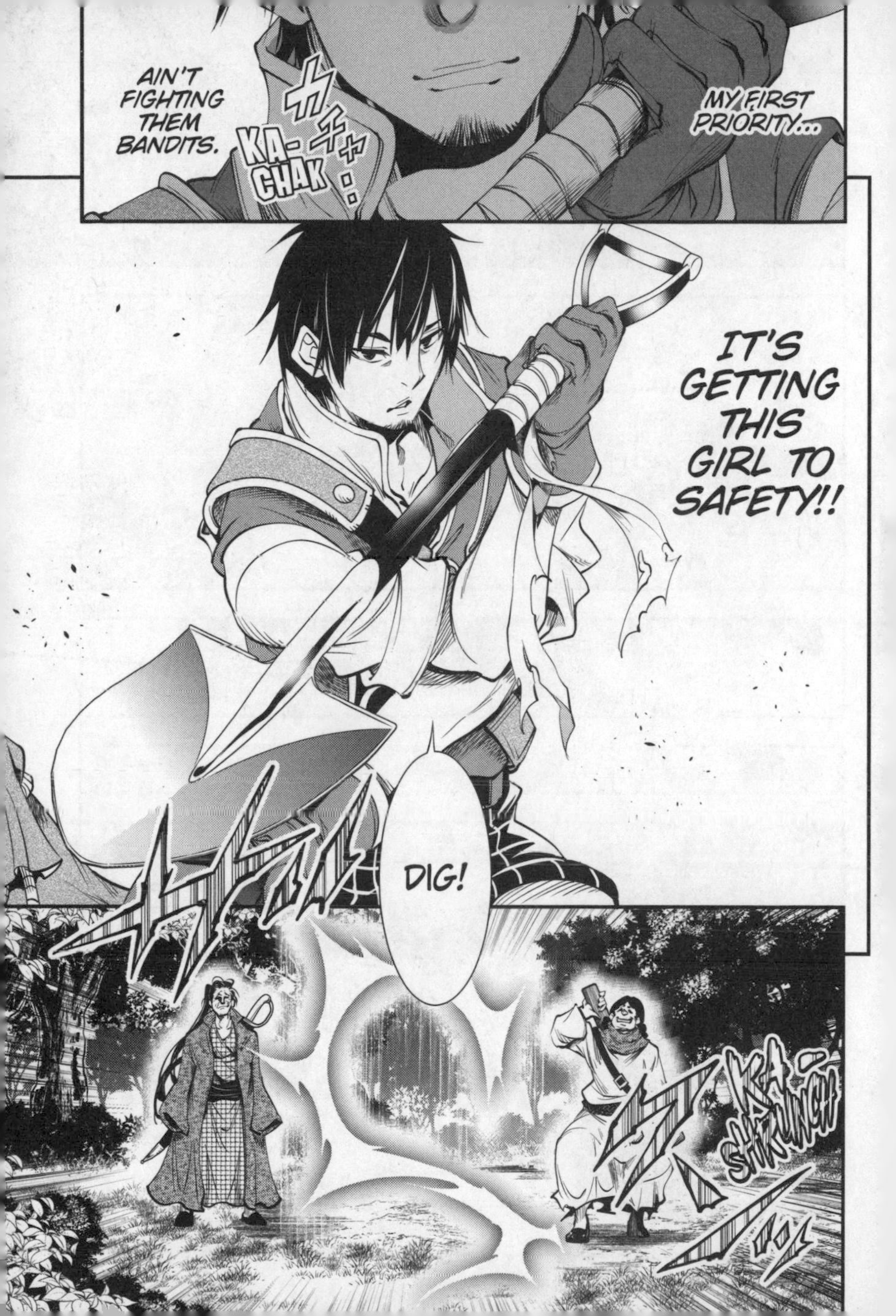
MY FIRST PRIORITY...
KA-CHAK
AIN'T FIGHTING THEM BANDITS.
IT'S GETTING THIS GIRL TO SAFETY!!
DIG!
KA-SHRUNCH

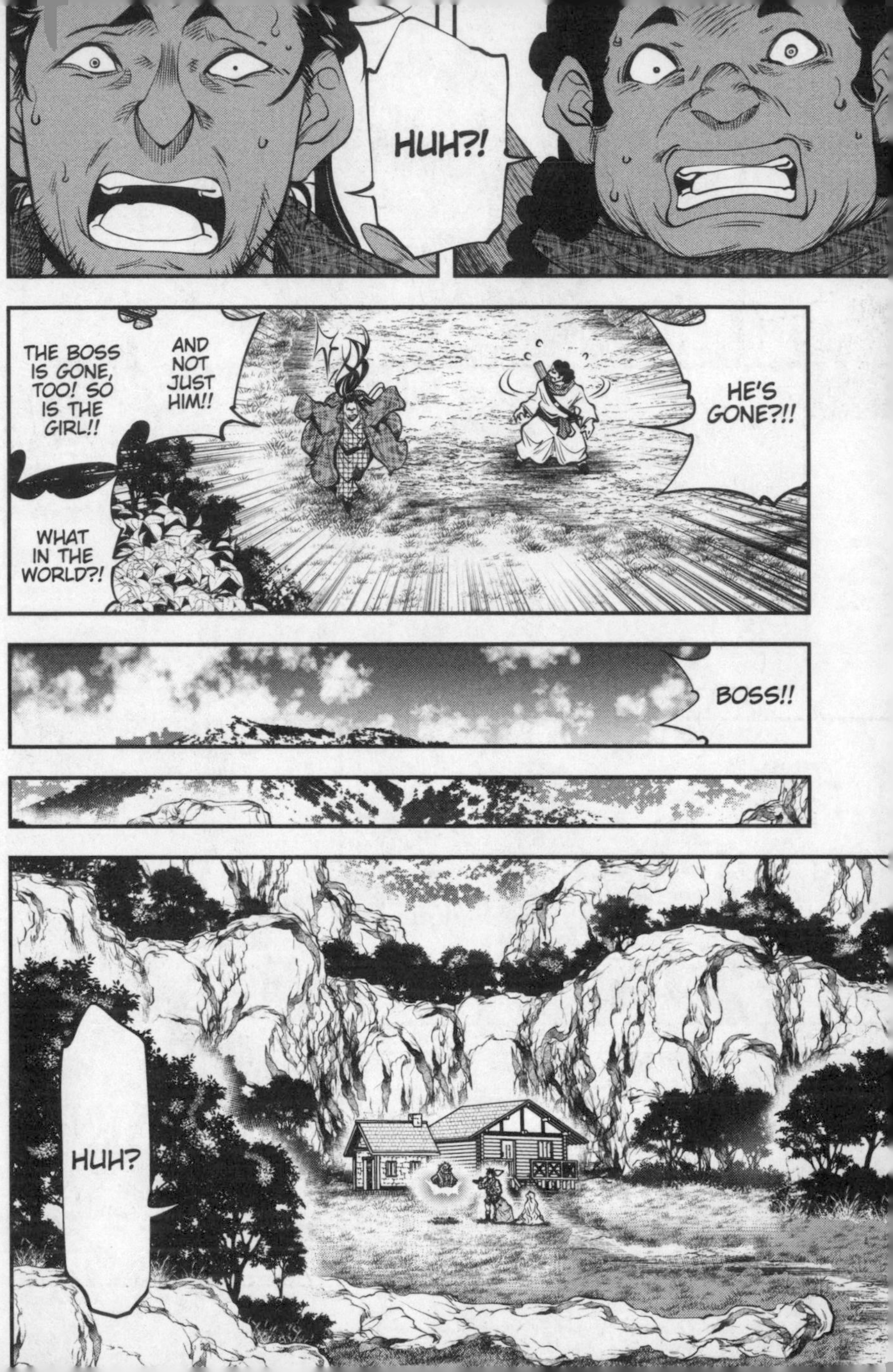
HUH?!
HE'S GONE?!!
AND NOT JUST HIM!!
THE BOSS IS GONE, TOO! SO IS THE GIRL!!
WHAT IN THE WORLD?!
BOSS!!
HUH?

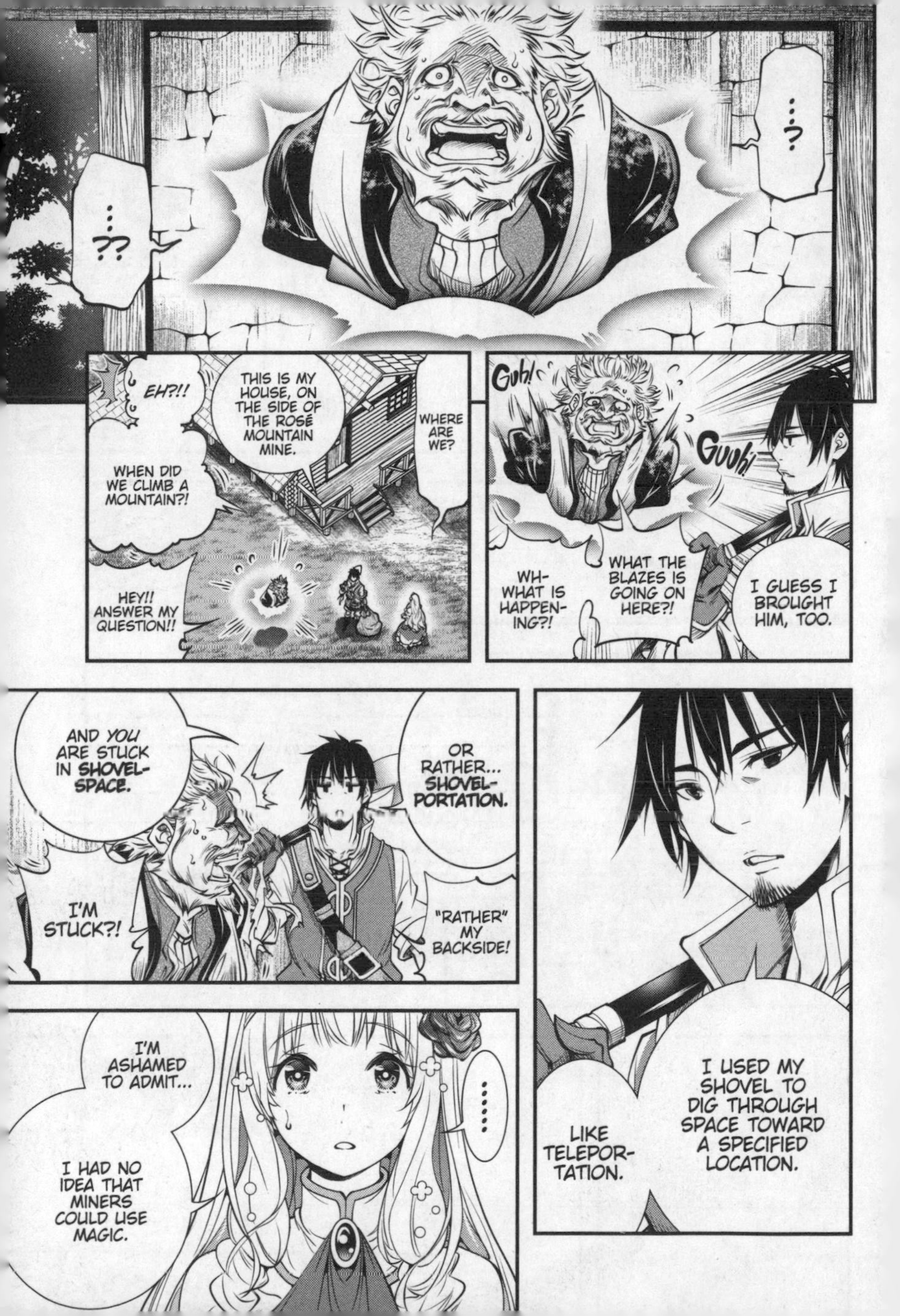
...?
...??
GUUH!
GUH!
I GUESS I BROUGHT HIM, TOO.
WHAT THE BLAZES IS GOING ON HERE?!
WH- WHAT IS HAPPENING?!
WHERE ARE WE?
THIS IS MY HOUSE, ON THE SIDE OF THE ROSÉ MOUNTAIN MINE.
EH?!!
WHEN DID WE CLIMB A MOUNTAIN?!
HEY!! ANSWER MY QUESTION!!
I USED MY SHOVEL TO DIG THROUGH SPACE TOWARD A SPECIFIED LOCATION.
LIKE TELEPORTATION.
OR RATHER... SHOVEL-PORTATION.
AND YOU ARE STUCK IN SHOVEL-SPACE.
"RATHER" MY BACKSIDE!
I'M STUCK?!
......
I'M ASHAMED TO ADMIT...
I HAD NO IDEA THAT MINERS COULD USE MAGIC.

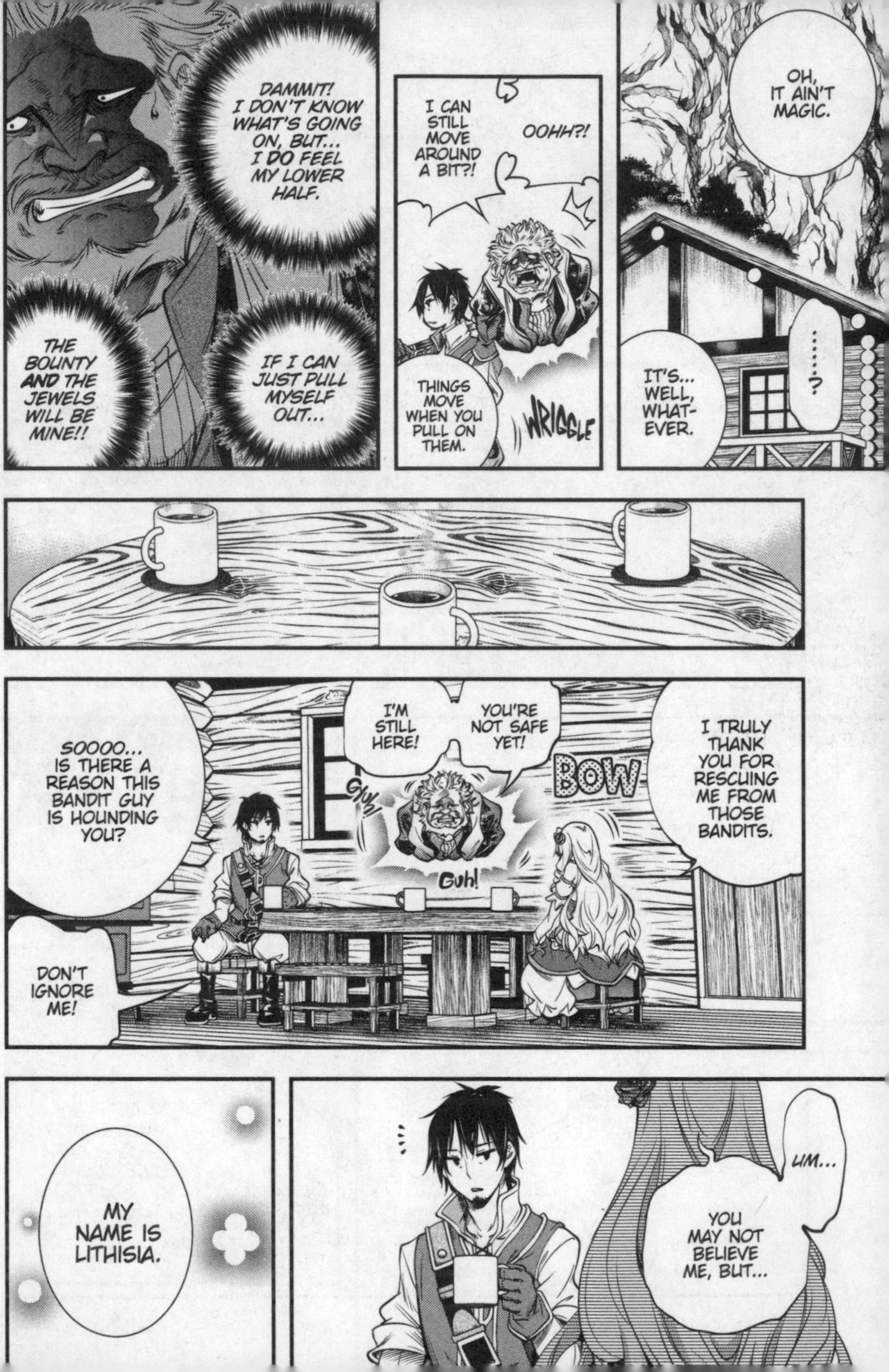
OH, IT AIN'T MAGIC.
......?
IT'S... WELL, WHAT-EVER.
OOHH?!
I CAN STILL MOVE AROUND A BIT?!
THINGS MOVE WHEN YOU PULL ON THEM.
WRIGGLE
DAMMIT! I DON'T KNOW WHAT'S GOING ON, BUT... I DO FEEL MY LOWER HALF.
IF I CAN JUST PULL MYSELF OUT...
THE BOUNTY AND THE JEWELS WILL BE MINE!!
I TRULY THANK YOU FOR RESCUING ME FROM THOSE BANDITS.
BOW
YOU'RE NOT SAFE YET!
I'M STILL HERE!
GYU
Guh!
SOOOO... IS THERE A REASON THIS BANDIT GUY IS HOUNDING YOU?
DON'T IGNORE ME!
UM...
YOU MAY NOT BELIEVE ME, BUT...
MY NAME IS LITHISIA.

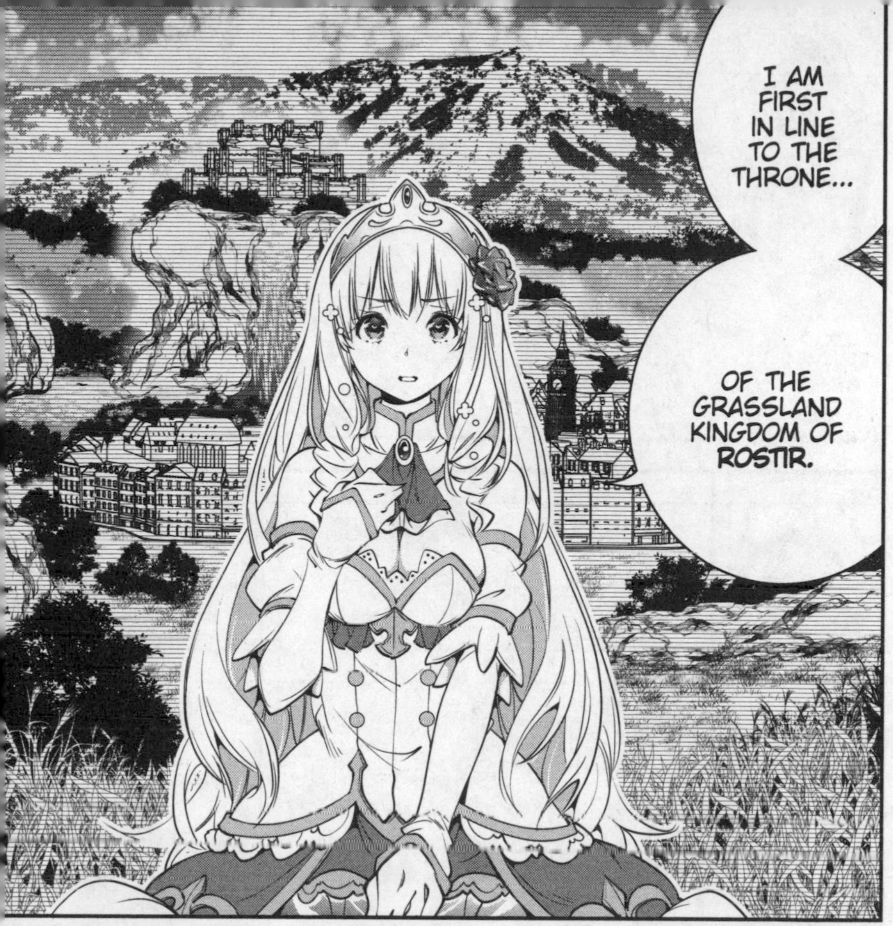
I AM FIRST IN LINE TO THE THRONE...
OF THE GRASSLAND KINGDOM OF ROSTIR.

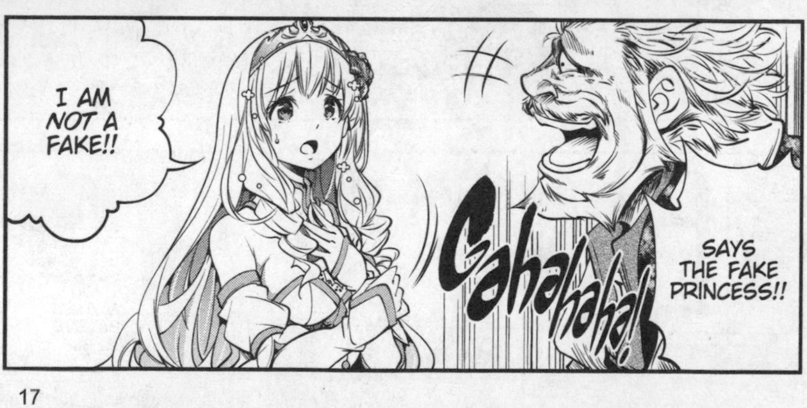
I AM NOT A FAKE!!
Gahahaha!
SAYS THE FAKE PRINCESS!!

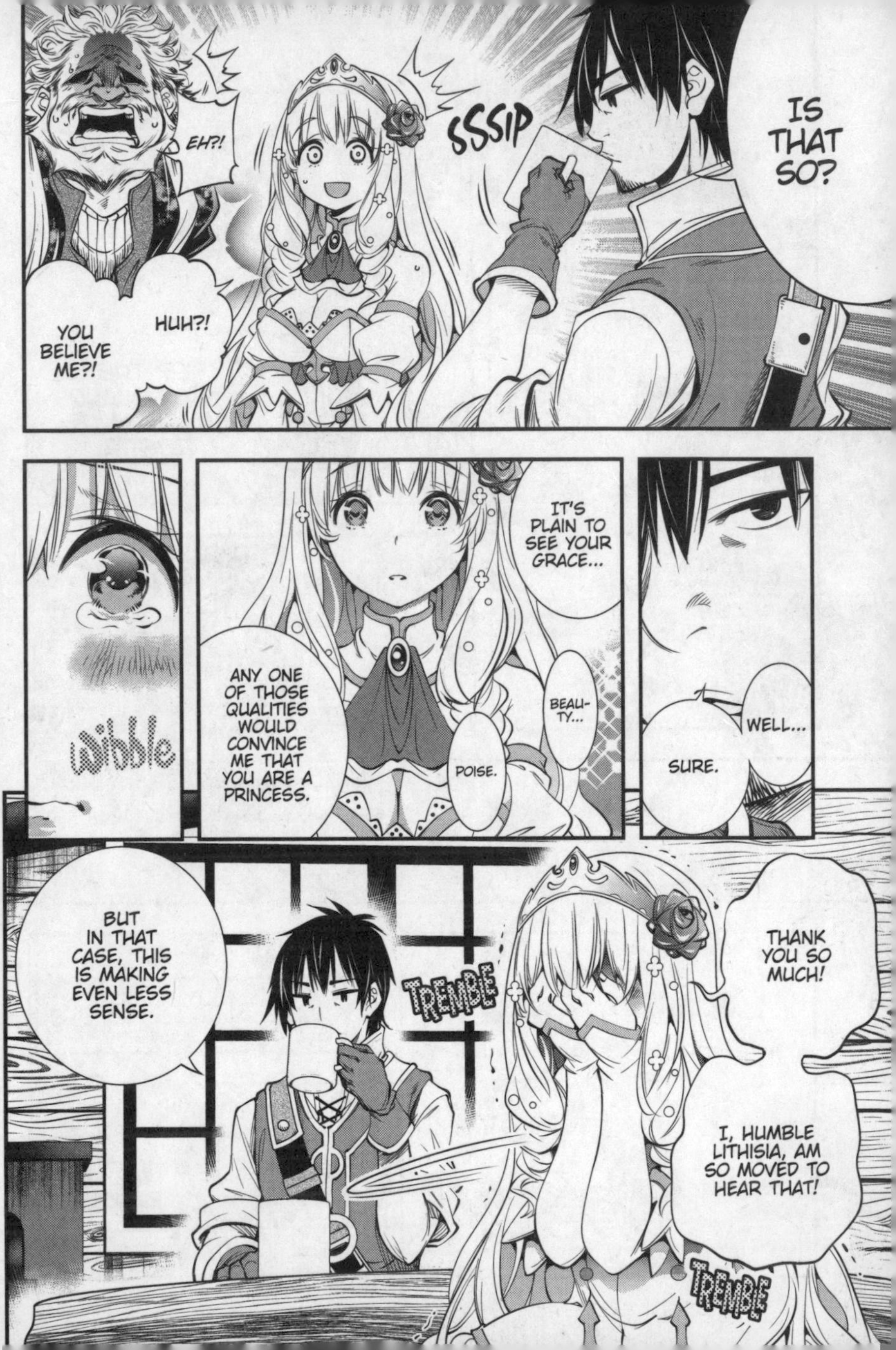
IS THAT SO?
SSSIP
EH?!
HUH?!
YOU BELIEVE ME?!
WELL...
SURE.
IT'S PLAIN TO SEE YOUR GRACE...
BEAU-TY...
POISE.
ANY ONE OF THOSE QUALITIES WOULD CONVINCE ME THAT YOU ARE A PRINCESS.
wibble
THANK YOU SO MUCH!
I, HUMBLE LITHISIA, AM SO MOVED TO HEAR THAT!
TREMBLE
TREMBLE
BUT IN THAT CASE, THIS IS MAKING EVEN LESS SENSE.

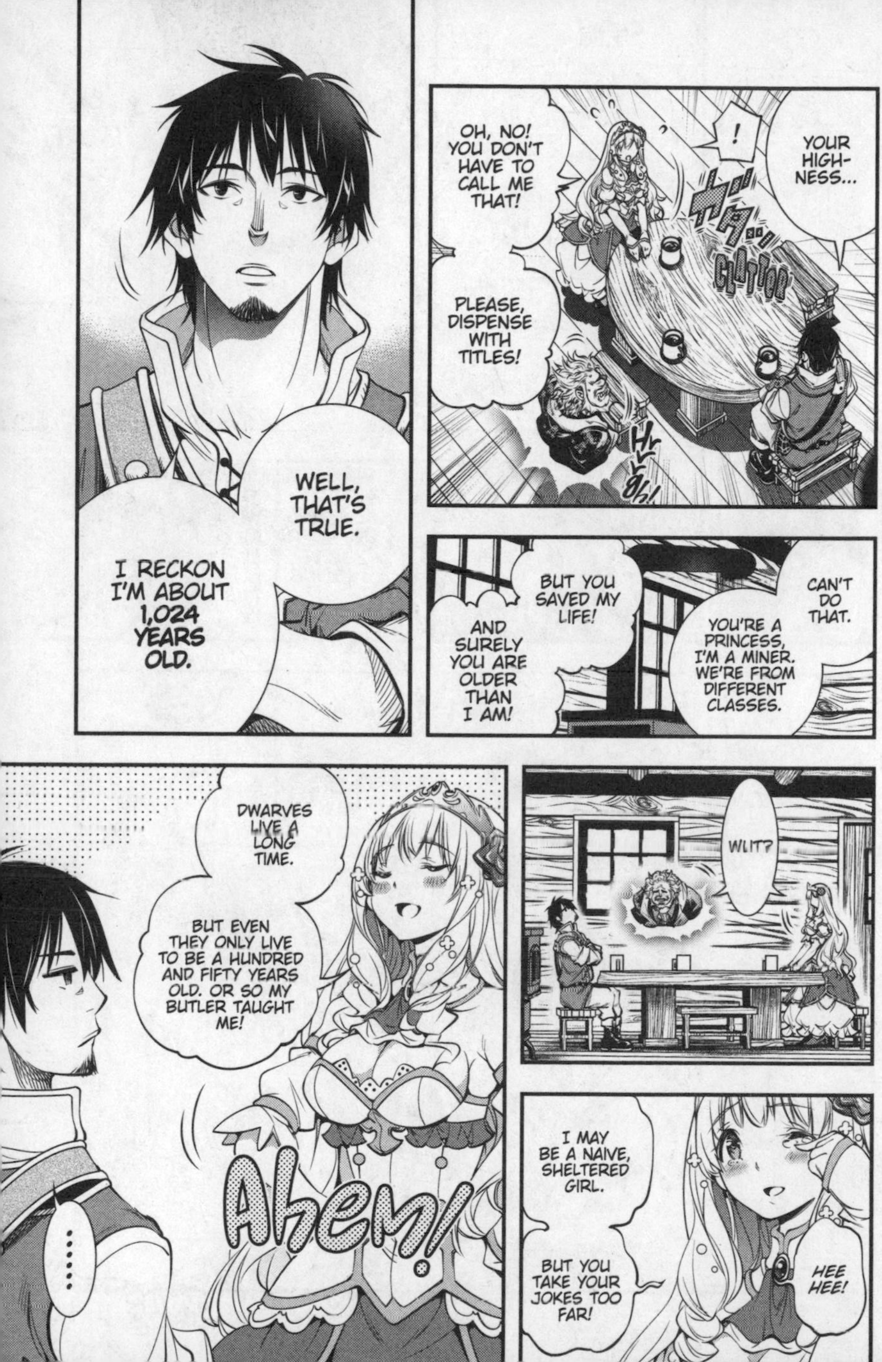
YOUR HIGHNESS...
!
CLATTER
OH, NO! YOU DON'T HAVE TO CALL ME THAT!
PLEASE, DISPENSE WITH TITLES!
CAN'T DO THAT.
YOU'RE A PRINCESS, I'M A MINER. WE'RE FROM DIFFERENT CLASSES.
BUT YOU SAVED MY LIFE!
AND SURELY YOU ARE OLDER THAN I AM!
WELL, THAT'S TRUE.
I RECKON I'M ABOUT 1,024 YEARS OLD.
WHAT?
I MAY BE A NAIVE, SHELTERED GIRL.
HEE HEE!
BUT YOU TAKE YOUR JOKES TOO FAR!
DWARVES LIVE A LONG TIME.
BUT EVEN THEY ONLY LIVE TO BE A HUNDRED AND FIFTY YEARS OLD. OR SO MY BUTLER TAUGHT ME!
Ahem!
......

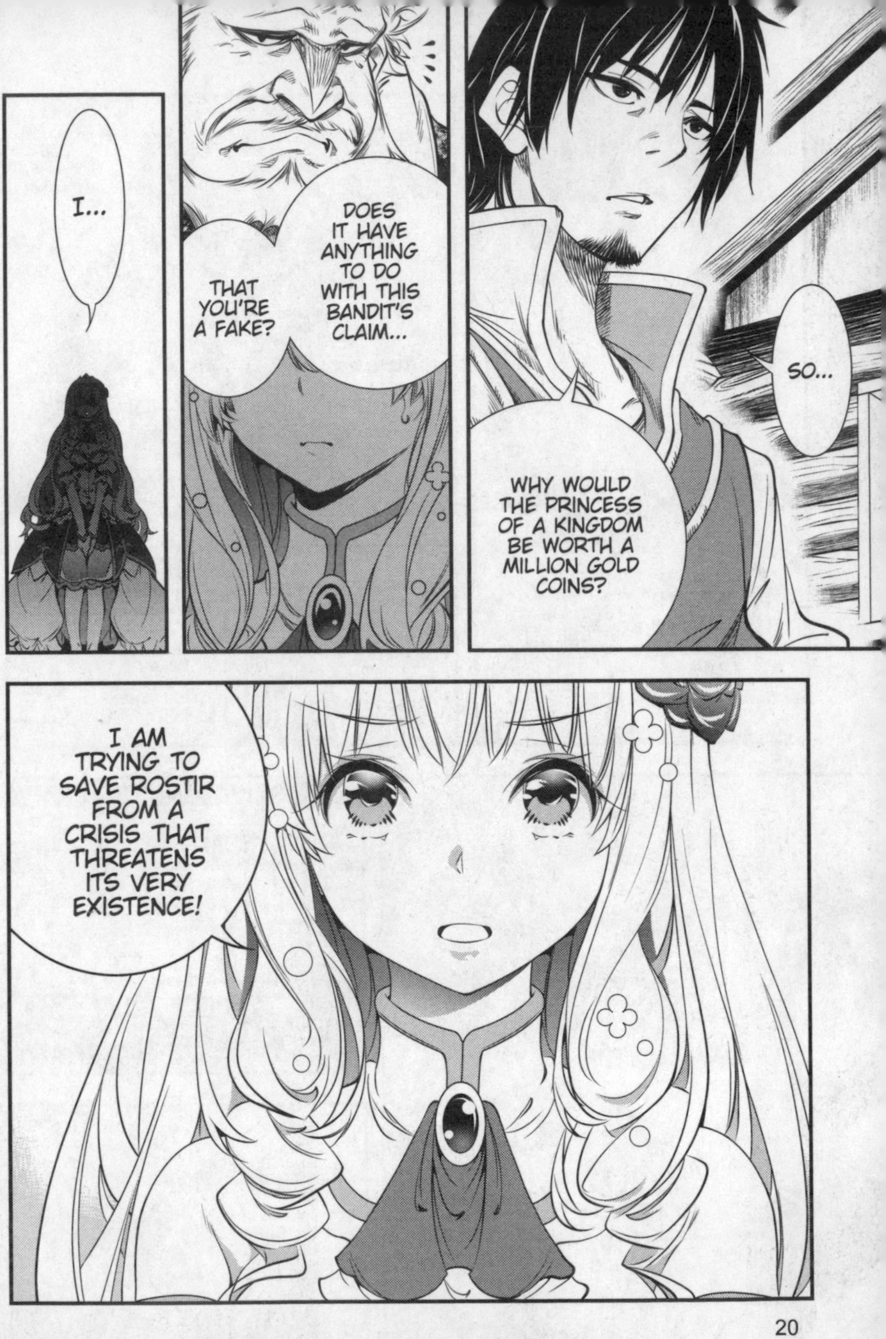
SO...
WHY WOULD THE PRINCESS OF A KINGDOM BE WORTH A MILLION GOLD COINS?
DOES IT HAVE ANYTHING TO DO WITH THIS BANDIT'S CLAIM...
THAT YOU'RE A FAKE?
I...
I AM TRYING TO SAVE ROSTIR FROM A CRISIS THAT THREATENS ITS VERY EXISTENCE!

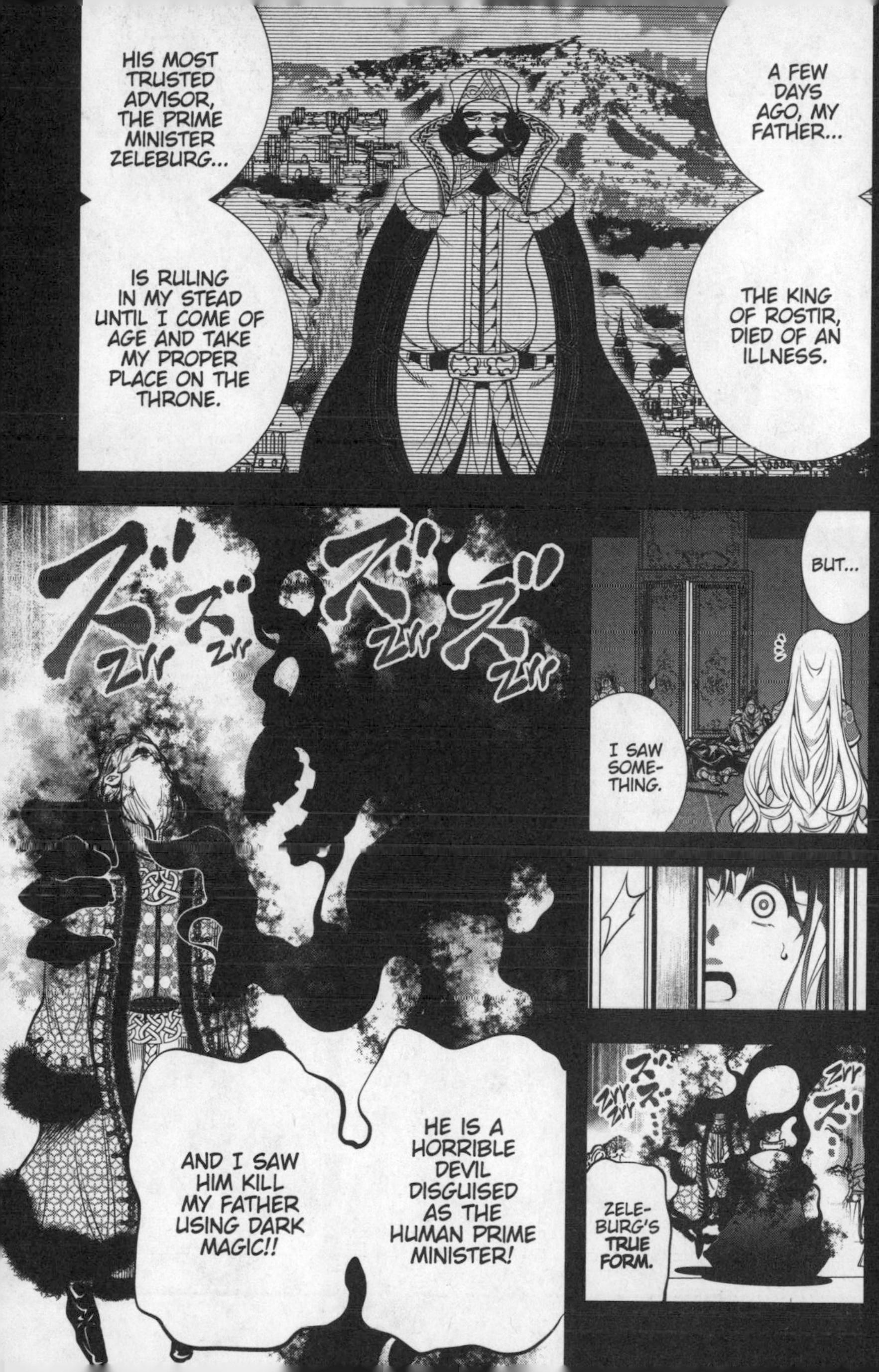
A FEW DAYS AGO, MY FATHER...
THE KING OF ROSTIR, DIED OF AN ILLNESS.
HIS MOST TRUSTED ADVISOR, THE PRIME MINISTER ZELEBURG...
IS RULING IN MY STEAD UNTIL I COME OF AGE AND TAKE MY PROPER PLACE ON THE THRONE.
BUT...
I SAW SOMETHING.
ZRR
ZRR ZRR
ZELEBURG'S TRUE FORM.
ZRR
ZRR
ZRR
ZRR
HE IS A HORRIBLE DEVIL DISGUISED AS THE HUMAN PRIME MINISTER!
AND I SAW HIM KILL MY FATHER USING DARK MAGIC!!

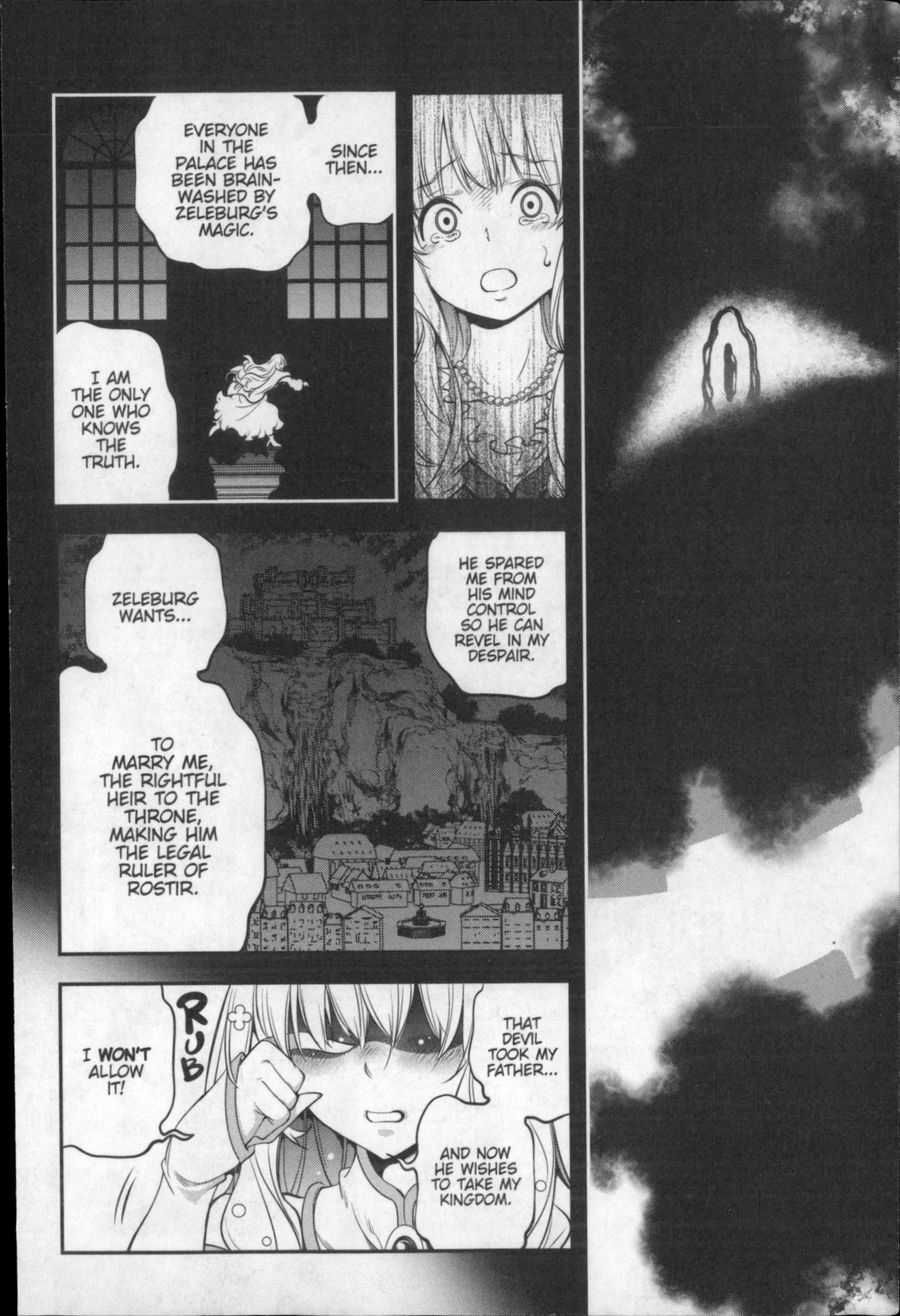
SINCE THEN...
EVERYONE IN THE PALACE HAS BEEN BRAIN-WASHED BY ZELEBURG'S MAGIC.
I AM THE ONLY ONE WHO KNOWS THE TRUTH.
HE SPARED ME FROM HIS MIND CONTROL SO HE CAN REVEL IN MY DESPAIR.
ZELEBURG WANTS...
TO MARRY ME, THE RIGHTFUL HEIR TO THE THRONE, MAKING HIM THE LEGAL RULER OF ROSTIR.
THAT DEVIL TOOK MY FATHER...
AND NOW HE WISHES TO TAKE MY KINGDOM.
RUB
I WON'T ALLOW IT!

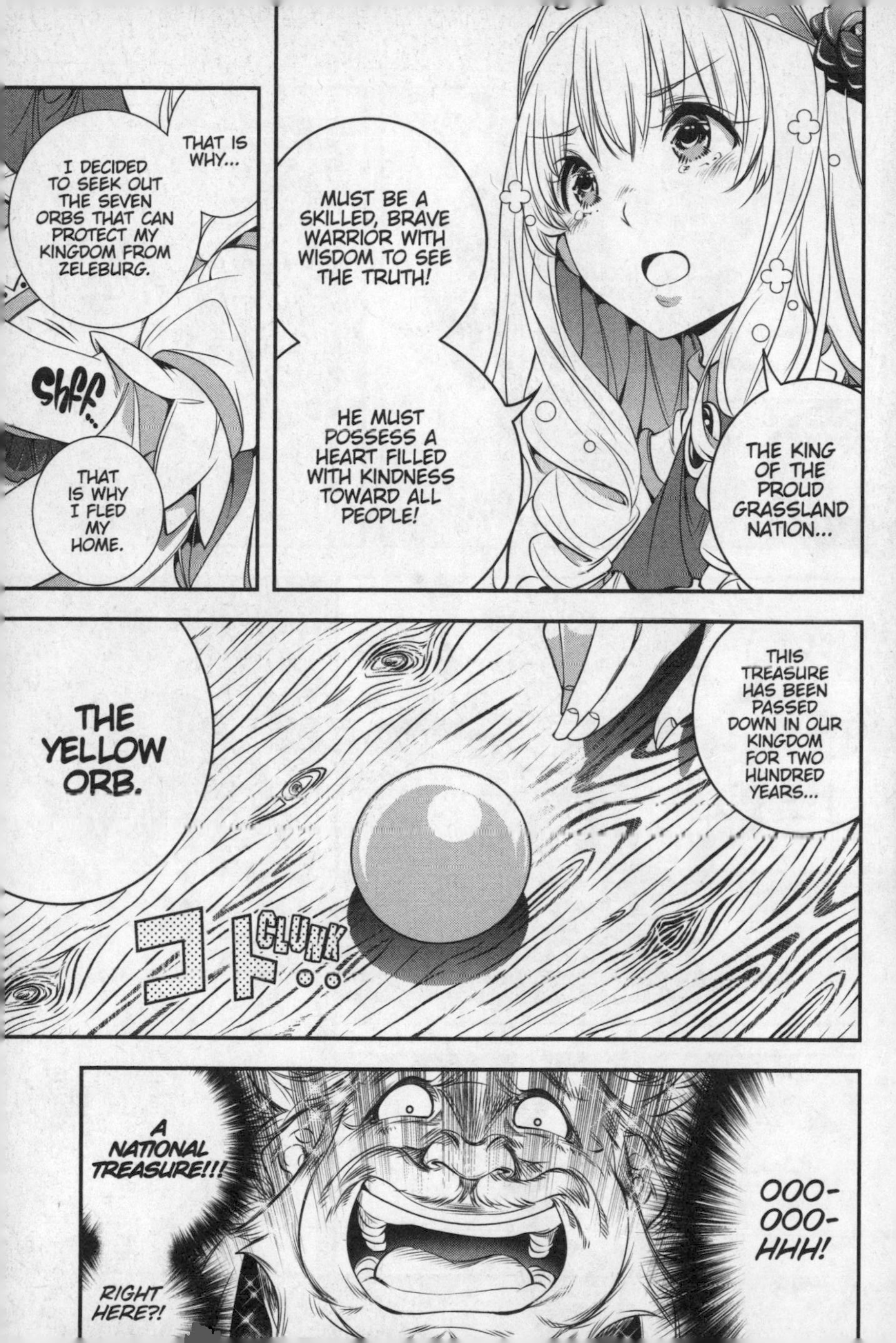
THE KING OF THE PROUD GRASSLAND NATION...
MUST BE A SKILLED, BRAVE WARRIOR WITH WISDOM TO SEE THE TRUTH!
HE MUST POSSESS A HEART FILLED WITH KINDNESS TOWARD ALL PEOPLE!
THAT IS WHY...
I DECIDED TO SEEK OUT THE SEVEN ORBS THAT CAN PROTECT MY KINGDOM FROM ZELEBURG.
Shff...
THAT IS WHY I FLED MY HOME.
THIS TREASURE HAS BEEN PASSED DOWN IN OUR KINGDOM FOR TWO HUNDRED YEARS...
THE YELLOW ORB.
コト CLUNK..
OOO-OOO-HHH!
A NATIONAL TREASURE!!!
RIGHT HERE?!

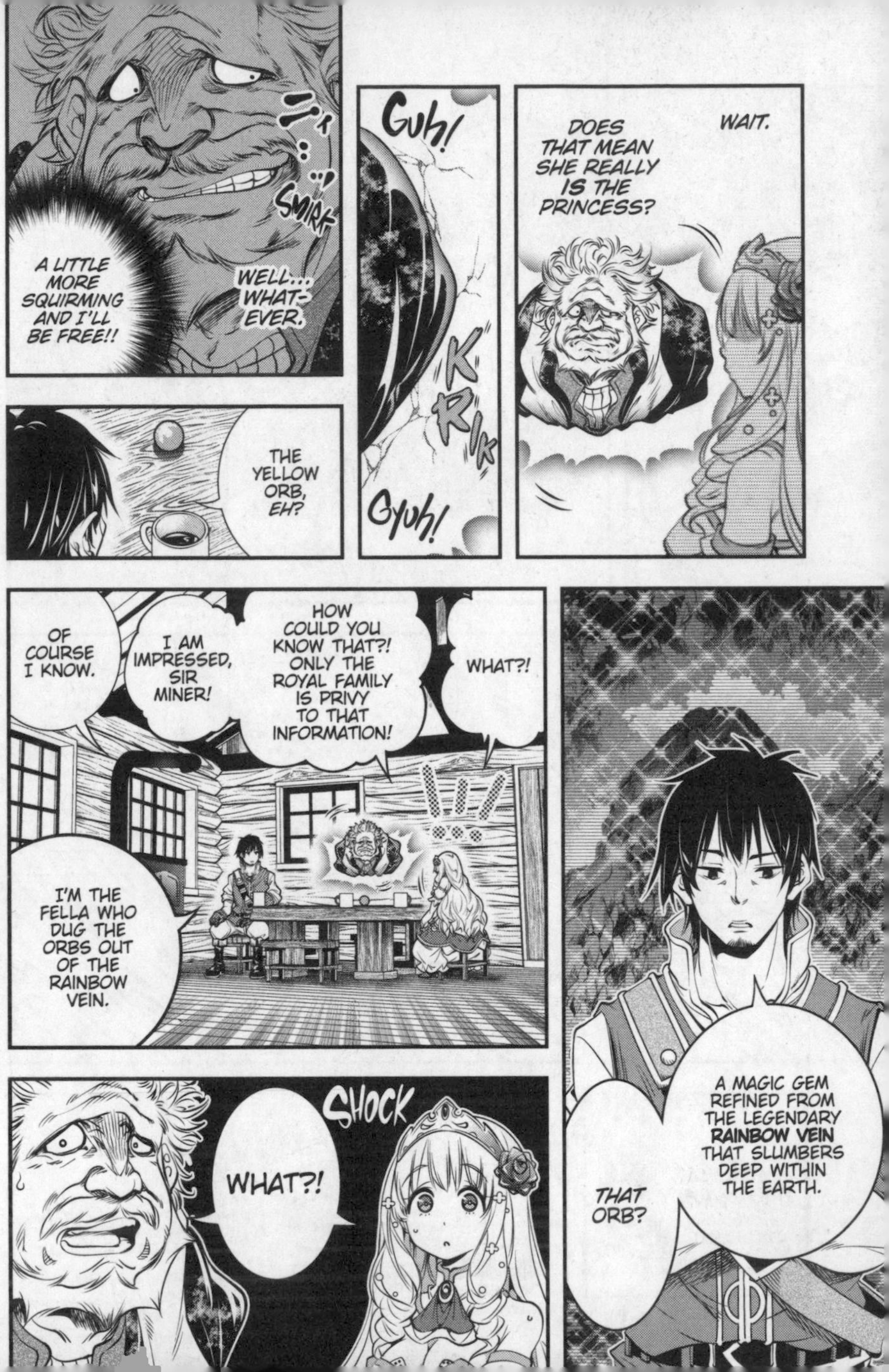
WAIT.
DOES THAT MEAN SHE REALLY IS THE PRINCESS?
GUH!
KRIK
GYUH!
SMIRK
WELL... WHATEVER.
A LITTLE MORE SQUIRMING AND I'LL BE FREE!!
THE YELLOW ORB, EH?
A MAGIC GEM REFINED FROM THE LEGENDARY **RAINBOW VEIN** THAT SLUMBERS DEEP WITHIN THE EARTH.
THAT ORB?
WHAT?!
HOW COULD YOU KNOW THAT?! ONLY THE ROYAL FAMILY IS PRIVY TO THAT INFORMATION!
I AM IMPRESSED, SIR MINER!
OF COURSE I KNOW.
I'M THE FELLA WHO DUG THE ORBS OUT OF THE RAINBOW VEIN.
SHOCK
WHAT?!

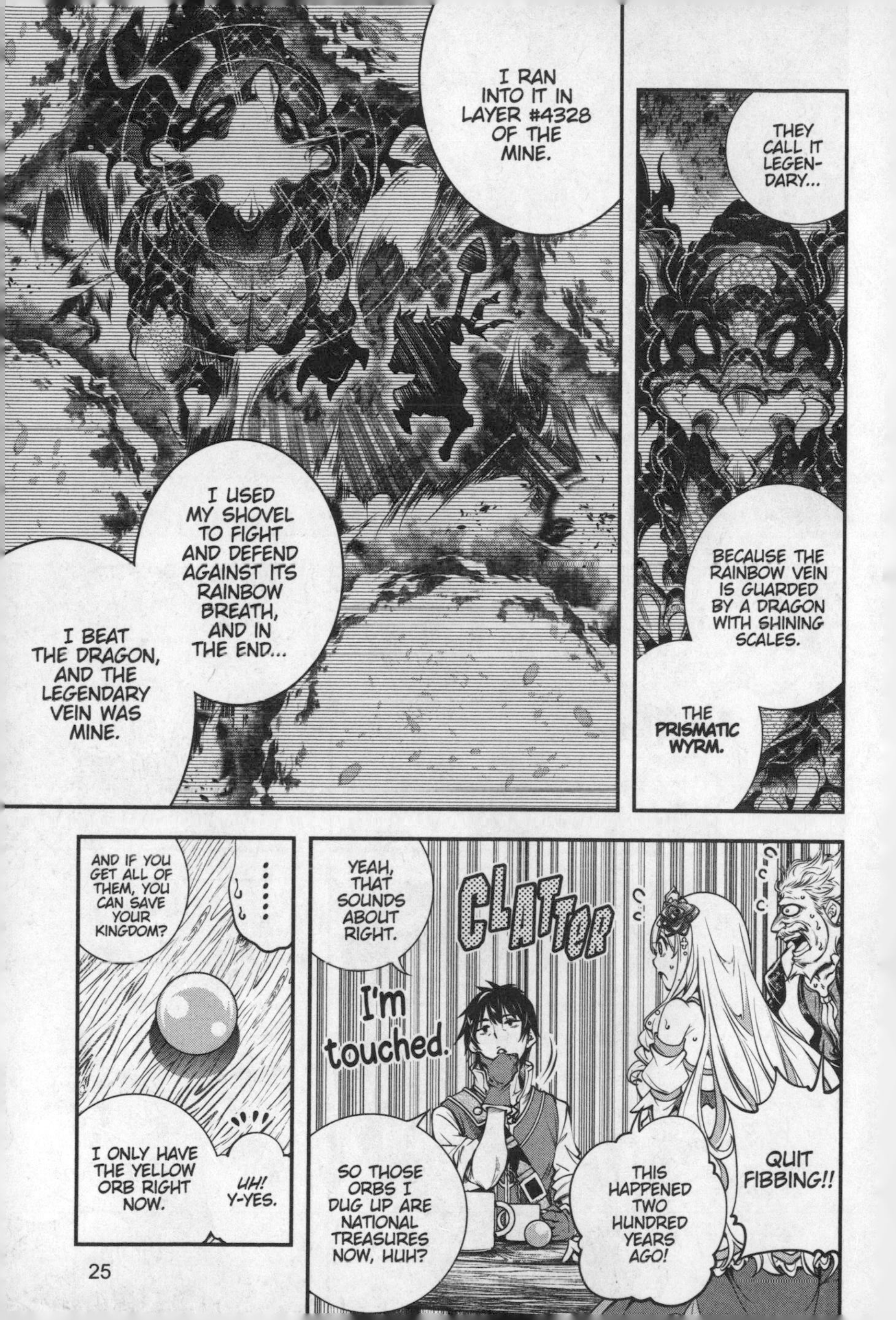
THEY CALL IT LEGEN-DARY...
BECAUSE THE RAINBOW VEIN IS GUARDED BY A DRAGON WITH SHINING SCALES.
THE PRISMATIC WYRM.
I RAN INTO IT IN LAYER #4328 OF THE MINE.
I USED MY SHOVEL TO FIGHT AND DEFEND AGAINST ITS RAINBOW BREATH, AND IN THE END...
I BEAT THE DRAGON, AND THE LEGENDARY VEIN WAS MINE.
CLATTER
QUIT FIBBING!!
THIS HAPPENED TWO HUNDRED YEARS AGO!
YEAH, THAT SOUNDS ABOUT RIGHT.
I'm touched.
SO THOSE ORBS I DUG UP ARE NATIONAL TREASURES NOW, HUH?
AND IF YOU GET ALL OF THEM, YOU CAN SAVE YOUR KINGDOM?
......
UH! Y-YES.
I ONLY HAVE THE YELLOW ORB RIGHT NOW.

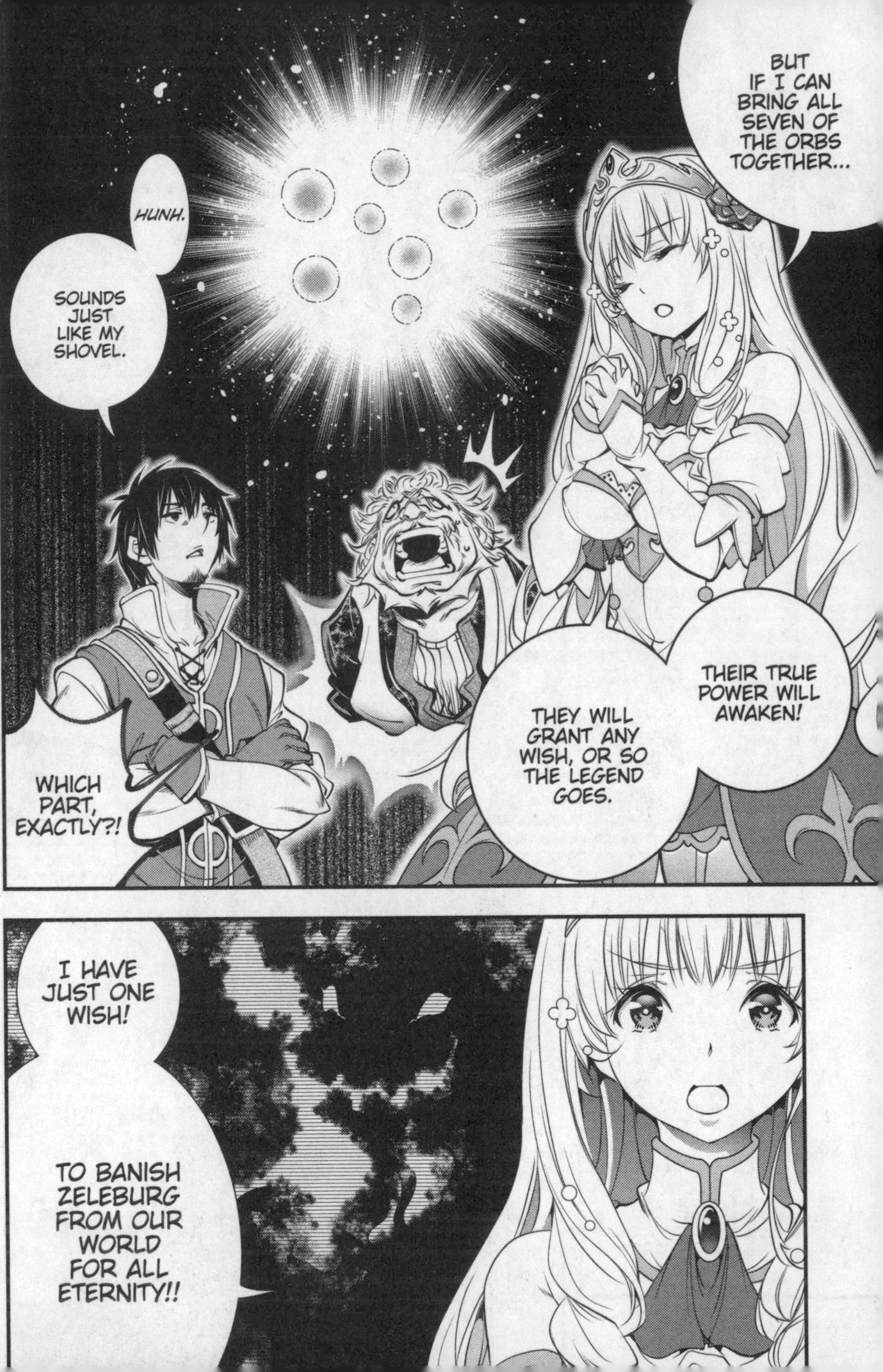
BUT IF I CAN BRING ALL SEVEN OF THE ORBS TOGETHER...
THEIR TRUE POWER WILL AWAKEN!
THEY WILL GRANT ANY WISH, OR SO THE LEGEND GOES.
HUNH.
SOUNDS JUST LIKE MY SHOVEL.
WHICH PART, EXACTLY?!
I HAVE JUST ONE WISH!
TO BANISH ZELEBURG FROM OUR WORLD FOR ALL ETERNITY!!

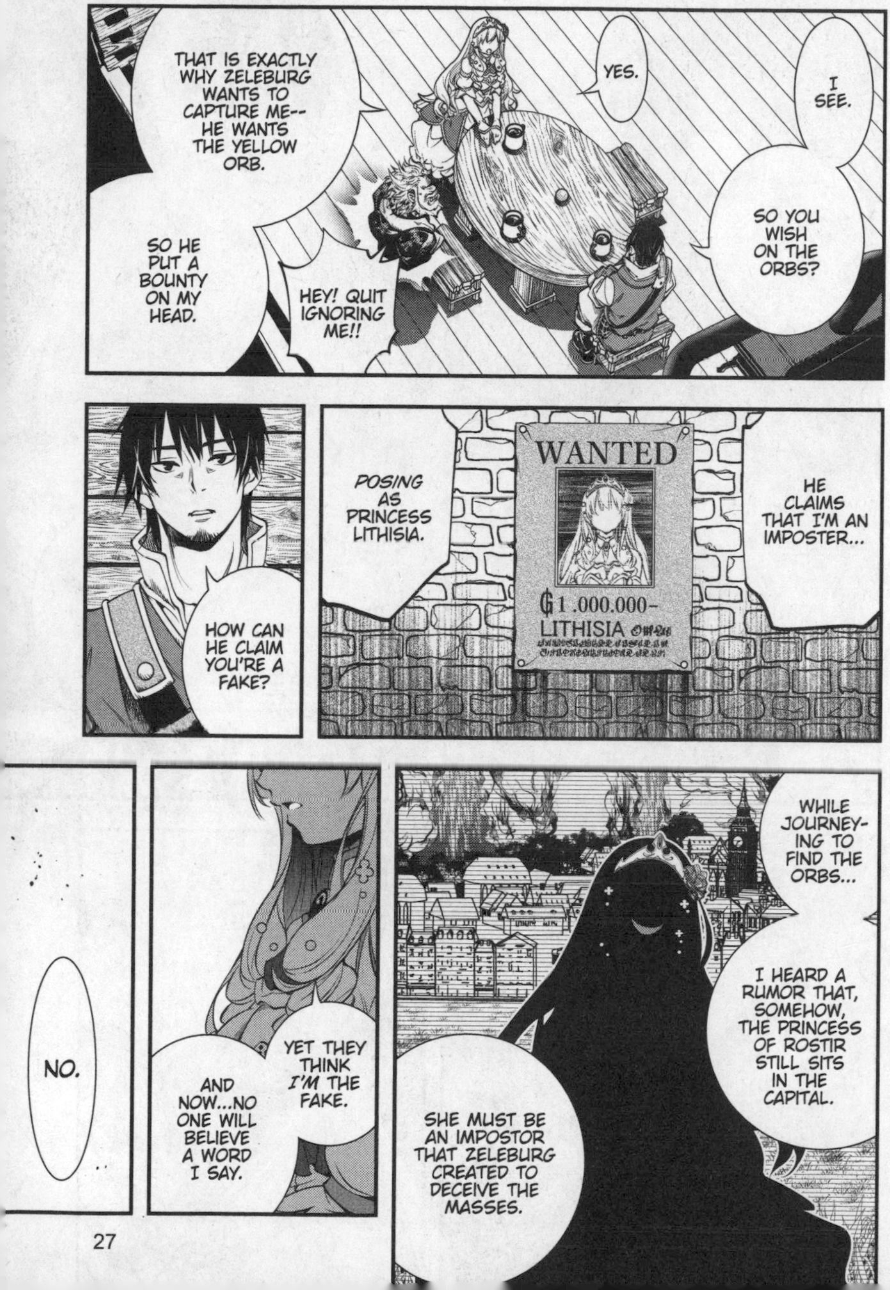
I SEE.
SO YOU WISH ON THE ORBS?
YES.
THAT IS EXACTLY WHY ZELEBURG WANTS TO CAPTURE ME-- HE WANTS THE YELLOW ORB.
HEY! QUIT IGNORING ME!!
SO HE PUT A BOUNTY ON MY HEAD.
HE CLAIMS THAT I'M AN IMPOSTER...
WANTED
₲1.000.000-
LITHISIA
POSING AS PRINCESS LITHISIA.
HOW CAN HE CLAIM YOU'RE A FAKE?
WHILE JOURNEYING TO FIND THE ORBS...
I HEARD A RUMOR THAT, SOMEHOW, THE PRINCESS OF ROSTIR STILL SITS IN THE CAPITAL.
SHE MUST BE AN IMPOSTOR THAT ZELEBURG CREATED TO DECEIVE THE MASSES.
YET THEY THINK *I'M* THE FAKE.
AND NOW...NO ONE WILL BELIEVE A WORD I SAY.
NO.

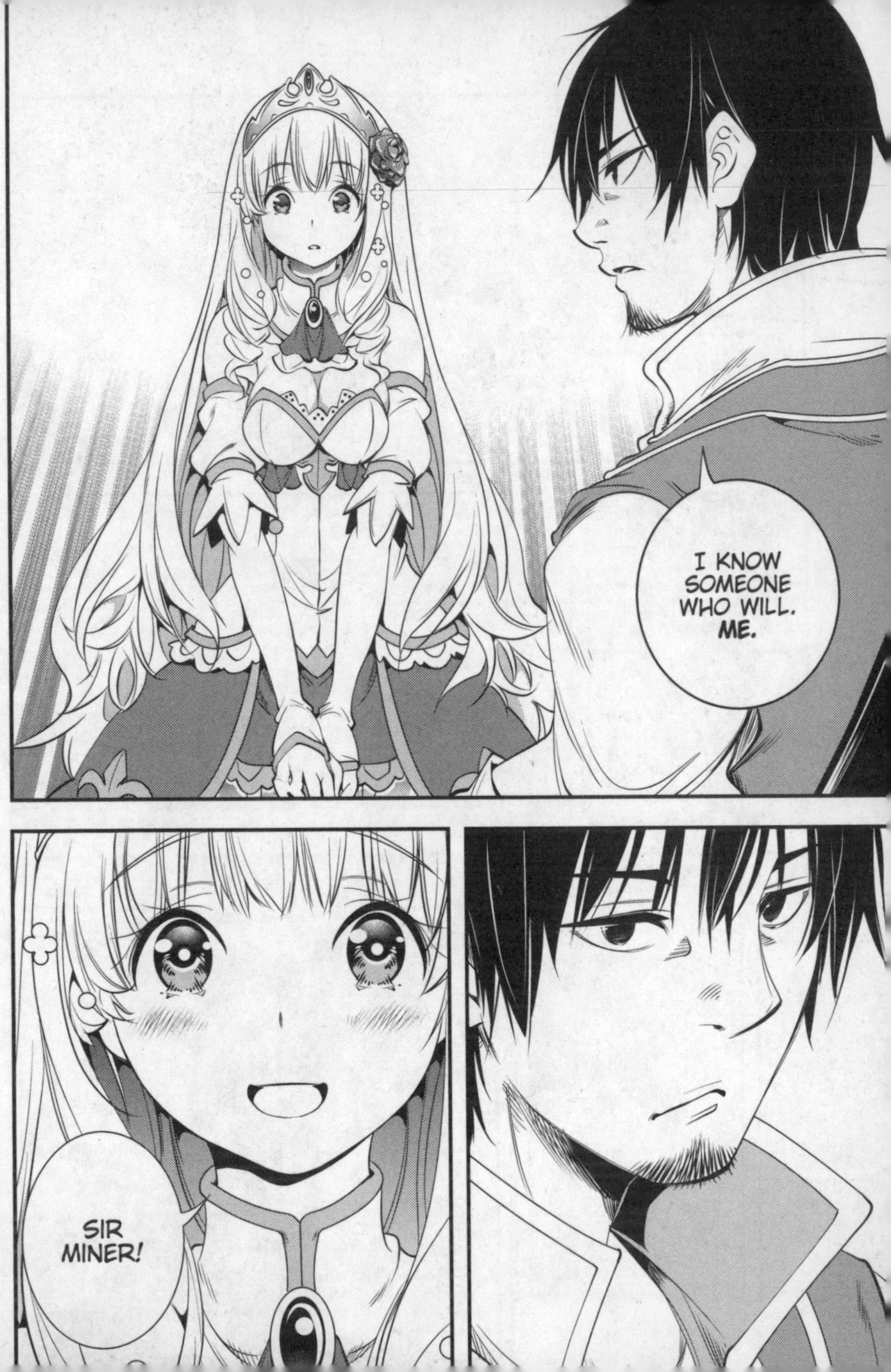
I KNOW SOMEONE WHO WILL. ME.
SIR MINER!

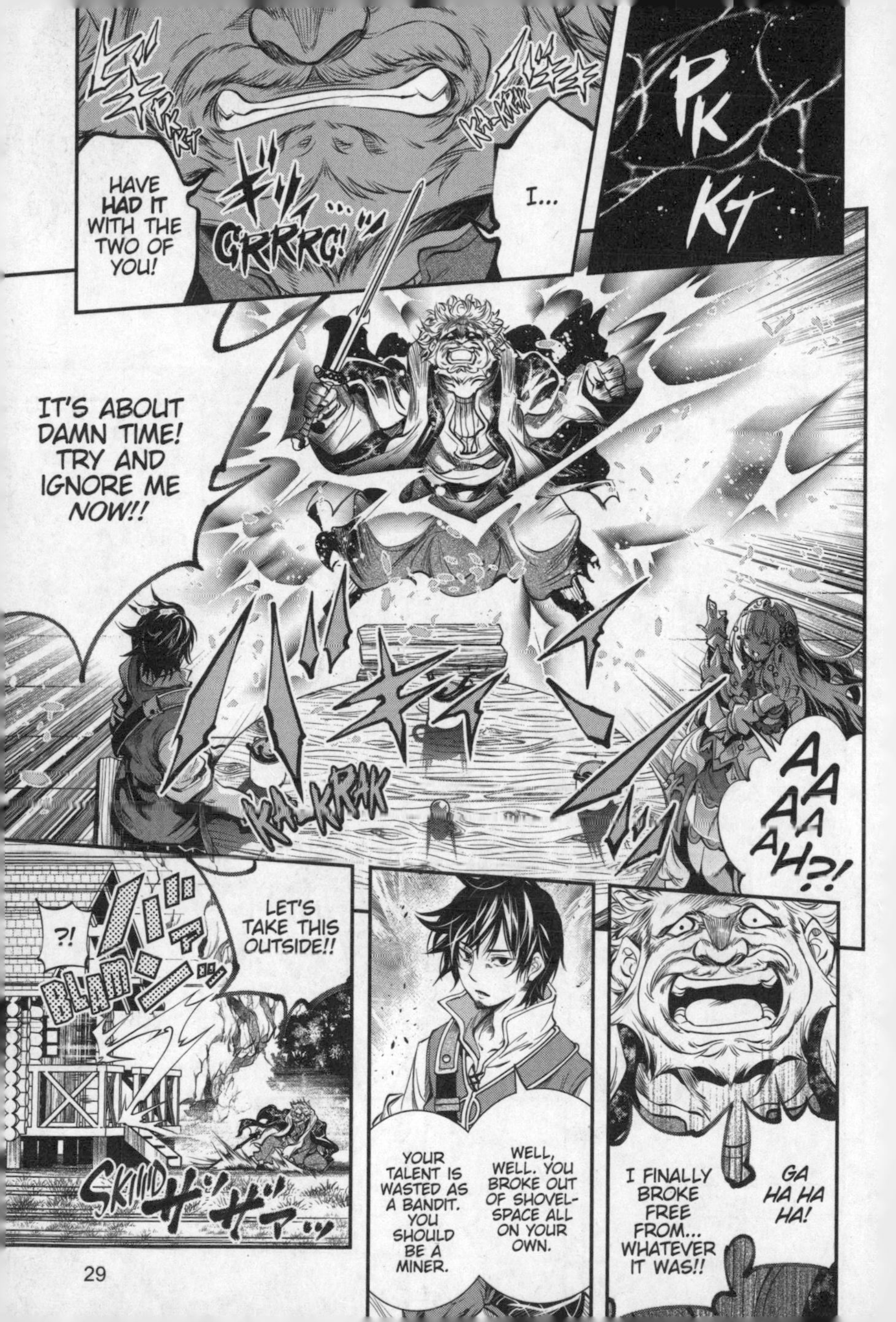
PK
KT
I...
KA-KRAK
PK KT
GRRRG!
HAVE HAD IT WITH THE TWO OF YOU!
AAAAAAH?!
KA-KRAK
IT'S ABOUT DAMN TIME! TRY AND IGNORE ME NOW!!
GA HA HA HA!
I FINALLY BROKE FREE FROM... WHATEVER IT WAS!!
WELL, WELL. YOU BROKE OUT OF SHOVEL-SPACE ALL ON YOUR OWN.
YOUR TALENT IS WASTED AS A BANDIT. YOU SHOULD BE A MINER.
LET'S TAKE THIS OUTSIDE!!
?!
BLAM
SKIIID

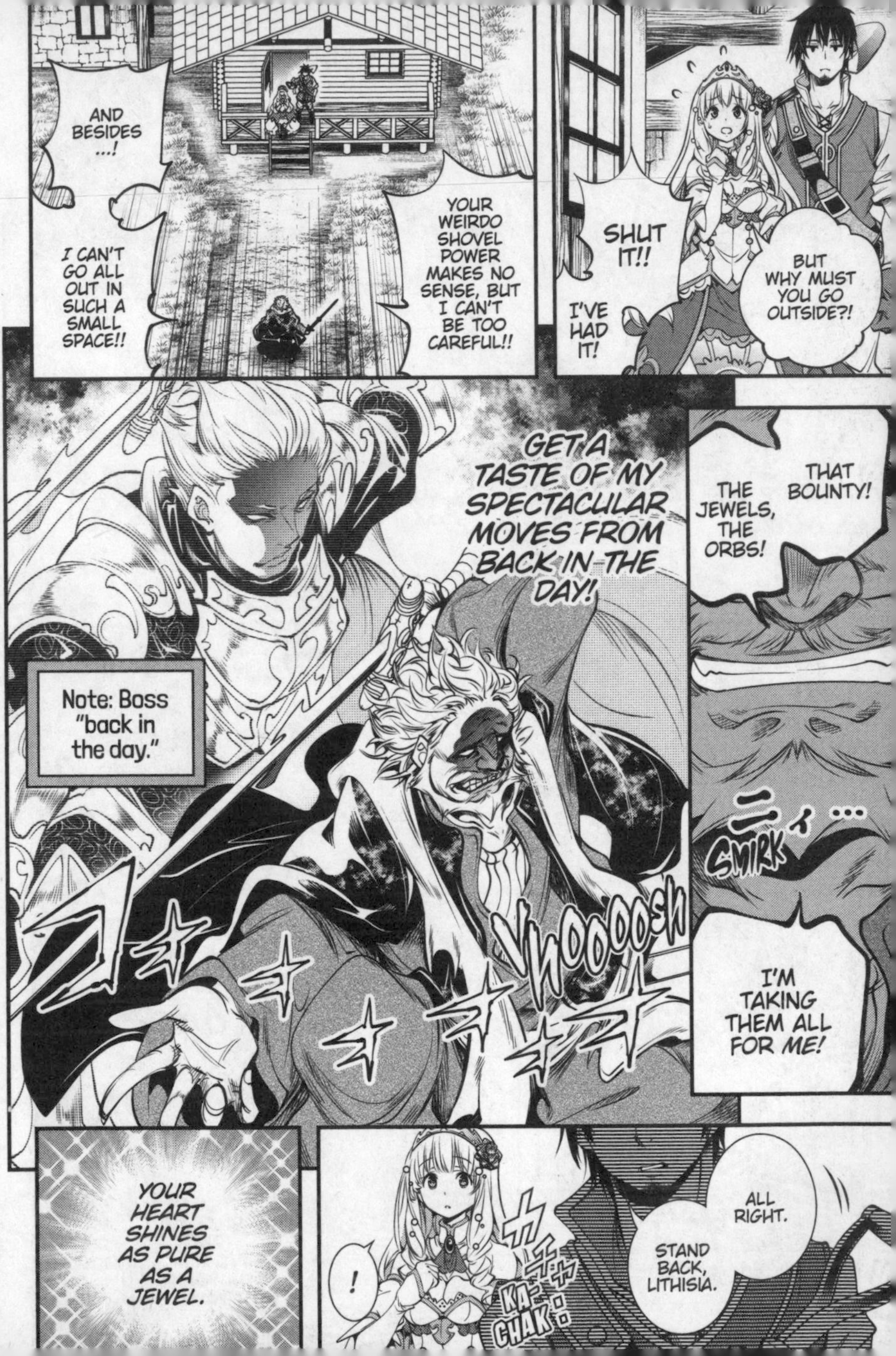
BUT WHY MUST YOU GO OUTSIDE?!
SHUT IT!!
I'VE HAD IT!
YOUR WEIRDO SHOVEL POWER MAKES NO SENSE, BUT I CAN'T BE TOO CAREFUL!!
AND BESIDES ...!
I CAN'T GO ALL OUT IN SUCH A SMALL SPACE!!
THAT BOUNTY!
THE JEWELS, THE ORBS!
SMIRK
I'M TAKING THEM ALL FOR ME!
GET A TASTE OF MY SPECTACULAR MOVES FROM BACK IN THE DAY!
Note: Boss "back in the day."
VHOOOOSH
ALL RIGHT.
STAND BACK, LITHISIA.
!
KA-CHAK!
YOUR HEART SHINES AS PURE AS A JEWEL.

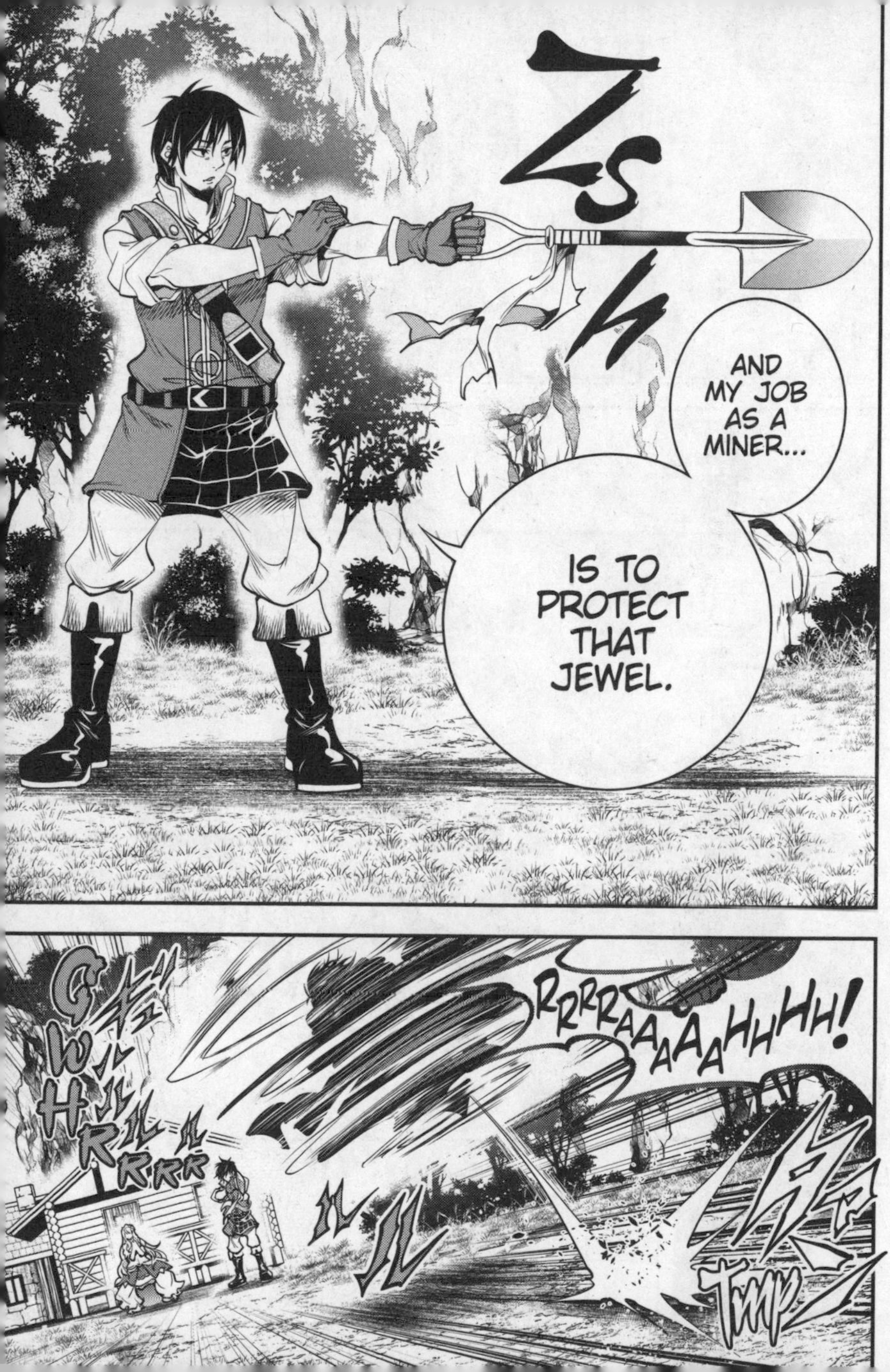
ZSH
AND MY JOB AS A MINER...
IS TO PROTECT THAT JEWEL.
TMP
RRRRAAAAAHHHHH!
GWHRRRR

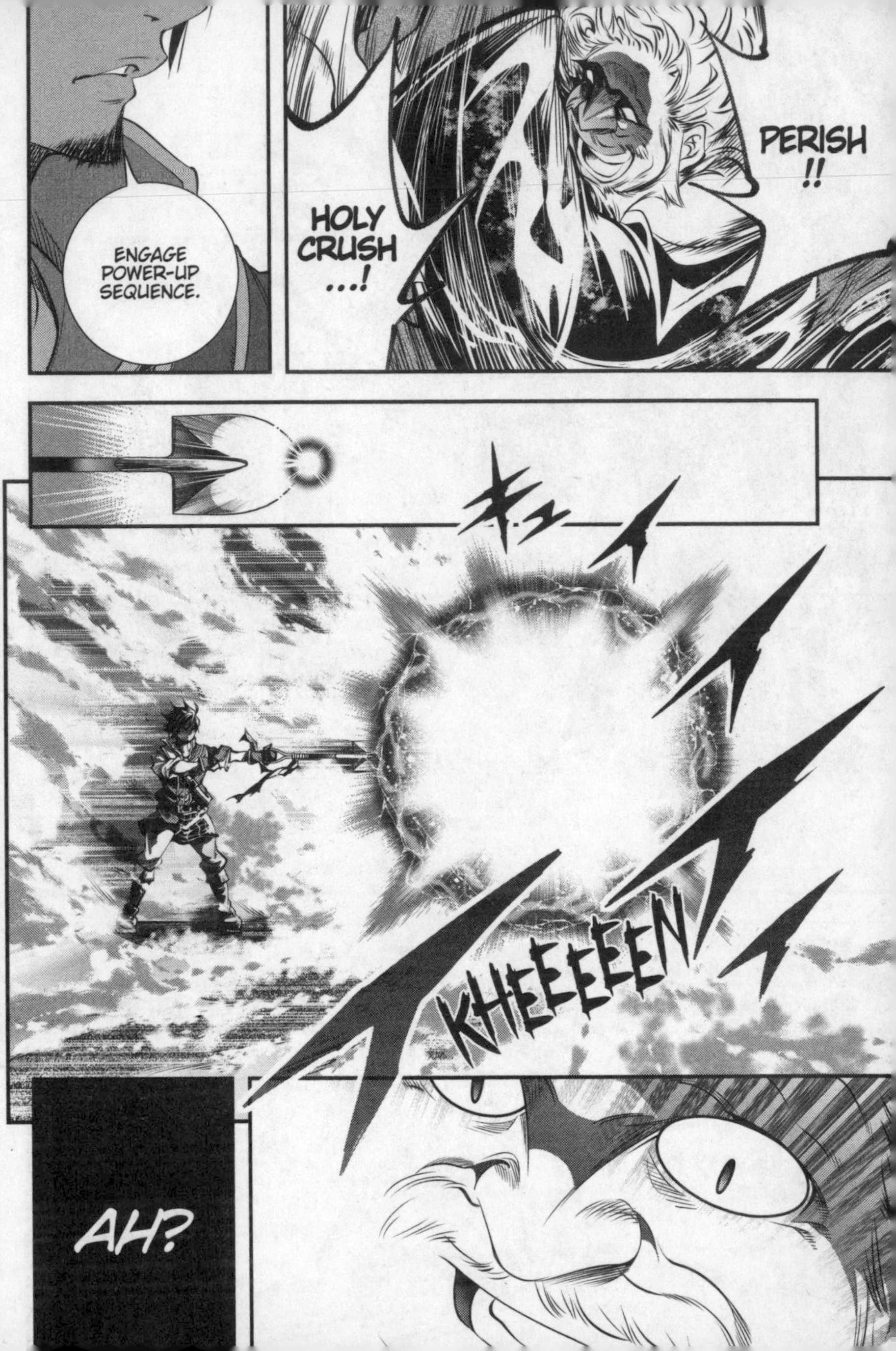
PERISH !!
HOLY CRUSH ...!
ENGAGE POWER-UP SEQUENCE.
KHEEEEEN
AH?

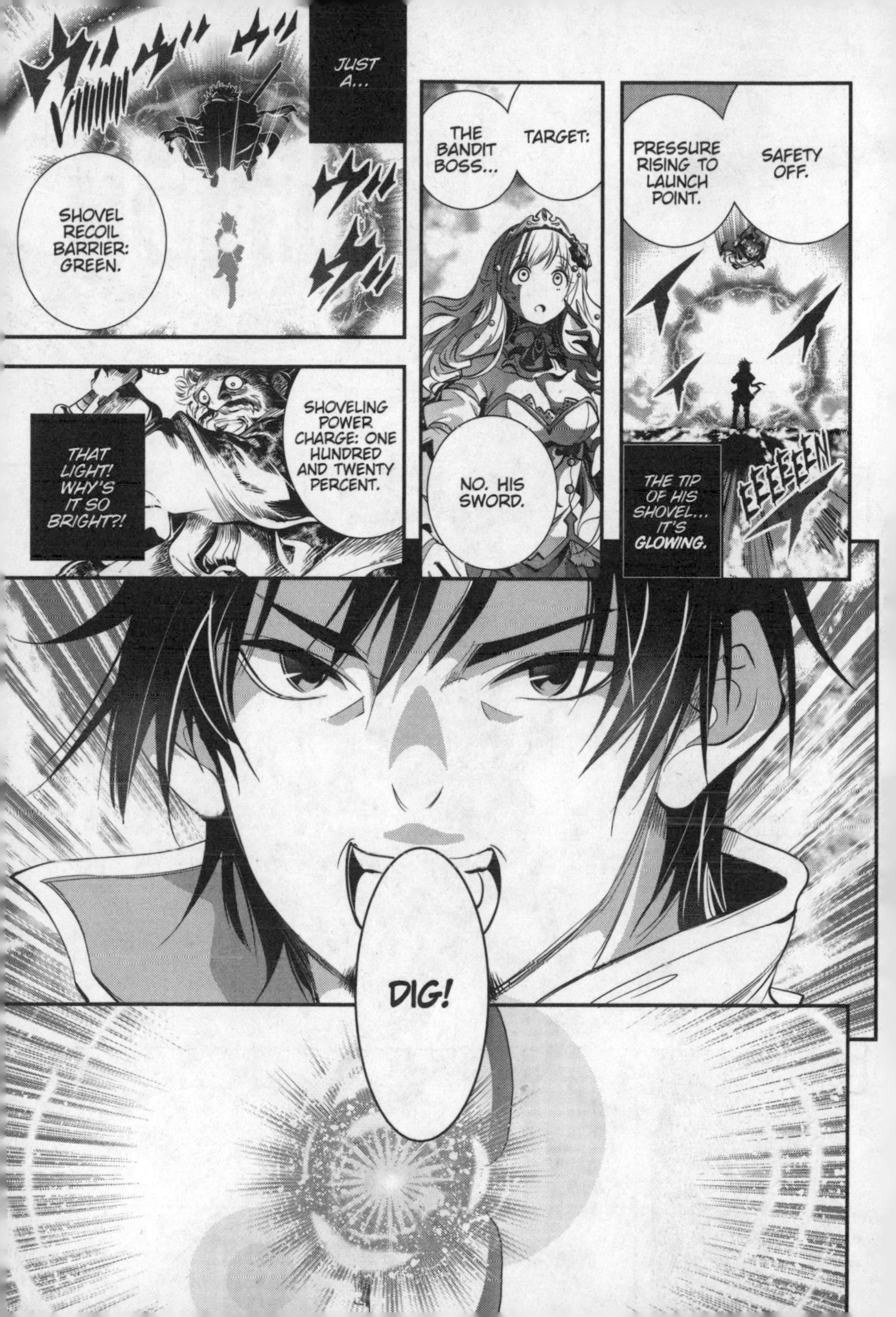
SAFETY OFF.
PRESSURE RISING TO LAUNCH POINT.
THE TIP OF HIS SHOVEL... IT'S GLOWING.
EEEEEEN
TARGET:
THE BANDIT BOSS...
NO. HIS SWORD.
JUST A...
SHOVEL RECOIL BARRIER: GREEN.
SHOVELING POWER CHARGE: ONE HUNDRED AND TWENTY PERCENT.
THAT LIGHT! WHY'S IT SO BRIGHT?!
DIG!

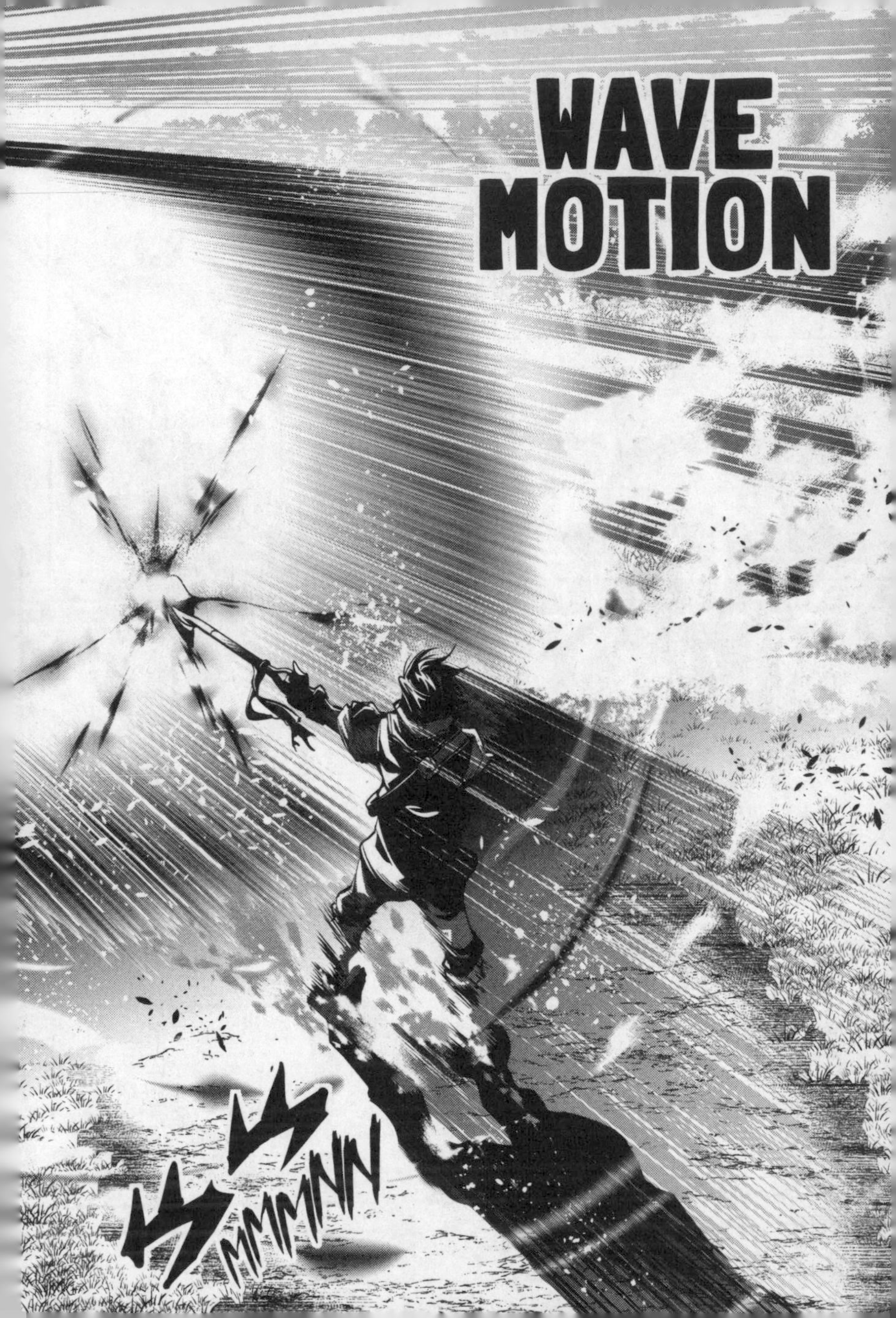
WAVE MOTION
SHWMMMNN

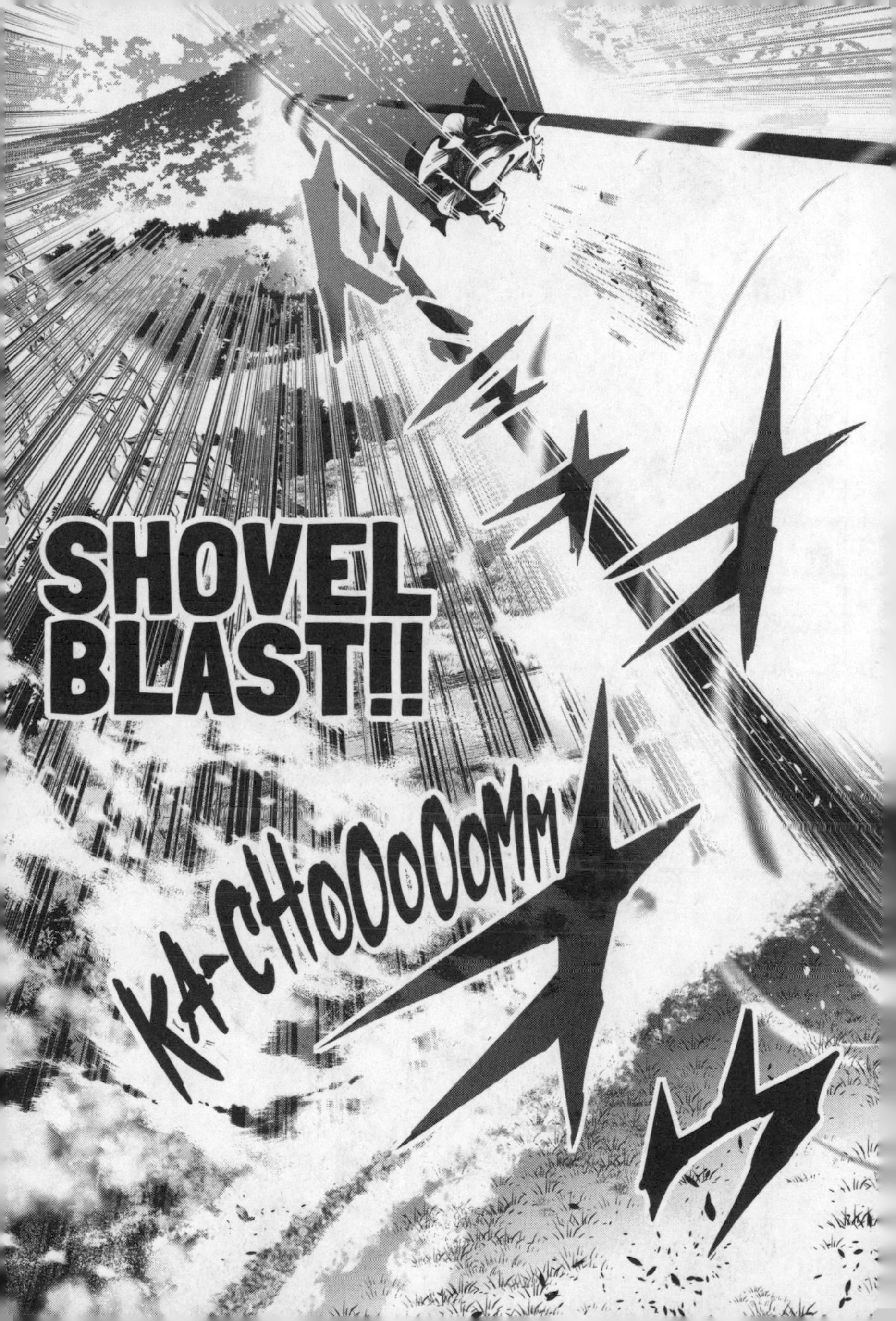
SHOVEL BLAST!!
KA-CHOOOOOOMM

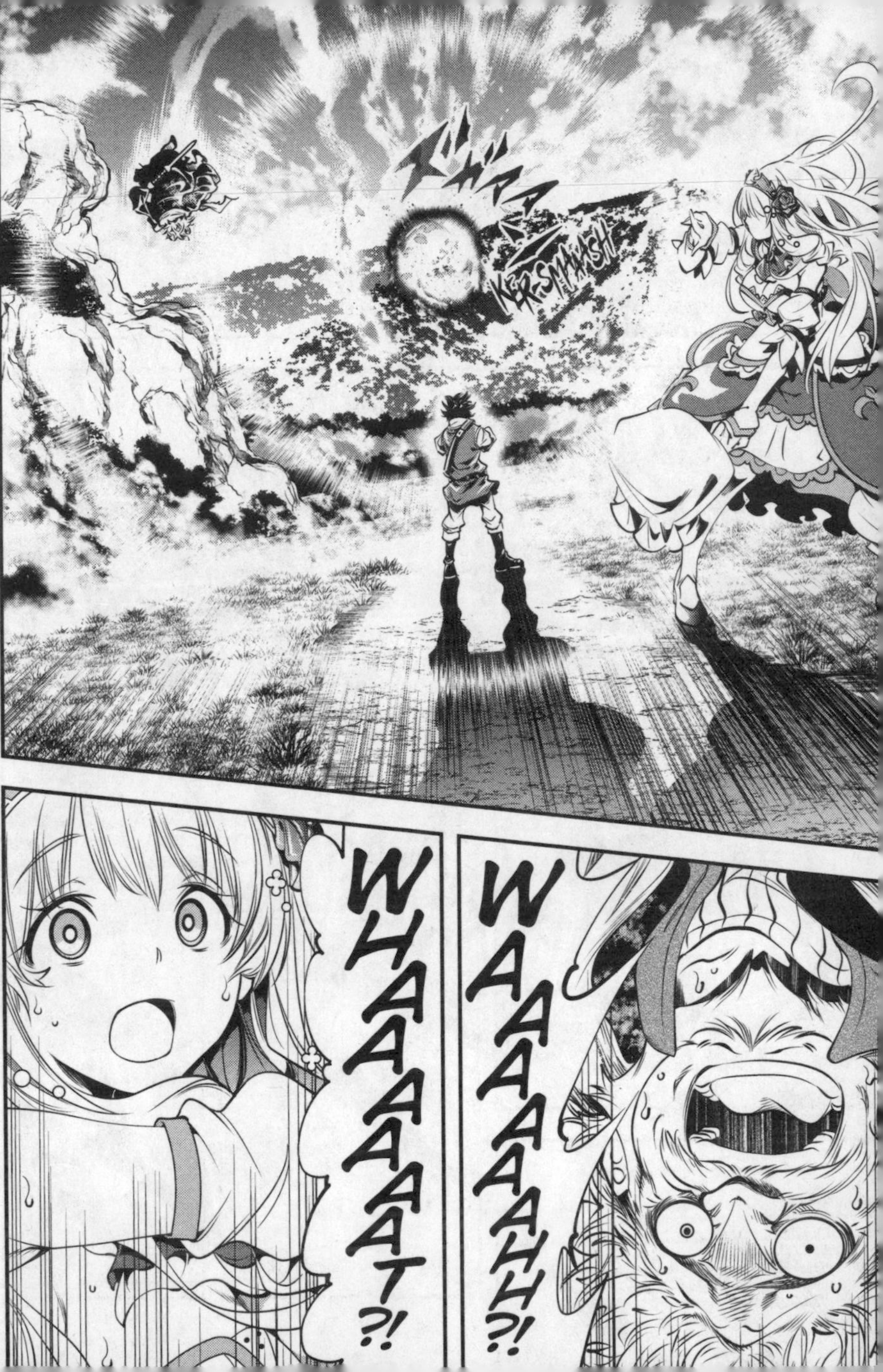
KER-SMAAASH
WAAAAAAAAH?!
WHAAAAAAT?!

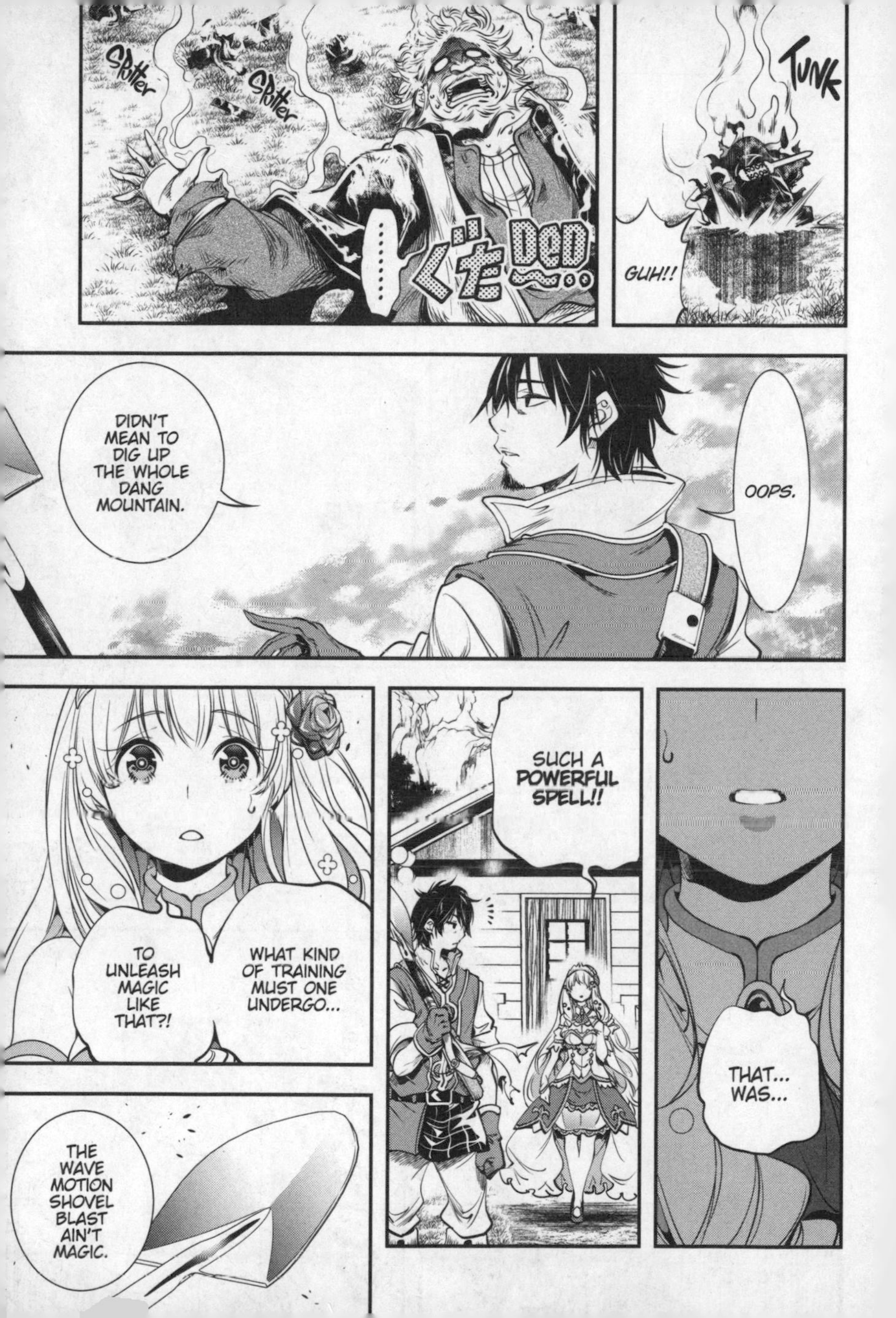
TUNK
GUH!!
Sputter
Sputter
......
ぐだDeD～‥
OOPS.
DIDN'T MEAN TO DIG UP THE WHOLE DANG MOUNTAIN.
THAT... WAS...
SUCH A POWERFUL SPELL!!
WHAT KIND OF TRAINING MUST ONE UNDERGO...
TO UNLEASH MAGIC LIKE THAT?!
THE WAVE MOTION SHOVEL BLAST AIN'T MAGIC.

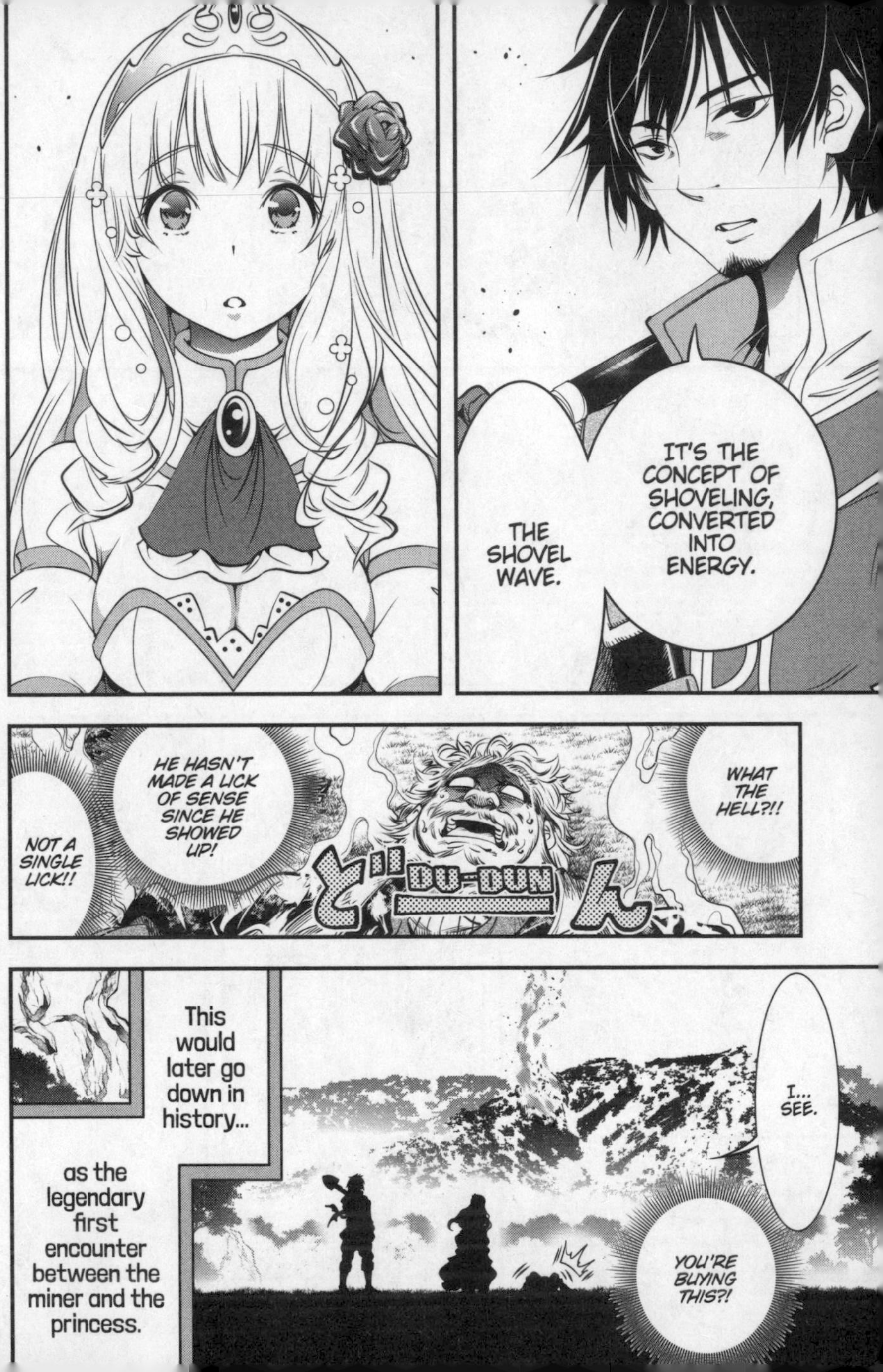
IT'S THE CONCEPT OF SHOVELING, CONVERTED INTO ENERGY.
THE SHOVEL WAVE.
WHAT THE HELL?!!
HE HASN'T MADE A LICK OF SENSE SINCE HE SHOWED UP!
NOT A SINGLE LICK!!
DU-DUN
I... SEE.
YOU'RE BUYING THIS?!
This would later go down in history...
as the legendary first encounter between the miner and the princess.

THE INVINCIBLE
SHOVEL

"WAVE MOTION SHOVEL BLAST!"
(˙ω˙)σ====★(゚д゚)∴.KA-CHOOOM

THE INVINCIBLE SHOVEL

"WAVE MOTION SHOVEL BLAST!"
(ˋ・ω・ˊ)♂=====★(ﾟДﾟ ;;;).:∴. KA-CHOOOM

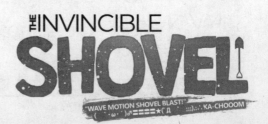

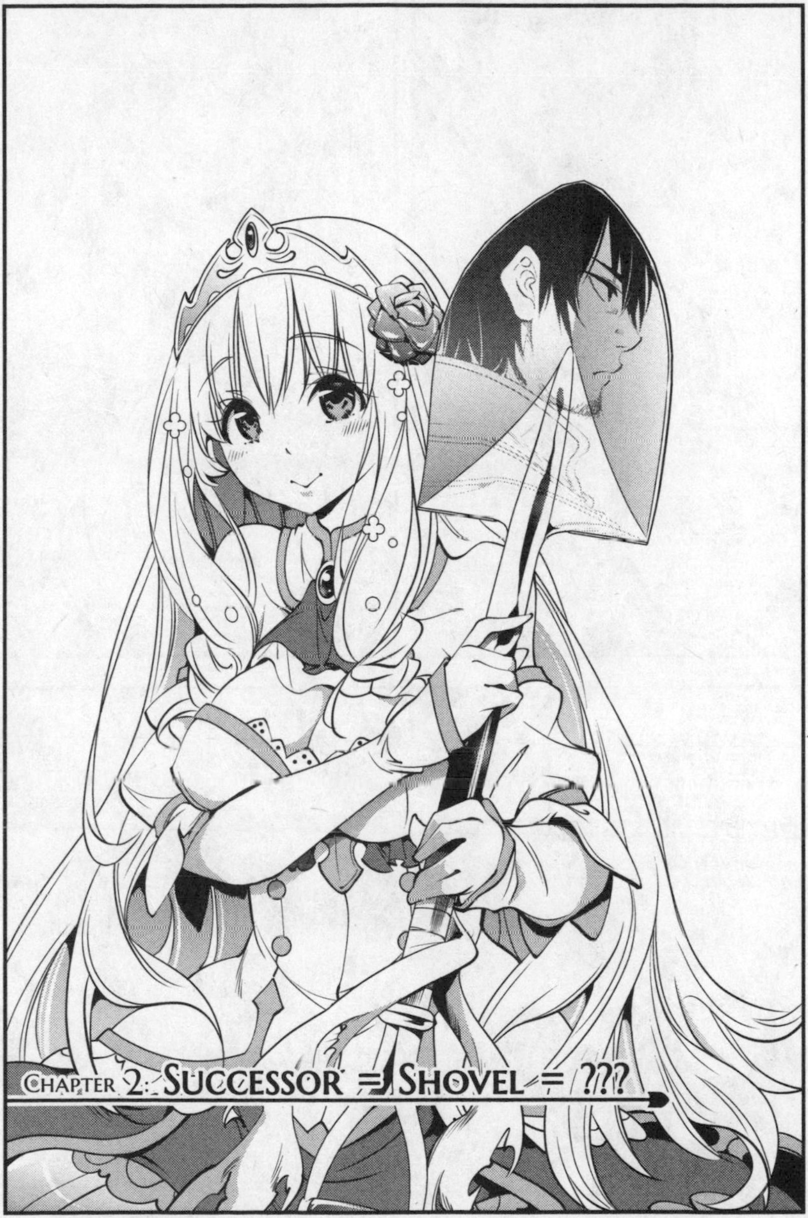
Chapter 2: Successor = Shovel = ???

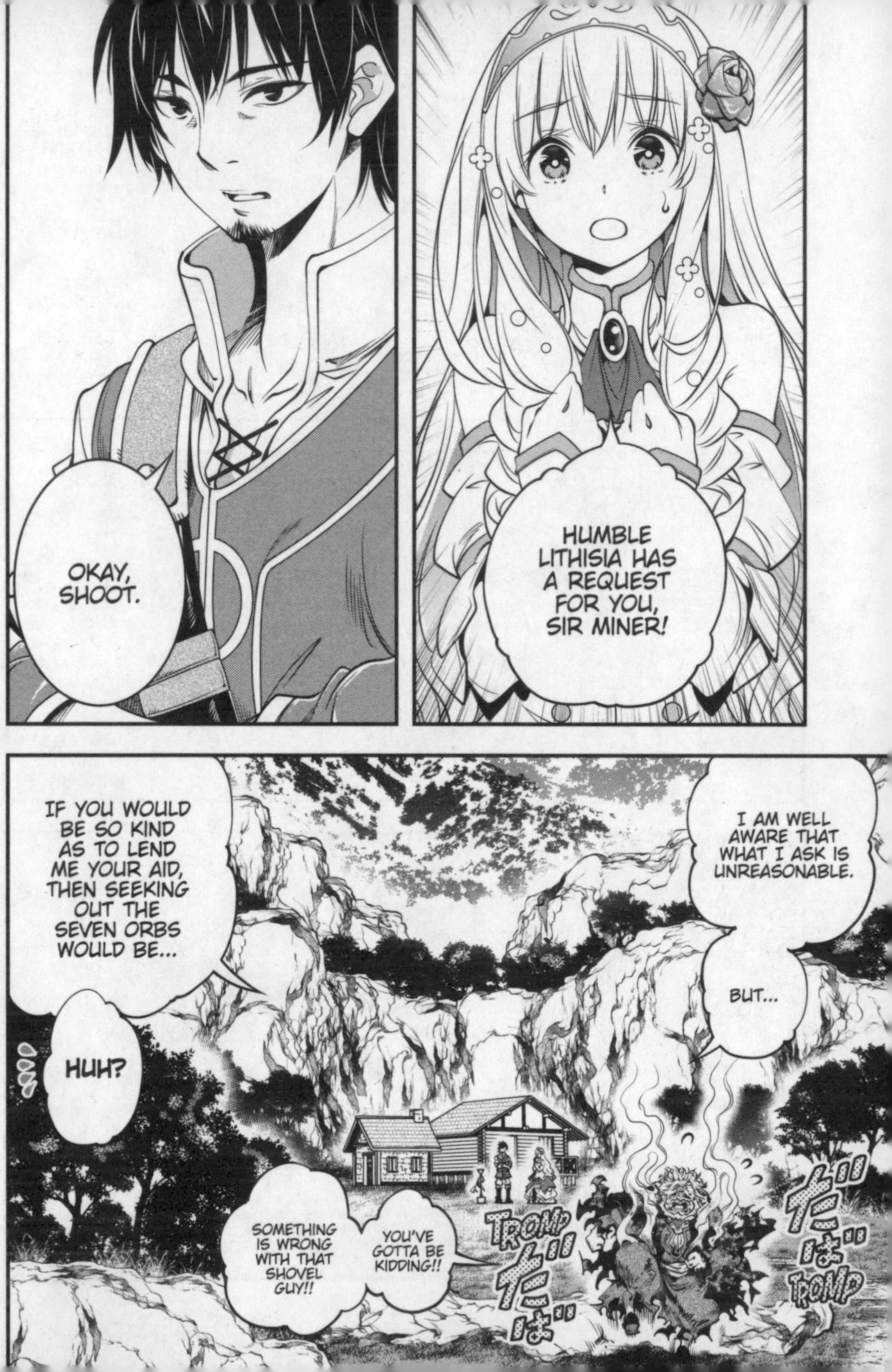
HUMBLE LITHISIA HAS A REQUEST FOR YOU, SIR MINER!
OKAY, SHOOT.
I AM WELL AWARE THAT WHAT I ASK IS UNREASONABLE.
BUT...
IF YOU WOULD BE SO KIND AS TO LEND ME YOUR AID, THEN SEEKING OUT THE SEVEN ORBS WOULD BE...
HUH?
TROMP
TROMP
YOU'VE GOTTA BE KIDDING!!
SOMETHING IS WRONG WITH THAT SHOVEL GUY!!

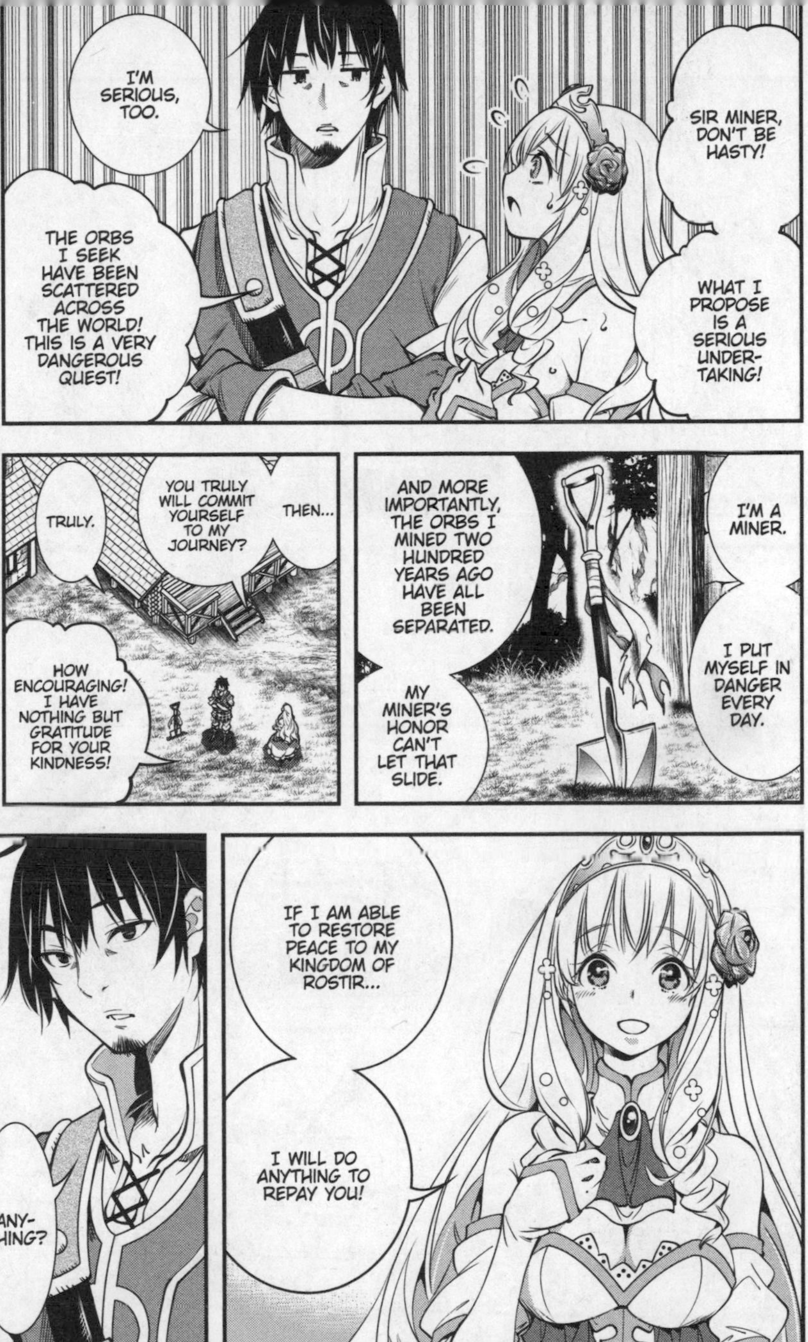
SIR MINER, DON'T BE HASTY!
WHAT I PROPOSE IS A SERIOUS UNDER-TAKING!
I'M SERIOUS, TOO.
THE ORBS I SEEK HAVE BEEN SCATTERED ACROSS THE WORLD! THIS IS A VERY DANGEROUS QUEST!
I'M A MINER.
I PUT MYSELF IN DANGER EVERY DAY.
AND MORE IMPORTANTLY, THE ORBS I MINED TWO HUNDRED YEARS AGO HAVE ALL BEEN SEPARATED.
MY MINER'S HONOR CAN'T LET THAT SLIDE.
THEN...
YOU TRULY WILL COMMIT YOURSELF TO MY JOURNEY?
TRULY.
HOW ENCOURAGING! I HAVE NOTHING BUT GRATITUDE FOR YOUR KINDNESS!
IF I AM ABLE TO RESTORE PEACE TO MY KINGDOM OF ROSTIR...
I WILL DO ANYTHING TO REPAY YOU!
ANY-THING?

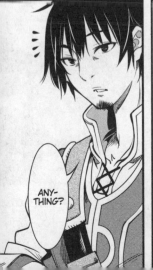

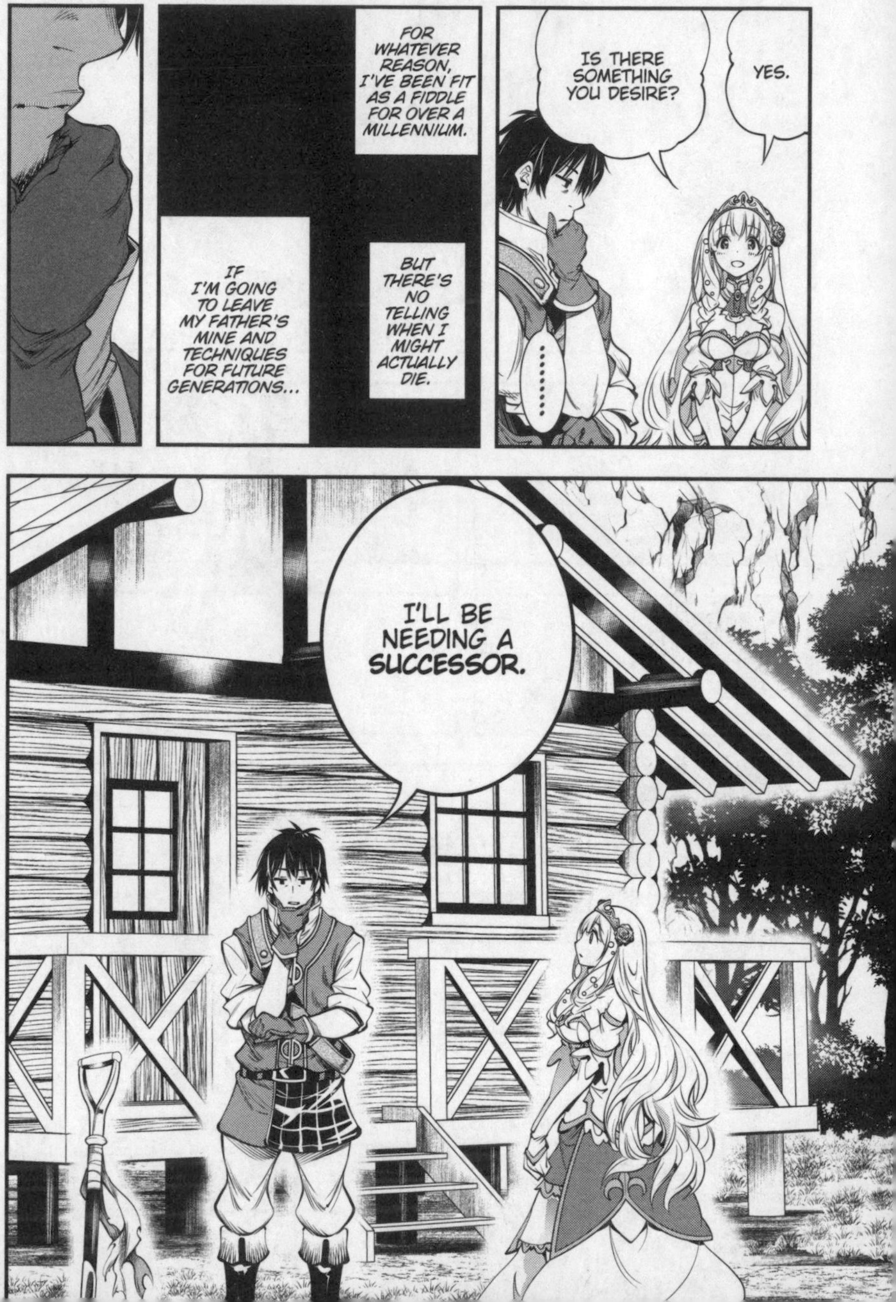
YES.
IS THERE SOMETHING YOU DESIRE?
......
FOR WHATEVER REASON, I'VE BEEN FIT AS A FIDDLE FOR OVER A MILLENNIUM.
BUT THERE'S NO TELLING WHEN I MIGHT ACTUALLY DIE.
IF I'M GOING TO LEAVE MY FATHER'S MINE AND TECHNIQUES FOR FUTURE GENERATIONS...
I'LL BE NEEDING A SUCCESSOR.

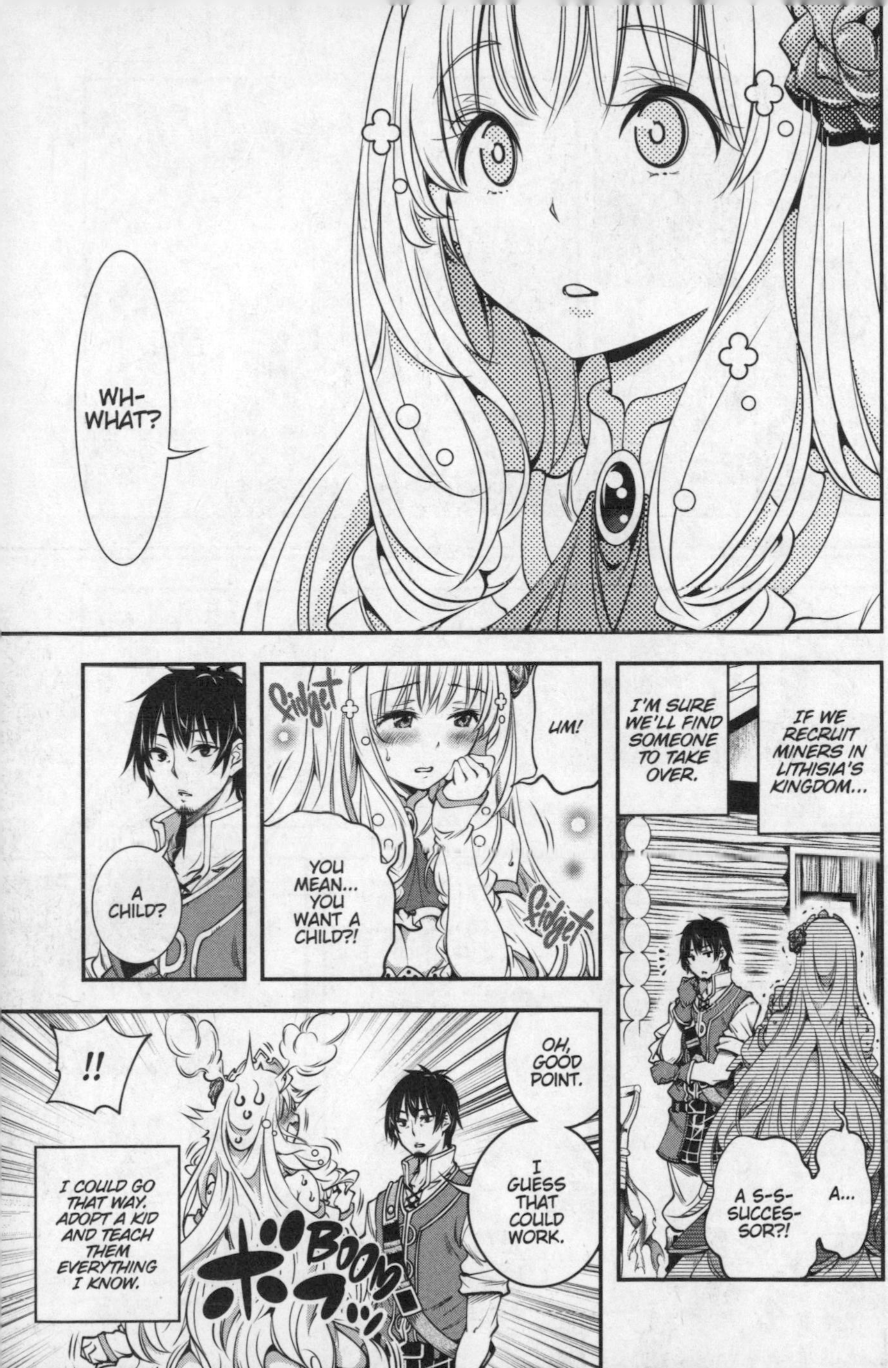
WH- WHAT?
IF WE RECRUIT MINERS IN LITHISIA'S KINGDOM...
I'M SURE WE'LL FIND SOMEONE TO TAKE OVER.
A...
A S-S-SUCCES-SOR?!
UM!
fidget
fidget
YOU MEAN... YOU WANT A CHILD?!
A CHILD?
OH, GOOD POINT.
I GUESS THAT COULD WORK.
!!
I COULD GO THAT WAY. ADOPT A KID AND TEACH THEM EVERYTHING I KNOW.
BOOM

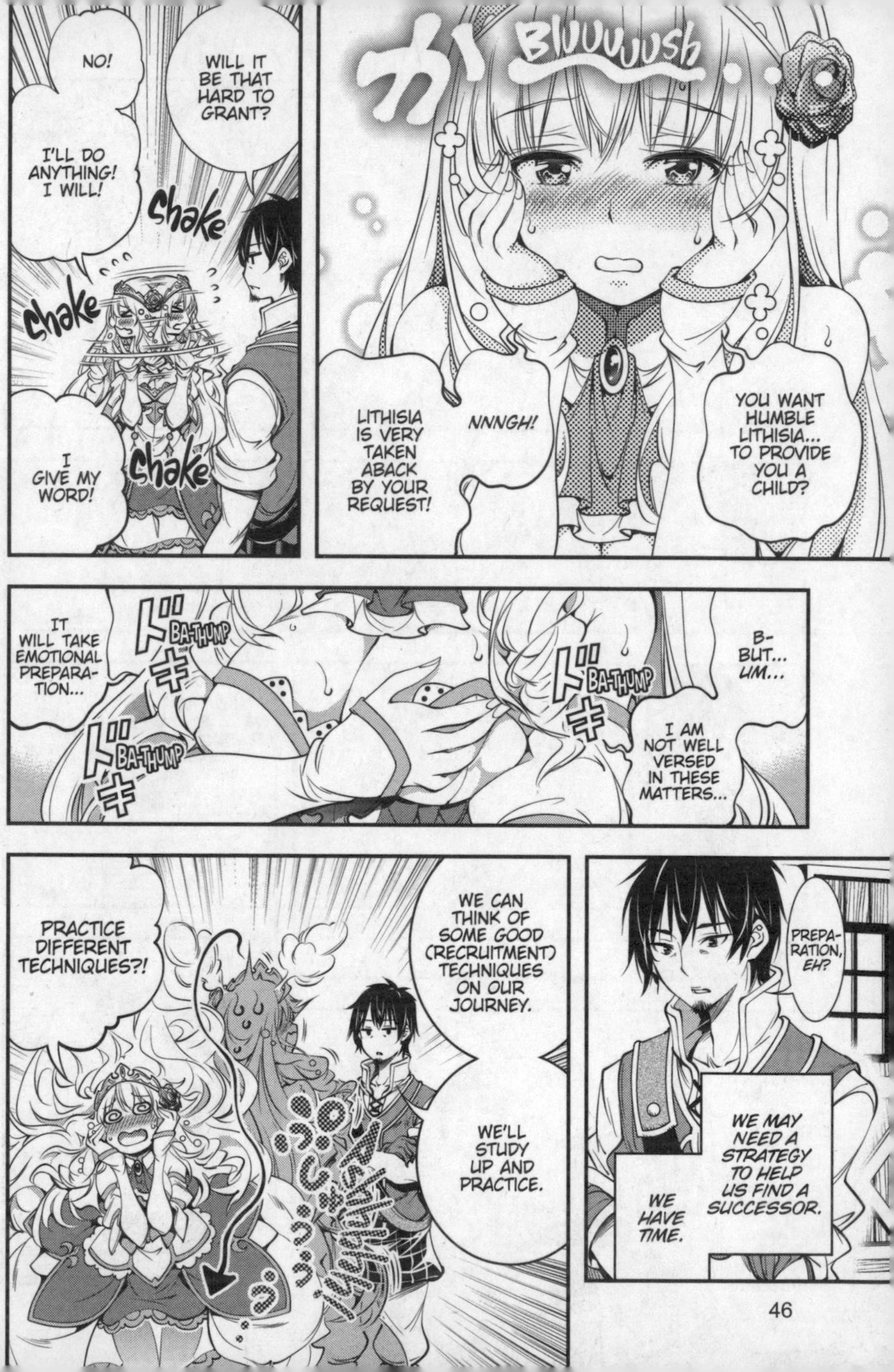
カ! Bluuuush
YOU WANT HUMBLE LITHISIA... TO PROVIDE YOU A CHILD?
NNNGH!
LITHISIA IS VERY TAKEN ABACK BY YOUR REQUEST!
WILL IT BE THAT HARD TO GRANT?
NO!
I'LL DO ANYTHING! I WILL!
Shake
Shake
I GIVE MY WORD!
Shake
B- BUT... UM...
I AM NOT WELL VERSED IN THESE MATTERS...
ドキ BA-THUMP
IT WILL TAKE EMOTIONAL PREPARATION...
ドキ BA-THUMP
ドキ BA-THUMP
PREPARATION, EH?
WE MAY NEED A STRATEGY TO HELP US FIND A SUCCESSOR.
WE HAVE TIME.
WE CAN THINK OF SOME GOOD (RECRUITMENT) TECHNIQUES ON OUR JOURNEY.
WE'LL STUDY UP AND PRACTICE.
PRACTICE DIFFERENT TECHNIQUES?!

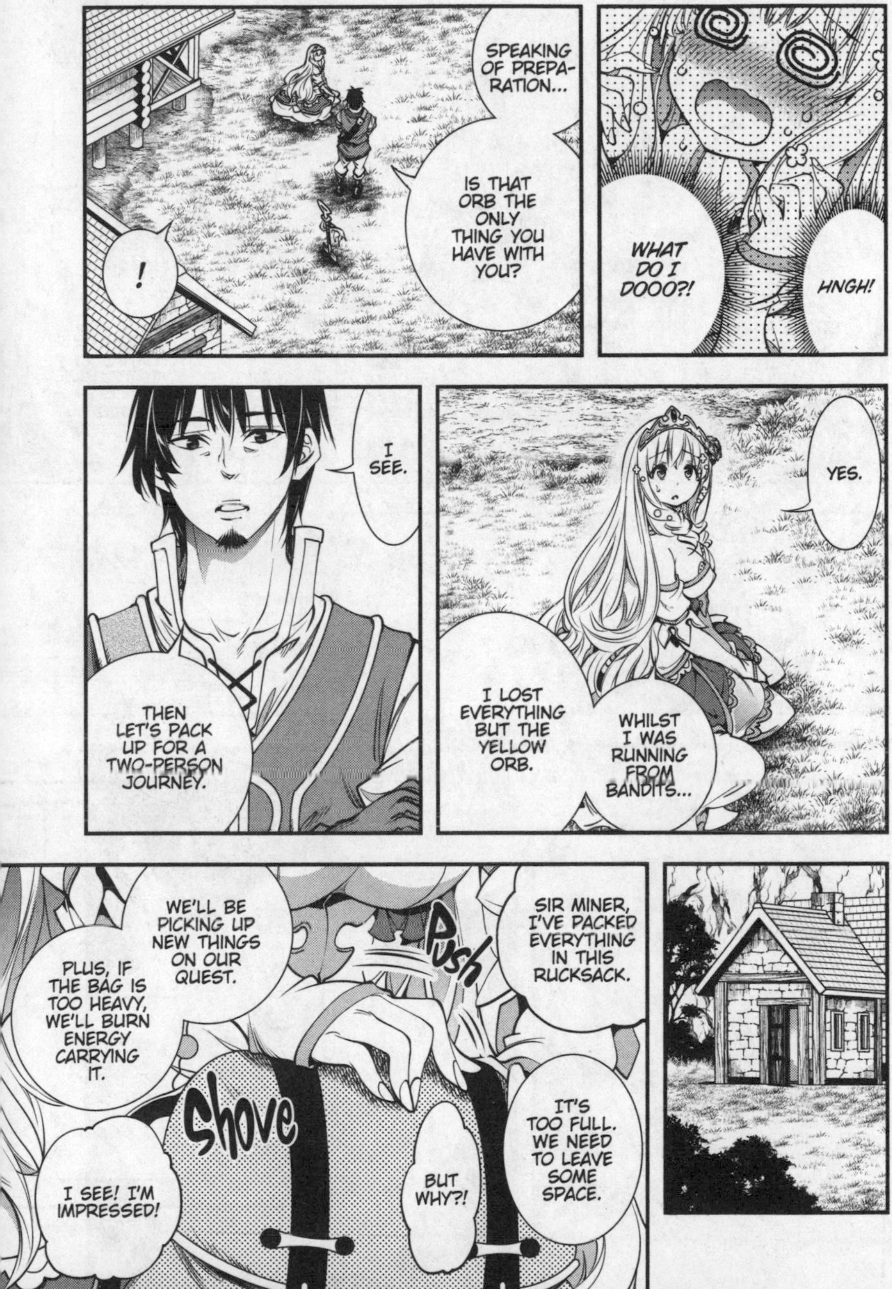
HNGH!
WHAT DO I DOOO?!
SPEAKING OF PREPA-RATION...
IS THAT ORB THE ONLY THING YOU HAVE WITH YOU?
!
YES.
WHILST I WAS RUNNING FROM BANDITS...
I LOST EVERYTHING BUT THE YELLOW ORB.
I SEE.
THEN LET'S PACK UP FOR A TWO-PERSON JOURNEY.
SIR MINER, I'VE PACKED EVERYTHING IN THIS RUCKSACK.
Push
IT'S TOO FULL. WE NEED TO LEAVE SOME SPACE.
BUT WHY?!
WE'LL BE PICKING UP NEW THINGS ON OUR QUEST.
PLUS, IF THE BAG IS TOO HEAVY, WE'LL BURN ENERGY CARRYING IT.
Shove
I SEE! I'M IMPRESSED!

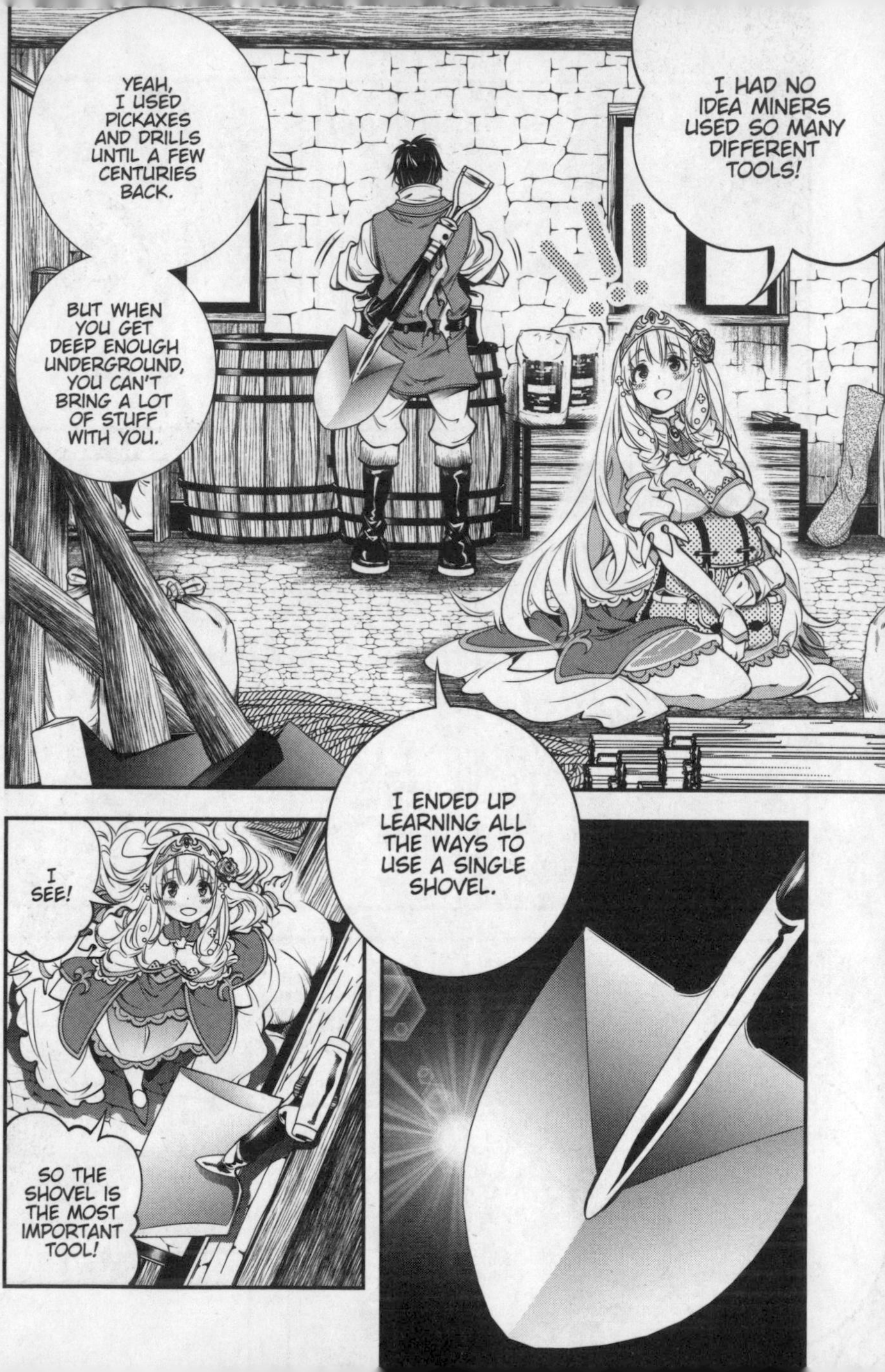
I HAD NO IDEA MINERS USED SO MANY DIFFERENT TOOLS!
YEAH, I USED PICKAXES AND DRILLS UNTIL A FEW CENTURIES BACK.
BUT WHEN YOU GET DEEP ENOUGH UNDERGROUND, YOU CAN'T BRING A LOT OF STUFF WITH YOU.
I ENDED UP LEARNING ALL THE WAYS TO USE A SINGLE SHOVEL.
I SEE!
SO THE SHOVEL IS THE MOST IMPORTANT TOOL!

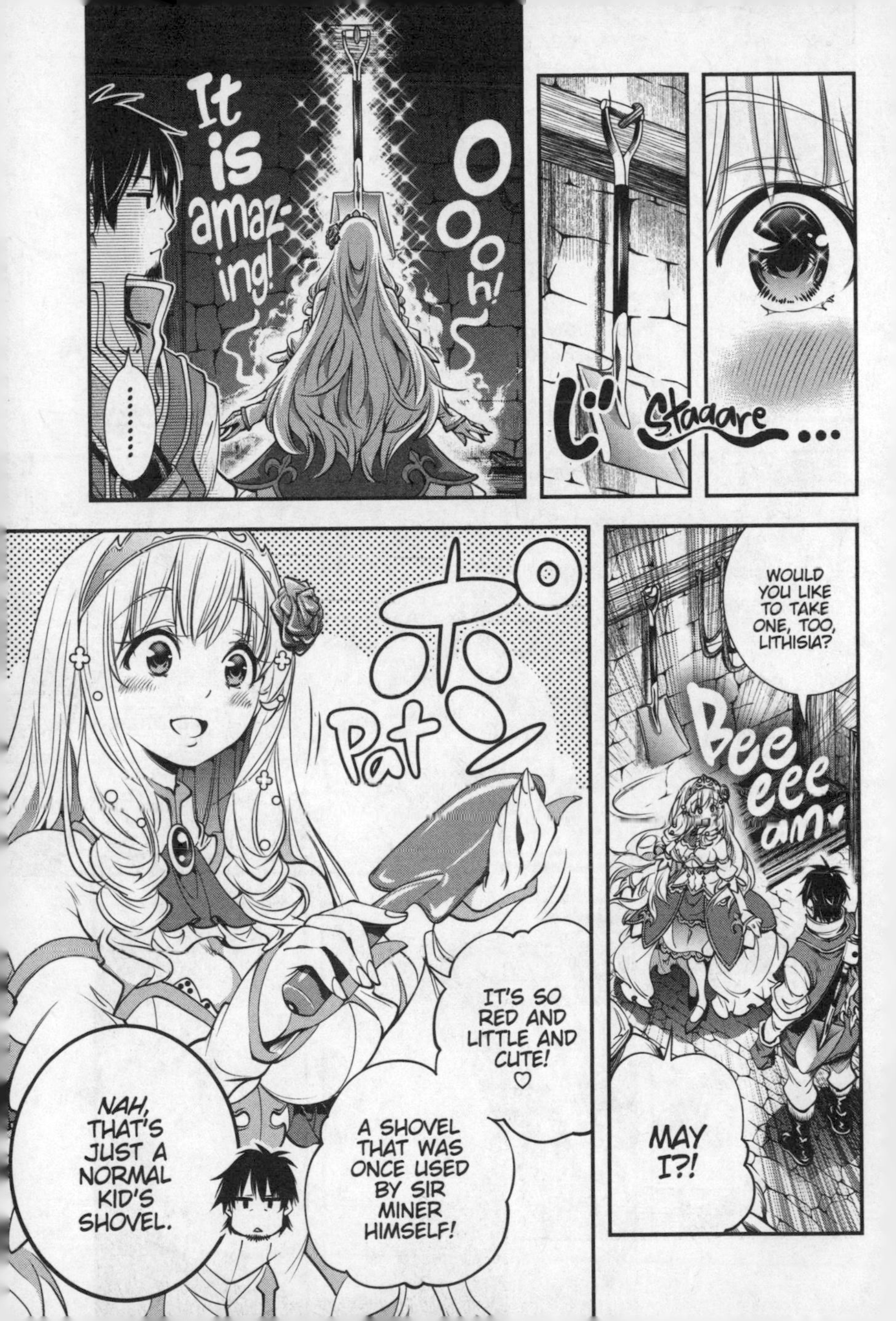
Staaare...
Oooh!
It is amazing!
......
WOULD YOU LIKE TO TAKE ONE, TOO, LITHISIA?
Beeeeeam
MAY I?!
Pat
IT'S SO RED AND LITTLE AND CUTE! ♡
A SHOVEL THAT WAS ONCE USED BY SIR MINER HIMSELF!
NAH, THAT'S JUST A NORMAL KID'S SHOVEL.

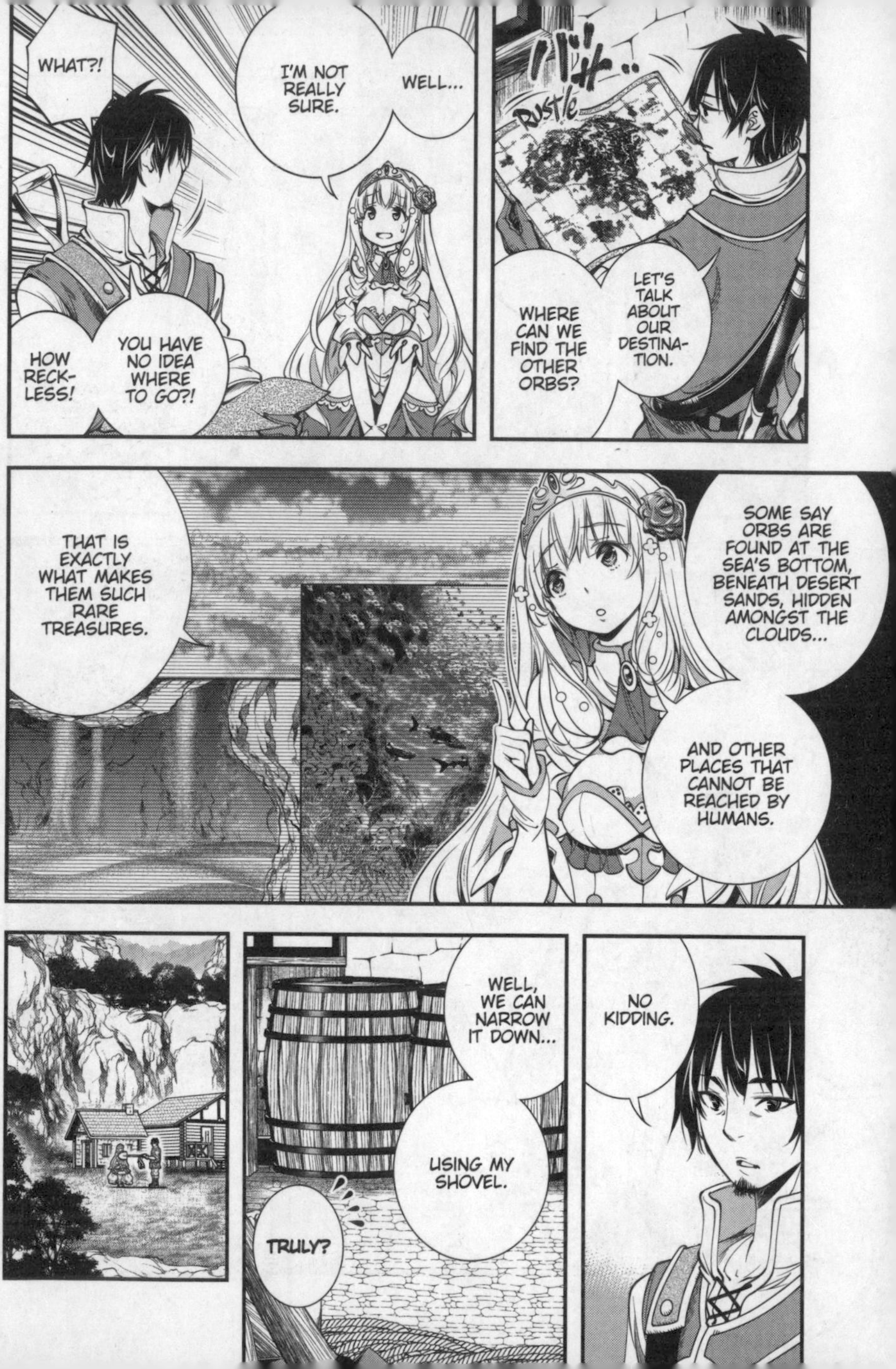
RUSTLE
LET'S TALK ABOUT OUR DESTINATION.
WHERE CAN WE FIND THE OTHER ORBS?
WELL...
I'M NOT REALLY SURE.
WHAT?!
YOU HAVE NO IDEA WHERE TO GO?!
HOW RECK-LESS!
SOME SAY ORBS ARE FOUND AT THE SEA'S BOTTOM, BENEATH DESERT SANDS, HIDDEN AMONGST THE CLOUDS...
AND OTHER PLACES THAT CANNOT BE REACHED BY HUMANS.
THAT IS EXACTLY WHAT MAKES THEM SUCH RARE TREASURES.
NO KIDDING.
WELL, WE CAN NARROW IT DOWN...
USING MY SHOVEL.
TRULY?

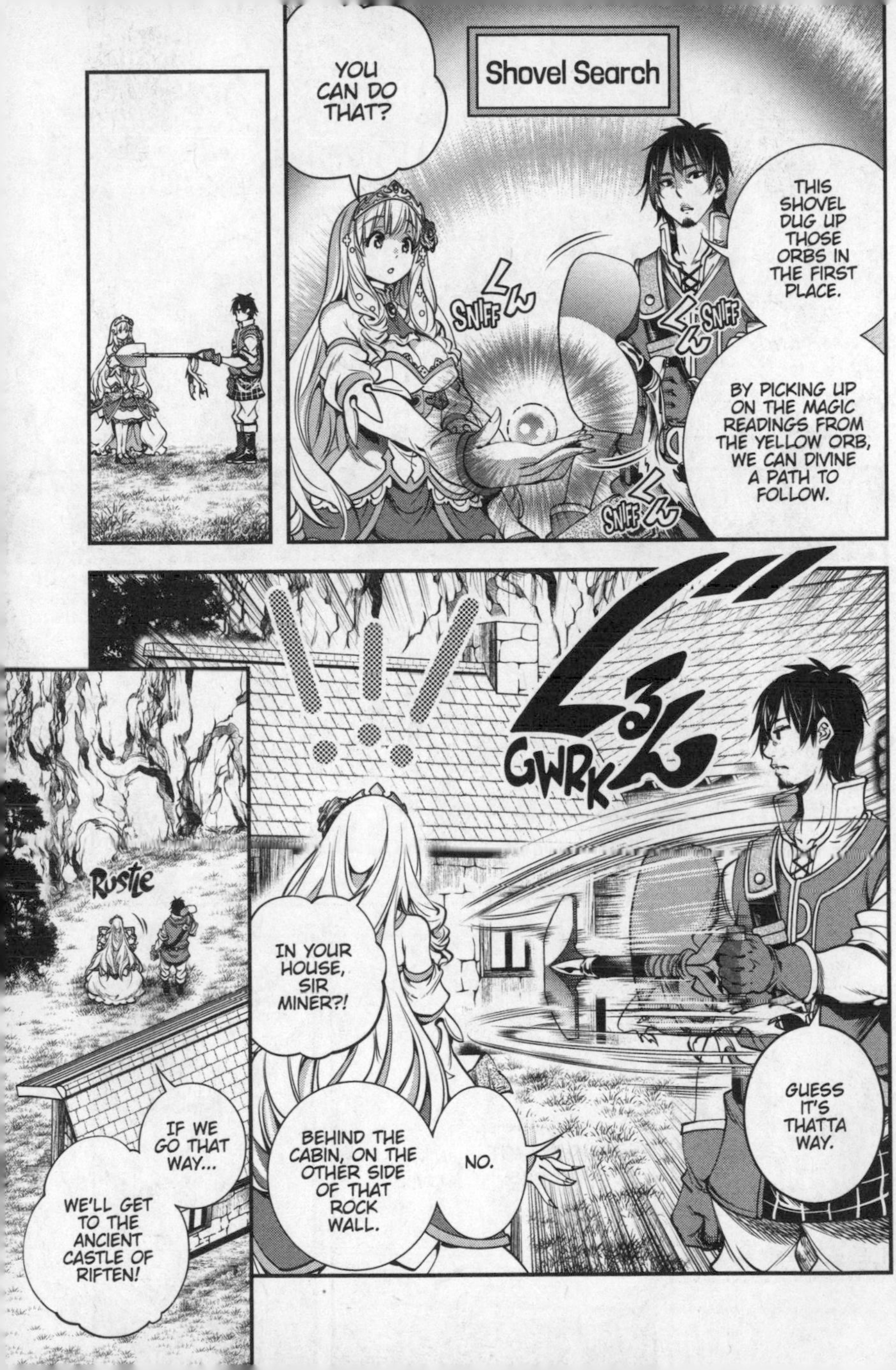
Shovel Search
YOU CAN DO THAT?
THIS SHOVEL DUG UP THOSE ORBS IN THE FIRST PLACE.
SNIFF
SNIFF
BY PICKING UP ON THE MAGIC READINGS FROM THE YELLOW ORB, WE CAN DIVINE A PATH TO FOLLOW.
SNIFF
GWRK
!!
GUESS IT'S THATTA WAY.
IN YOUR HOUSE, SIR MINER?!
NO.
BEHIND THE CABIN, ON THE OTHER SIDE OF THAT ROCK WALL.
RUSTLE
IF WE GO THAT WAY...
WE'LL GET TO THE ANCIENT CASTLE OF RIFTEN!

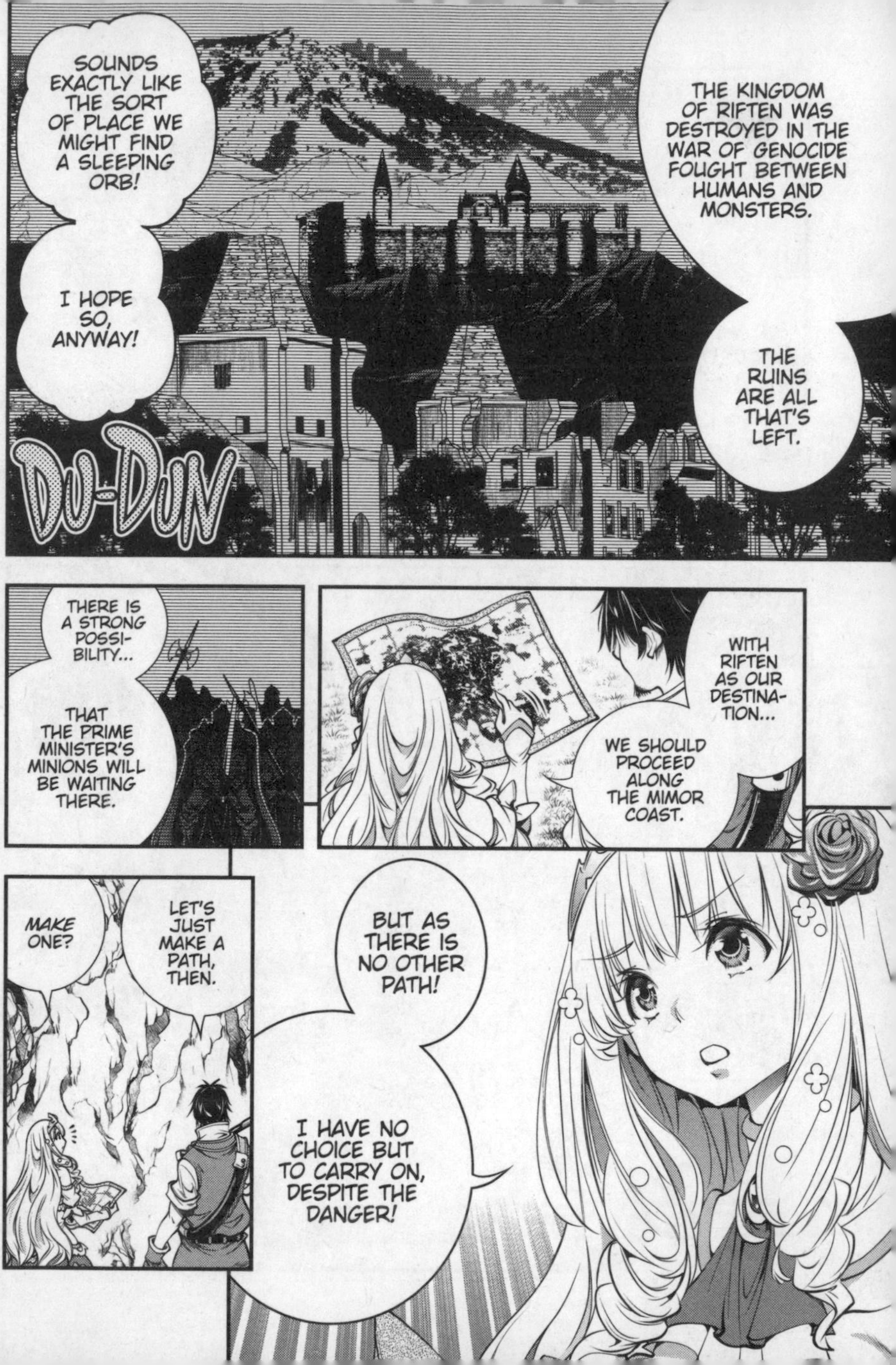
THE KINGDOM OF RIFTEN WAS DESTROYED IN THE WAR OF GENOCIDE FOUGHT BETWEEN HUMANS AND MONSTERS.
THE RUINS ARE ALL THAT'S LEFT.
SOUNDS EXACTLY LIKE THE SORT OF PLACE WE MIGHT FIND A SLEEPING ORB!
I HOPE SO, ANYWAY!
DU-DON
WITH RIFTEN AS OUR DESTINATION...
WE SHOULD PROCEED ALONG THE MIMOR COAST.
THERE IS A STRONG POSSIBILITY...
THAT THE PRIME MINISTER'S MINIONS WILL BE WAITING THERE.
BUT AS THERE IS NO OTHER PATH!
I HAVE NO CHOICE BUT TO CARRY ON, DESPITE THE DANGER!
LET'S JUST MAKE A PATH, THEN.
MAKE ONE?

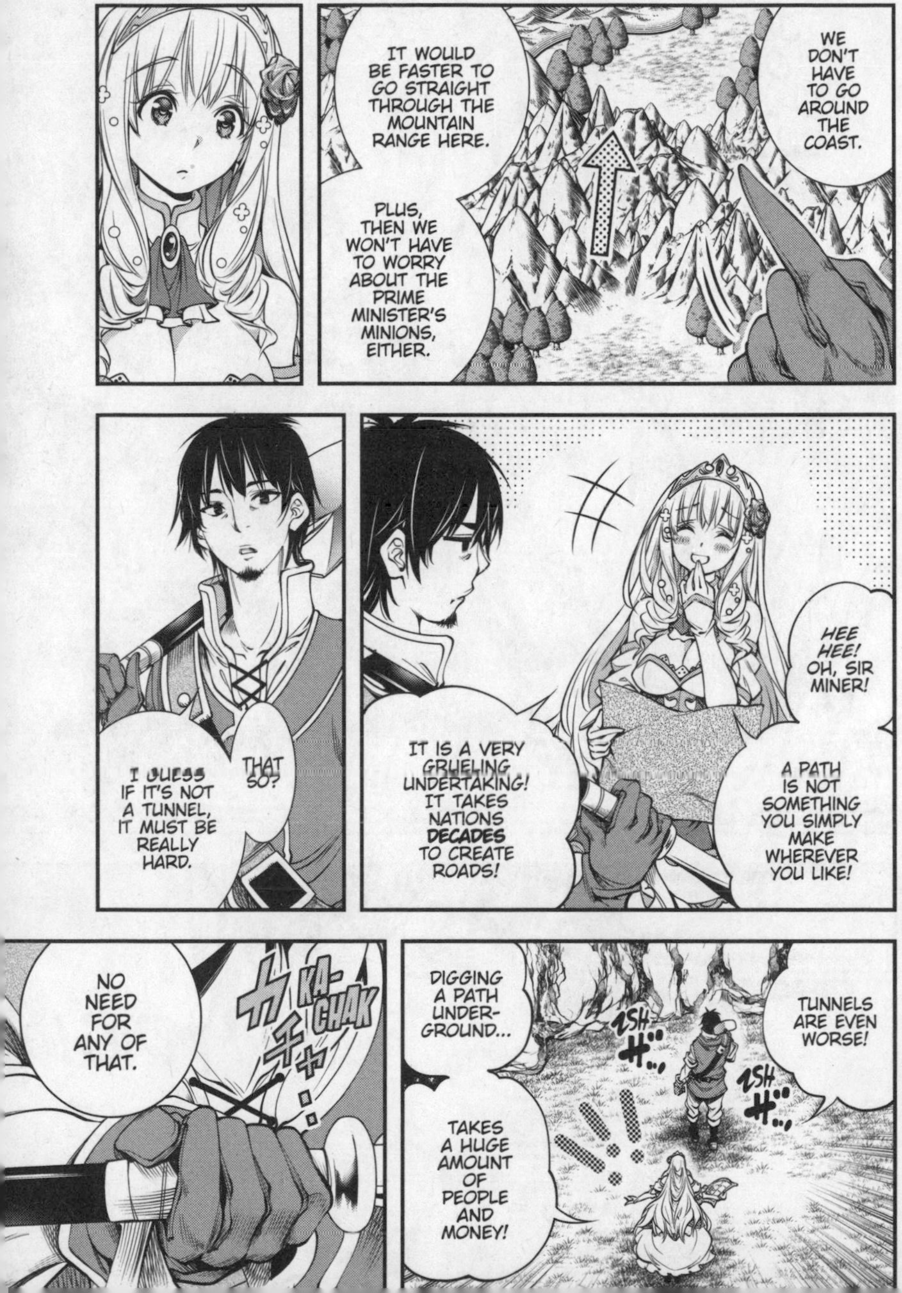
WE DON'T HAVE TO GO AROUND THE COAST.
IT WOULD BE FASTER TO GO STRAIGHT THROUGH THE MOUNTAIN RANGE HERE.
PLUS, THEN WE WON'T HAVE TO WORRY ABOUT THE PRIME MINISTER'S MINIONS, EITHER.
HEE HEE! OH, SIR MINER!
A PATH IS NOT SOMETHING YOU SIMPLY MAKE WHEREVER YOU LIKE!
IT IS A VERY GRUELING UNDERTAKING! IT TAKES NATIONS **DECADES** TO CREATE ROADS!
THAT SO?
I GUESS IF IT'S NOT A TUNNEL, IT MUST BE REALLY HARD.
TUNNELS ARE EVEN WORSE!
ZSH
ZSH
DIGGING A PATH UNDER-GROUND...
TAKES A HUGE AMOUNT OF PEOPLE AND MONEY!
KA-CHAK
NO NEED FOR ANY OF THAT.

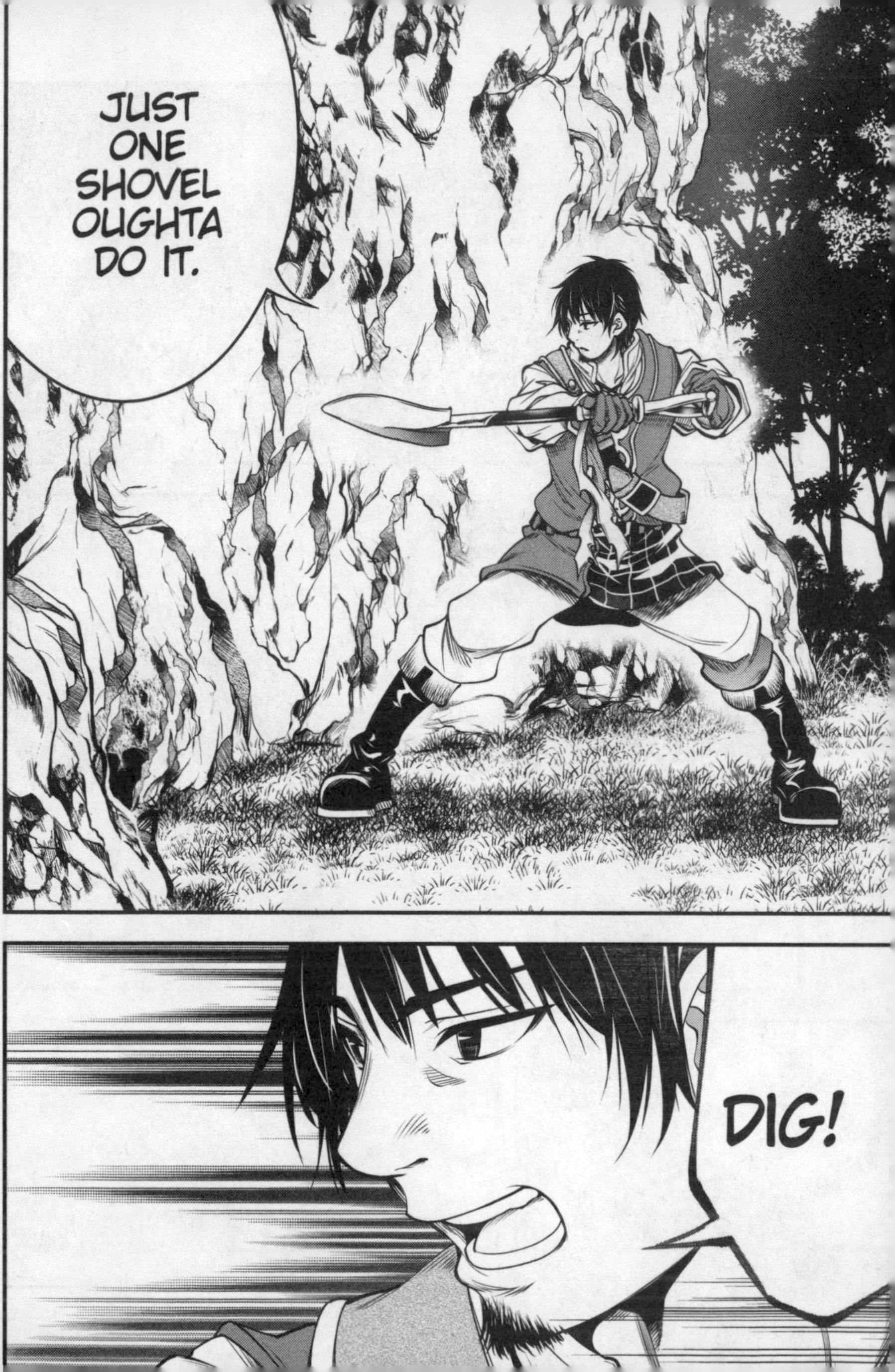
JUST ONE SHOVEL OUGHTA DO IT.
DIG!

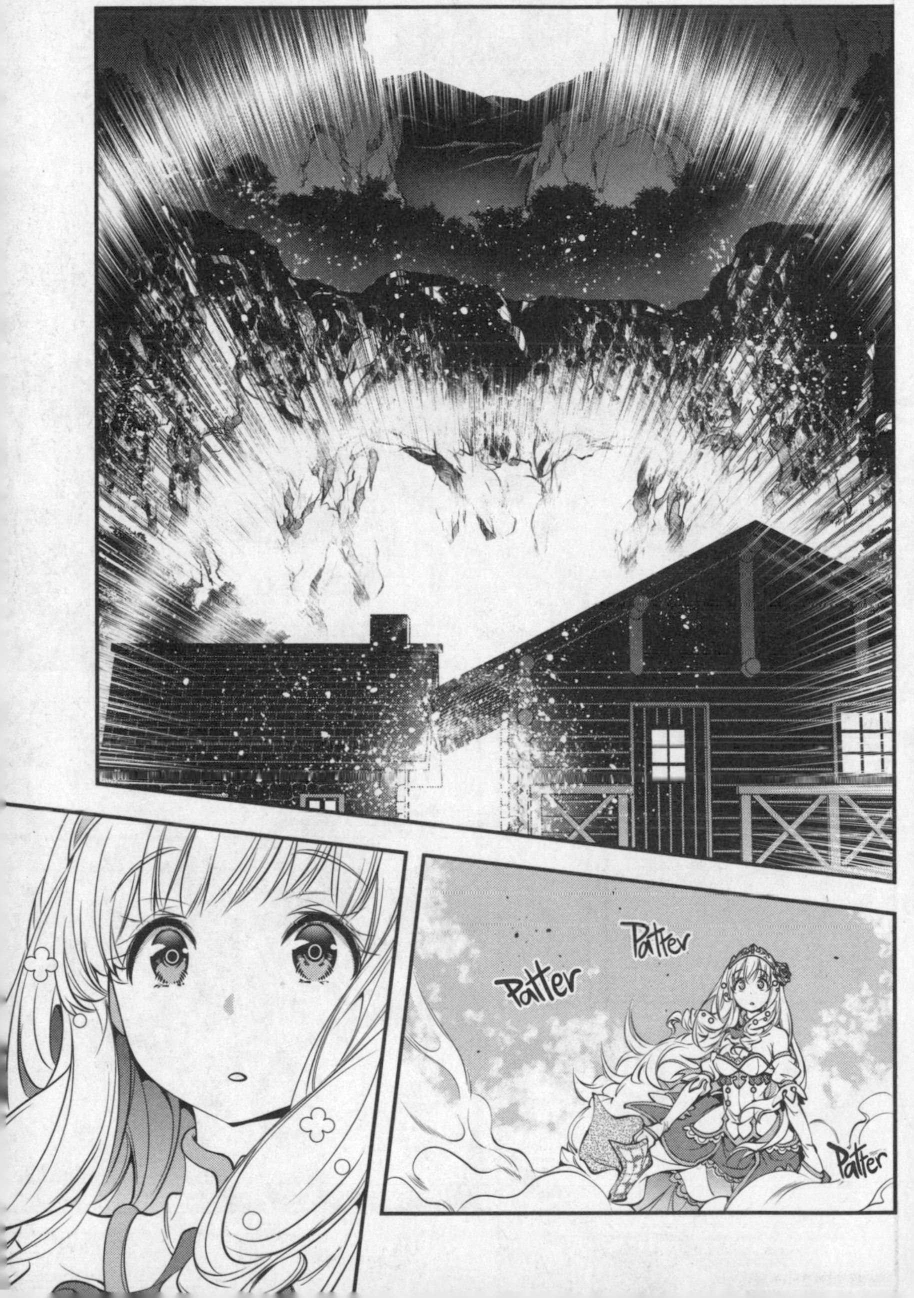
Patter
Patter
Patter

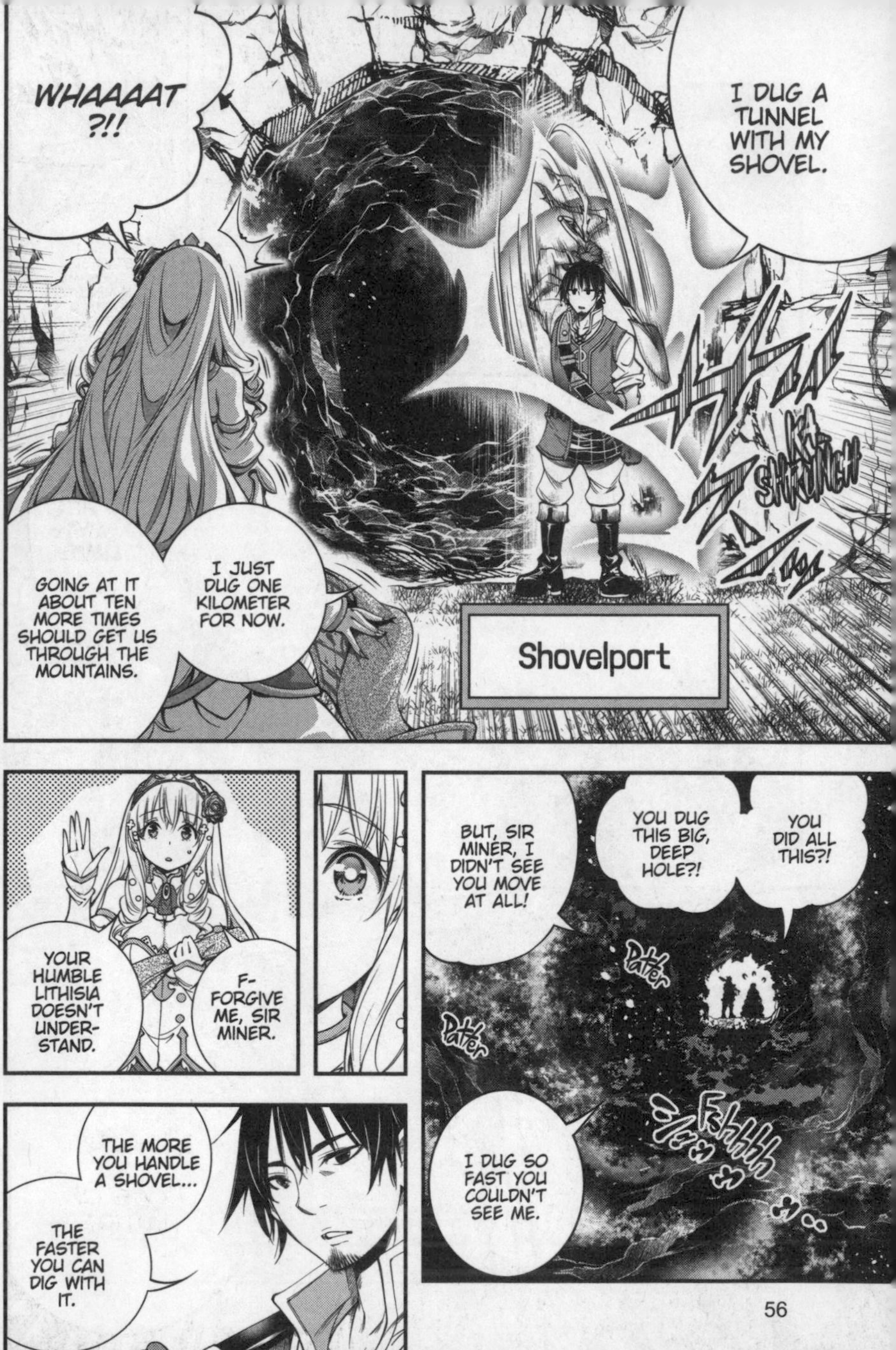
I DUG A TUNNEL WITH MY SHOVEL.
KA-SHRUNCH
WHAAAAT?!!
I JUST DUG ONE KILOMETER FOR NOW.
GOING AT IT ABOUT TEN MORE TIMES SHOULD GET US THROUGH THE MOUNTAINS.
Shovelport
YOU DID ALL THIS?!
YOU DUG THIS BIG, DEEP HOLE?!
BUT, SIR MINER, I DIDN'T SEE YOU MOVE AT ALL!
Patter
Patter
Fshhhhh
I DUG SO FAST YOU COULDN'T SEE ME.
F-FORGIVE ME, SIR MINER.
YOUR HUMBLE LITHISIA DOESN'T UNDER-STAND.
THE MORE YOU HANDLE A SHOVEL...
THE FASTER YOU CAN DIG WITH IT.

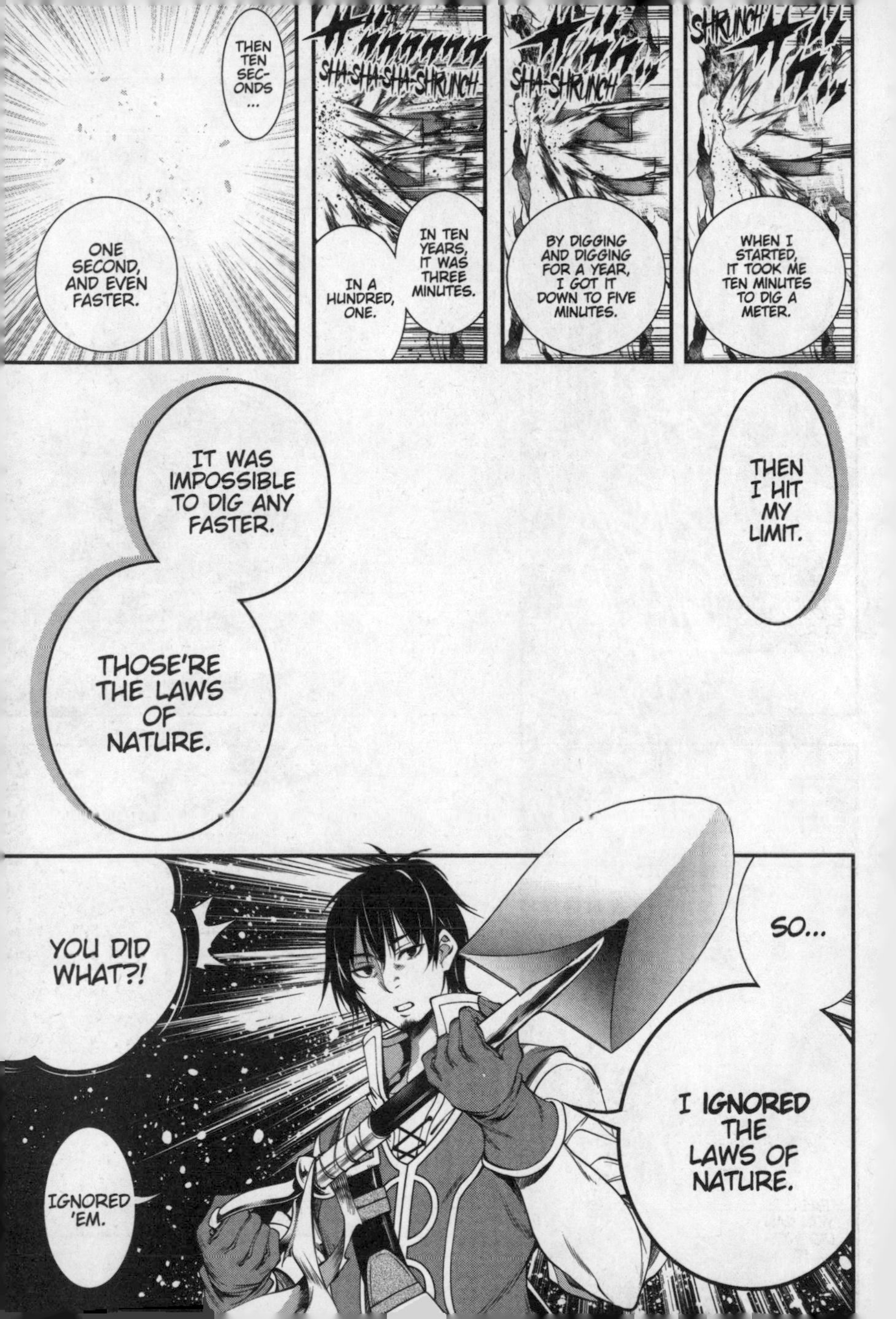
SHRUNCH
WHEN I STARTED, IT TOOK ME TEN MINUTES TO DIG A METER.
SHA-SHRUNCH
BY DIGGING AND DIGGING FOR A YEAR, I GOT IT DOWN TO FIVE MINUTES.
SHA-SHA-SHA-SHRUNCH
IN TEN YEARS, IT WAS THREE MINUTES.
IN A HUNDRED, ONE.
THEN TEN SEC-ONDS ...
ONE SECOND, AND EVEN FASTER.
THEN I HIT MY LIMIT.
IT WAS IMPOSSIBLE TO DIG ANY FASTER.
THOSE'RE THE LAWS OF NATURE.
SO...
I IGNORED THE LAWS OF NATURE.
YOU DID WHAT?!
IGNORED 'EM.

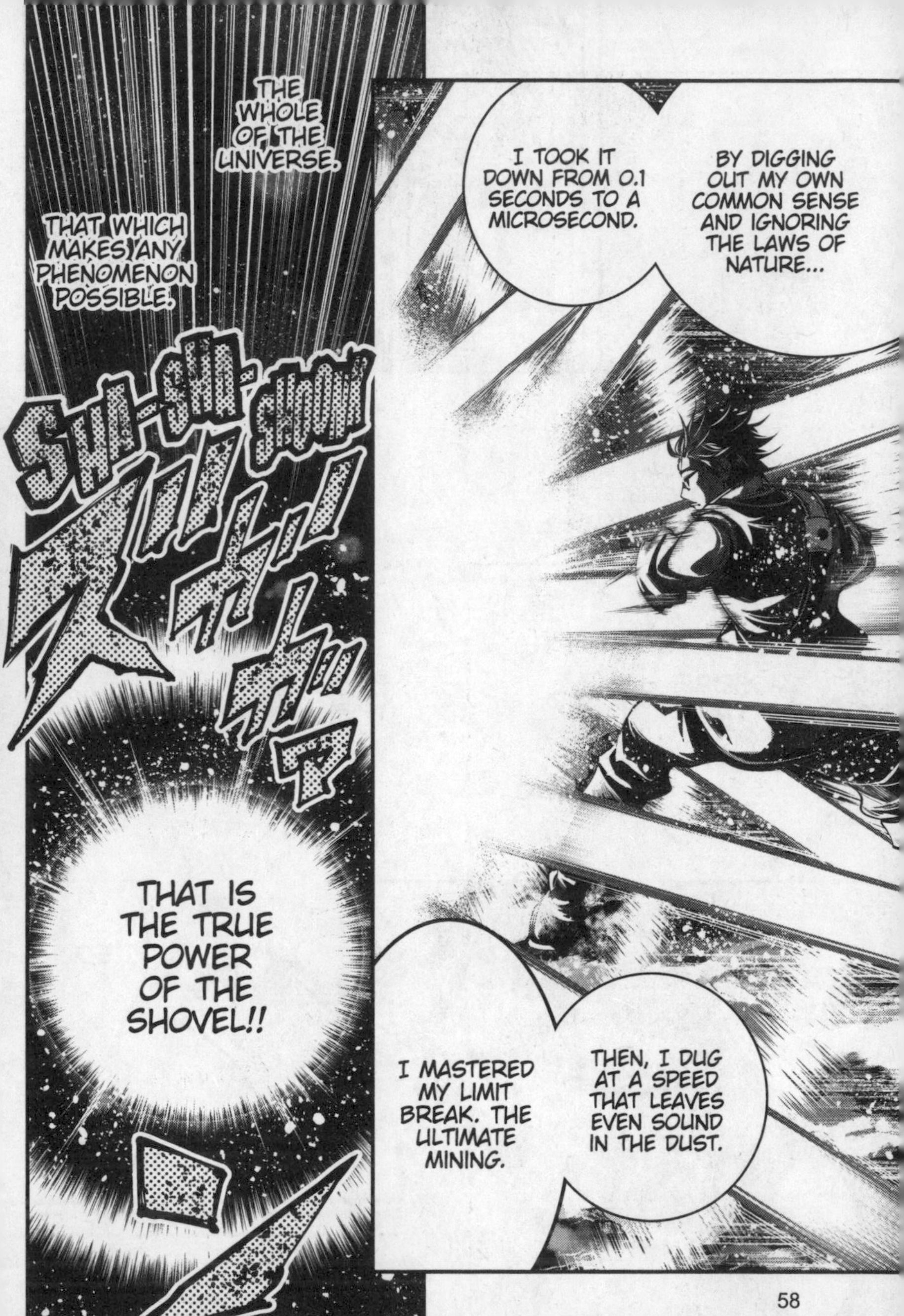
BY DIGGING OUT MY OWN COMMON SENSE AND IGNORING THE LAWS OF NATURE...
I TOOK IT DOWN FROM 0.1 SECONDS TO A MICROSECOND.
THEN, I DUG AT A SPEED THAT LEAVES EVEN SOUND IN THE DUST.
I MASTERED MY LIMIT BREAK. THE ULTIMATE MINING.
THE WHOLE OF THE UNIVERSE.
THAT WHICH MAKES ANY PHENOMENON POSSIBLE.
SHA-SHA-SHOOM!!
THAT IS THE TRUE POWER OF THE SHOVEL!!

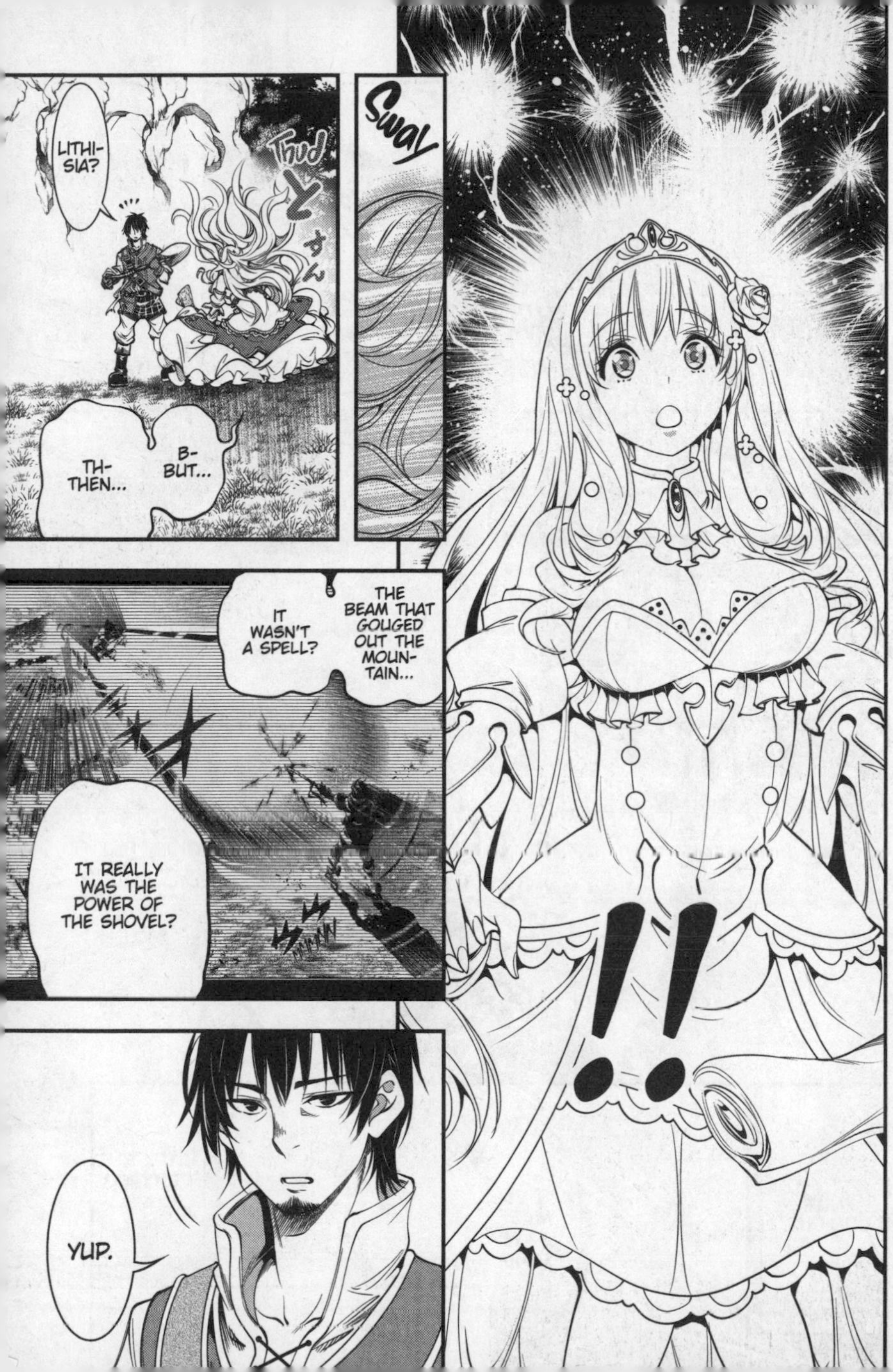
!!
SWAY
THUD
LITHISIA?
B-BUT...
TH-THEN...
THE BEAM THAT GOUGED OUT THE MOUNTAIN...
IT WASN'T A SPELL?
IT REALLY WAS THE POWER OF THE SHOVEL?
YUP.

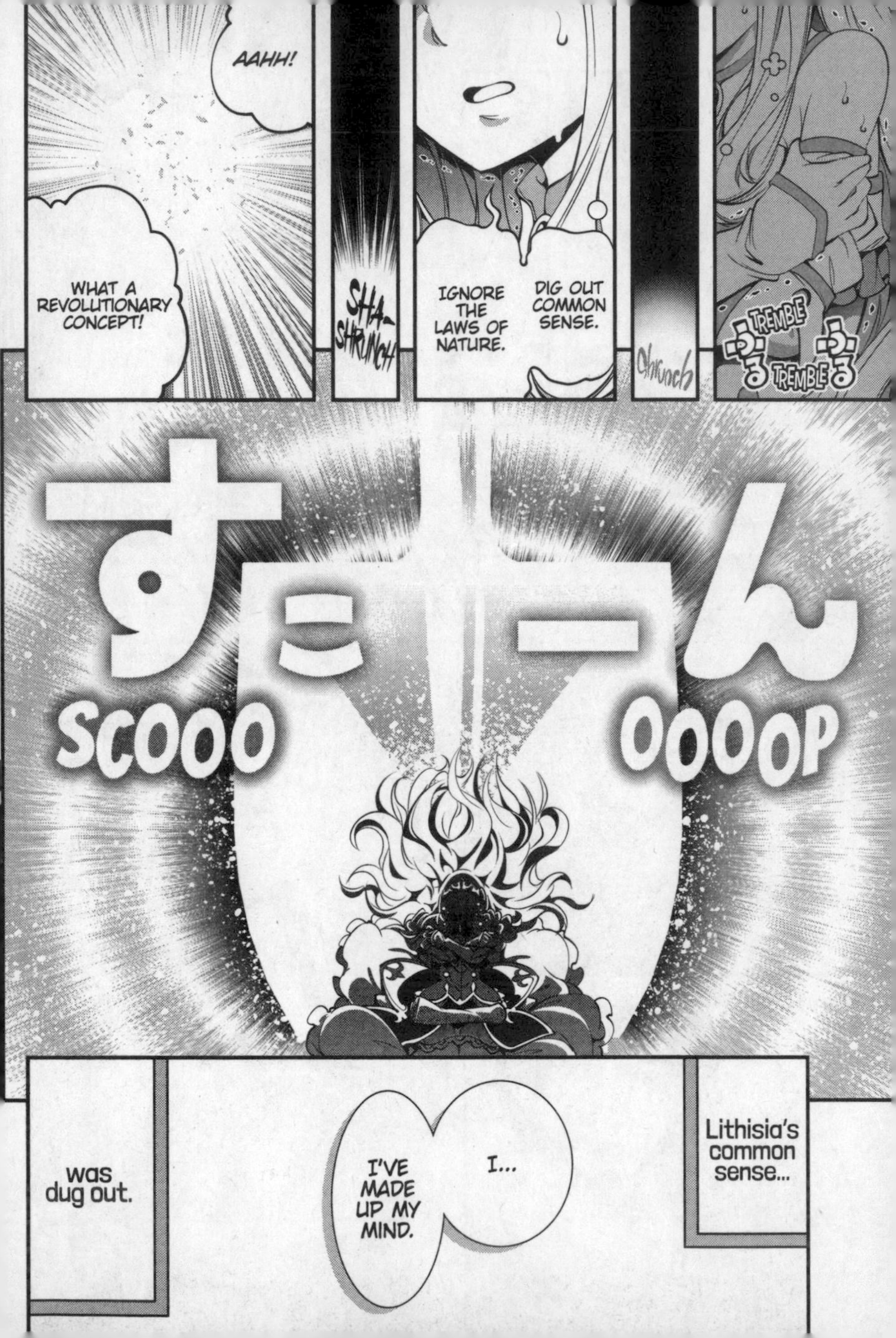
TREMBLE
TREMBLE
Shrunch
DIG OUT COMMON SENSE.
IGNORE THE LAWS OF NATURE.
SHA-SHRUNCH
AAHH!
WHAT A REVOLUTIONARY CONCEPT!
すーーん
SCOOO OOOOP
Lithisia's common sense...
I...
I'VE MADE UP MY MIND.
was dug out.

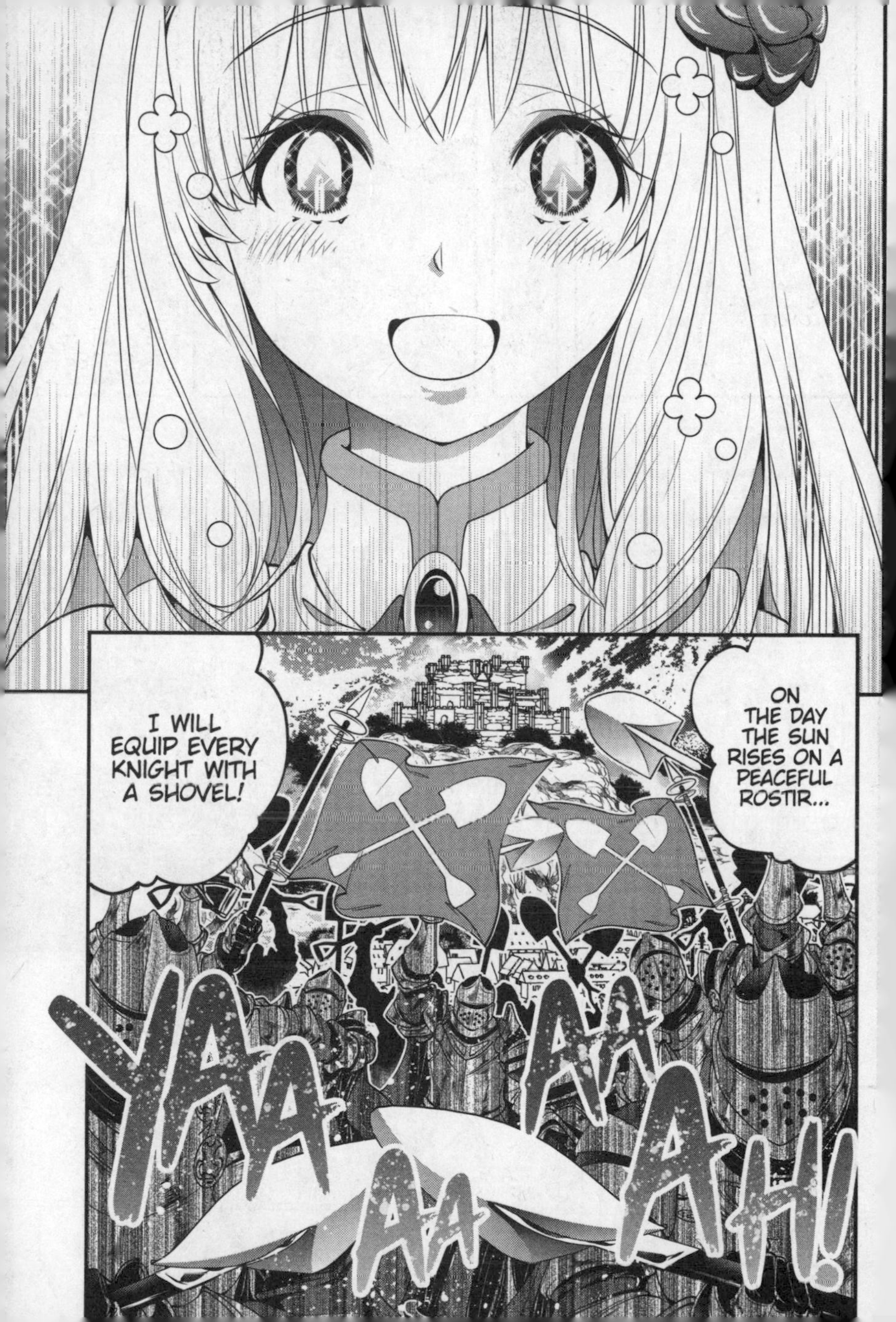
ON THE DAY THE SUN RISES ON A PEACEFUL ROSTIR...
I WILL EQUIP EVERY KNIGHT WITH A SHOVEL!
YAAAAAAAAAH!

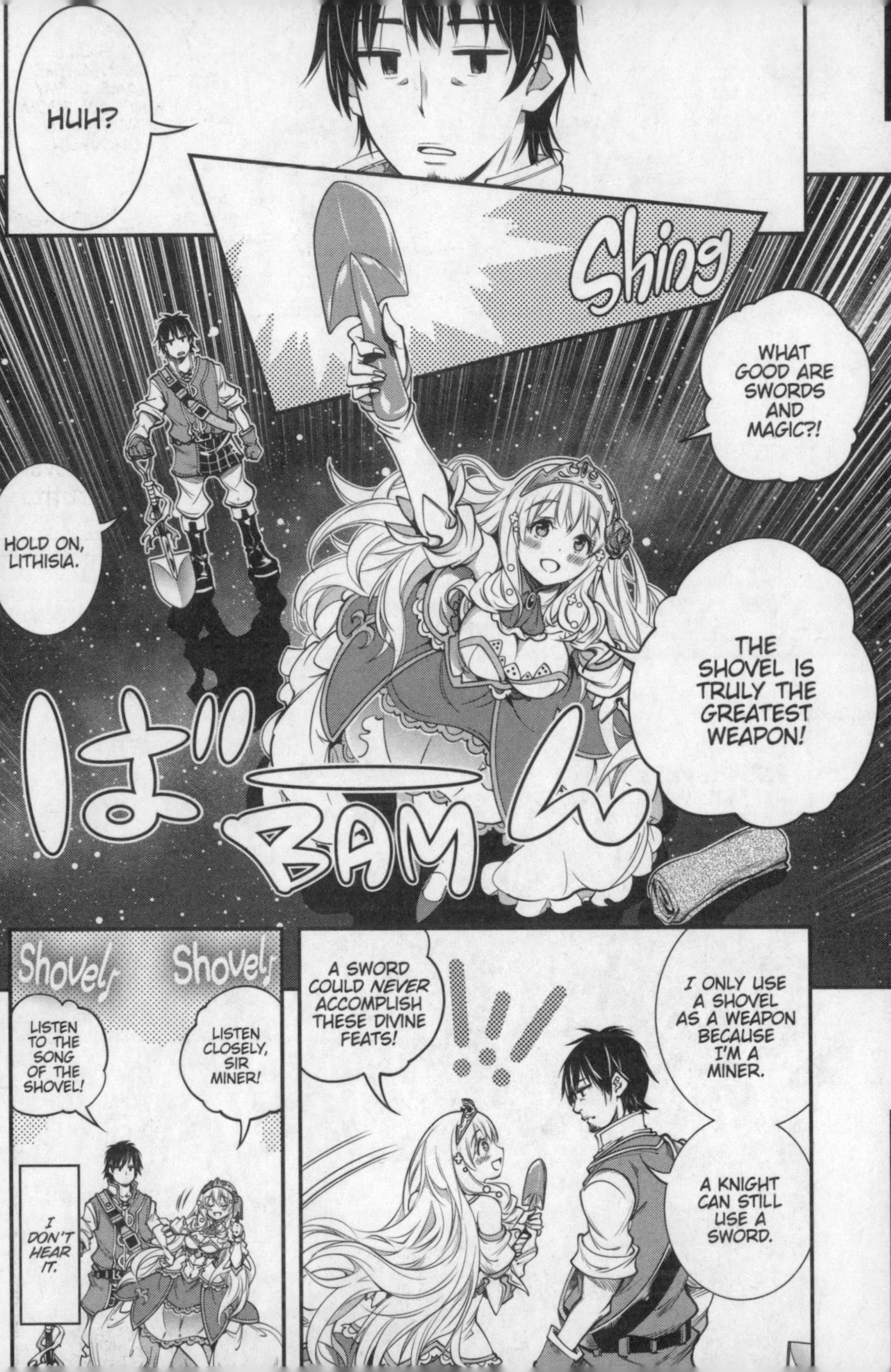
HUH?
Shing
WHAT GOOD ARE SWORDS AND MAGIC?!
THE SHOVEL IS TRULY THE GREATEST WEAPON!
HOLD ON, LITHISIA.
ばーん
BAM
I ONLY USE A SHOVEL AS A WEAPON BECAUSE I'M A MINER.
A KNIGHT CAN STILL USE A SWORD.
!!!
A SWORD COULD *NEVER* ACCOMPLISH THESE DIVINE FEATS!
Shovel♪
Shovel♪
LISTEN CLOSELY, SIR MINER!
LISTEN TO THE SONG OF THE SHOVEL!
I DON'T HEAR IT.

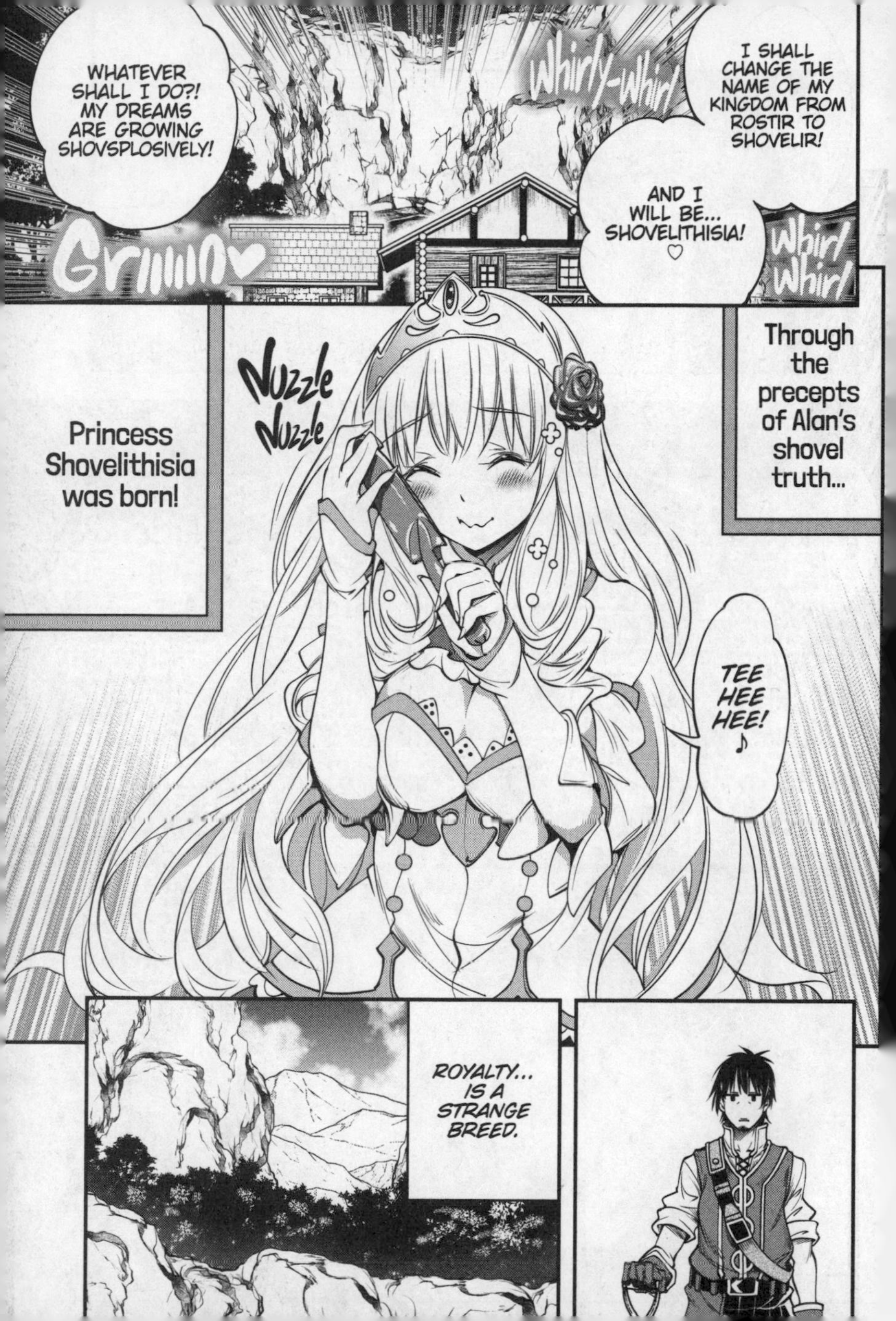

I SHALL CHANGE THE NAME OF MY KINGDOM FROM ROSTIR TO SHOVELIR!
whirly-whirl
AND I WILL BE... SHOVELITHISIA! ♡
whirl whirl
WHATEVER SHALL I DO?! MY DREAMS ARE GROWING SHOVSPLOSIVELY!
Grinnn♥
Through the precepts of Alan's shovel truth...
Nuzzle Nuzzle
Princess Shovelithisia was born!
TEE HEE HEE! ♪
ROYALTY... IS A STRANGE BREED.

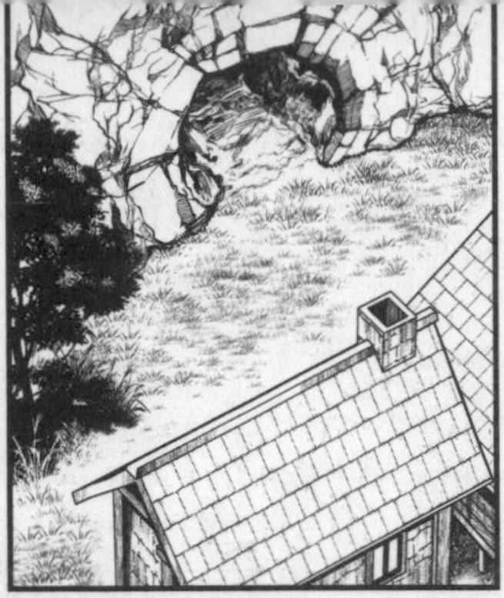

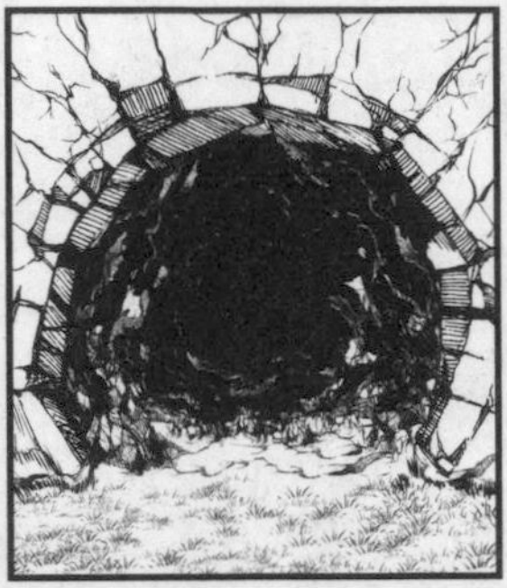

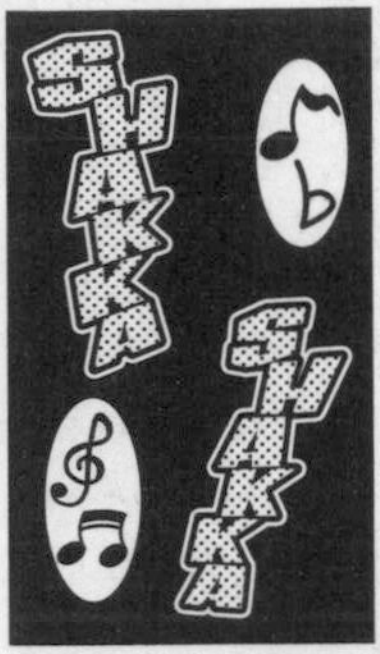
SHAKA
SHAKA

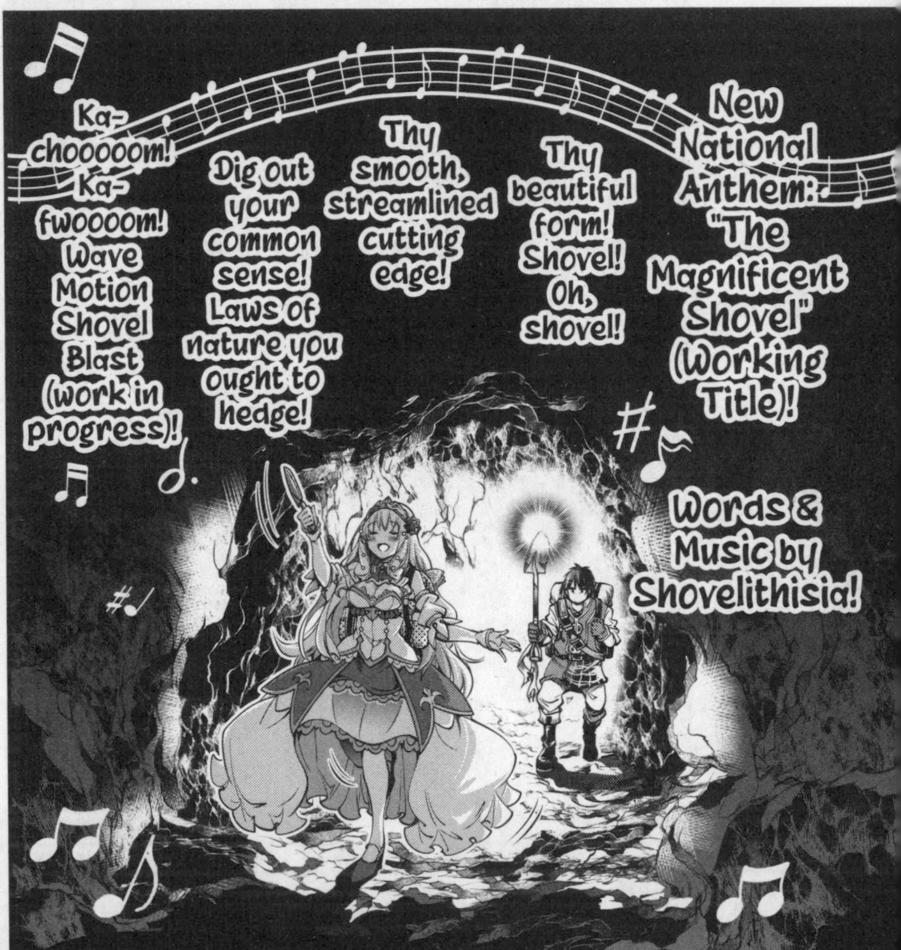
New National Anthem: "The Magnificent Shovel" (Working Title)!
Thy beautiful form! Shovel! Oh, shovel!
Thy smooth, streamlined cutting edge!
Dig out your common sense! Laws of nature you ought to hedge!
Ka-chooooom! Ka-fwoooom! Wave Motion Shovel Blast (work in progress)!
Words & Music by Shovelithisia!

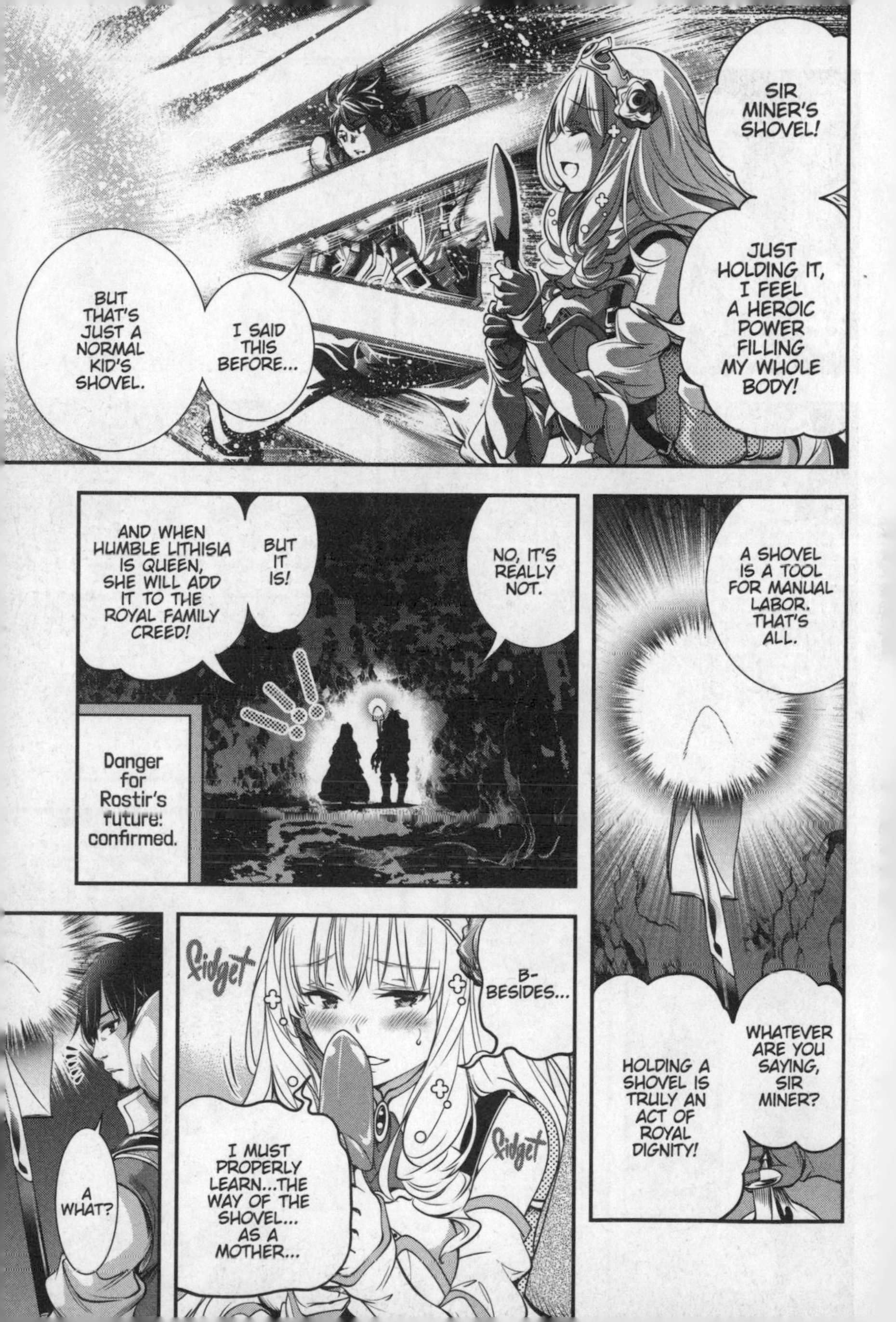
SIR MINER'S SHOVEL!
JUST HOLDING IT, I FEEL A HEROIC POWER FILLING MY WHOLE BODY!
I SAID THIS BEFORE...
BUT THAT'S JUST A NORMAL KID'S SHOVEL.
A SHOVEL IS A TOOL FOR MANUAL LABOR. THAT'S ALL.
WHATEVER ARE YOU SAYING, SIR MINER?
HOLDING A SHOVEL IS TRULY AN ACT OF ROYAL DIGNITY!
NO, IT'S REALLY NOT.
BUT IT IS!
AND WHEN HUMBLE LITHISIA IS QUEEN, SHE WILL ADD IT TO THE ROYAL FAMILY CREED!
Danger for Rostir's future: confirmed.
fidget
B-BESIDES...
fidget
I MUST PROPERLY LEARN...THE WAY OF THE SHOVEL... AS A MOTHER...
A WHAT?

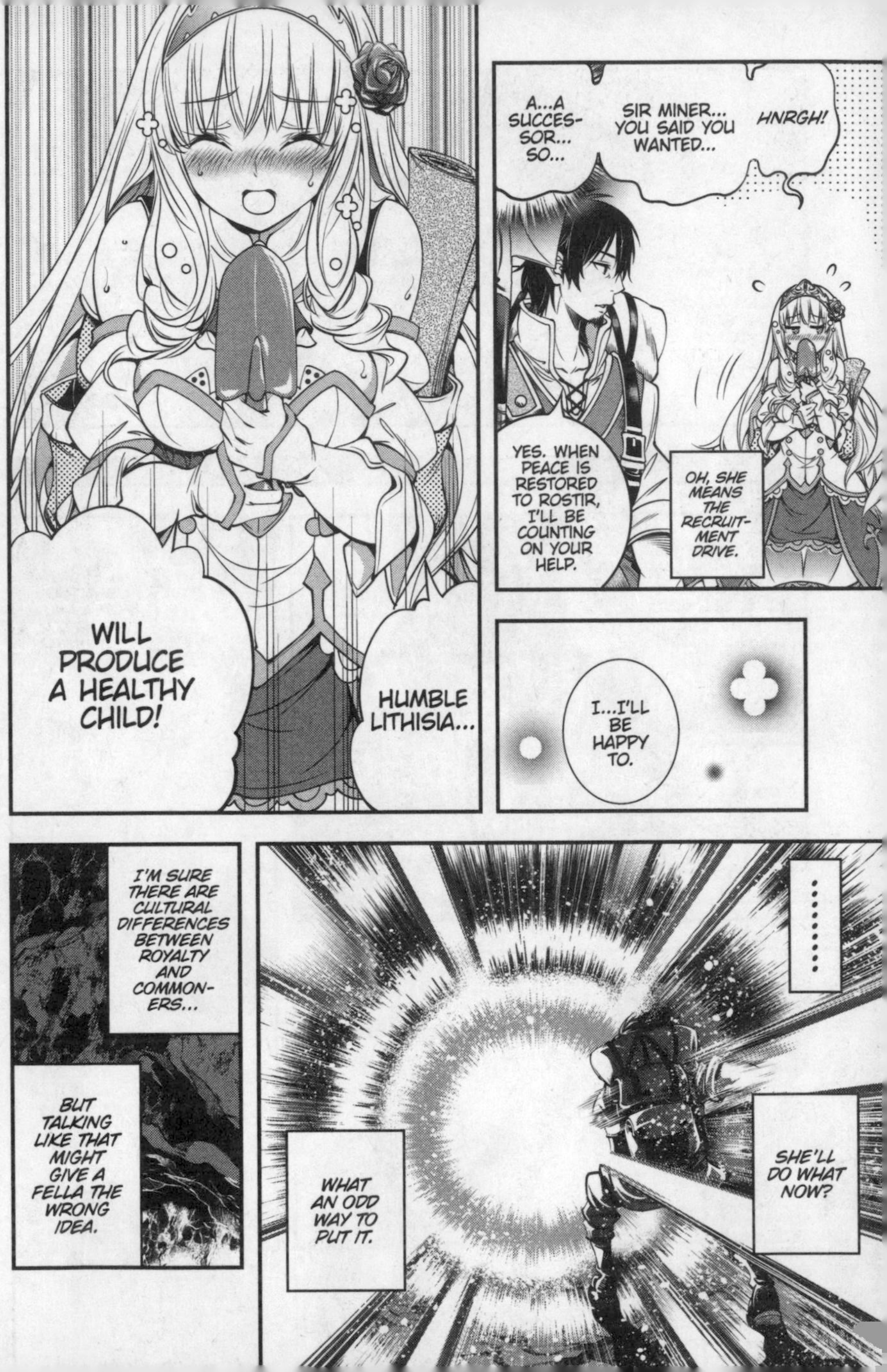
HNRGH!
SIR MINER... YOU SAID YOU WANTED...
A...A SUCCES-SOR... SO...
OH, SHE MEANS THE RECRUIT-MENT DRIVE.
YES. WHEN PEACE IS RESTORED TO ROSTIR, I'LL BE COUNTING ON YOUR HELP.
I...I'LL BE HAPPY TO.
HUMBLE LITHISIA...
WILL PRODUCE A HEALTHY CHILD!
....
SHE'LL DO WHAT NOW?
WHAT AN ODD WAY TO PUT IT.
I'M SURE THERE ARE CULTURAL DIFFERENCES BETWEEN ROYALTY AND COMMON-ERS...
BUT TALKING LIKE THAT MIGHT GIVE A FELLA THE WRONG IDEA.

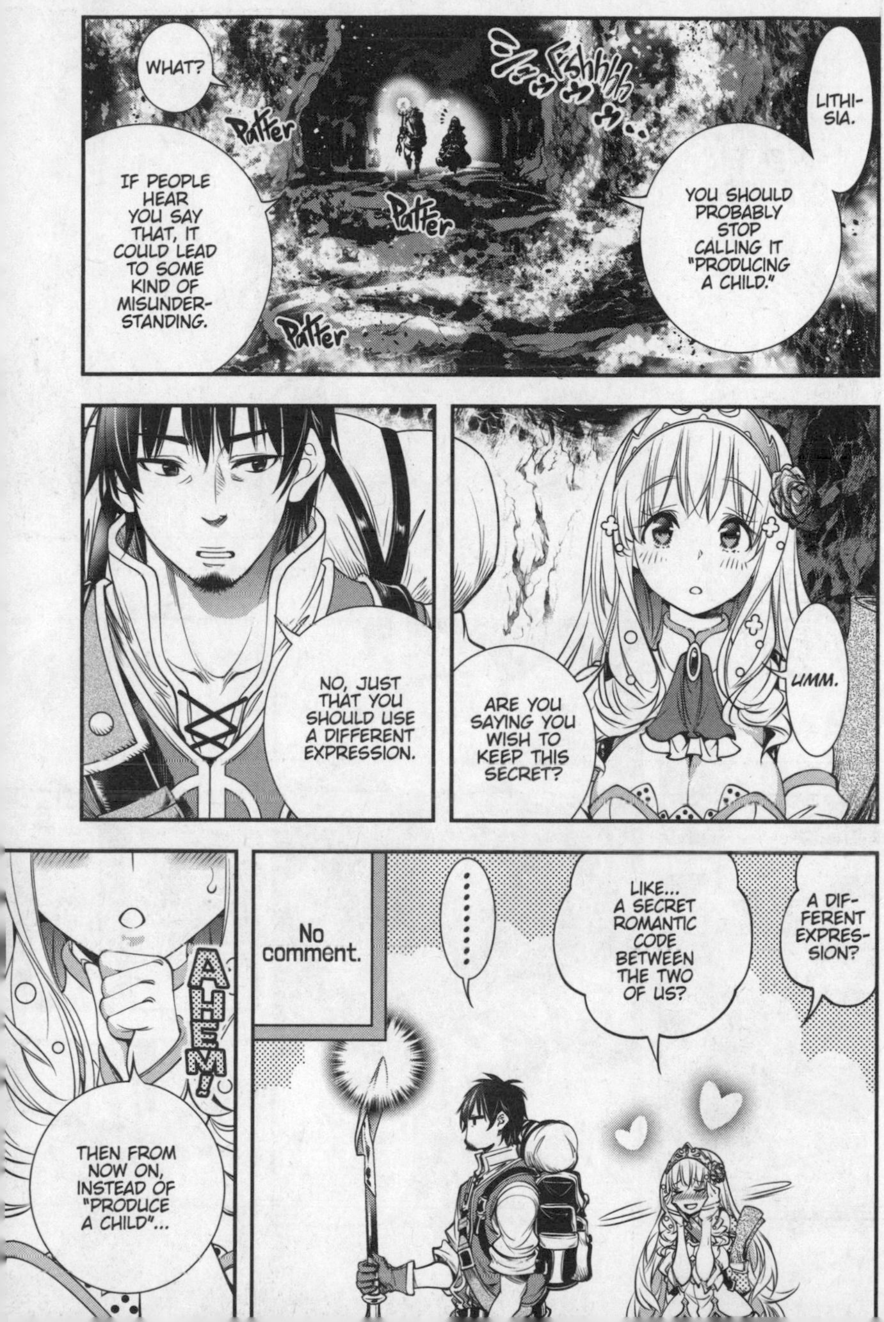
LITHI-SIA.
Fshhhhh
YOU SHOULD PROBABLY STOP CALLING IT "PRODUCING A CHILD."
WHAT?
IF PEOPLE HEAR YOU SAY THAT, IT COULD LEAD TO SOME KIND OF MISUNDER-STANDING.
Patter
Patter
Patter
UMM.
ARE YOU SAYING YOU WISH TO KEEP THIS SECRET?
NO, JUST THAT YOU SHOULD USE A DIFFERENT EXPRESSION.
A DIF-FERENT EXPRES-SION?
LIKE... A SECRET ROMANTIC CODE BETWEEN THE TWO OF US?
....
No comment.
AHEM!
THEN FROM NOW ON, INSTEAD OF "PRODUCE A CHILD"...

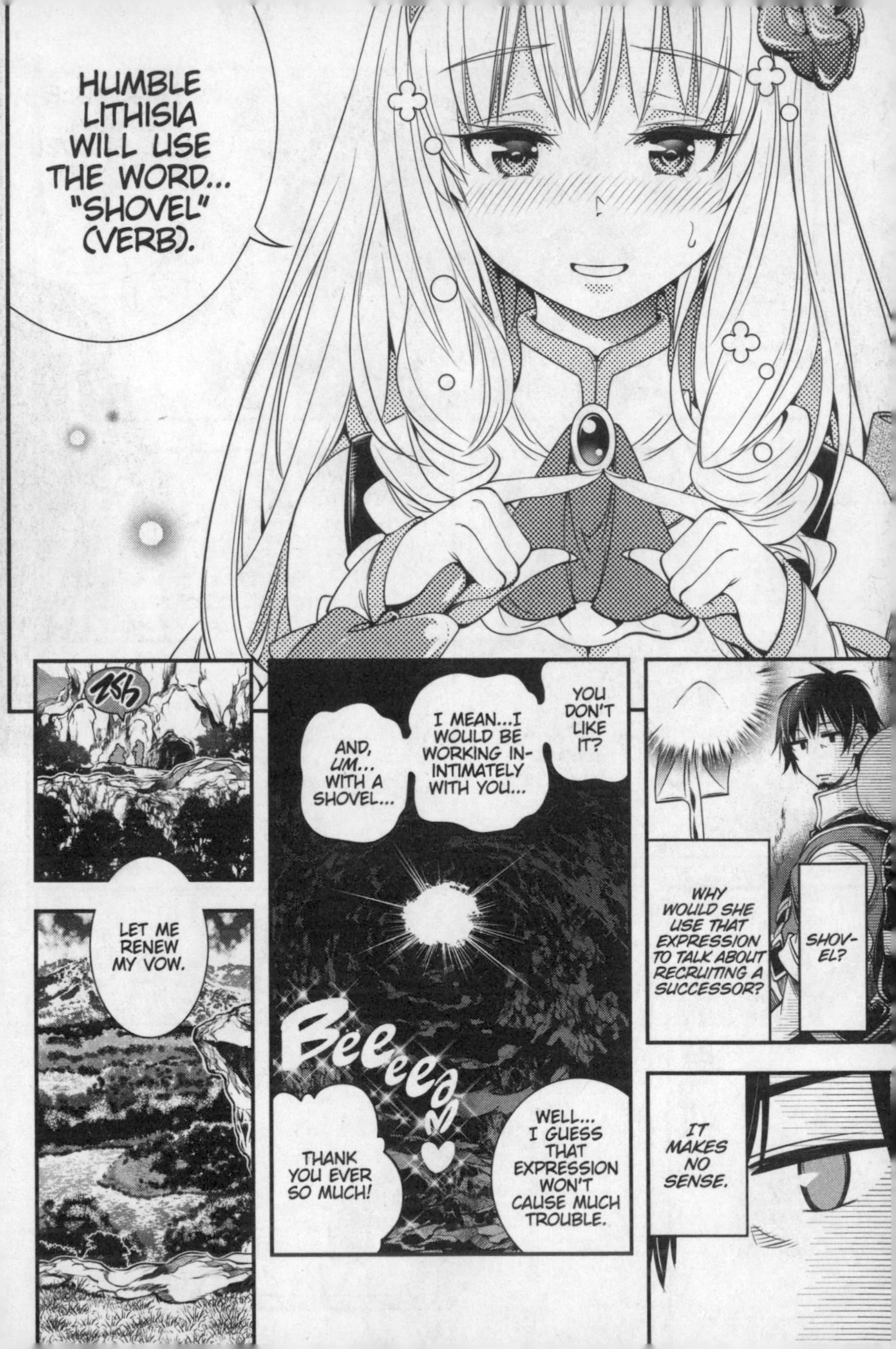
HUMBLE LITHISIA WILL USE THE WORD... "SHOVEL" (VERB).
SHOV-EL?
WHY WOULD SHE USE THAT EXPRESSION TO TALK ABOUT RECRUITING A SUCCESSOR?
IT MAKES NO SENSE.
YOU DON'T LIKE IT?
I MEAN...I WOULD BE WORKING IN-INTIMATELY WITH YOU...
AND, UM... WITH A SHOVEL...
Beeeeam
WELL... I GUESS THAT EXPRESSION WON'T CAUSE MUCH TROUBLE.
THANK YOU EVER SO MUCH!
LET ME RENEW MY VOW.

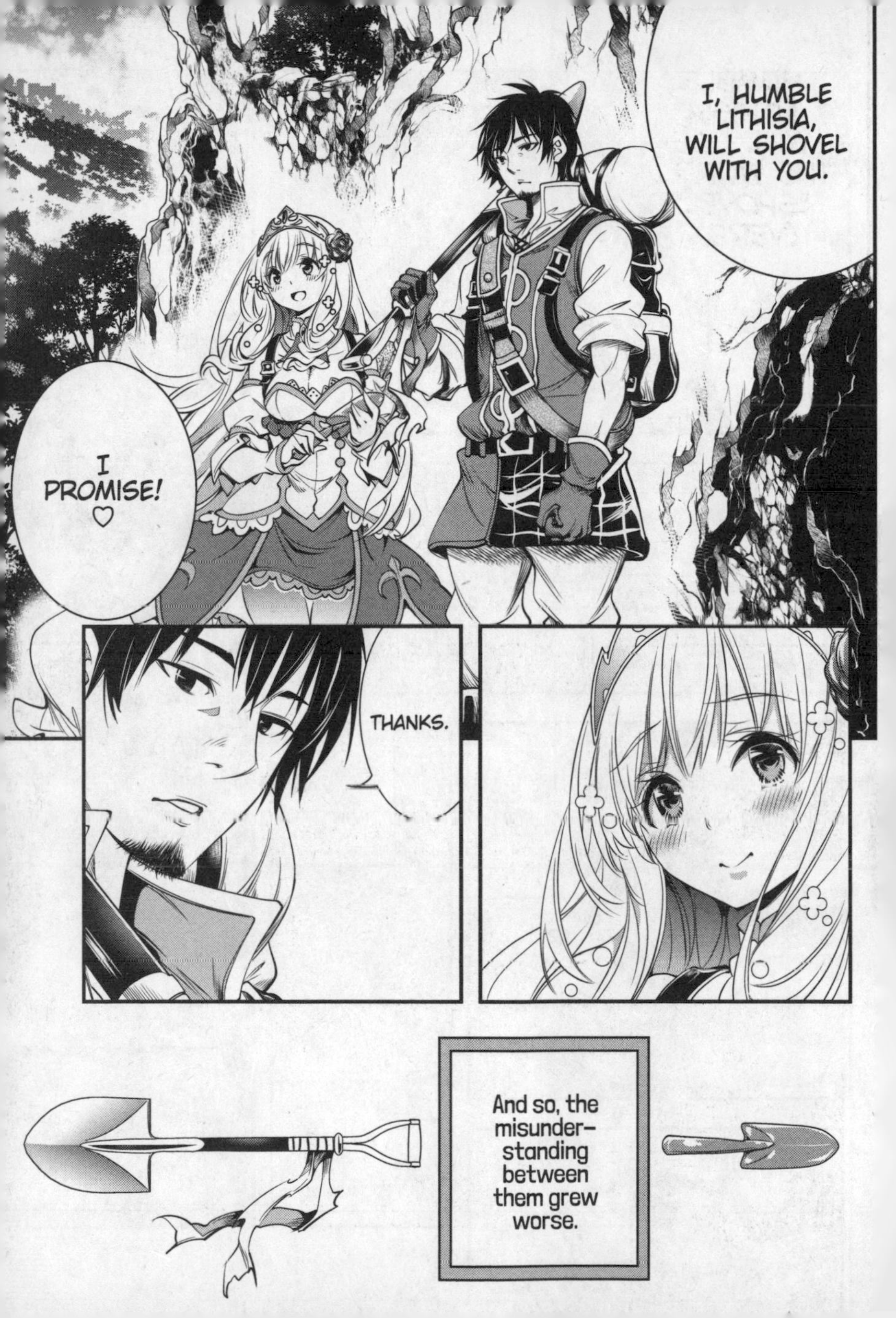
I, HUMBLE LITHISIA, WILL SHOVEL WITH YOU.
I PROMISE! ♡
THANKS.
And so, the misunder-standing between them grew worse.

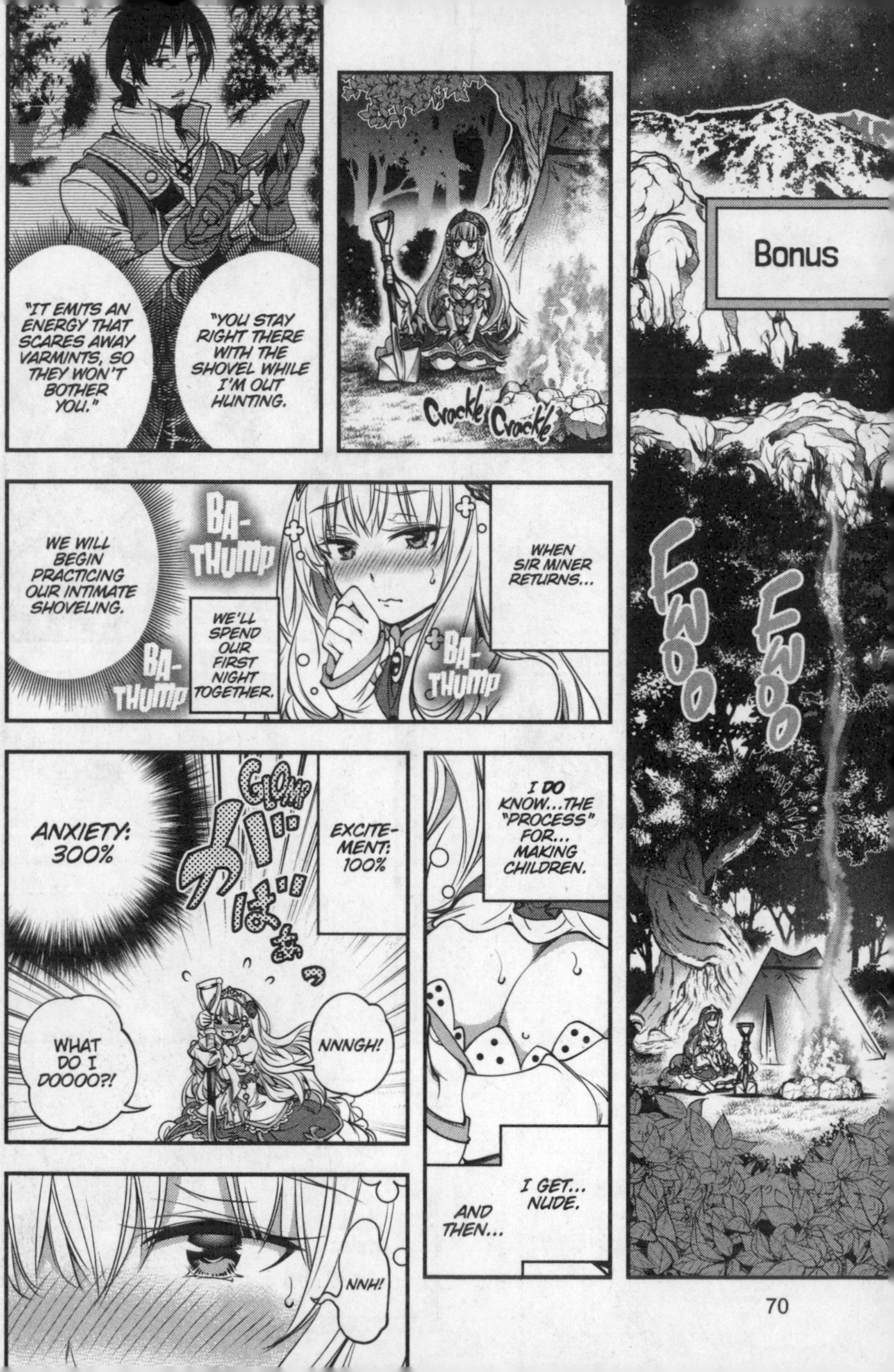

Bonus
FWOO
FWOO
Crackle Crackle
"YOU STAY RIGHT THERE WITH THE SHOVEL WHILE I'M OUT HUNTING.
"IT EMITS AN ENERGY THAT SCARES AWAY VARMINTS, SO THEY WON'T BOTHER YOU."
WHEN SIR MINER RETURNS...
BA-THUMP
WE'LL SPEND OUR FIRST NIGHT TOGETHER.
BA-THUMP
WE WILL BEGIN PRACTICING OUR INTIMATE SHOVELING.
BA-THUMP
I DO KNOW...THE "PROCESS" FOR... MAKING CHILDREN.
I GET... NUDE.
AND THEN...
EXCITEMENT: 100%
GLOMP
ANXIETY: 300%
NNNGH!
WHAT DO I DOOOO?!
NNH!

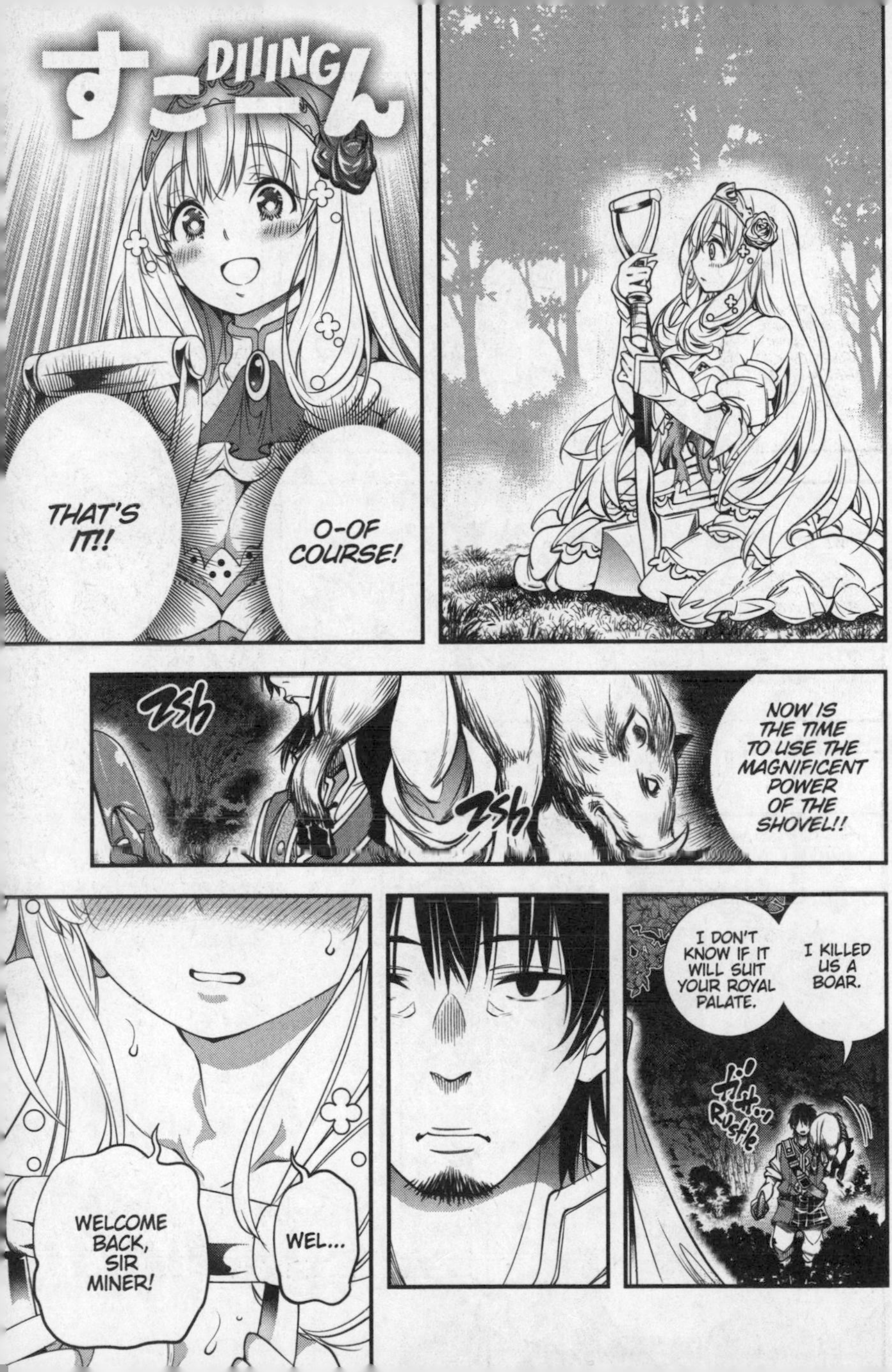

すこーん
DIIING
O-OF COURSE!
THAT'S IT!!
NOW IS THE TIME TO USE THE MAGNIFICENT POWER OF THE SHOVEL!!
ZSH
ZSH
I KILLED US A BOAR.
I DON'T KNOW IF IT WILL SUIT YOUR ROYAL PALATE.
RUSTLE
WEL...
WELCOME BACK, SIR MINER!

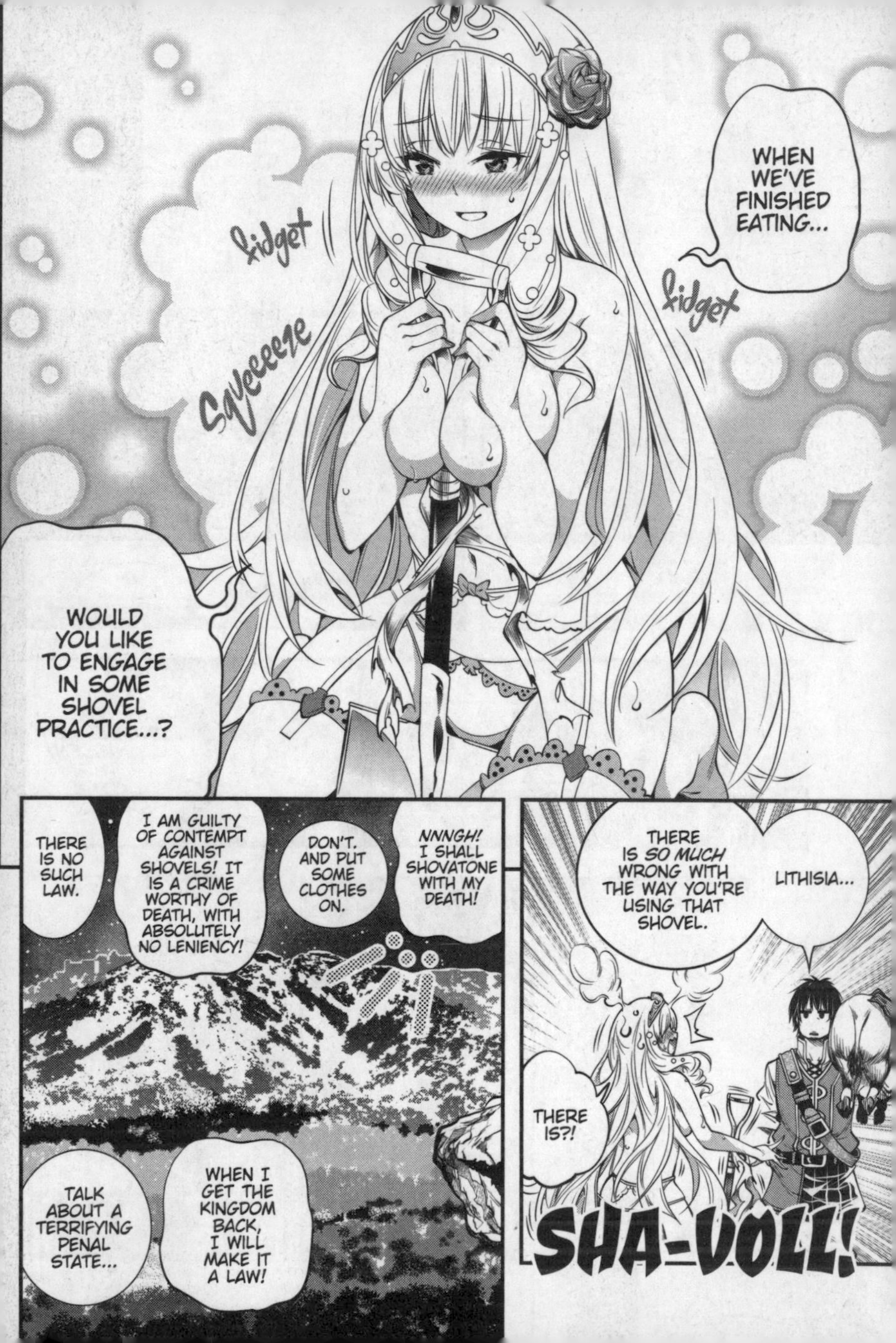
WHEN WE'VE FINISHED EATING...
fidget
fidget
Squeeeeze
WOULD YOU LIKE TO ENGAGE IN SOME SHOVEL PRACTICE...?
LITHISIA...
THERE IS *SO MUCH* WRONG WITH THE WAY YOU'RE USING THAT SHOVEL.
THERE IS?!
SHA-VOLL!
NNNGH! I SHALL SHOVATONE WITH MY DEATH!
DON'T. AND PUT SOME CLOTHES ON.
I AM GUILTY OF CONTEMPT AGAINST SHOVELS! IT IS A CRIME WORTHY OF DEATH, WITH ABSOLUTELY NO LENIENCY!
THERE IS NO SUCH LAW.
WHEN I GET THE KINGDOM BACK, I WILL MAKE IT A LAW!
TALK ABOUT A TERRIFYING PENAL STATE...

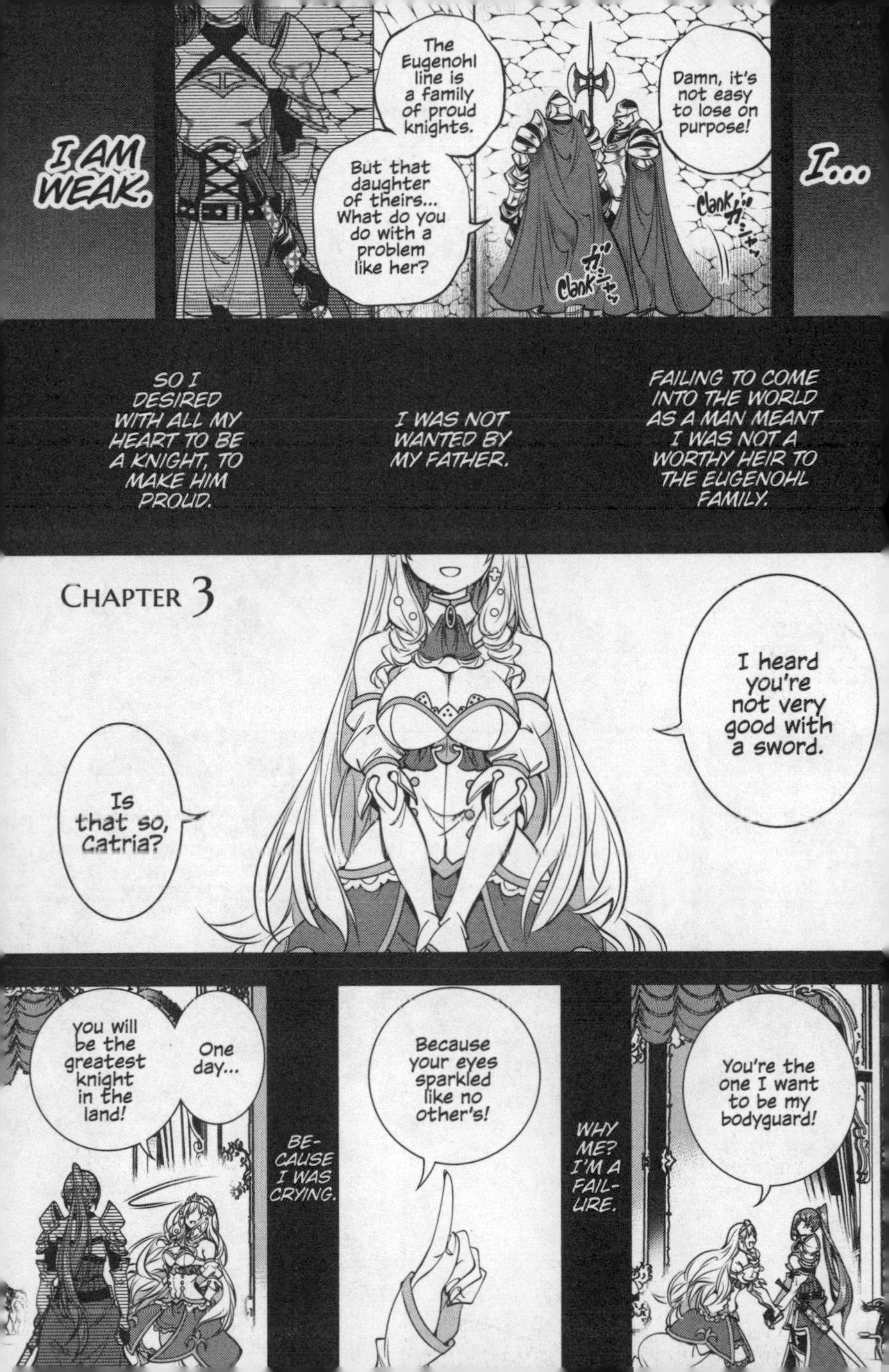
I...
Damn, it's not easy to lose on purpose!
Clank ガシャッ
Clank ガシャッ
The Eugenohl line is a family of proud knights.
But that daughter of theirs... What do you do with a problem like her?
I AM WEAK.
FAILING TO COME INTO THE WORLD AS A MAN MEANT I WAS NOT A WORTHY HEIR TO THE EUGENOHL FAMILY.
I WAS NOT WANTED BY MY FATHER.
SO I DESIRED WITH ALL MY HEART TO BE A KNIGHT, TO MAKE HIM PROUD.
CHAPTER 3
I heard you're not very good with a sword.
Is that so, Catria?
You're the one I want to be my bodyguard!
WHY ME? I'M A FAILURE.
Because your eyes sparkled like no other's!
BECAUSE I WAS CRYING.
One day...
you will be the greatest knight in the land!

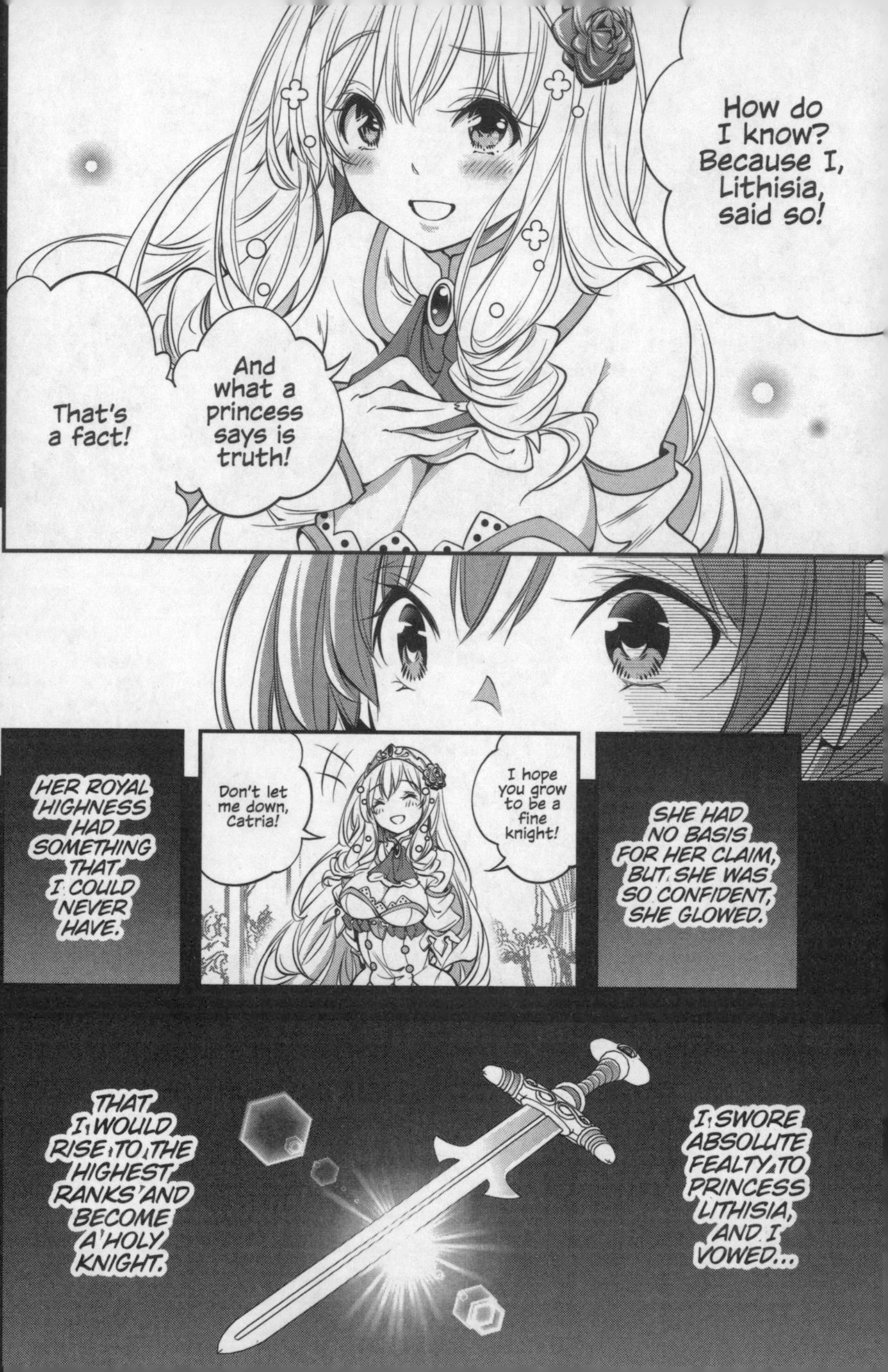
How do I know? Because I, Lithisia, said so!
And what a princess says is truth!
That's a fact!
SHE HAD NO BASIS FOR HER CLAIM, BUT SHE WAS SO CONFIDENT, SHE GLOWED.
I hope you grow to be a fine knight!
Don't let me down, Catria!
HER ROYAL HIGHNESS HAD SOMETHING THAT I COULD NEVER HAVE.
I SWORE ABSOLUTE FEALTY TO PRINCESS LITHISIA, AND I VOWED...
THAT I WOULD RISE TO THE HIGHEST RANKS AND BECOME A HOLY KNIGHT.

THE INVINCIBLE

SHOVEL

"WAVE MOTION SHOVEL BLAST!"
(·ω·)つ=͟͟͞͞ ☆（ д ）：：).KA-CHOOOM

THE INVINCIBLE SHOVEL

"WAVE MOTION SHOVEL BLAST!" (　´・ω・｀)♂＝＝＝＝★(ﾟДﾟ ;;;).:∴. KA-CHOOOM

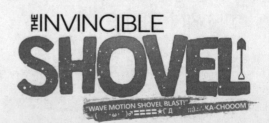

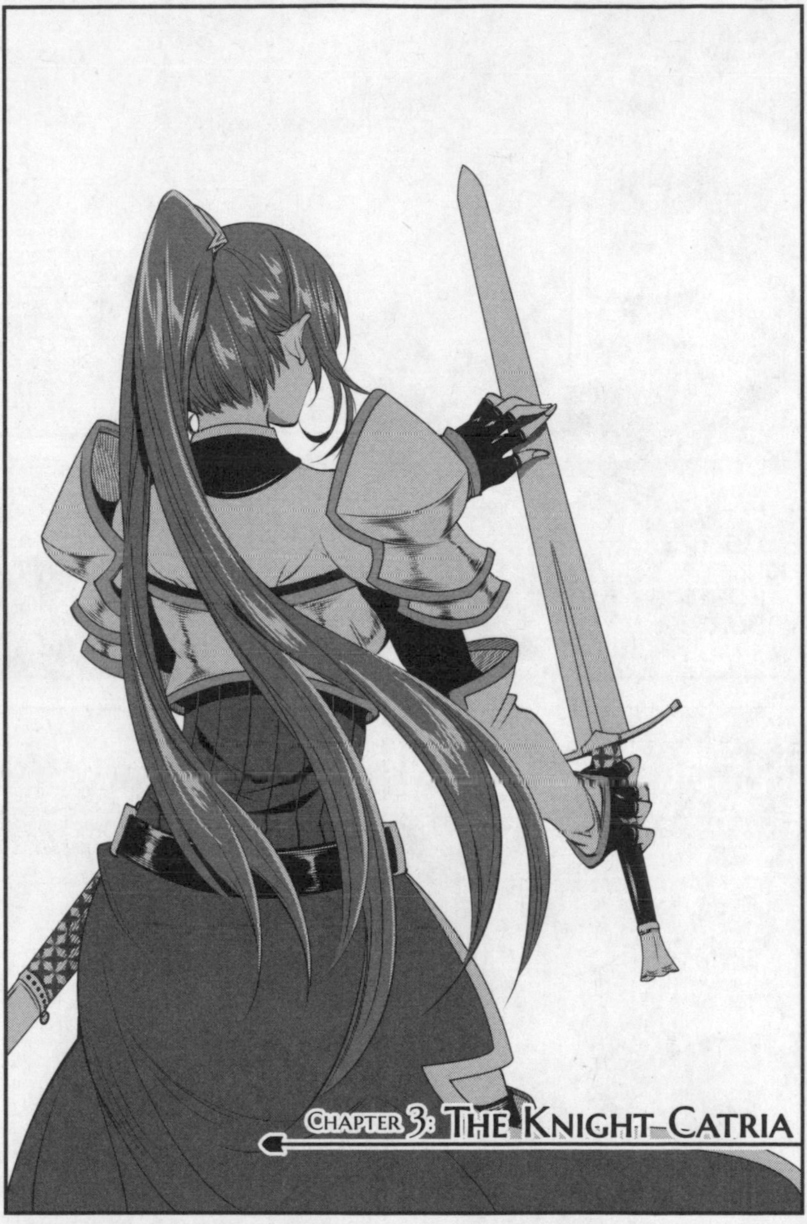
Chapter 3: The Knight Catria

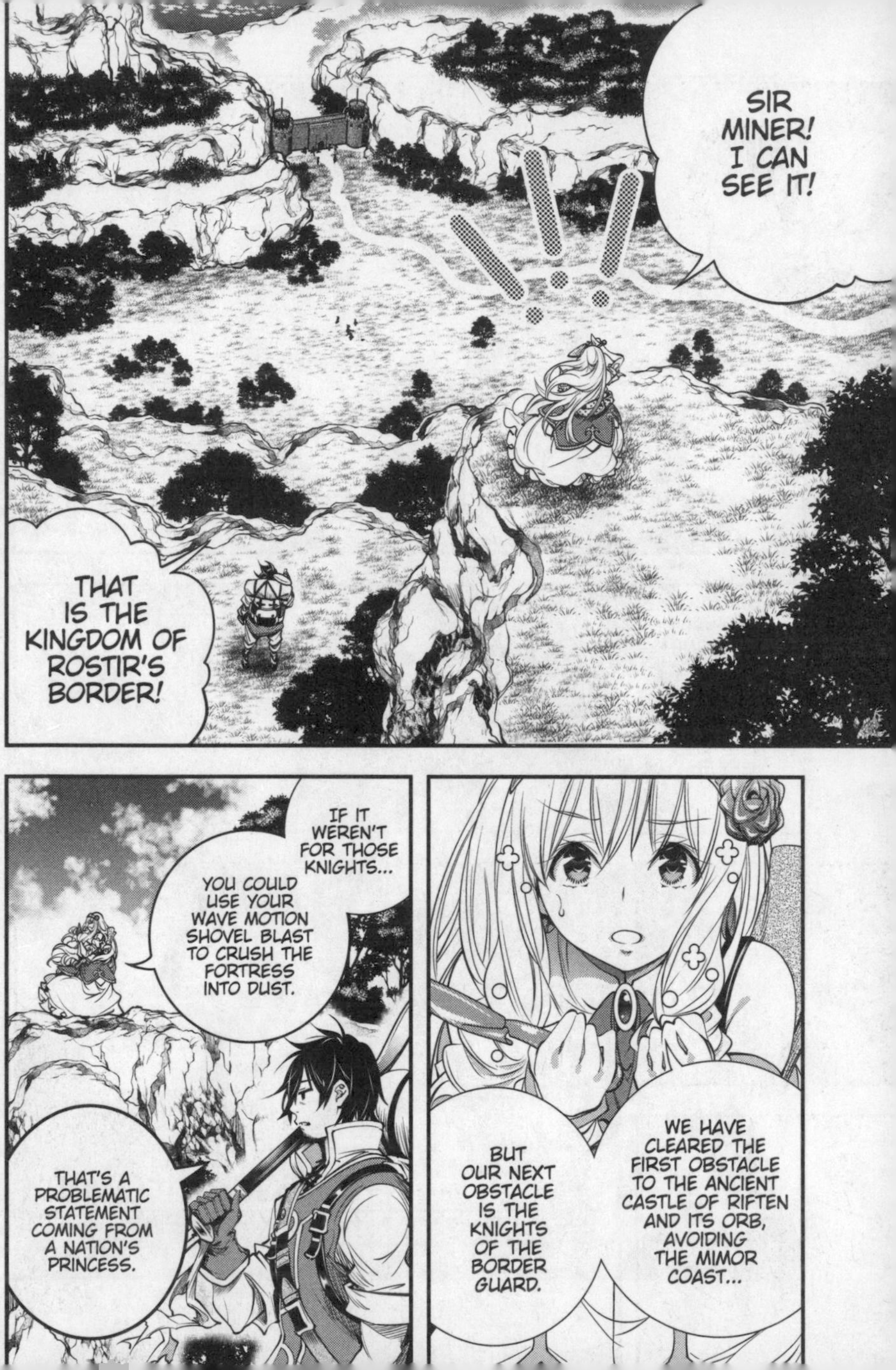
SIR MINER! I CAN SEE IT!
!!
THAT IS THE KINGDOM OF ROSTIR'S BORDER!
WE HAVE CLEARED THE FIRST OBSTACLE TO THE ANCIENT CASTLE OF RIFTEN AND ITS ORB, AVOIDING THE MIMOR COAST...
BUT OUR NEXT OBSTACLE IS THE KNIGHTS OF THE BORDER GUARD.
IF IT WEREN'T FOR THOSE KNIGHTS...
YOU COULD USE YOUR WAVE MOTION SHOVEL BLAST TO CRUSH THE FORTRESS INTO DUST.
THAT'S A PROBLEMATIC STATEMENT COMING FROM A NATION'S PRINCESS.

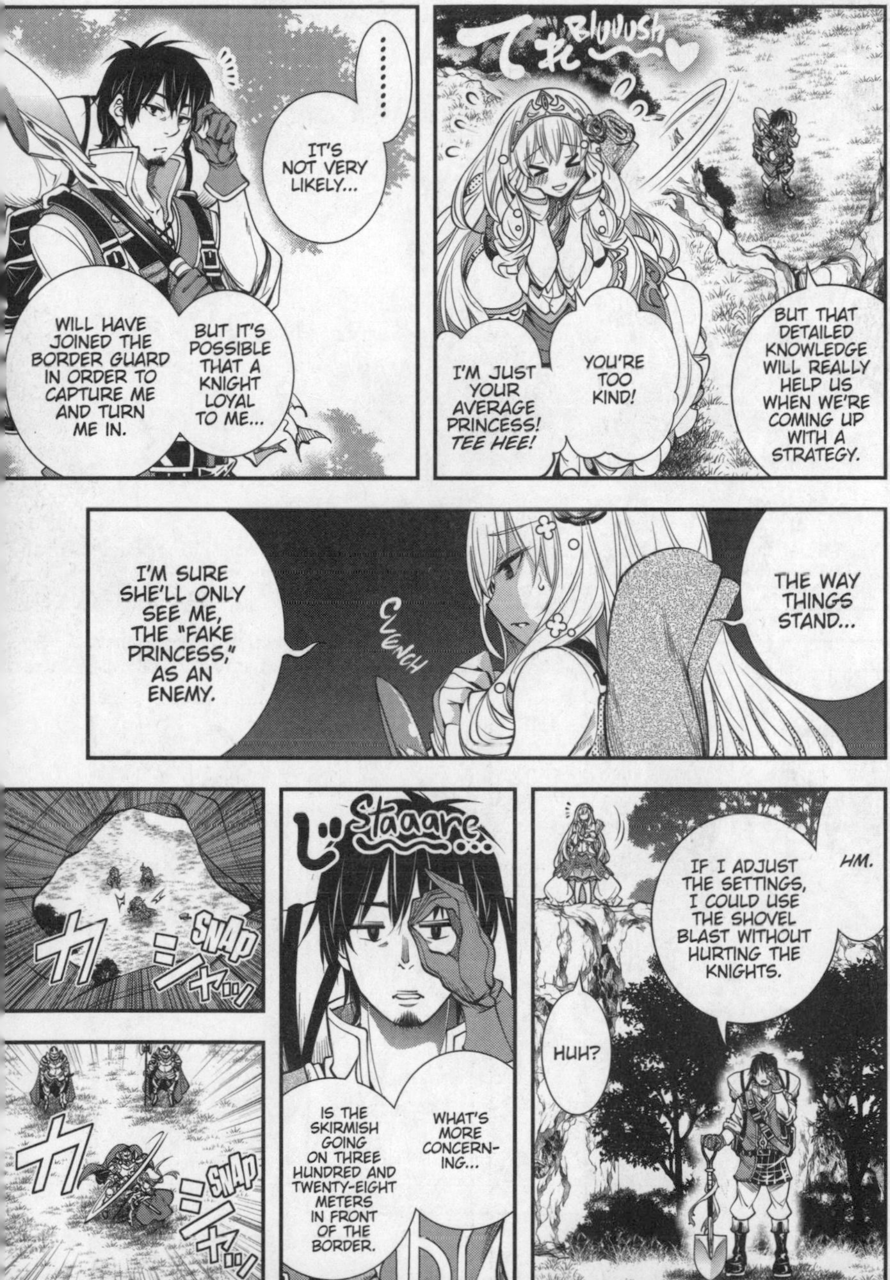
てれ
BLUUUSH~♥
BUT THAT DETAILED KNOWLEDGE WILL REALLY HELP US WHEN WE'RE COMING UP WITH A STRATEGY.
YOU'RE TOO KIND!
I'M JUST YOUR AVERAGE PRINCESS! TEE HEE!
......
IT'S NOT VERY LIKELY...
BUT IT'S POSSIBLE THAT A KNIGHT LOYAL TO ME...
WILL HAVE JOINED THE BORDER GUARD IN ORDER TO CAPTURE ME AND TURN ME IN.
THE WAY THINGS STAND...
CLENCH
I'M SURE SHE'LL ONLY SEE ME, THE "FAKE PRINCESS," AS AN ENEMY.
HM.
IF I ADJUST THE SETTINGS, I COULD USE THE SHOVEL BLAST WITHOUT HURTING THE KNIGHTS.
HUH?
じ
Staaare...
WHAT'S MORE CONCERNING...
IS THE SKIRMISH GOING ON THREE HUNDRED AND TWENTY-EIGHT METERS IN FRONT OF THE BORDER.
カシャッ
SNAP
カシャッ
SNAP

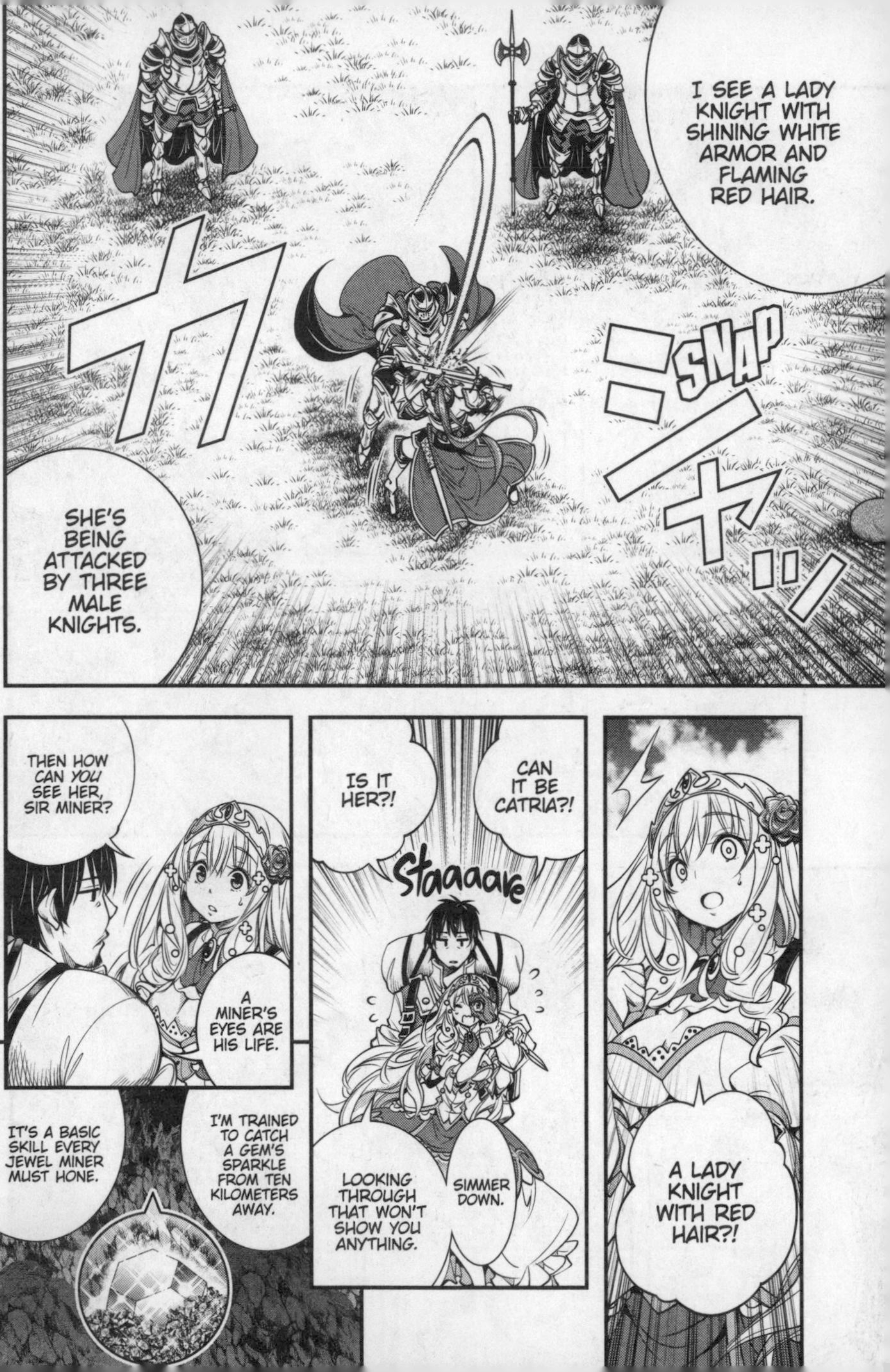
I SEE A LADY KNIGHT WITH SHINING WHITE ARMOR AND FLAMING RED HAIR.
SNAP
SHE'S BEING ATTACKED BY THREE MALE KNIGHTS.
A LADY KNIGHT WITH RED HAIR?!
CAN IT BE CATRIA?!
IS IT HER?!
Staaaare
SIMMER DOWN.
LOOKING THROUGH THAT WON'T SHOW YOU ANYTHING.
THEN HOW CAN *YOU* SEE HER, SIR MINER?
A MINER'S EYES ARE HIS LIFE.
I'M TRAINED TO CATCH A GEM'S SPARKLE FROM TEN KILOMETERS AWAY.
IT'S A BASIC SKILL EVERY JEWEL MINER MUST HONE.

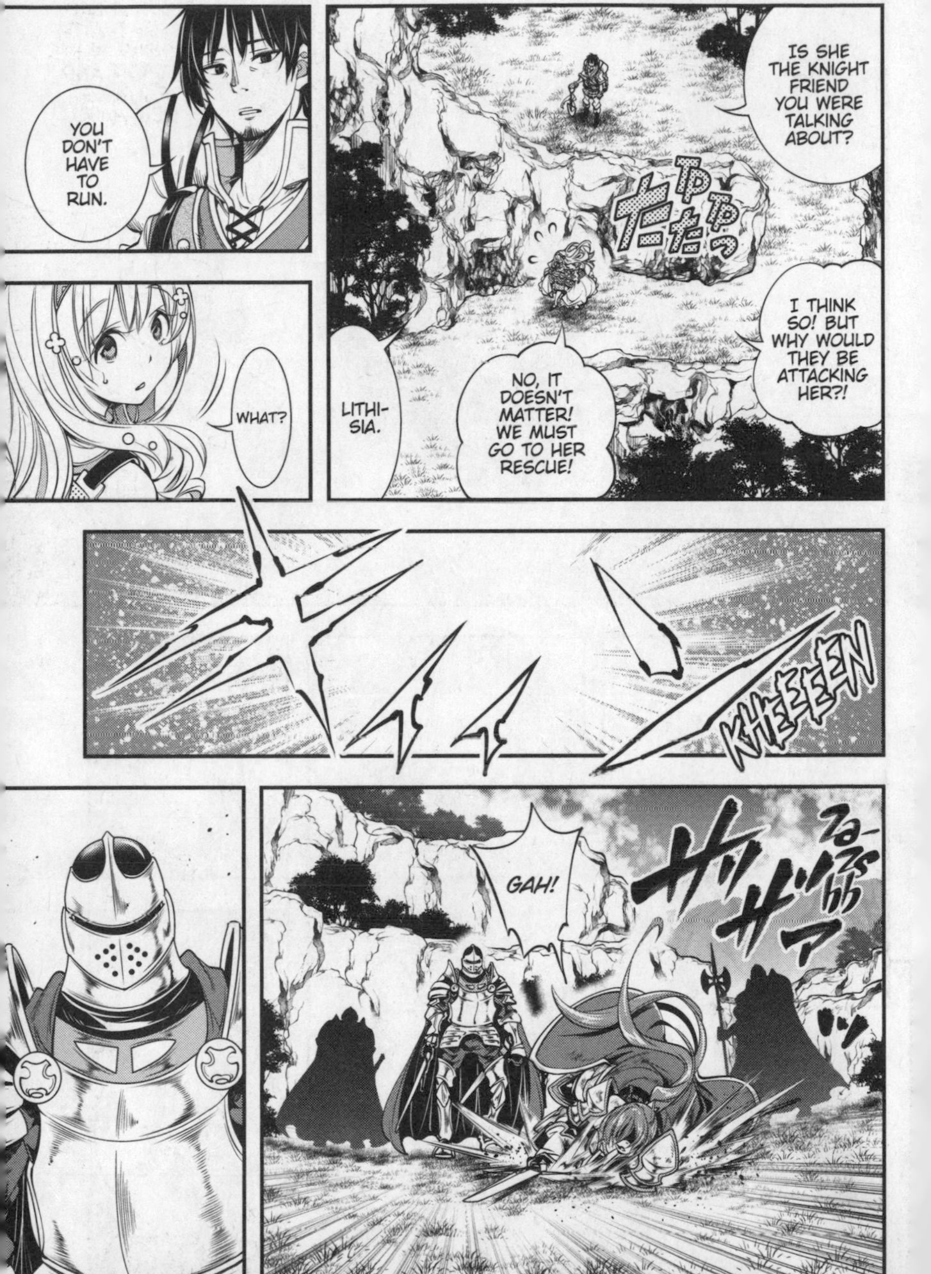
IS SHE THE KNIGHT FRIEND YOU WERE TALKING ABOUT?
I THINK SO! BUT WHY WOULD THEY BE ATTACKING HER?!
NO, IT DOESN'T MATTER! WE MUST GO TO HER RESCUE!
LITHI-SIA.
YOU DON'T HAVE TO RUN.
WHAT?
KHEEEEN
GAH!

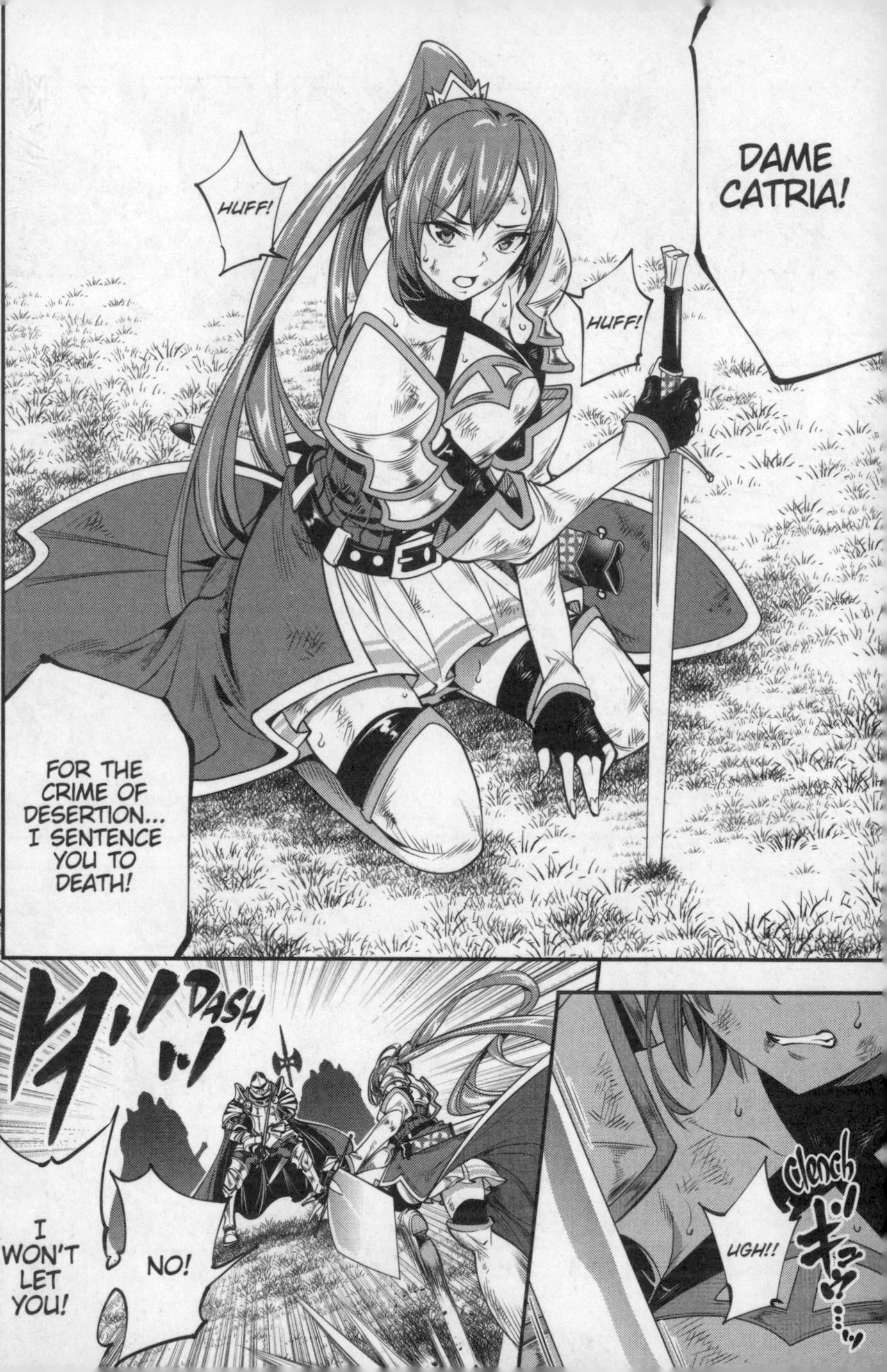
DAME CATRIA!
HUFF!
HUFF!
FOR THE CRIME OF DESERTION... I SENTENCE YOU TO DEATH!
UGH!!
clench
DASH
NO!
I WON'T LET YOU!

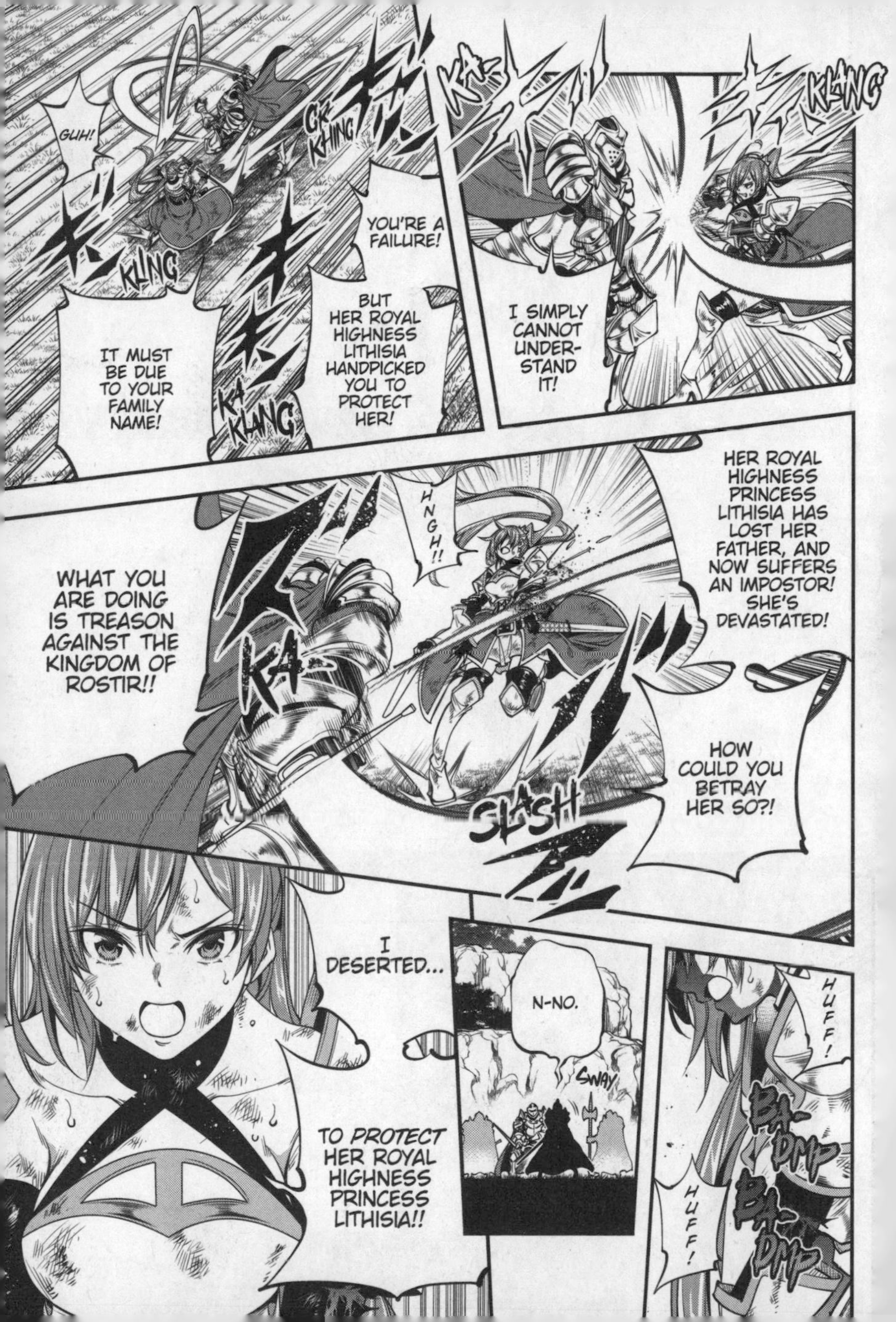
KLANG
KA-
I SIMPLY CANNOT UNDER-STAND IT!
YOU'RE A FAILURE!
BUT HER ROYAL HIGHNESS LITHISIA HANDPICKED YOU TO PROTECT HER!
GK KHING
GUH!
KLING
KA KLANG
IT MUST BE DUE TO YOUR FAMILY NAME!
HER ROYAL HIGHNESS PRINCESS LITHISIA HAS LOST HER FATHER, AND NOW SUFFERS AN IMPOSTOR! SHE'S DEVASTATED!
HNGH!!
WHAT YOU ARE DOING IS TREASON AGAINST THE KINGDOM OF ROSTIR!!
KA
HOW COULD YOU BETRAY HER SO?!
SLASH
HUFF!
BA-DMP
BA-DMP
HUFF!
N-NO.
SWAY
I DESERTED...
TO PROTECT HER ROYAL HIGHNESS PRINCESS LITHISIA!!

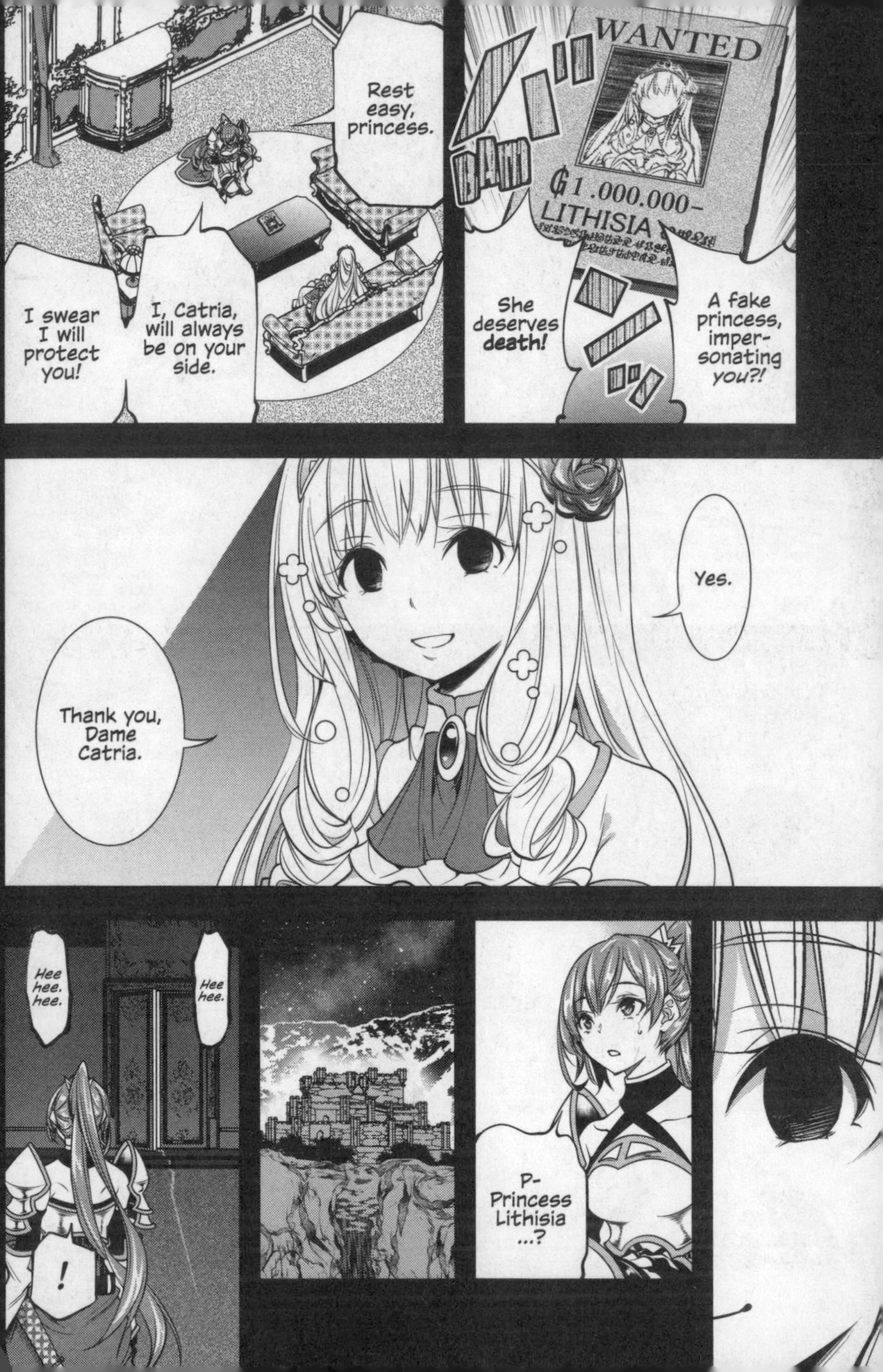
WANTED
₲1.000.000-
LITHISIA
BAM
A fake princess, imper-sonating you?!
She deserves **death!**
Rest easy, princess.
I, Catria, will always be on your side.
I swear I will protect you!
Yes.
Thank you, Dame Catria.
P-Princess Lithisia ...?
Hee hee.
Hee hee. hee.
!

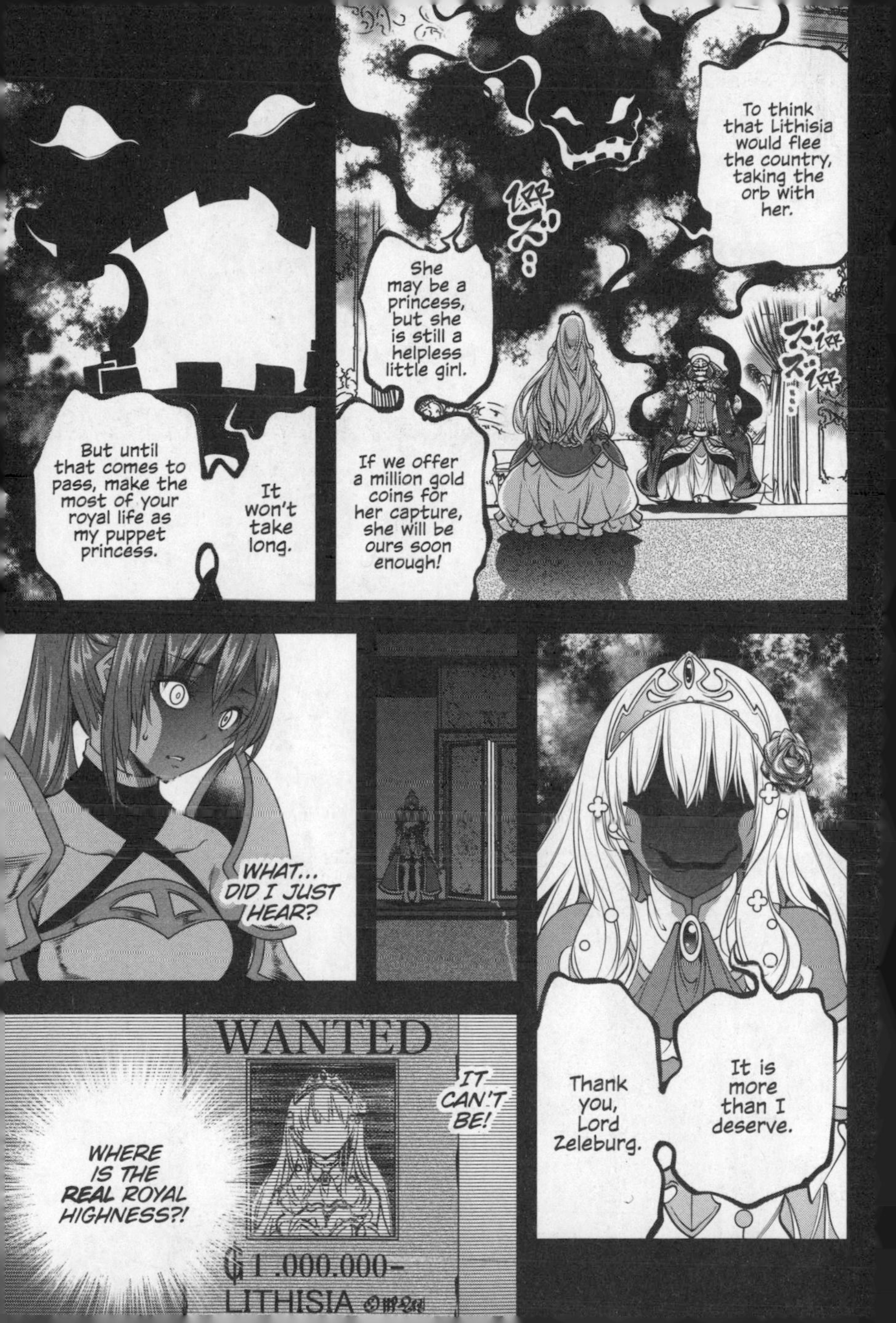
To think that Lithisia would flee the country, taking the orb with her.
She may be a princess, but she is still a helpless little girl.
If we offer a million gold coins for her capture, she will be ours soon enough!
It won't take long.
But until that comes to pass, make the most of your royal life as my puppet princess.
It is more than I deserve.
Thank you, Lord Zeleburg.
WHAT... DID I JUST HEAR?
WANTED
IT CAN'T BE!
WHERE IS THE REAL ROYAL HIGHNESS?!
₲1.000.000-
LITHISIA

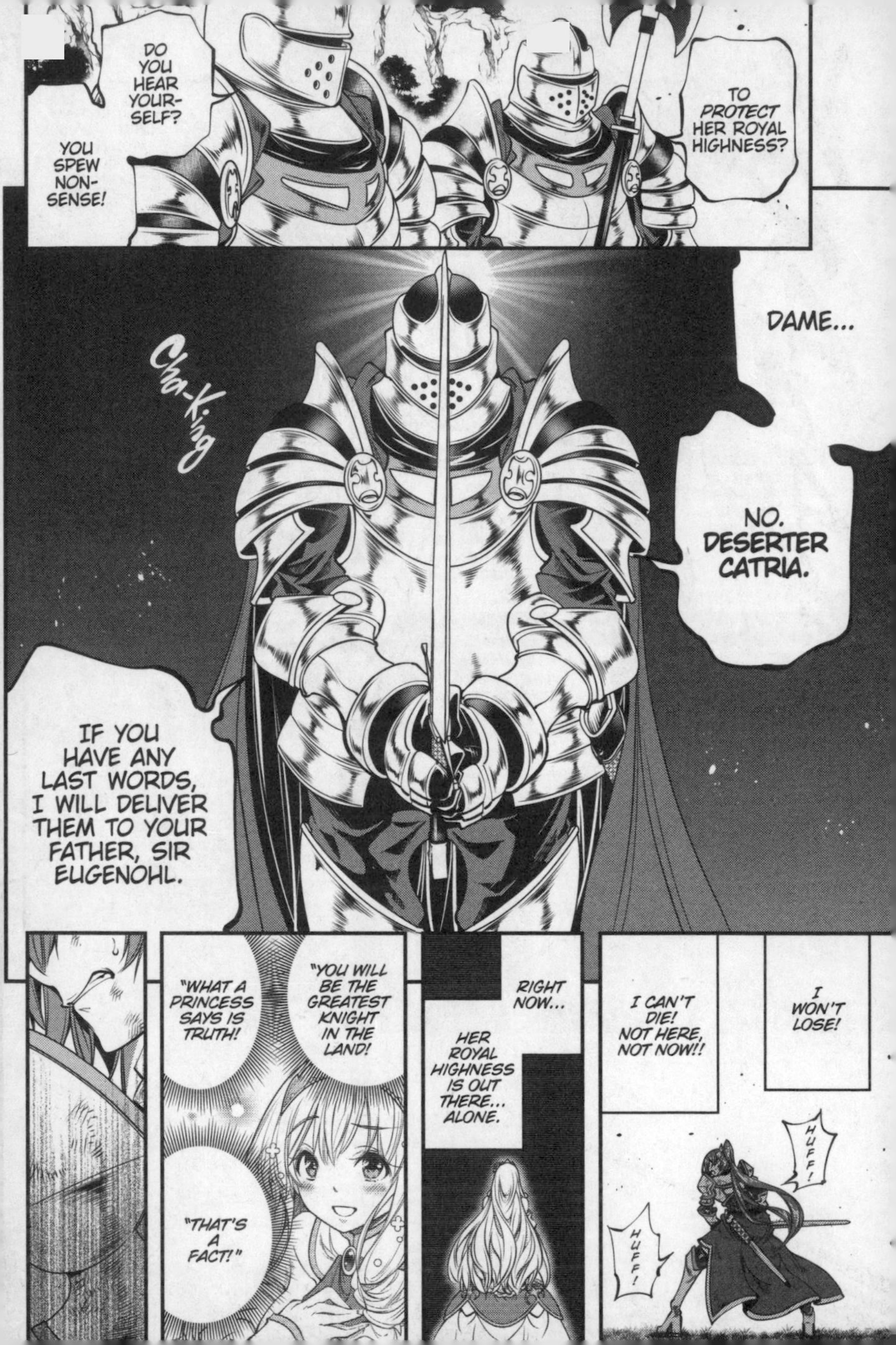
TO PROTECT HER ROYAL HIGHNESS?
DO YOU HEAR YOURSELF?
YOU SPEW NONSENSE!
DAME...
NO. DESERTER CATRIA.
Cha-King
IF YOU HAVE ANY LAST WORDS, I WILL DELIVER THEM TO YOUR FATHER, SIR EUGENOHL.
I WON'T LOSE!
I CAN'T DIE! NOT HERE, NOT NOW!!
HUFF!
HUFF!
RIGHT NOW...
HER ROYAL HIGHNESS IS OUT THERE... ALONE.
"YOU WILL BE THE GREATEST KNIGHT IN THE LAND!
"WHAT A PRINCESS SAYS IS TRUTH!
"THAT'S A FACT!"

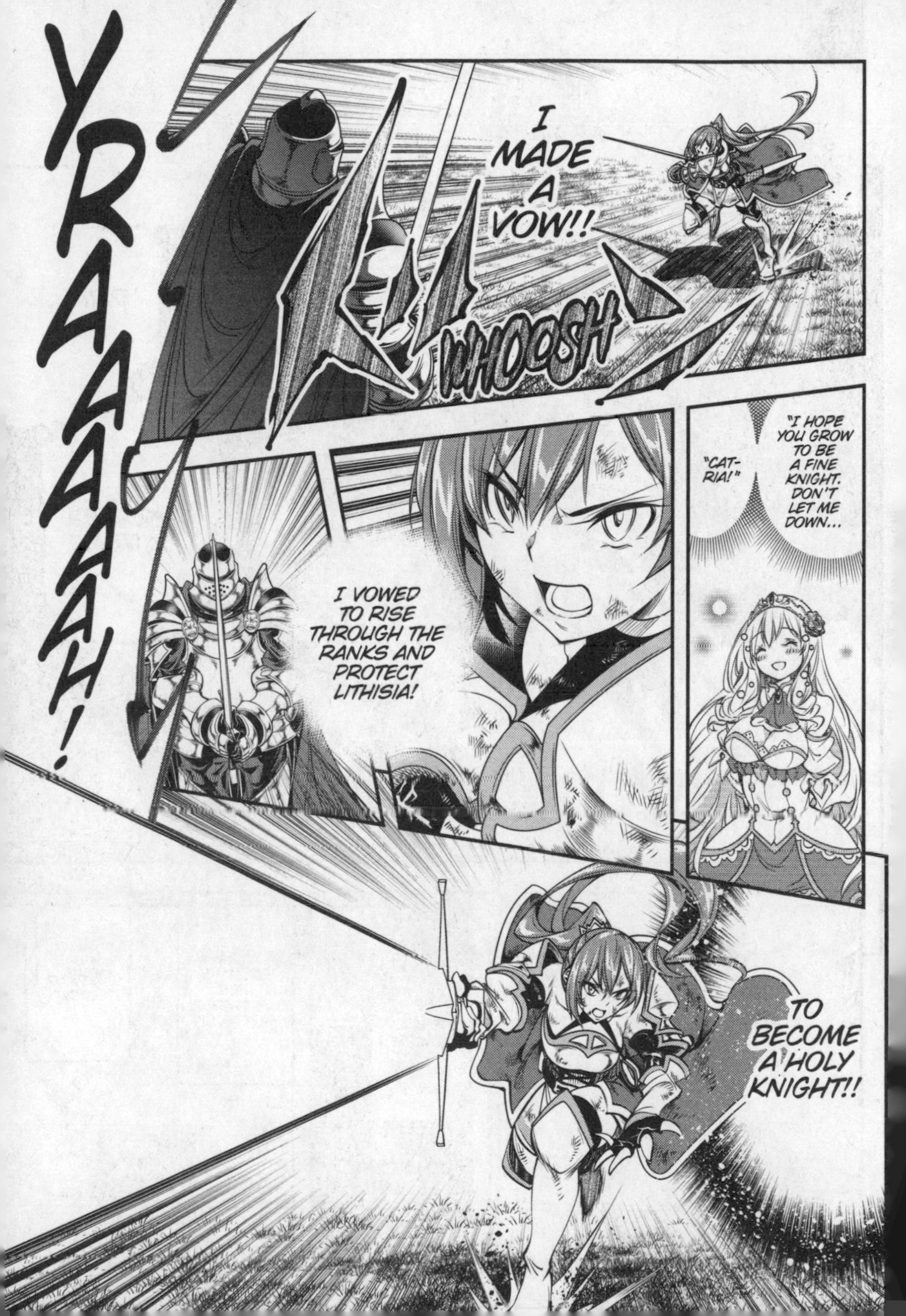

I MADE A VOW!!
WHOOSH
YRAAAAAAH!
"I HOPE YOU GROW TO BE A FINE KNIGHT. DON'T LET ME DOWN…
"CAT-RIA!"
I VOWED TO RISE THROUGH THE RANKS AND PROTECT LITHISIA!
TO BECOME A HOLY KNIGHT!!

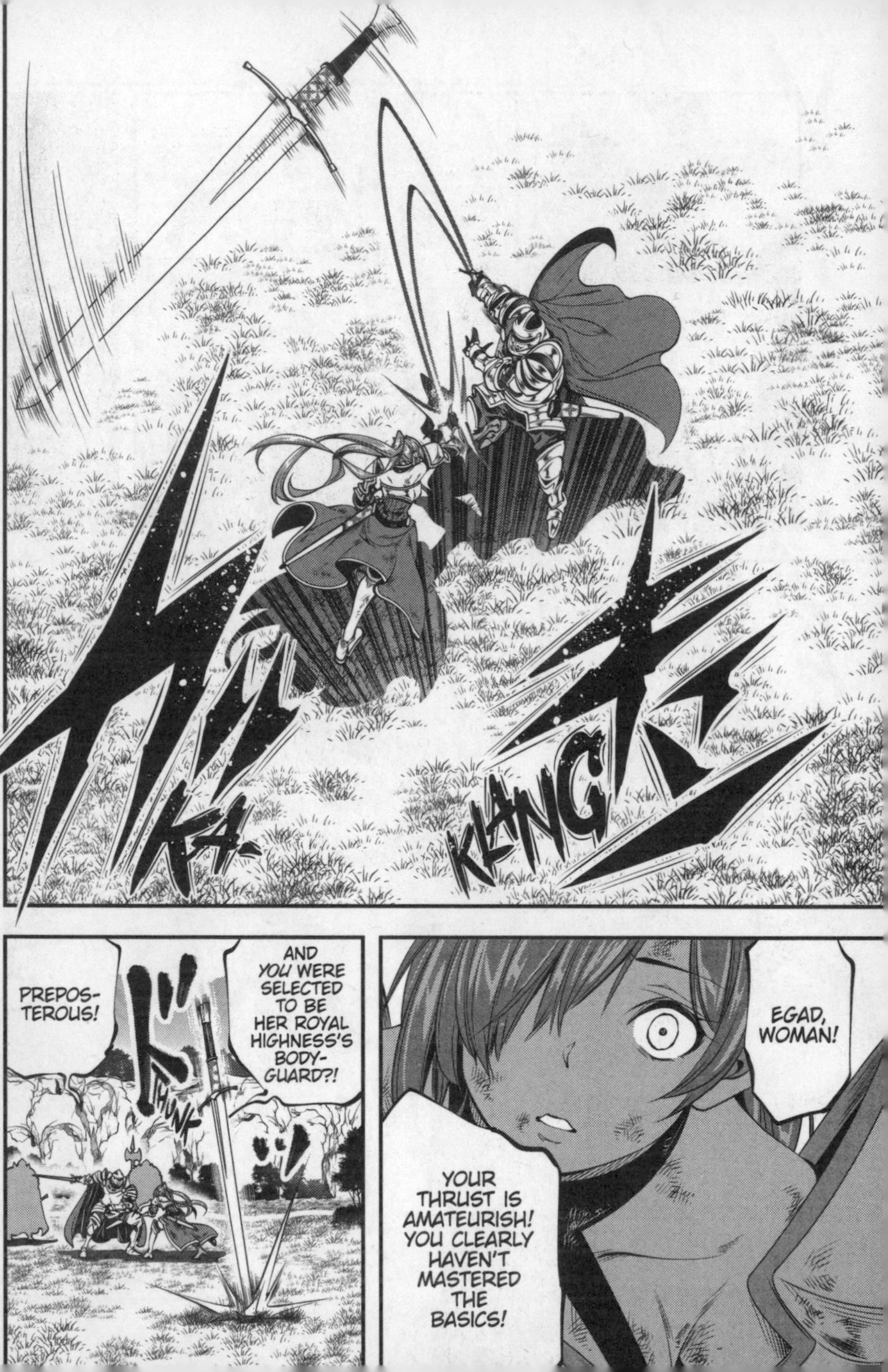
KA-
KLANG
EGAD, WOMAN!
YOUR THRUST IS AMATEURISH! YOU CLEARLY HAVEN'T MASTERED THE BASICS!
AND YOU WERE SELECTED TO BE HER ROYAL HIGHNESS'S BODY-GUARD?!
PREPOS-TEROUS!
THUNK

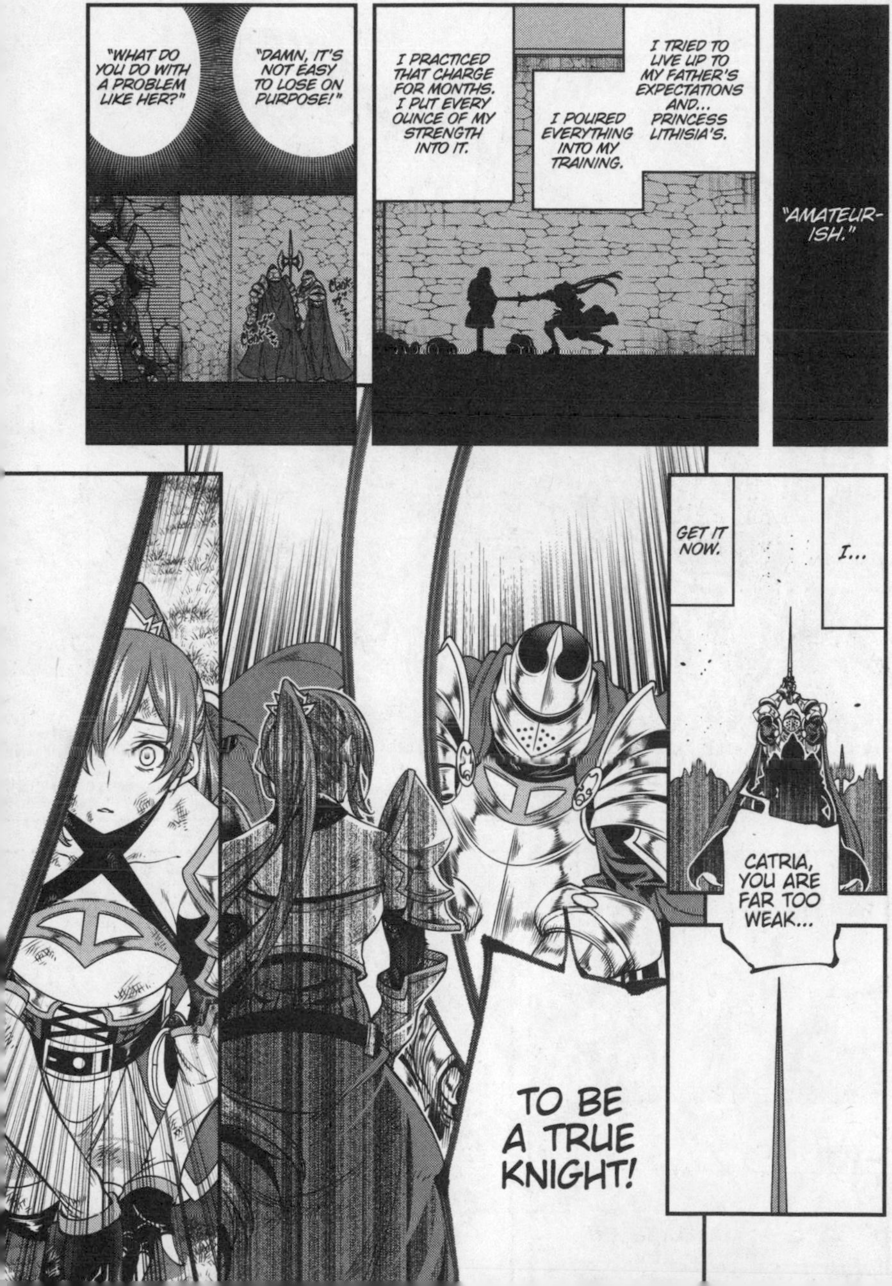
"AMATEURISH."
I TRIED TO LIVE UP TO MY FATHER'S EXPECTATIONS AND... PRINCESS LITHISIA'S.
I POURED EVERYTHING INTO MY TRAINING.
I PRACTICED THAT CHARGE FOR MONTHS. I PUT EVERY OUNCE OF MY STRENGTH INTO IT.
"DAMN, IT'S NOT EASY TO LOSE ON PURPOSE!"
"WHAT DO YOU DO WITH A PROBLEM LIKE HER?"
I...
GET IT NOW.
CATRIA, YOU ARE FAR TOO WEAK...
TO BE A TRUE KNIGHT!

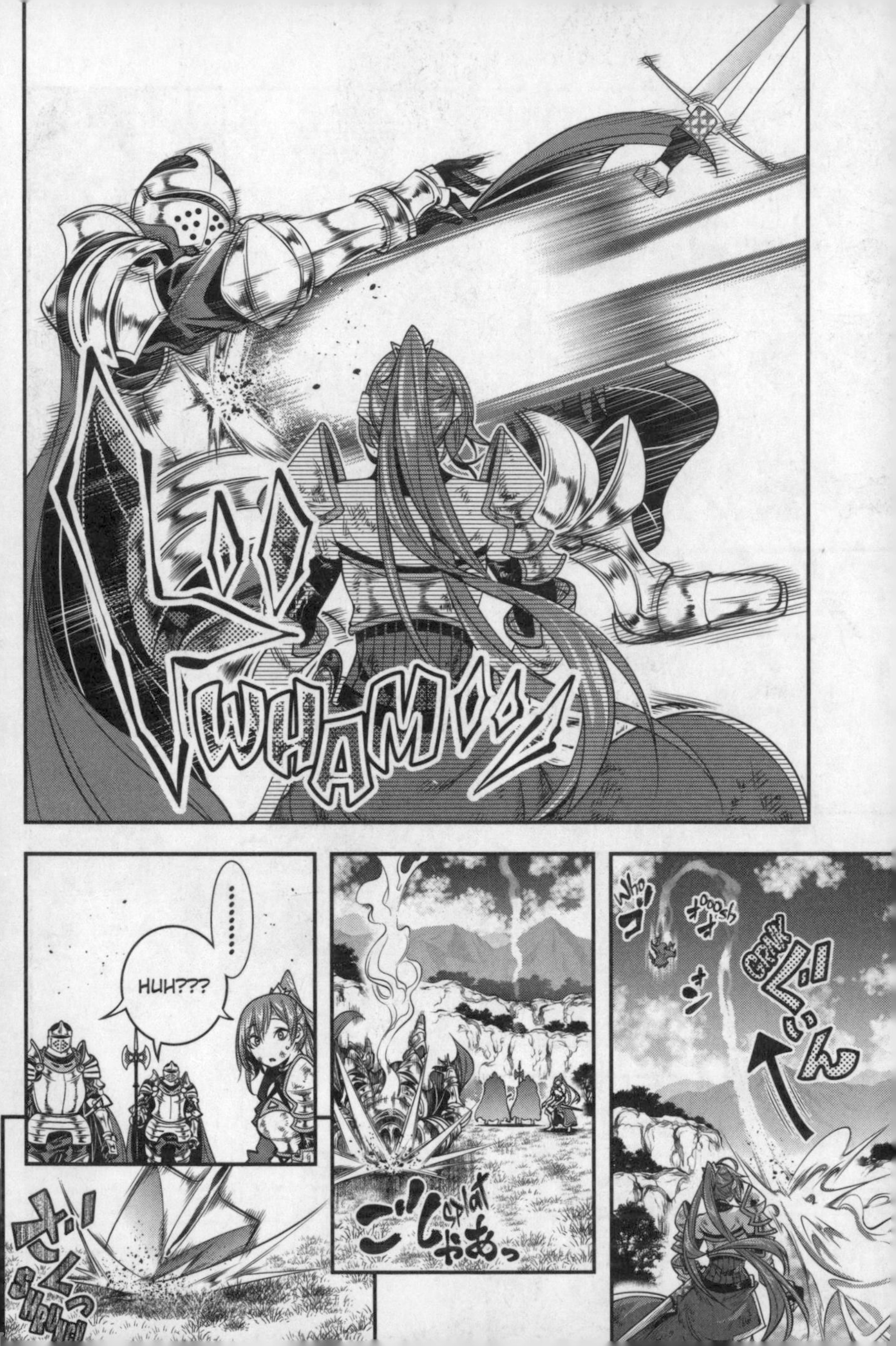
WHAM
Who ゴ
whoosh オオ
オン
ぐいん
splat
ごしゃあっ
....
HUH???
ざくっ

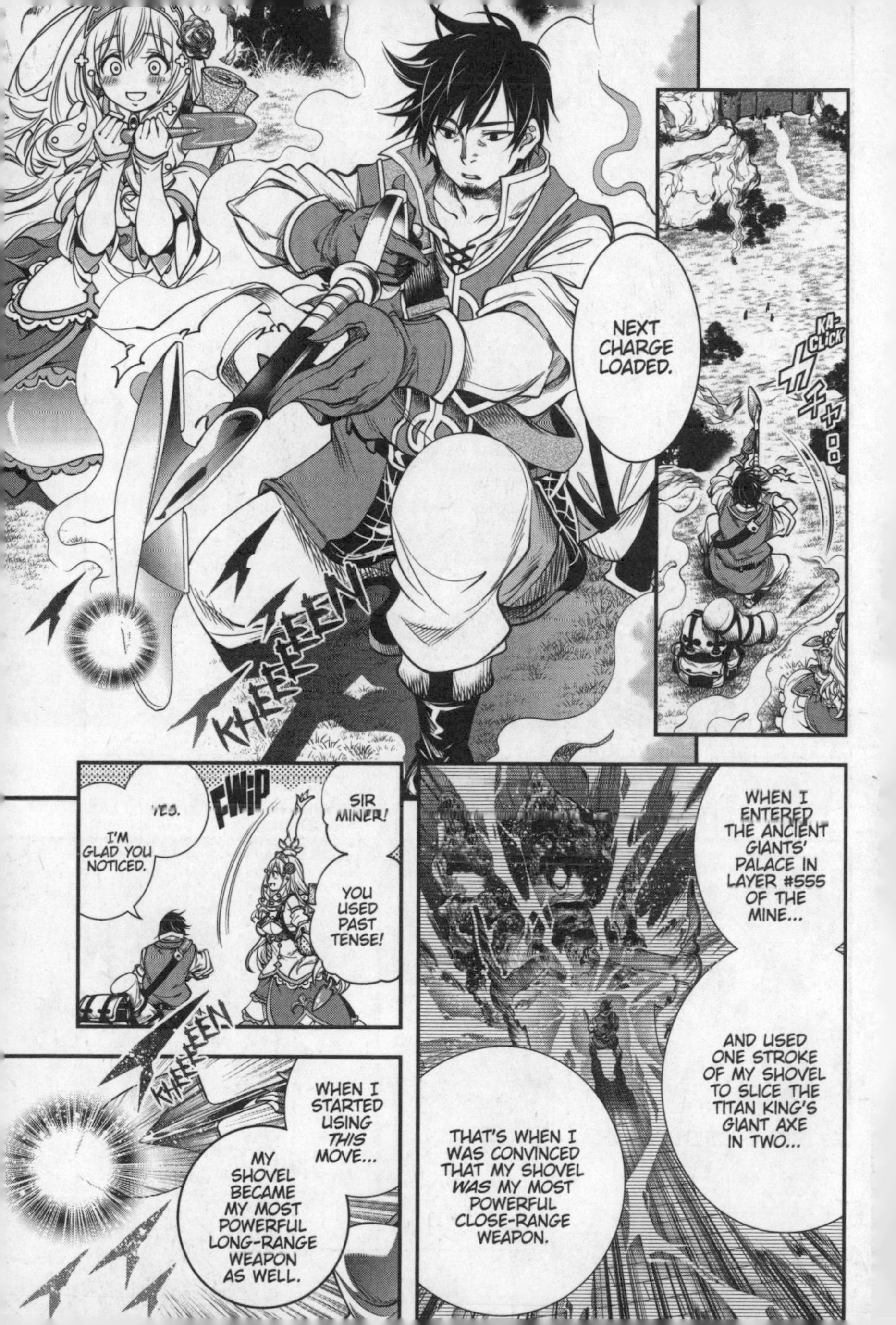
KA-CLICK
NEXT CHARGE LOADED.
KHEEEEEN
WHEN I ENTERED THE ANCIENT GIANTS' PALACE IN LAYER #555 OF THE MINE...
AND USED ONE STROKE OF MY SHOVEL TO SLICE THE TITAN KING'S GIANT AXE IN TWO...
THAT'S WHEN I WAS CONVINCED THAT MY SHOVEL *WAS* MY MOST POWERFUL CLOSE-RANGE WEAPON.
SIR MINER!
YOU USED PAST TENSE!
FWIP
YES.
I'M GLAD YOU NOTICED.
KHEEEEEN
WHEN I STARTED USING *THIS* MOVE...
MY SHOVEL BECAME MY MOST POWERFUL LONG-RANGE WEAPON AS WELL.

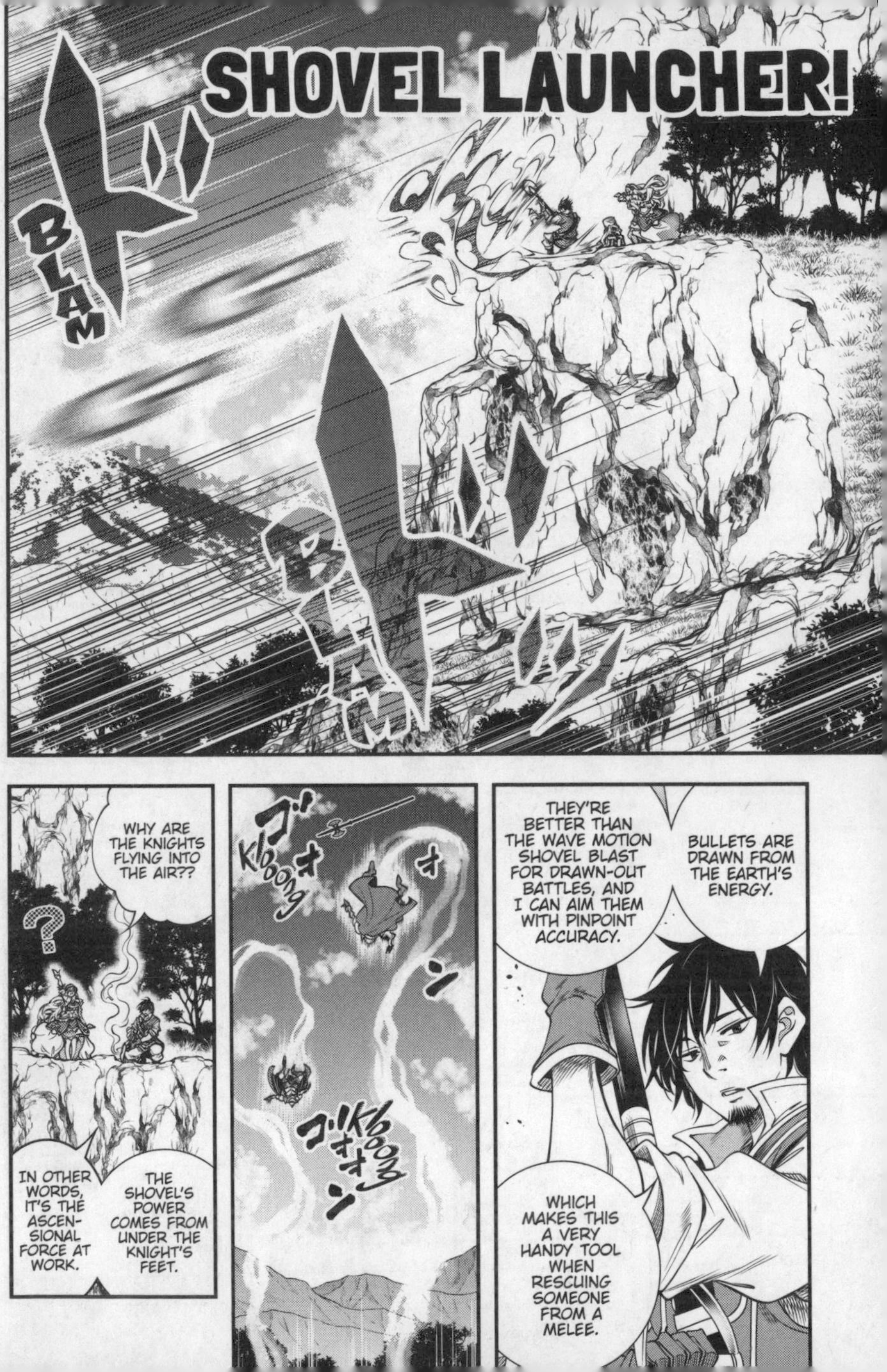

SHOVEL LAUNCHER!
BLAM
BULLETS ARE DRAWN FROM THE EARTH'S ENERGY.
THEY'RE BETTER THAN THE WAVE MOTION SHOVEL BLAST FOR DRAWN-OUT BATTLES, AND I CAN AIM THEM WITH PINPOINT ACCURACY.
WHICH MAKES THIS A VERY HANDY TOOL WHEN RESCUING SOMEONE FROM A MELEE.
ゴオオン
Kboong
ゴオオン
Kboong
WHY ARE THE KNIGHTS FLYING INTO THE AIR??
?
THE SHOVEL'S POWER COMES FROM UNDER THE KNIGHT'S FEET.
IN OTHER WORDS, IT'S THE ASCEN-SIONAL FORCE AT WORK.

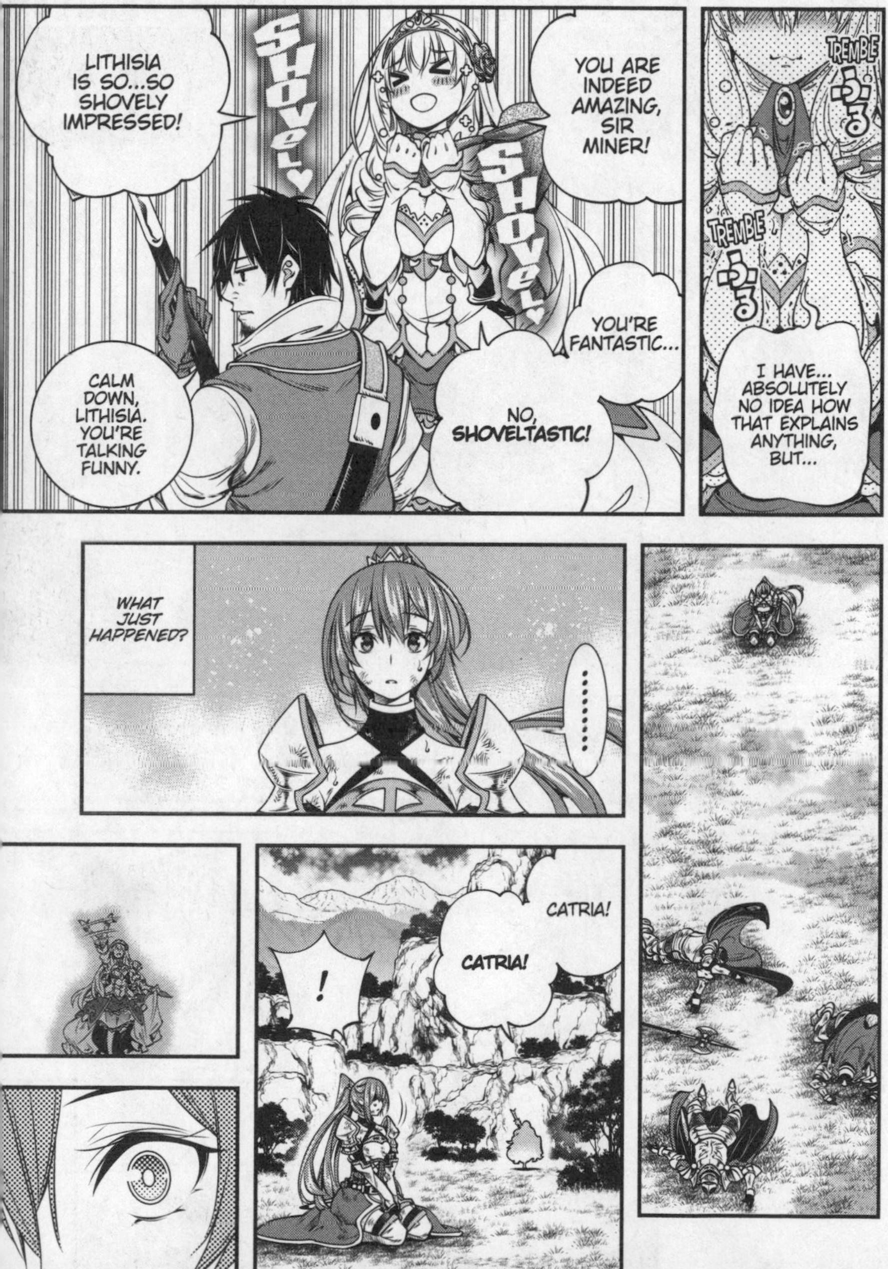
TREMBLE
ぷる
TREMBLE
ぷる
I HAVE... ABSOLUTELY NO IDEA HOW THAT EXPLAINS ANYTHING, BUT...
YOU ARE INDEED AMAZING, SIR MINER!
SHOVEL♥
SHOVEL♥
LITHISIA IS SO...SO SHOVELY IMPRESSED!
YOU'RE FANTASTIC...
NO, SHOVELTASTIC!
CALM DOWN, LITHISIA. YOU'RE TALKING FUNNY.
......
WHAT JUST HAPPENED?
CATRIA!
CATRIA!
!

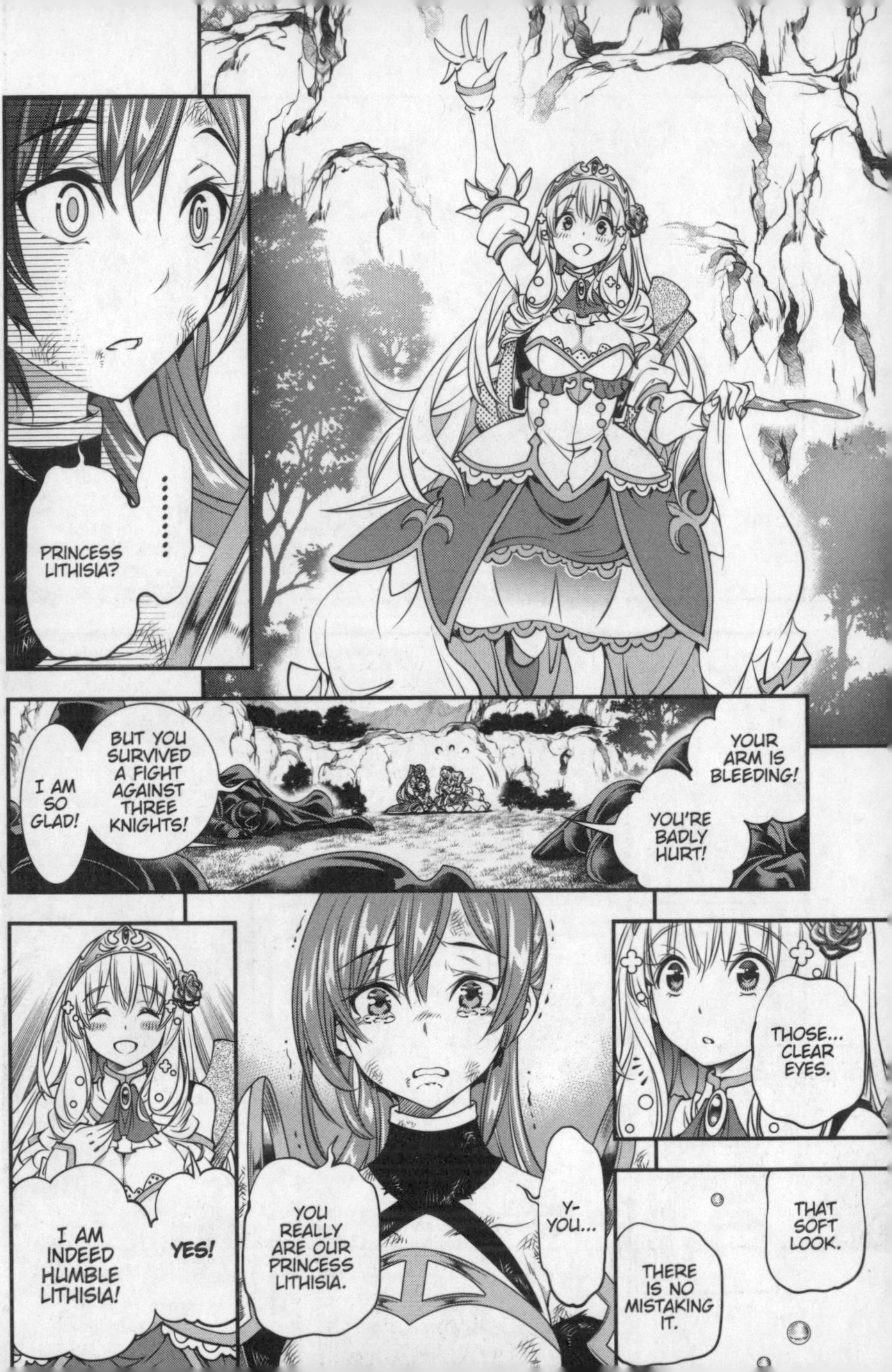
......
PRINCESS LITHISIA?
YOUR ARM IS BLEEDING!
YOU'RE BADLY HURT!
BUT YOU SURVIVED A FIGHT AGAINST THREE KNIGHTS!
I AM SO GLAD!
THOSE... CLEAR EYES.
THAT SOFT LOOK.
THERE IS NO MISTAKING IT.
Y-YOU...
YOU REALLY ARE OUR PRINCESS LITHISIA.
YES!
I AM INDEED HUMBLE LITHISIA!

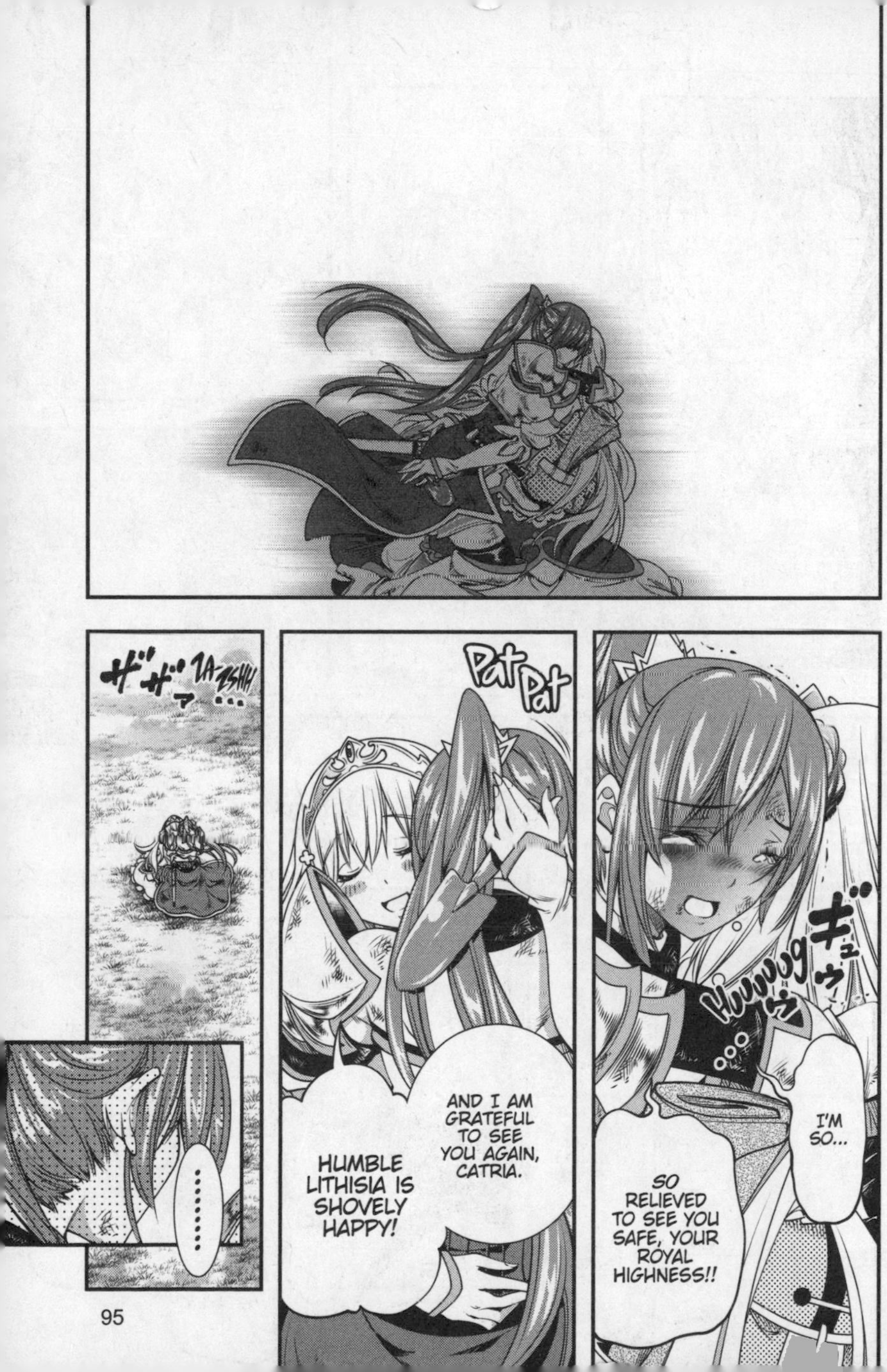
ギュウゥ
HUUUUUG
I'M SO...
SO RELIEVED TO SEE YOU SAFE, YOUR ROYAL HIGHNESS!!
Pat Pat
AND I AM GRATEFUL TO SEE YOU AGAIN, CATRIA.
HUMBLE LITHISIA IS SHOVELY HAPPY!
ザザァ
ZA-ZSHH...
....

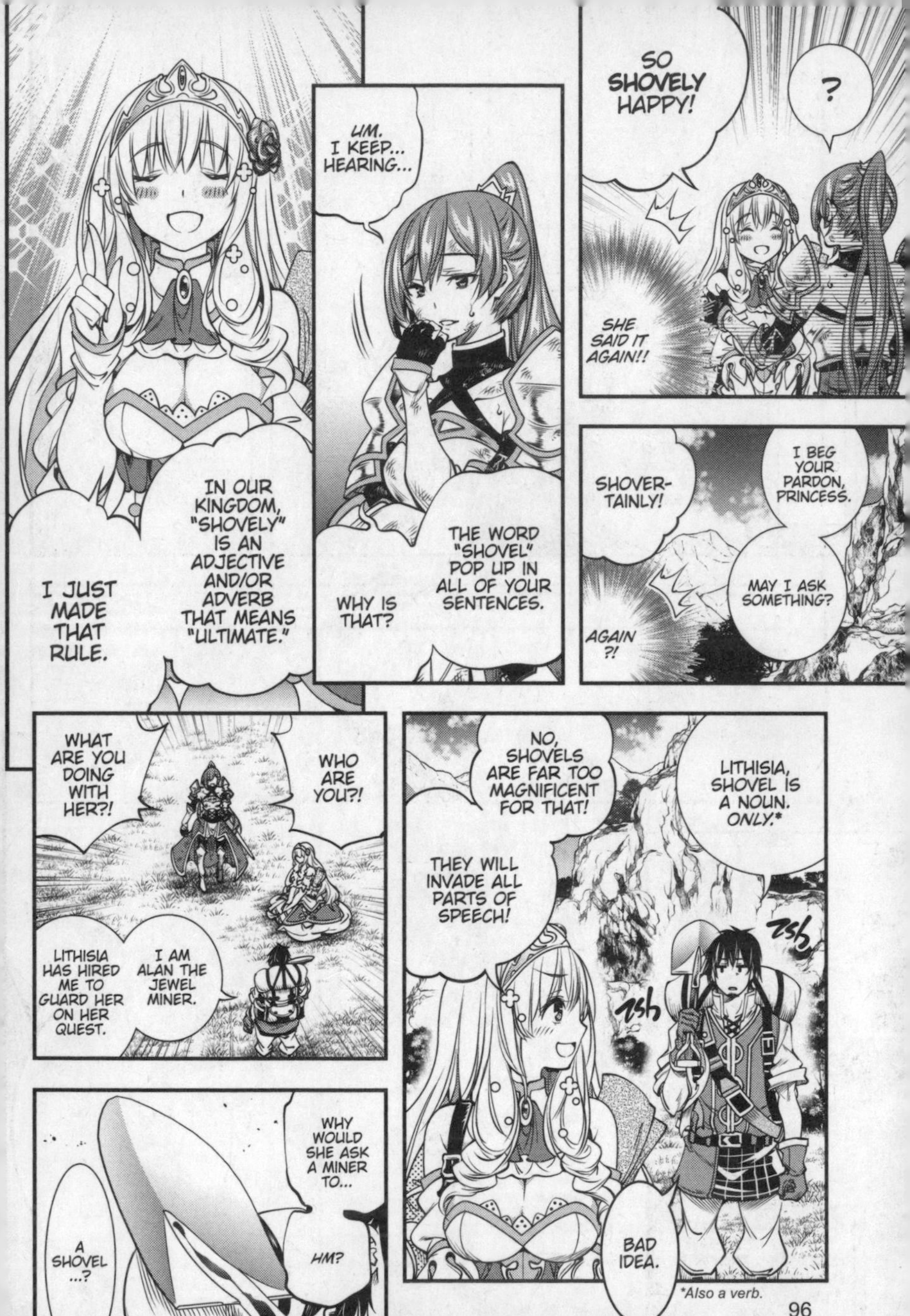
?
SO SHOVELY HAPPY!
SHE SAID IT AGAIN!!
I BEG YOUR PARDON, PRINCESS.
MAY I ASK SOMETHING?
SHOVER-TAINLY!
AGAIN ?!
UM. I KEEP... HEARING...
THE WORD "SHOVEL" POP UP IN ALL OF YOUR SENTENCES.
WHY IS THAT?
IN OUR KINGDOM, "SHOVELY" IS AN ADJECTIVE AND/OR ADVERB THAT MEANS "ULTIMATE."
I JUST MADE THAT RULE.
LITHISIA, SHOVEL IS A NOUN. ONLY.*
NO, SHOVELS ARE FAR TOO MAGNIFICENT FOR THAT!
THEY WILL INVADE ALL PARTS OF SPEECH!
zsh
zsh
BAD IDEA.
WHO ARE YOU?!
WHAT ARE YOU DOING WITH HER?!
I AM ALAN THE JEWEL MINER.
LITHISIA HAS HIRED ME TO GUARD HER ON HER QUEST.
WHY WOULD SHE ASK A MINER TO...
HM?
A SHOVEL ...?

*Also a verb.

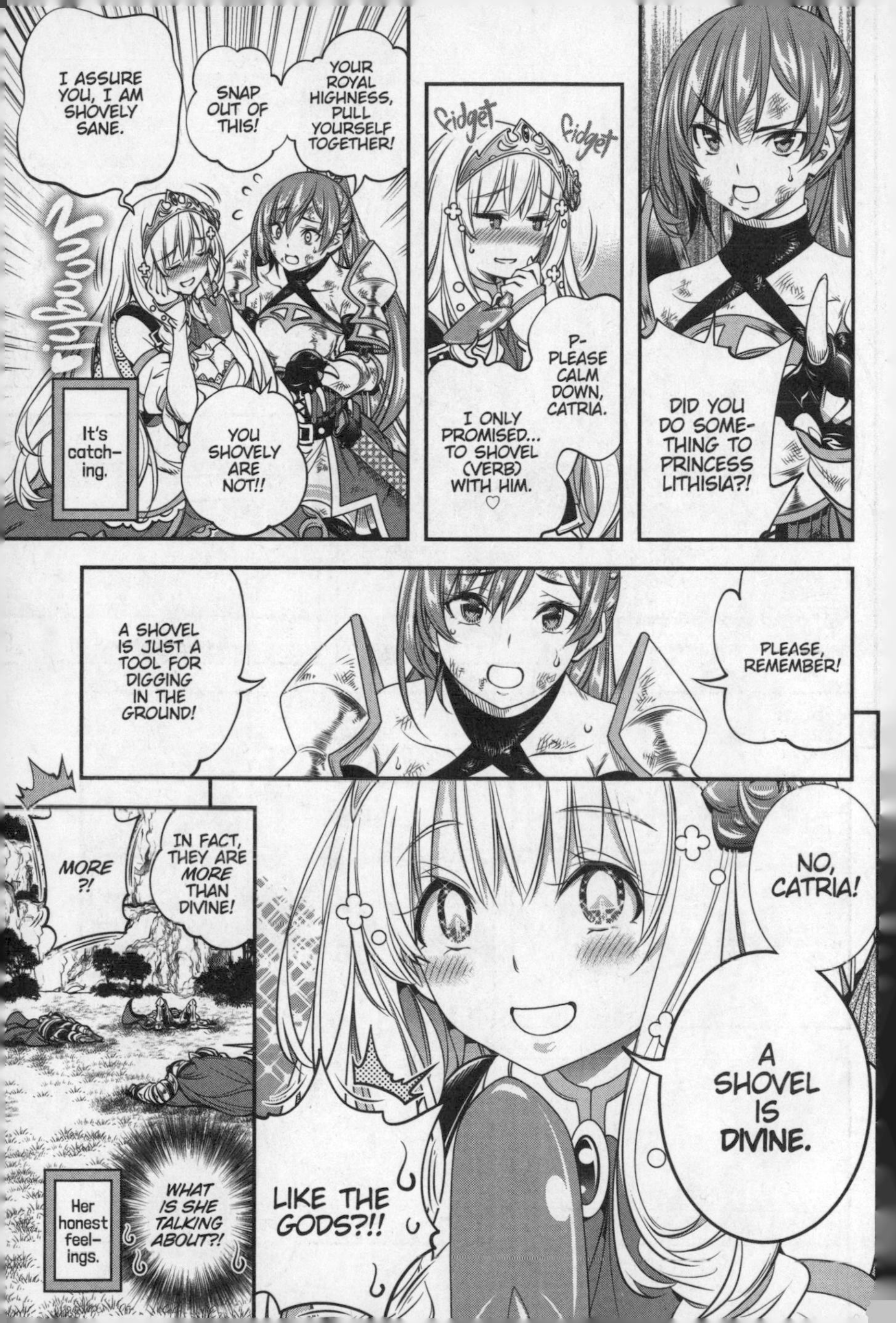
DID YOU DO SOME-THING TO PRINCESS LITHISIA?!
Fidget fidget
P-PLEASE CALM DOWN, CATRIA.
I ONLY PROMISED... TO SHOVEL (VERB) WITH HIM. ♡
YOUR ROYAL HIGHNESS, PULL YOURSELF TOGETHER!
SNAP OUT OF THIS!
I ASSURE YOU, I AM SHOVELY SANE.
Snuggle
YOU SHOVELY ARE NOT!!
It's catch-ing.
PLEASE, REMEMBER!
A SHOVEL IS JUST A TOOL FOR DIGGING IN THE GROUND!
NO, CATRIA!
A SHOVEL IS DIVINE.
LIKE THE GODS?!!
IN FACT, THEY ARE MORE THAN DIVINE!
MORE ?!
WHAT IS SHE TALKING ABOUT?!
Her honest feel-ings.

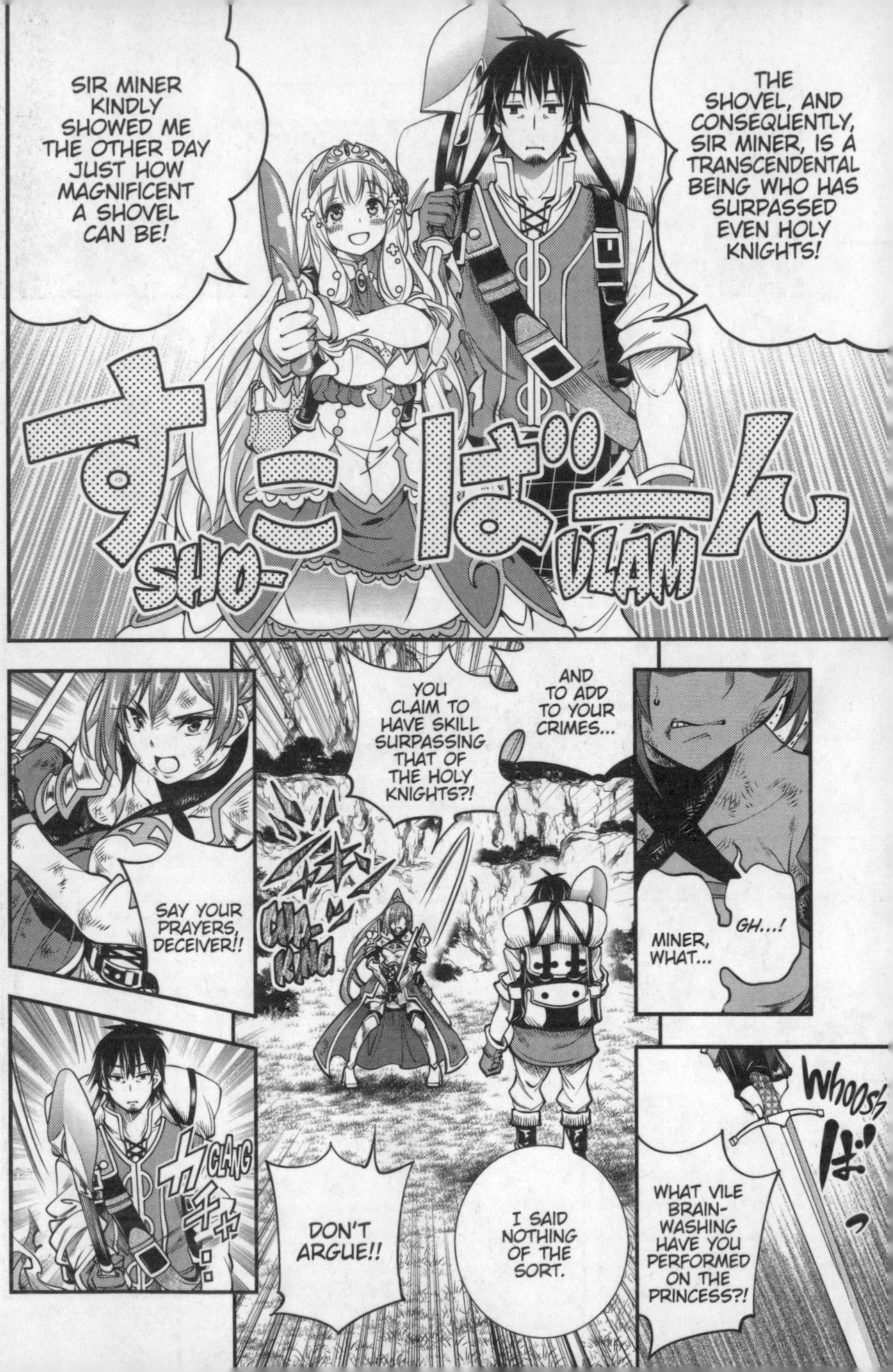
THE SHOVEL, AND CONSEQUENTLY, SIR MINER, IS A TRANSCENDENTAL BEING WHO HAS SURPASSED EVEN HOLY KNIGHTS!
SIR MINER KINDLY SHOWED ME THE OTHER DAY JUST HOW MAGNIFICENT A SHOVEL CAN BE!
すごーばーん
SHO-
VLAM
GH...!
MINER, WHAT...
Whoosh
WHAT VILE BRAIN-WASHING HAVE YOU PERFORMED ON THE PRINCESS?!
AND TO ADD TO YOUR CRIMES...
YOU CLAIM TO HAVE SKILL SURPASSING THAT OF THE HOLY KNIGHTS?!
CHA-KING
I SAID NOTHING OF THE SORT.
DON'T ARGUE!!
SAY YOUR PRAYERS, DECEIVER!!
CLANG

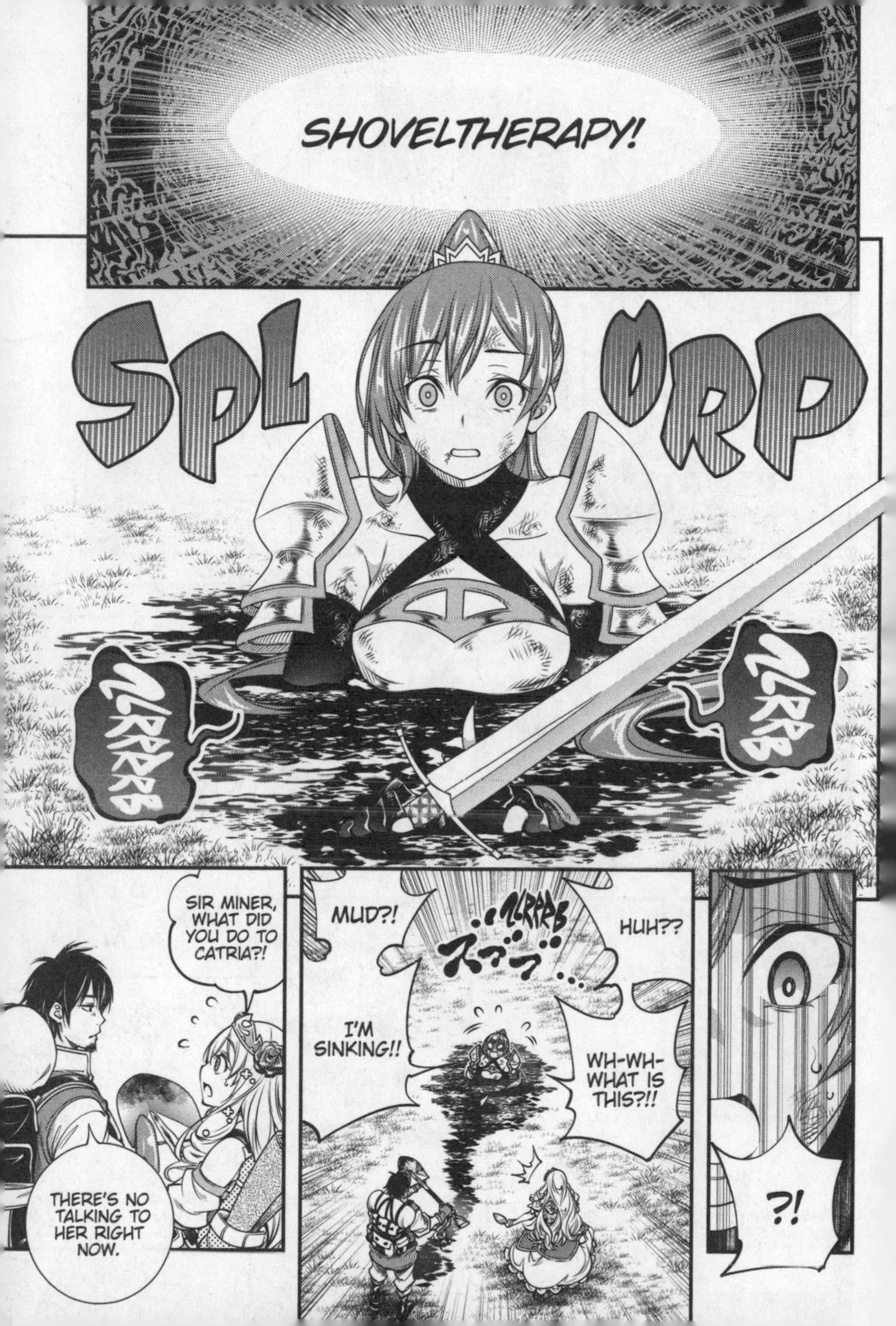

SHOVELTHERAPY!
SPLORP
ZLRRB
ZLRRRRB
?!
HUH??
MUD?!
ZLRRRB
WH-WH-WHAT IS THIS?!!
I'M SINKING!!
SIR MINER, WHAT DID YOU DO TO CATRIA?!
THERE'S NO TALKING TO HER RIGHT NOW.

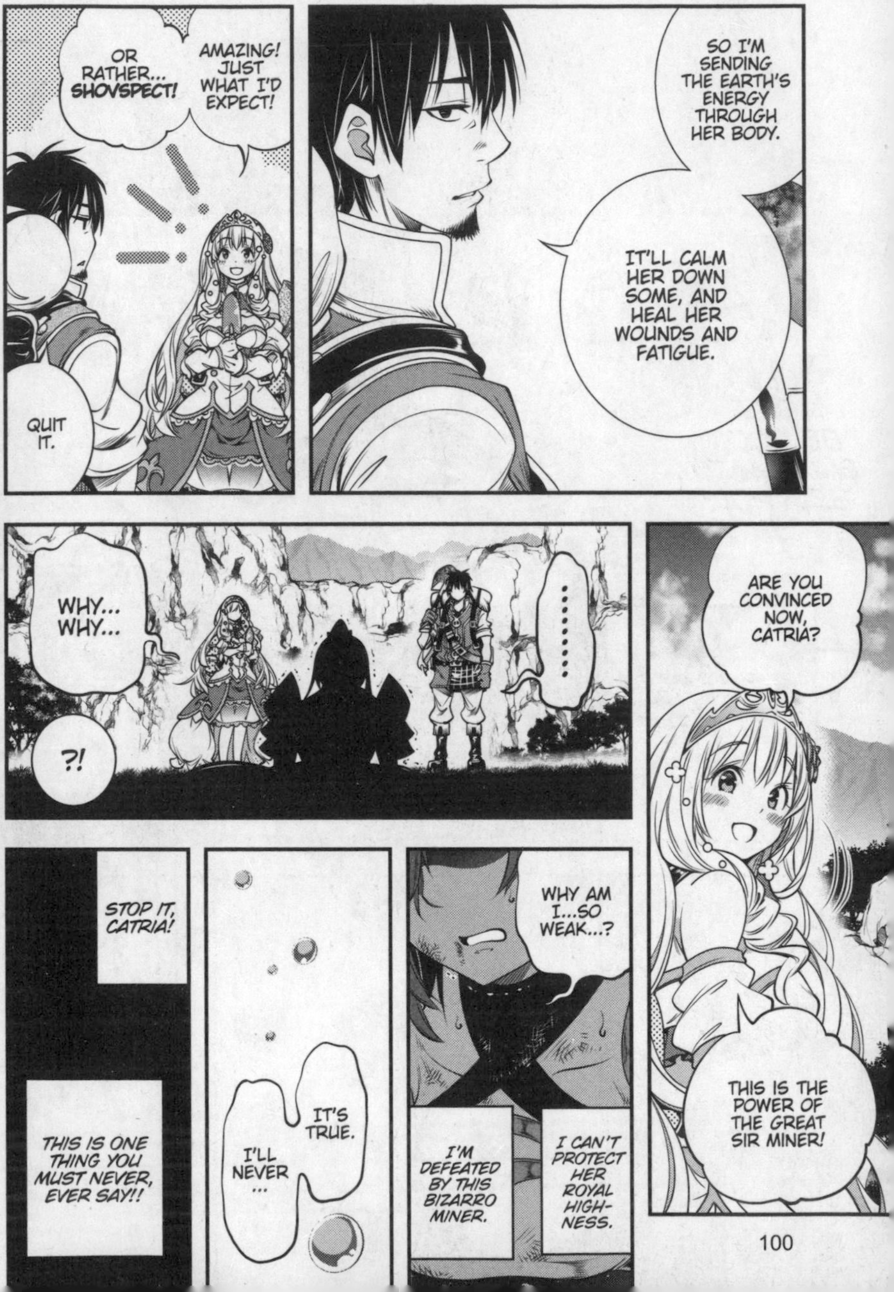
SO I'M SENDING THE EARTH'S ENERGY THROUGH HER BODY.
IT'LL CALM HER DOWN SOME, AND HEAL HER WOUNDS AND FATIGUE.
AMAZING! JUST WHAT I'D EXPECT!
OR RATHER... SHOVSPECT!
QUIT IT.
ARE YOU CONVINCED NOW, CATRIA?
THIS IS THE POWER OF THE GREAT SIR MINER!
....
WHY... WHY...
?!
WHY AM I...SO WEAK...?
I CAN'T PROTECT HER ROYAL HIGH-NESS.
I'M DEFEATED BY THIS BIZARRO MINER.
IT'S TRUE.
I'LL NEVER ...
STOP IT, CATRIA!
THIS IS ONE THING YOU MUST NEVER, EVER SAY!!

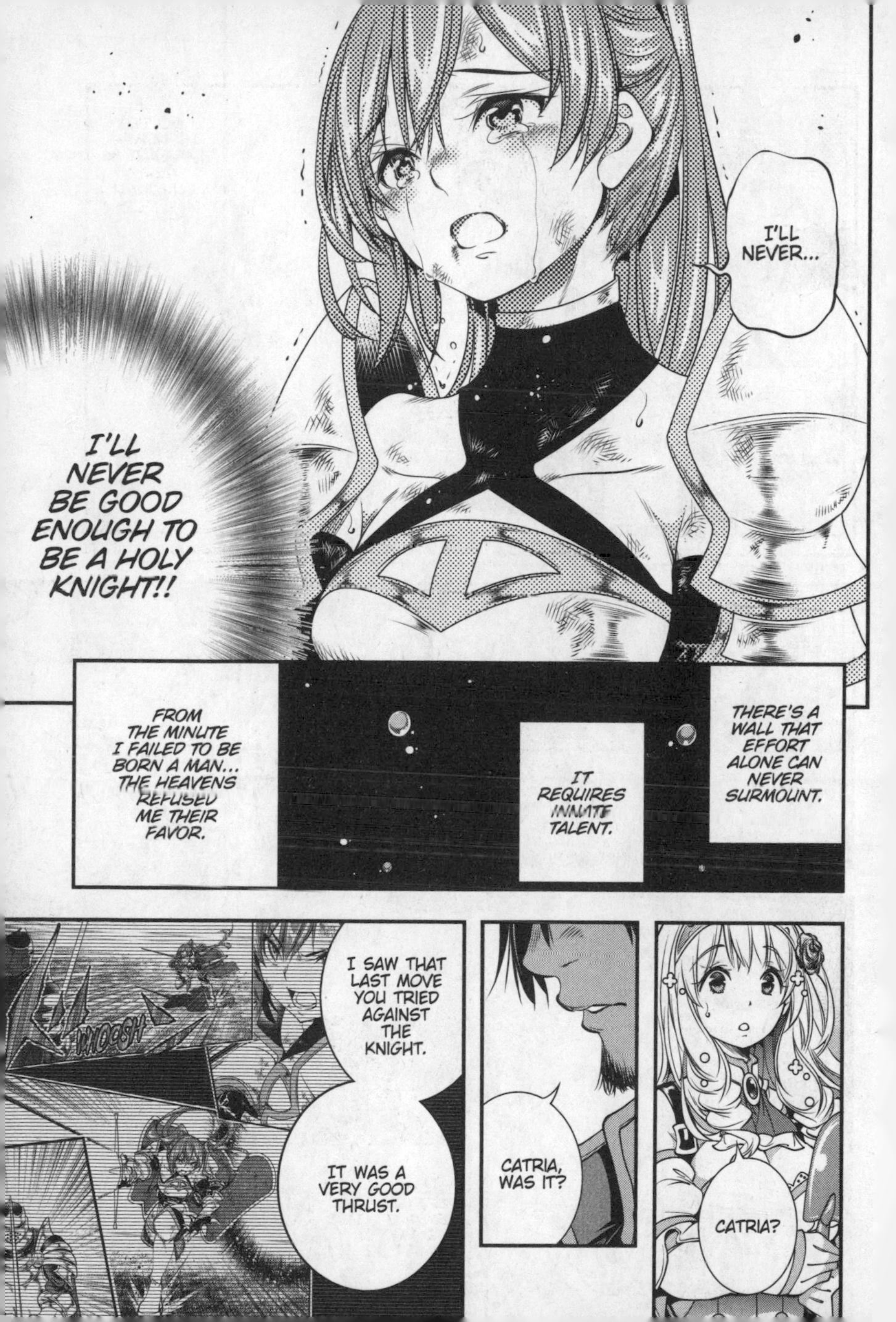
I'LL NEVER...
I'LL NEVER BE GOOD ENOUGH TO BE A HOLY KNIGHT!!
THERE'S A WALL THAT EFFORT ALONE CAN NEVER SURMOUNT.
IT REQUIRES INNATE TALENT.
FROM THE MINUTE I FAILED TO BE BORN A MAN... THE HEAVENS REFUSED ME THEIR FAVOR.
CATRIA?
CATRIA, WAS IT?
I SAW THAT LAST MOVE YOU TRIED AGAINST THE KNIGHT.
WHOOSH
IT WAS A VERY GOOD THRUST.

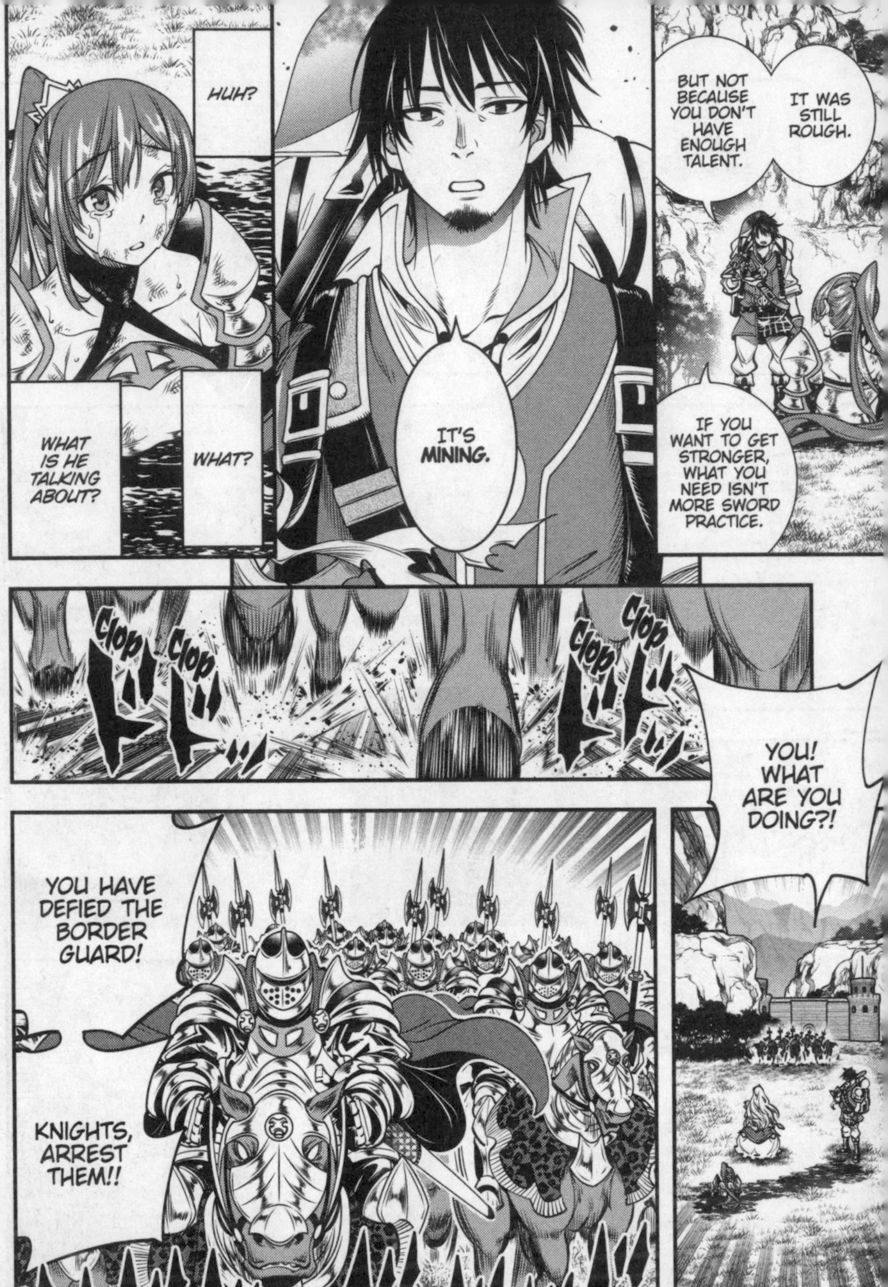
IT WAS STILL ROUGH.
BUT NOT BECAUSE YOU DON'T HAVE ENOUGH TALENT.
IF YOU WANT TO GET STRONGER, WHAT YOU NEED ISN'T MORE SWORD PRACTICE.
IT'S MINING.
HUH?
WHAT?
WHAT IS HE TALKING ABOUT?
CLOP CLOP
CLOP CLOP
YOU! WHAT ARE YOU DOING?!
YOU HAVE DEFIED THE BORDER GUARD!
KNIGHTS, ARREST THEM!!
CLOP CLOP CLOP CLOP CLOP CLOP CLOP

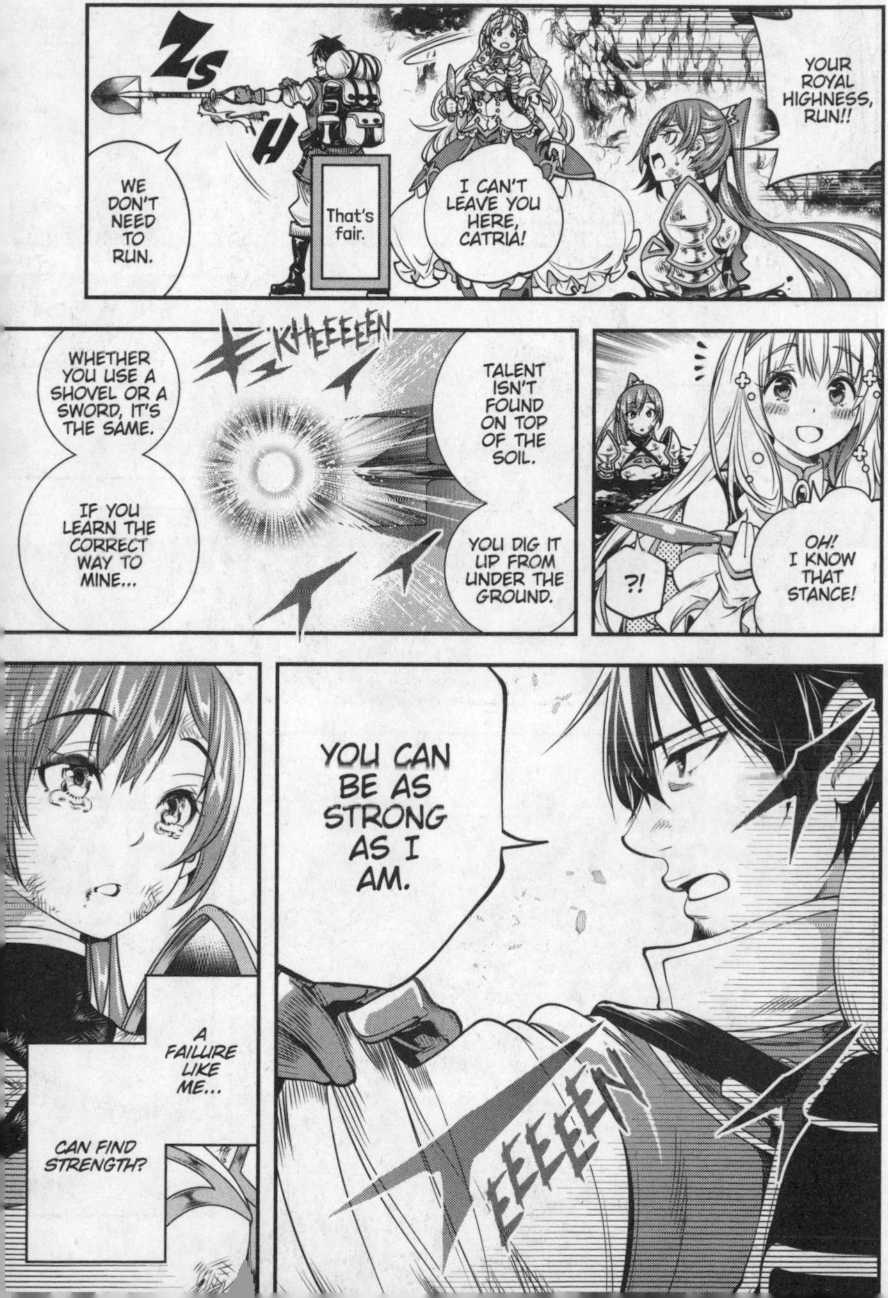
YOUR ROYAL HIGHNESS, RUN!!
I CAN'T LEAVE YOU HERE, CATRIA!
That's fair.
ZSH
WE DON'T NEED TO RUN.
OH! I KNOW THAT STANCE!
?!
TALENT ISN'T FOUND ON TOP OF THE SOIL.
YOU DIG IT UP FROM UNDER THE GROUND.
KYEEEEEN
WHETHER YOU USE A SHOVEL OR A SWORD, IT'S THE SAME.
IF YOU LEARN THE CORRECT WAY TO MINE...
YOU CAN BE AS STRONG AS I AM.
EEEEEN
A FAILURE LIKE ME...
CAN FIND STRENGTH?

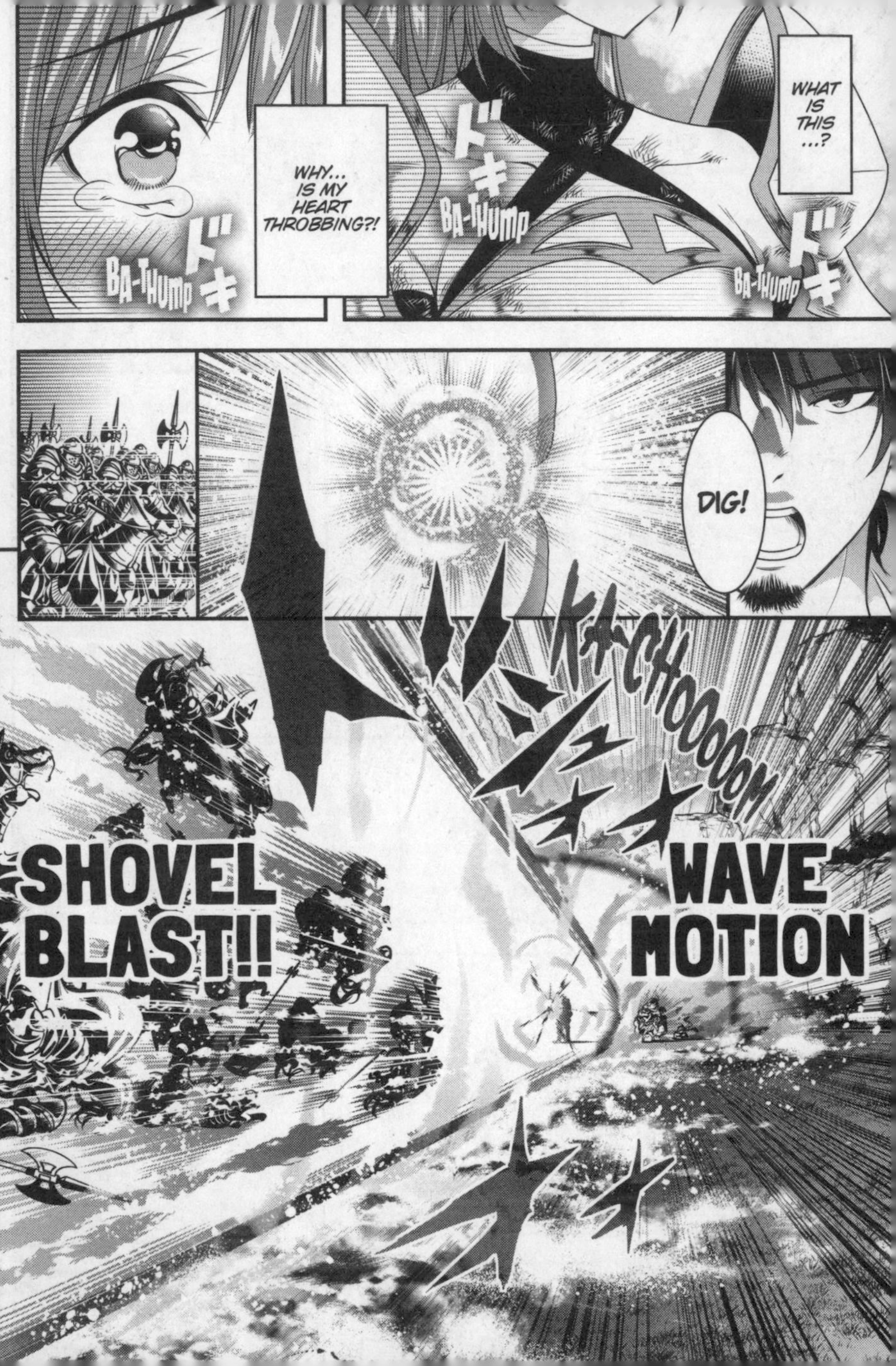
WHAT IS THIS ...?
ドキ
BA-THUMP
ドキ
BA-THUMP
WHY... IS MY HEART THROBBING?!
ドキ
BA-THUMP
DIG!
KA-CHOOOOOM
WAVE MOTION
SHOVEL BLAST!!

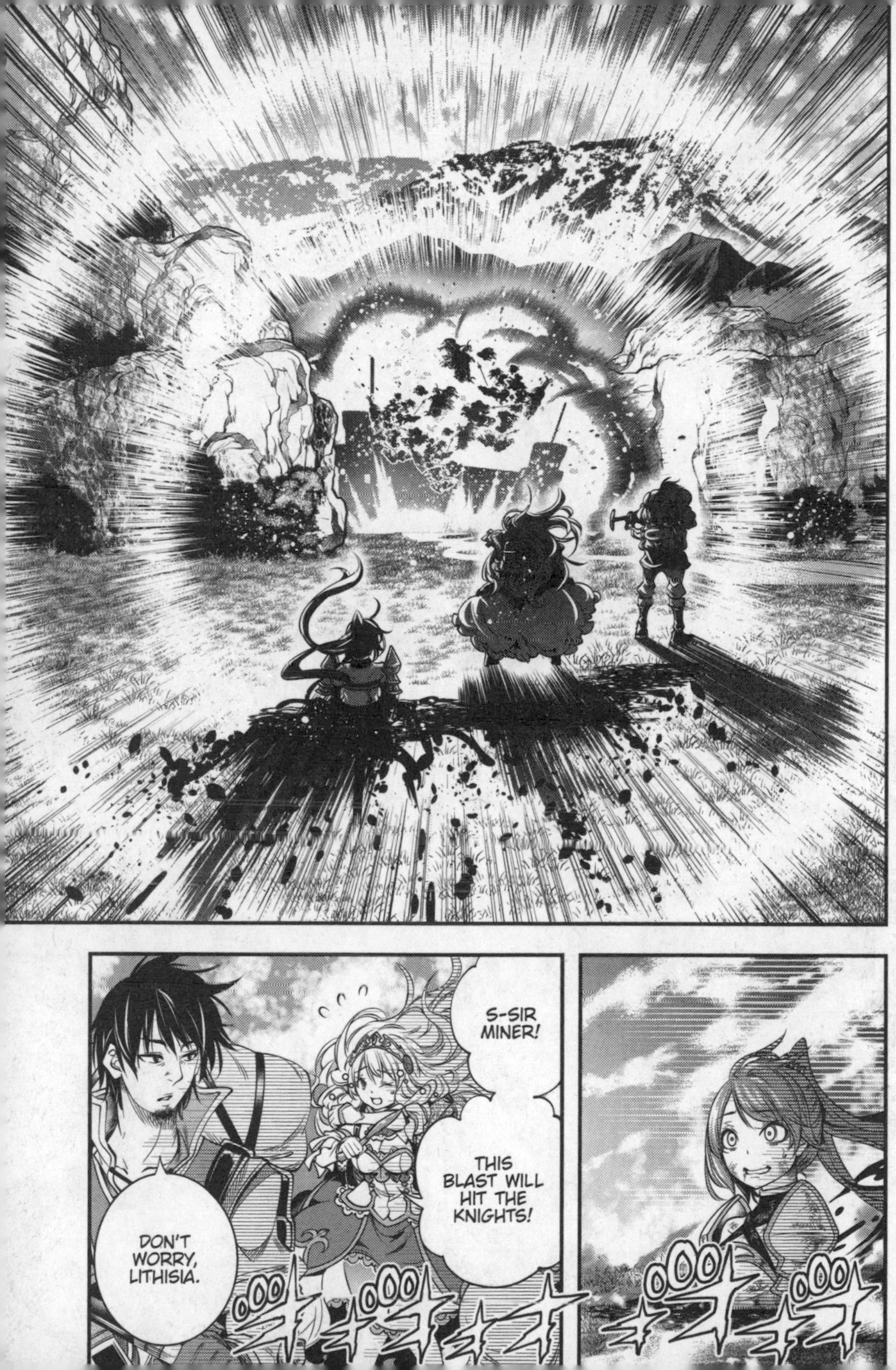
S-SIR MINER!
THIS BLAST WILL HIT THE KNIGHTS!
DON'T WORRY, LITHISIA.

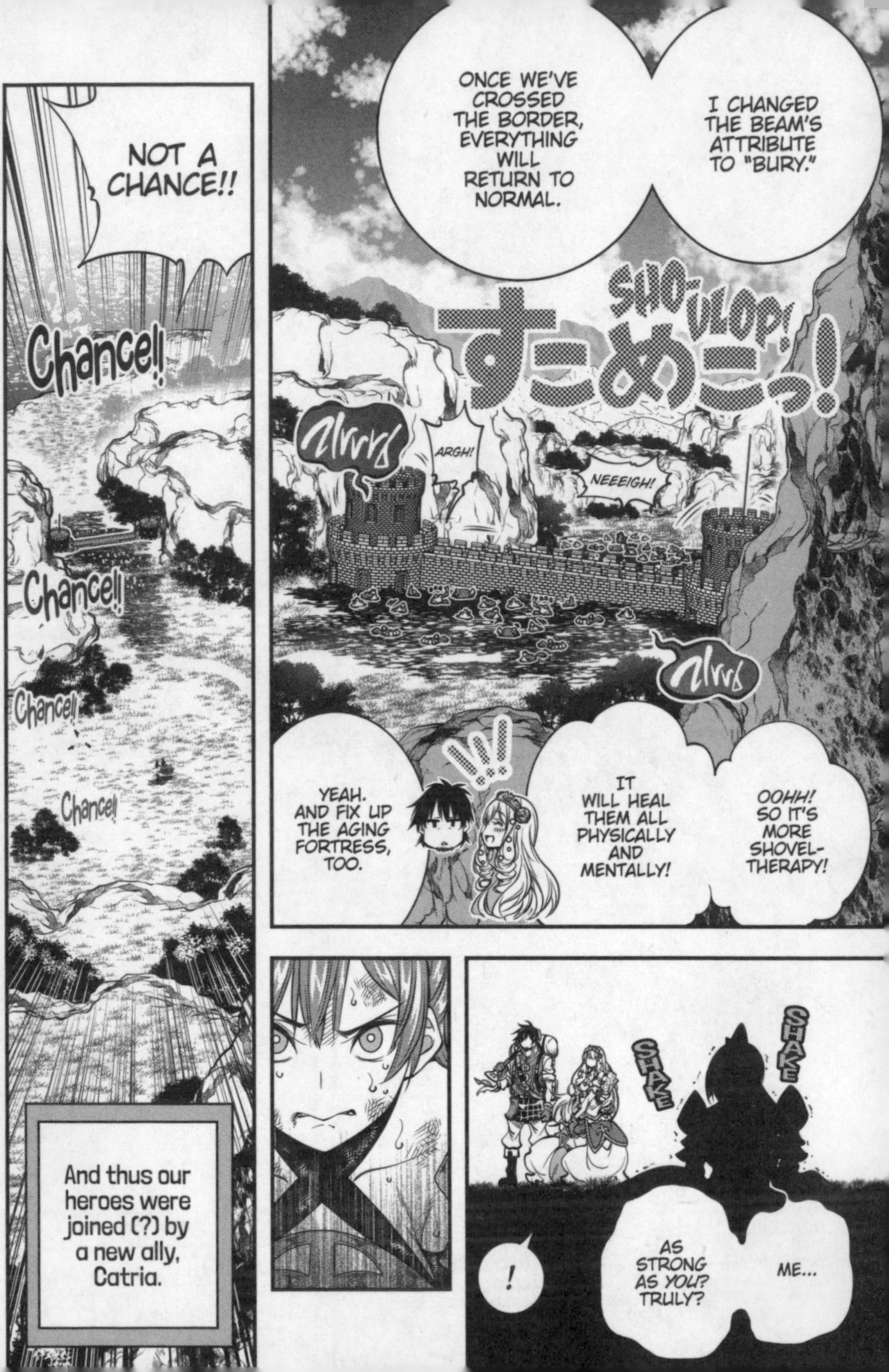
I CHANGED THE BEAM'S ATTRIBUTE TO "BURY."
ONCE WE'VE CROSSED THE BORDER, EVERYTHING WILL RETURN TO NORMAL.
SHO-ULOP!
ARGH!
NEEEIGH!
OOHH! SO IT'S MORE SHOVEL-THERAPY!
IT WILL HEAL THEM ALL PHYSICALLY AND MENTALLY!
YEAH. AND FIX UP THE AGING FORTRESS, TOO.
SHAKE
SHAKE
ME...
AS STRONG AS YOU? TRULY?
!
NOT A CHANCE!!
Chance!!
Chance!!
Chance!!
Chance!!
And thus our heroes were joined (?) by a new ally, Catria.

THE INVINCIBLE

SHOVEL

"WAVE MOTION SHOVEL BLAST!"

(˙ ˙ω˙ ˙)♂=====★(゛Д ゛ ;;;);.;˙. KA-CHOOOM

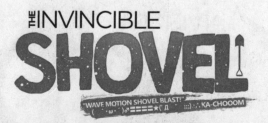

THE INVINCIBLE

SHOVEL

"WAVE MOTION SHOVEL BLAST!"
(˙ω˙)୨ ≡≡≡≡★(д   ;;;):.˙. KA-CHOOOM

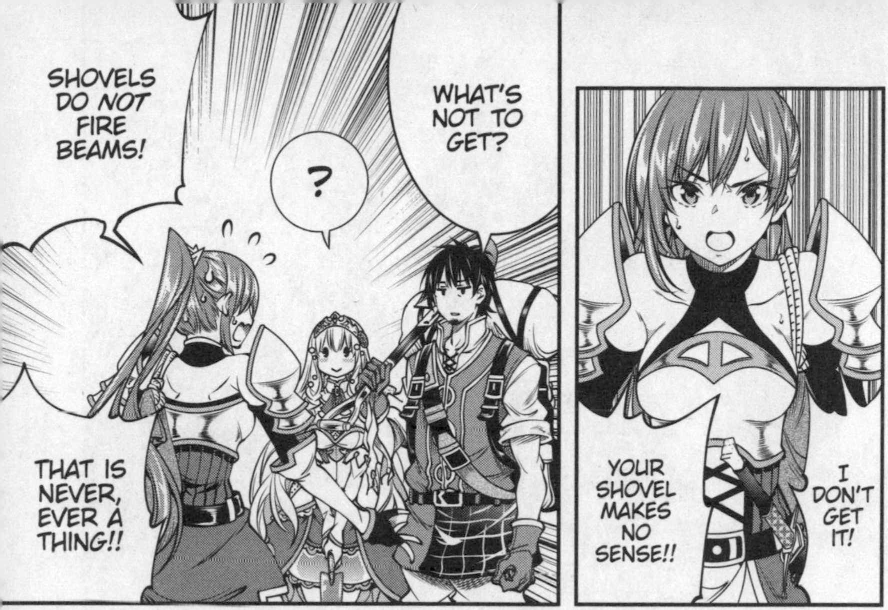
I DON'T GET IT!
YOUR SHOVEL MAKES NO SENSE!!
WHAT'S NOT TO GET?
?
SHOVELS DO *NOT* FIRE BEAMS!
THAT IS NEVER, EVER A THING!!

Chapter 4: Out of Control x Wild Delusions x Shovel Practice

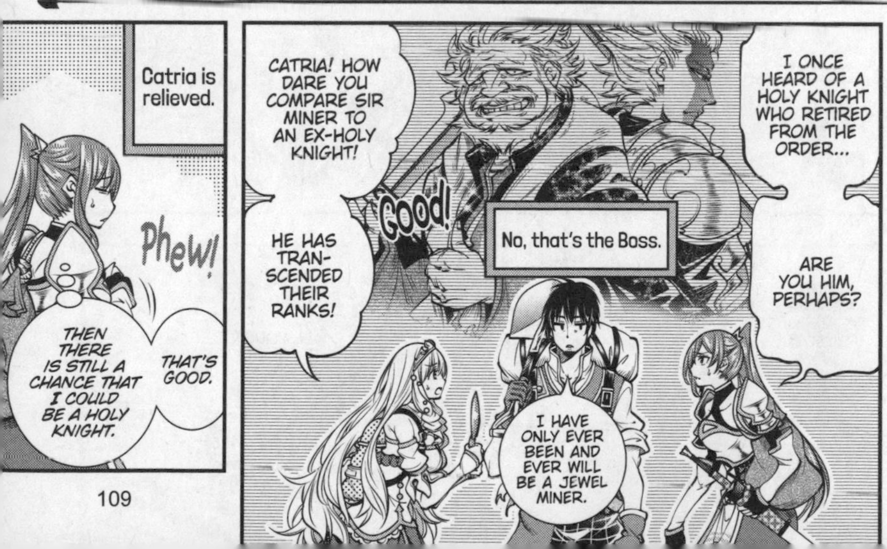
I ONCE HEARD OF A HOLY KNIGHT WHO RETIRED FROM THE ORDER...
ARE YOU HIM, PERHAPS?
CATRIA! HOW DARE YOU COMPARE SIR MINER TO AN EX-HOLY KNIGHT!
GOOD!
No, that's the Boss.
HE HAS TRAN-SCENDED THEIR RANKS!
I HAVE ONLY EVER BEEN AND EVER WILL BE A JEWEL MINER.
Catria is relieved.
Phew!
THAT'S GOOD.
THEN THERE IS STILL A CHANCE THAT I COULD BE A HOLY KNIGHT.

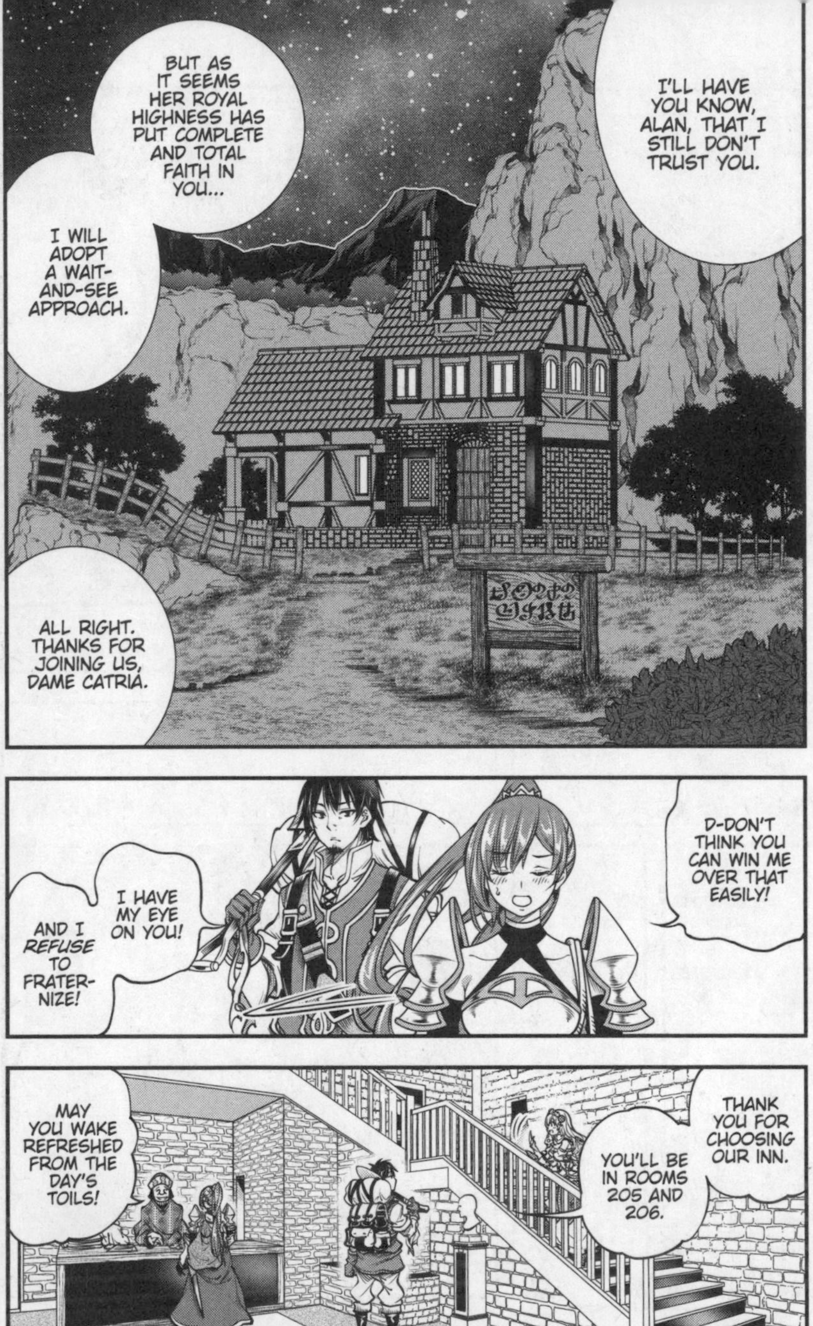
I'LL HAVE YOU KNOW, ALAN, THAT I STILL DON'T TRUST YOU.
BUT AS IT SEEMS HER ROYAL HIGHNESS HAS PUT COMPLETE AND TOTAL FAITH IN YOU...
I WILL ADOPT A WAIT-AND-SEE APPROACH.
ALL RIGHT. THANKS FOR JOINING US, DAME CATRIA.
D-DON'T THINK YOU CAN WIN ME OVER THAT EASILY!
I HAVE MY EYE ON YOU!
AND I *REFUSE* TO FRATER-NIZE!
THANK YOU FOR CHOOSING OUR INN.
YOU'LL BE IN ROOMS 205 AND 206.
MAY YOU WAKE REFRESHED FROM THE DAY'S TOILS!

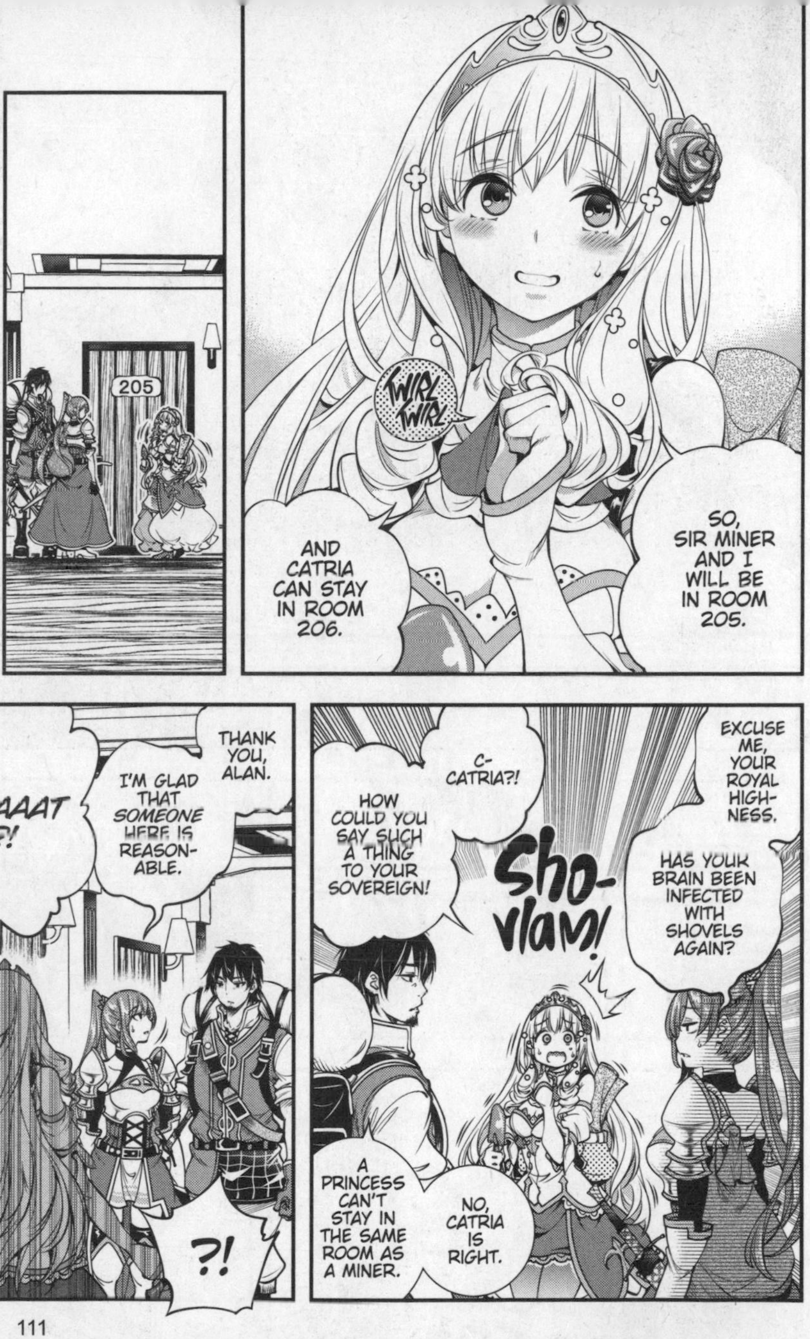
SO, SIR MINER AND I WILL BE IN ROOM 205.
TWIRL TWIRL
AND CATRIA CAN STAY IN ROOM 206.
205
EXCUSE ME, YOUR ROYAL HIGHNESS.
HAS YOUR BRAIN BEEN INFECTED WITH SHOVELS AGAIN?
C-CATRIA?!
HOW COULD YOU SAY SUCH A THING TO YOUR SOVEREIGN!
Sho-vlam!
NO, CATRIA IS RIGHT.
A PRINCESS CAN'T STAY IN THE SAME ROOM AS A MINER.
THANK YOU, ALAN.
I'M GLAD THAT SOMEONE HERE IS REASONABLE.
WHAAAT?!
?!

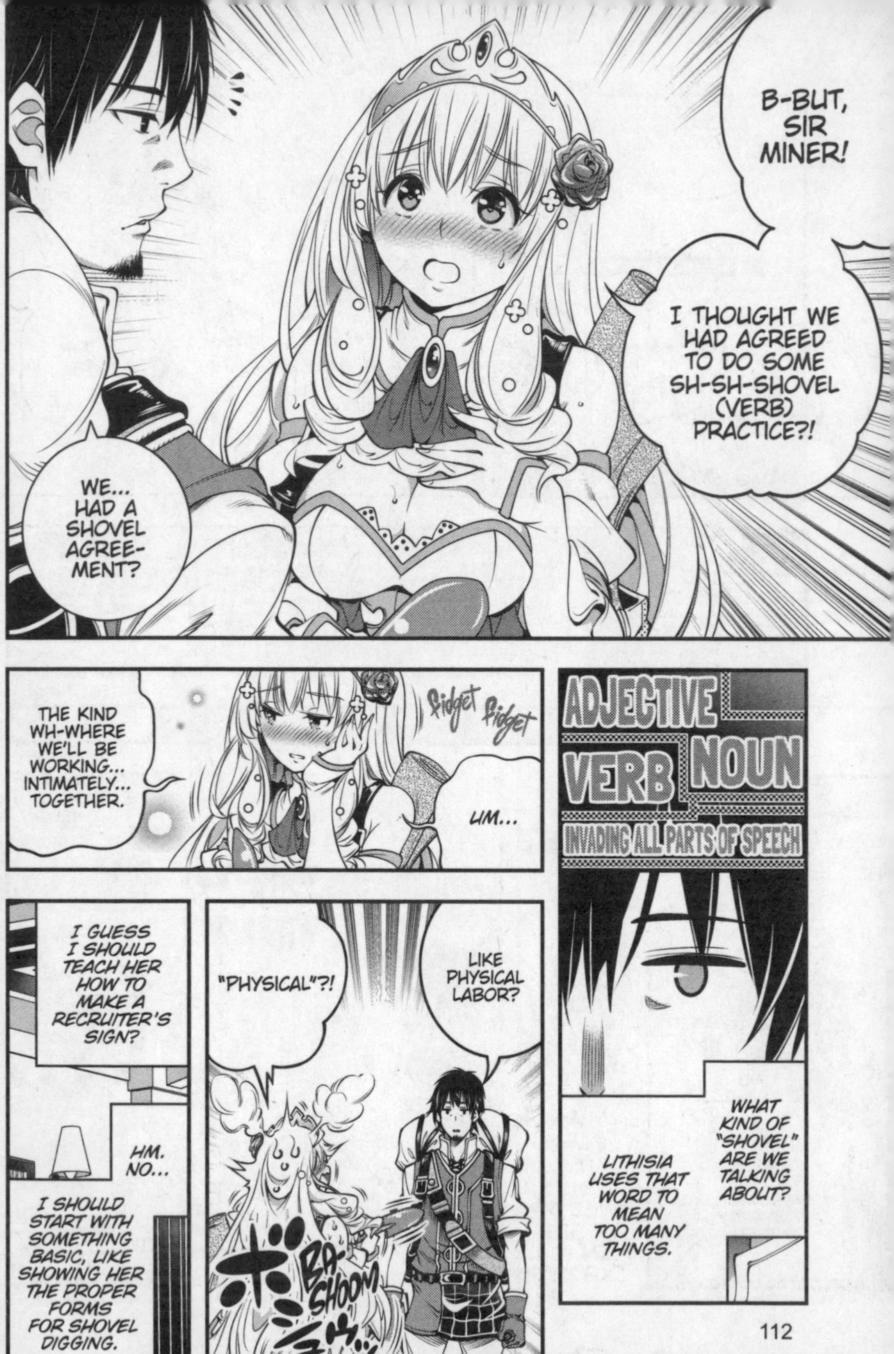
B-BUT, SIR MINER!
I THOUGHT WE HAD AGREED TO DO SOME SH-SH-SHOVEL (VERB) PRACTICE?!
WE... HAD A SHOVEL AGREEMENT?
ADJECTIVE
VERB NOUN
INVADING ALL PARTS OF SPEECH
WHAT KIND OF "SHOVEL" ARE WE TALKING ABOUT?
LITHISIA USES THAT WORD TO MEAN TOO MANY THINGS.
UM...
fidget fidget
THE KIND WH-WHERE WE'LL BE WORKING... INTIMATELY... TOGETHER.
LIKE PHYSICAL LABOR?
"PHYSICAL"?!
BA-SHOOM
I GUESS I SHOULD TEACH HER HOW TO MAKE A RECRUITER'S SIGN?
HM. NO...
I SHOULD START WITH SOMETHING BASIC, LIKE SHOWING HER THE PROPER FORMS FOR SHOVEL DIGGING.

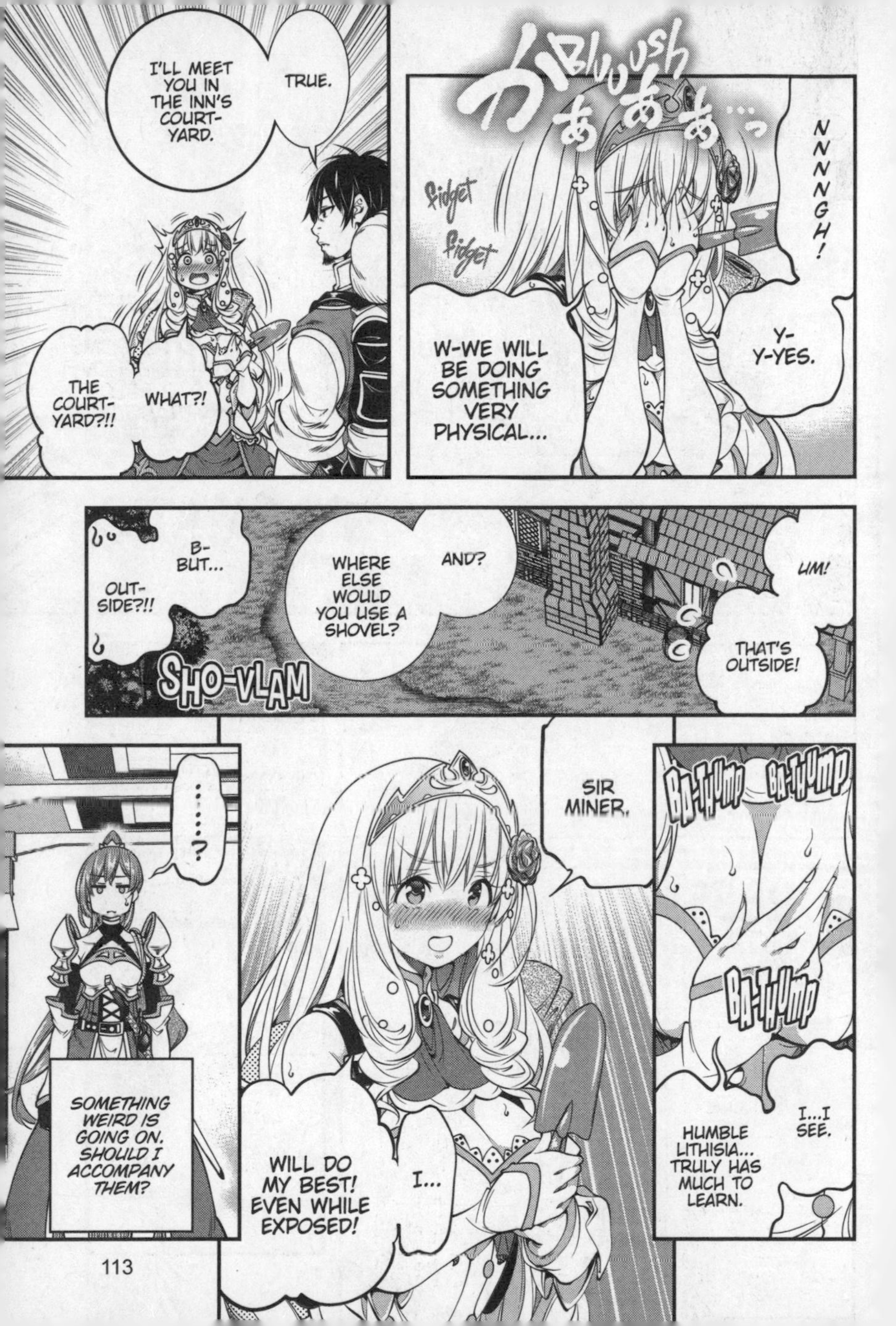
かあああ…っ
BLUUUSH
NNNNGH!
fidget
fidget
Y-Y-YES.
W-WE WILL BE DOING SOMETHING VERY PHYSICAL...
TRUE.
I'LL MEET YOU IN THE INN'S COURT-YARD.
WHAT?!
THE COURT-YARD?!!
UM!
THAT'S OUTSIDE!
AND?
WHERE ELSE WOULD YOU USE A SHOVEL?
B-BUT...
OUT-SIDE?!!
SHO-VLAM
BA-THUMP
BA-THUMP
BA-THUMP
I...I SEE.
HUMBLE LITHISIA... TRULY HAS MUCH TO LEARN.
SIR MINER.
I...
WILL DO MY BEST! EVEN WHILE EXPOSED!
......?
SOMETHING WEIRD IS GOING ON. SHOULD I ACCOMPANY THEM?

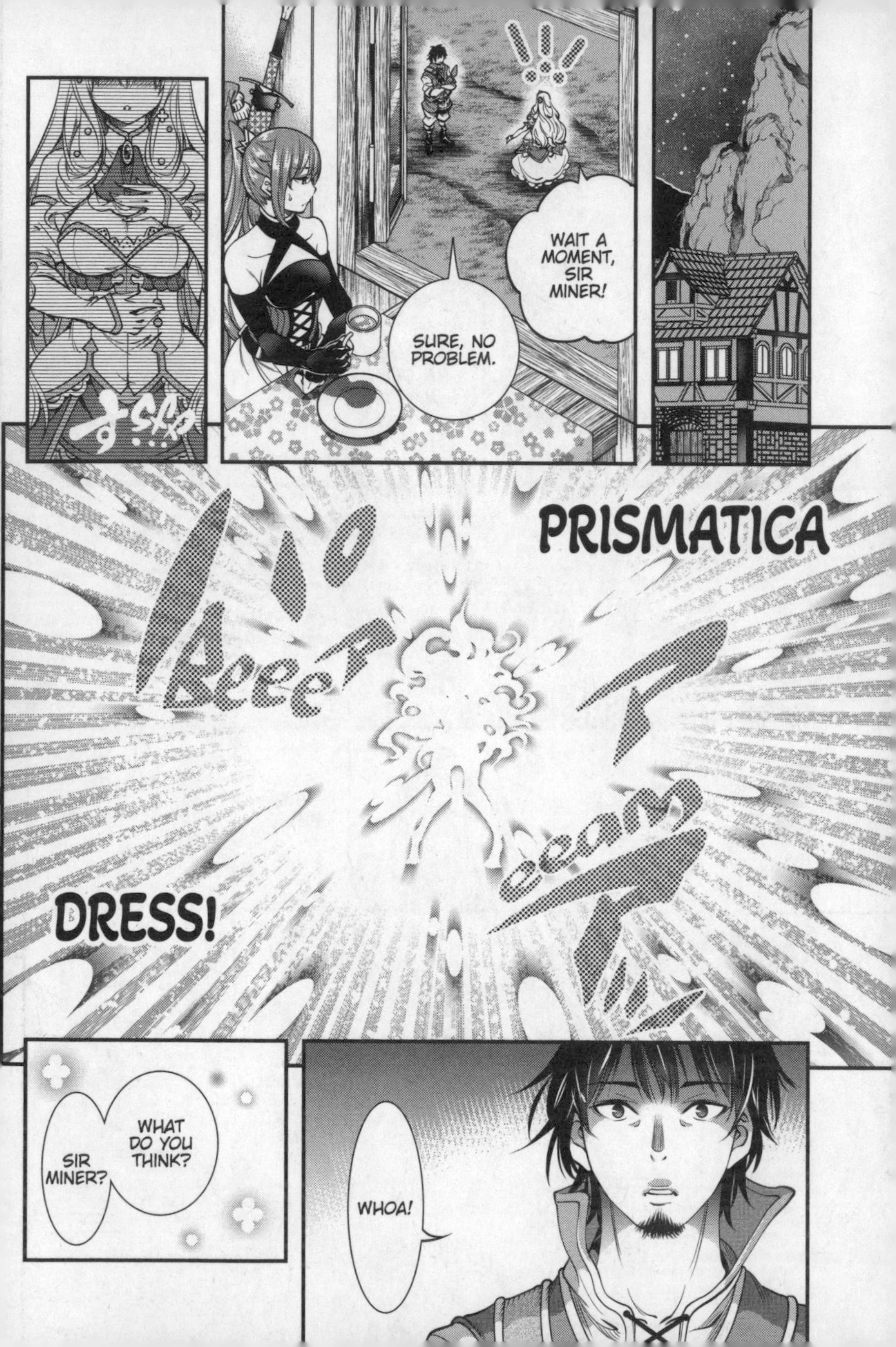
WAIT A MOMENT, SIR MINER!
SURE, NO PROBLEM.
PRISMATICA
DRESS!
WHOA!
WHAT DO YOU THINK?
SIR MINER?

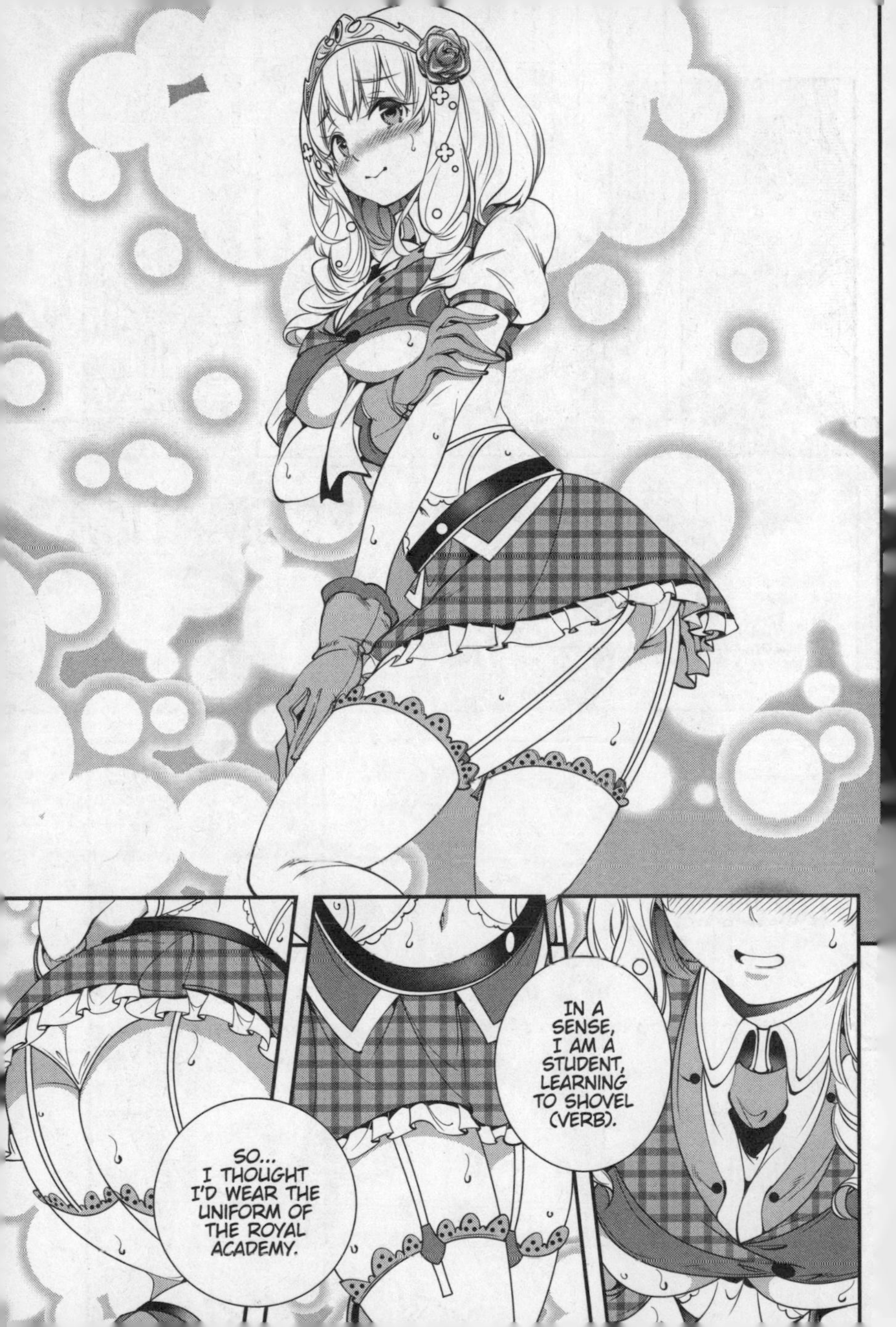
IN A SENSE, I AM A STUDENT, LEARNING TO SHOVEL (VERB).
SO... I THOUGHT I'D WEAR THE UNIFORM OF THE ROYAL ACADEMY.

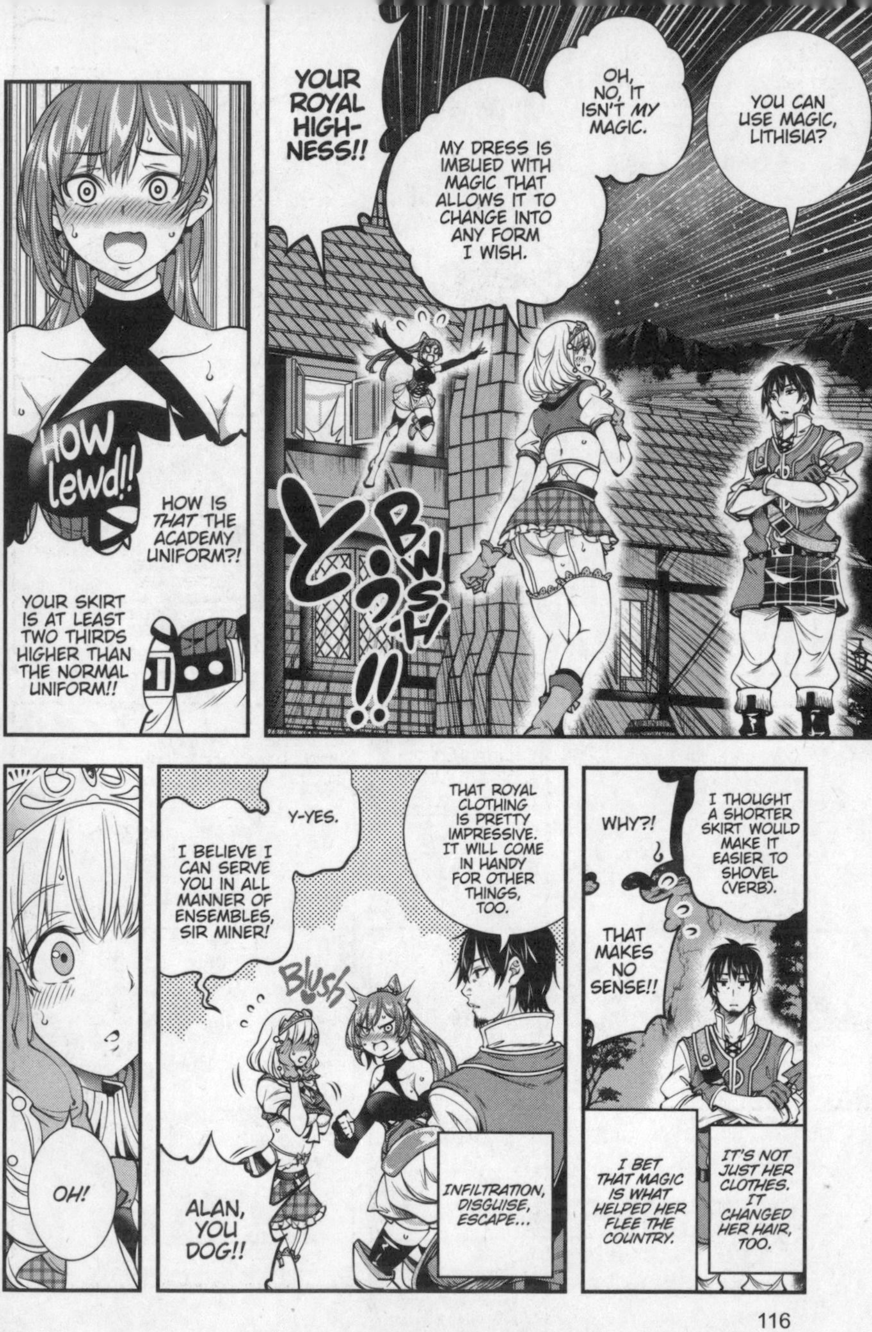
YOU CAN USE MAGIC, LITHISIA?
OH, NO, IT ISN'T *MY* MAGIC.
MY DRESS IS IMBUED WITH MAGIC THAT ALLOWS IT TO CHANGE INTO ANY FORM I WISH.
YOUR ROYAL HIGH-NESS!!
BWSH!!
HOW lewd!!
HOW IS *THAT* THE ACADEMY UNIFORM?!
YOUR SKIRT IS AT LEAST TWO THIRDS HIGHER THAN THE NORMAL UNIFORM!!
I THOUGHT A SHORTER SKIRT WOULD MAKE IT EASIER TO SHOVEL (VERB).
WHY?!
THAT MAKES NO SENSE!!
IT'S NOT JUST HER CLOTHES. IT CHANGED HER HAIR, TOO.
I BET THAT MAGIC IS WHAT HELPED HER FLEE THE COUNTRY.
THAT ROYAL CLOTHING IS PRETTY IMPRESSIVE. IT WILL COME IN HANDY FOR OTHER THINGS, TOO.
Y-YES.
I BELIEVE I CAN SERVE YOU IN ALL MANNER OF ENSEMBLES, SIR MINER!
Blush
INFILTRATION, DISGUISE, ESCAPE...
ALAN, YOU DOG!!
OH!

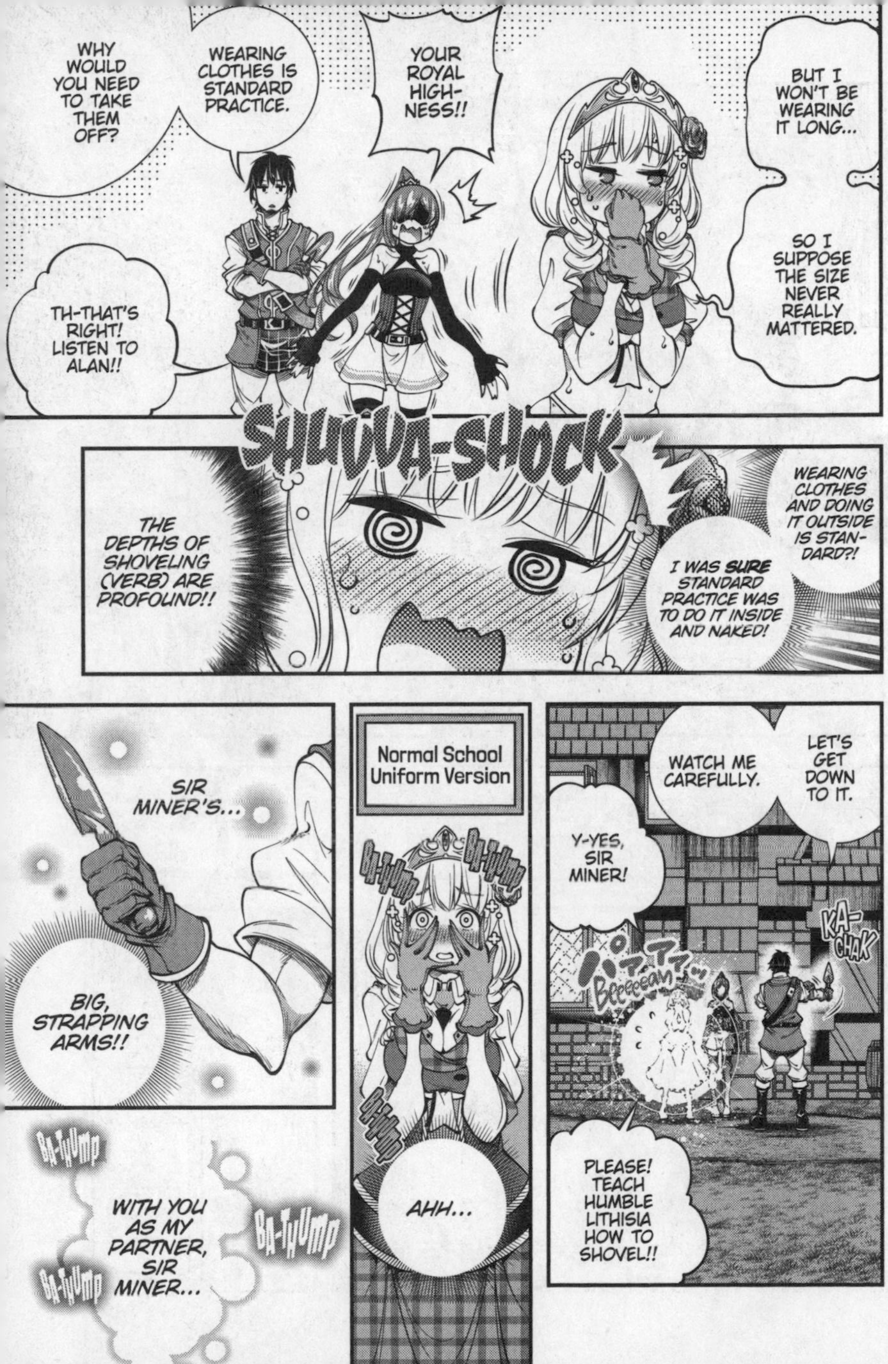
BUT I WON'T BE WEARING IT LONG...
SO I SUPPOSE THE SIZE NEVER REALLY MATTERED.
YOUR ROYAL HIGH-NESS!!
WEARING CLOTHES IS STANDARD PRACTICE.
WHY WOULD YOU NEED TO TAKE THEM OFF?
TH-THAT'S RIGHT! LISTEN TO ALAN!!
SHUVVA-SHOCK
WEARING CLOTHES AND DOING IT OUTSIDE IS STAN-DARD?!
I WAS **SURE** STANDARD PRACTICE WAS TO DO IT INSIDE AND NAKED!
THE DEPTHS OF SHOVELING (VERB) ARE PROFOUND!!
LET'S GET DOWN TO IT.
WATCH ME CAREFULLY.
Y-YES, SIR MINER!
KA-CHAK
PLEASE! TEACH HUMBLE LITHISIA HOW TO SHOVEL!!
Normal School Uniform Version
BA-THUMP
BA-THUMP
AHH...
SIR MINER'S...
BIG, STRAPPING ARMS!!
BA-THUMP
WITH YOU AS MY PARTNER, SIR MINER...
BA-THUMP
BA-THUMP

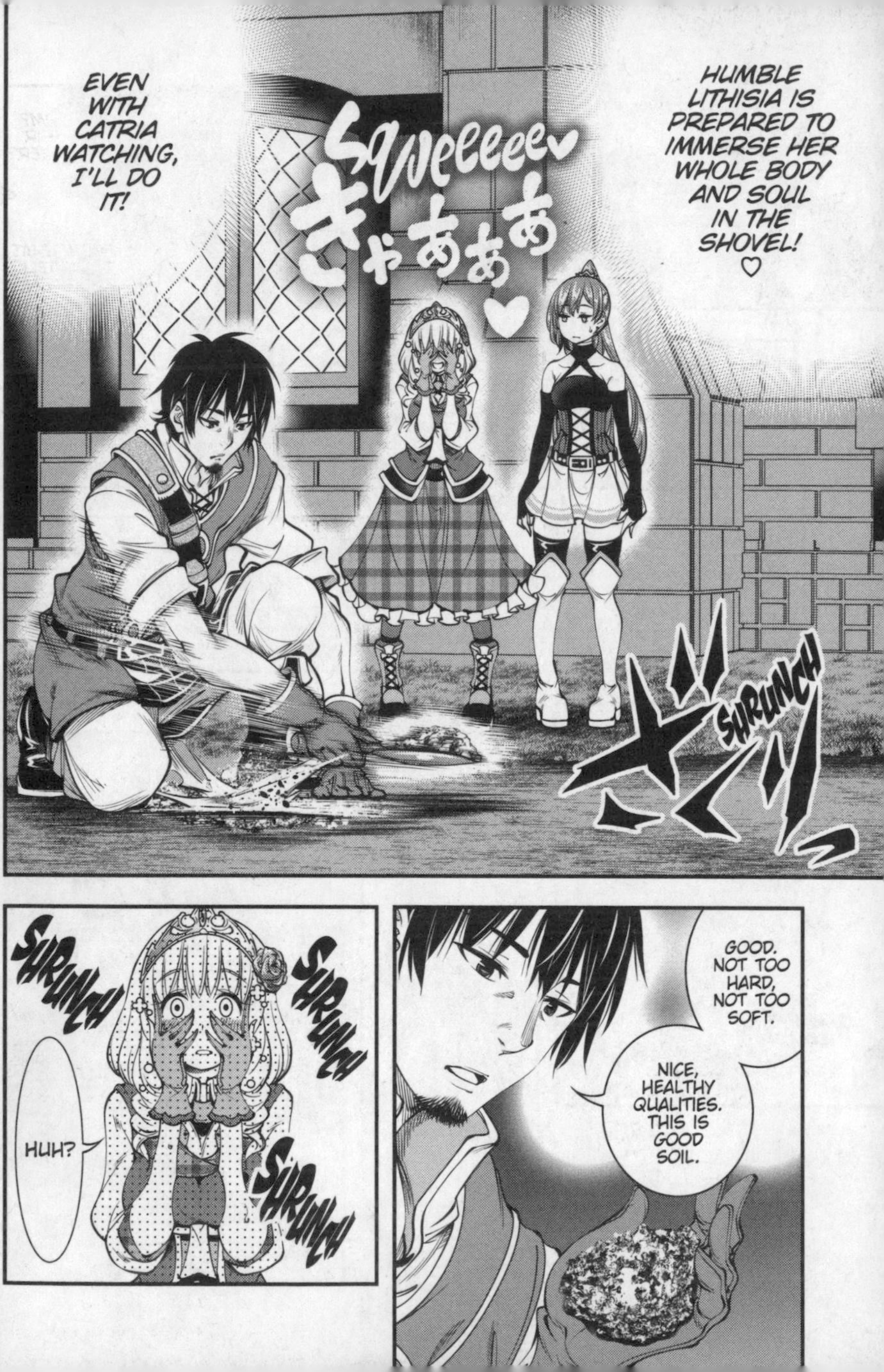
HUMBLE LITHISIA IS PREPARED TO IMMERSE HER WHOLE BODY AND SOUL IN THE SHOVEL! ♡
Sqweeee♥
きゃあああ♥
EVEN WITH CATRIA WATCHING, I'LL DO IT!
SURUNCH
GOOD. NOT TOO HARD, NOT TOO SOFT.
NICE, HEALTHY QUALITIES. THIS IS GOOD SOIL.
SURUNCH
SURUNCH
HUH?
SURUNCH
SURUNCH

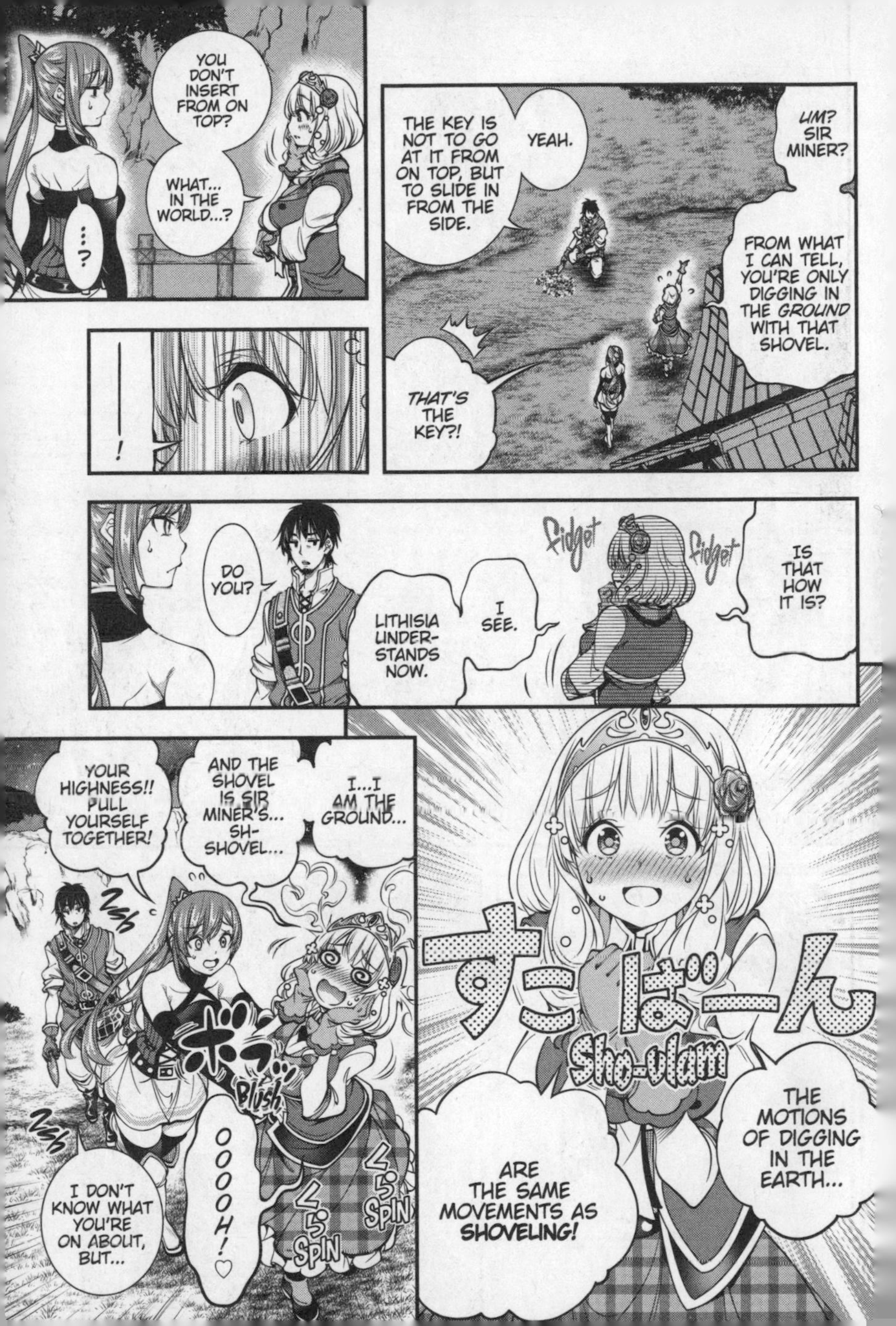
UM? SIR MINER?
FROM WHAT I CAN TELL, YOU'RE ONLY DIGGING IN THE *GROUND* WITH THAT SHOVEL.
YEAH.
THE KEY IS NOT TO GO AT IT FROM ON TOP, BUT TO SLIDE IN FROM THE SIDE.
THAT'S THE KEY?!
YOU DON'T INSERT FROM ON TOP?
WHAT... IN THE WORLD...?
...?
—!
IS THAT HOW IT IS?
fidget fidget
I SEE.
LITHISIA UNDERSTANDS NOW.
DO YOU?
すこぱーん
Sho-vlam
THE MOTIONS OF DIGGING IN THE EARTH...
ARE THE SAME MOVEMENTS AS SHOVELING!
I...I AM THE GROUND...
AND THE SHOVEL IS SIR MINER'S... SH-SHOVEL...
YOUR HIGHNESS!! PULL YOURSELF TOGETHER!
ボッ
Blush
OOOOOH!♡
くら SPIN
くら SPIN
I DON'T KNOW WHAT YOU'RE ON ABOUT, BUT...

SIR MINER ...?

HUH?

ShP

THIS HERE... IS THE PROPER WAY TO HOLD A SHOVEL.

CAN YOU REMEMBER THAT, LITHISIA?

PRESS

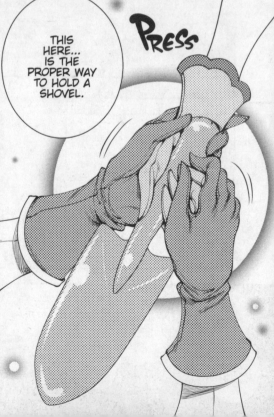

....

I CAN.

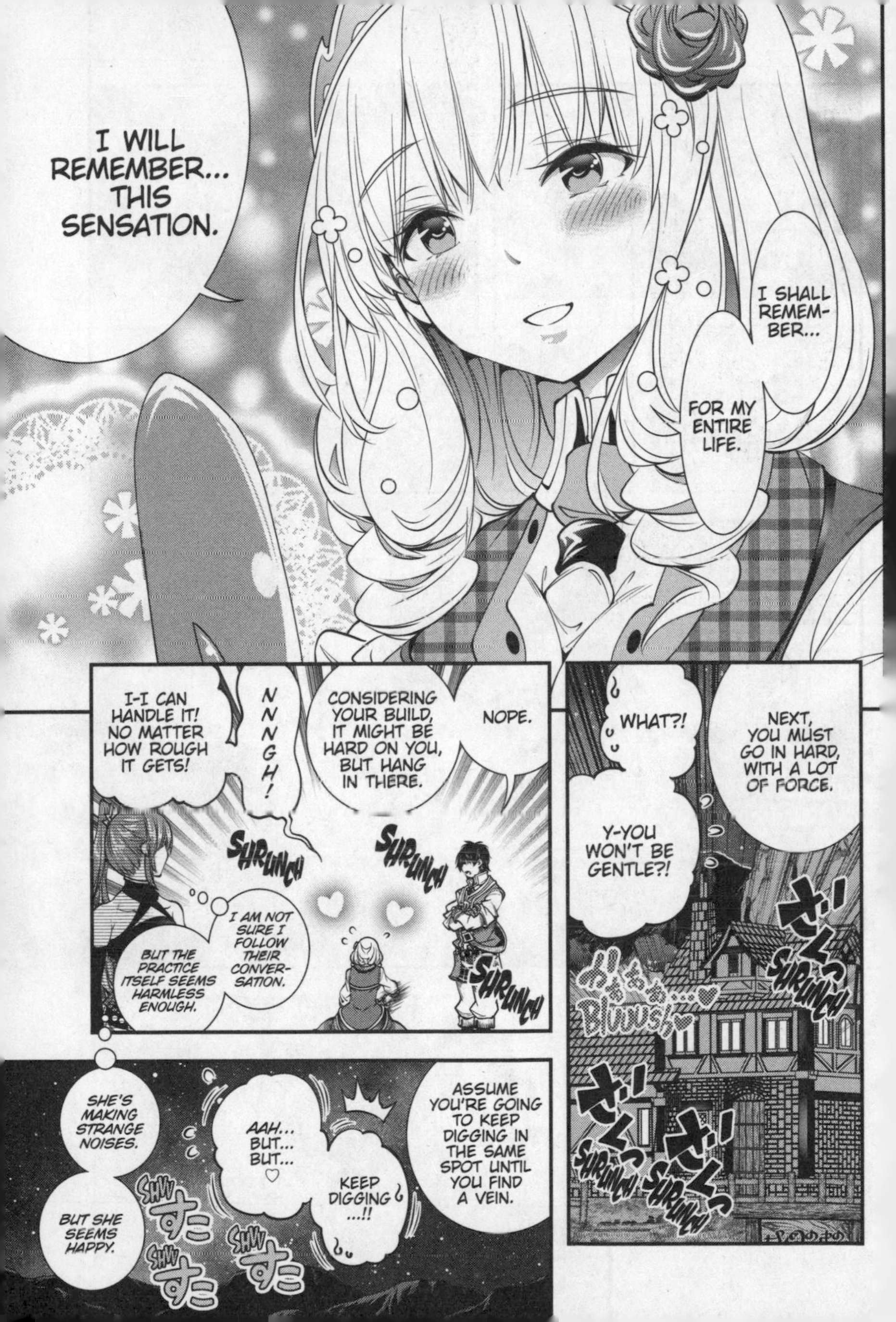
I SHALL REMEMBER...
FOR MY ENTIRE LIFE.
I WILL REMEMBER... THIS SENSATION.
NEXT, YOU MUST GO IN HARD, WITH A LOT OF FORCE.
WHAT?!
Y-YOU WON'T BE GENTLE?!
ざくっ SHRUNCH
わぁぁ…♥ Bluuush♥
ざくっ SHRUNCH
ざくっ SHRUNCH
NOPE.
CONSIDERING YOUR BUILD, IT MIGHT BE HARD ON YOU, BUT HANG IN THERE.
NNNGH!
I-I CAN HANDLE IT! NO MATTER HOW ROUGH IT GETS!
SHRUNCH
SHRUNCH
SHRUNCH
I AM NOT SURE I FOLLOW THEIR CONVERSATION.
BUT THE PRACTICE ITSELF SEEMS HARMLESS ENOUGH.
ASSUME YOU'RE GOING TO KEEP DIGGING IN THE SAME SPOT UNTIL YOU FIND A VEIN.
KEEP DIGGING ...!!
AAH... BUT... BUT... ♡
SHE'S MAKING STRANGE NOISES.
BUT SHE SEEMS HAPPY.
SHVV すこ
SHVV すこ
SHVV すこ

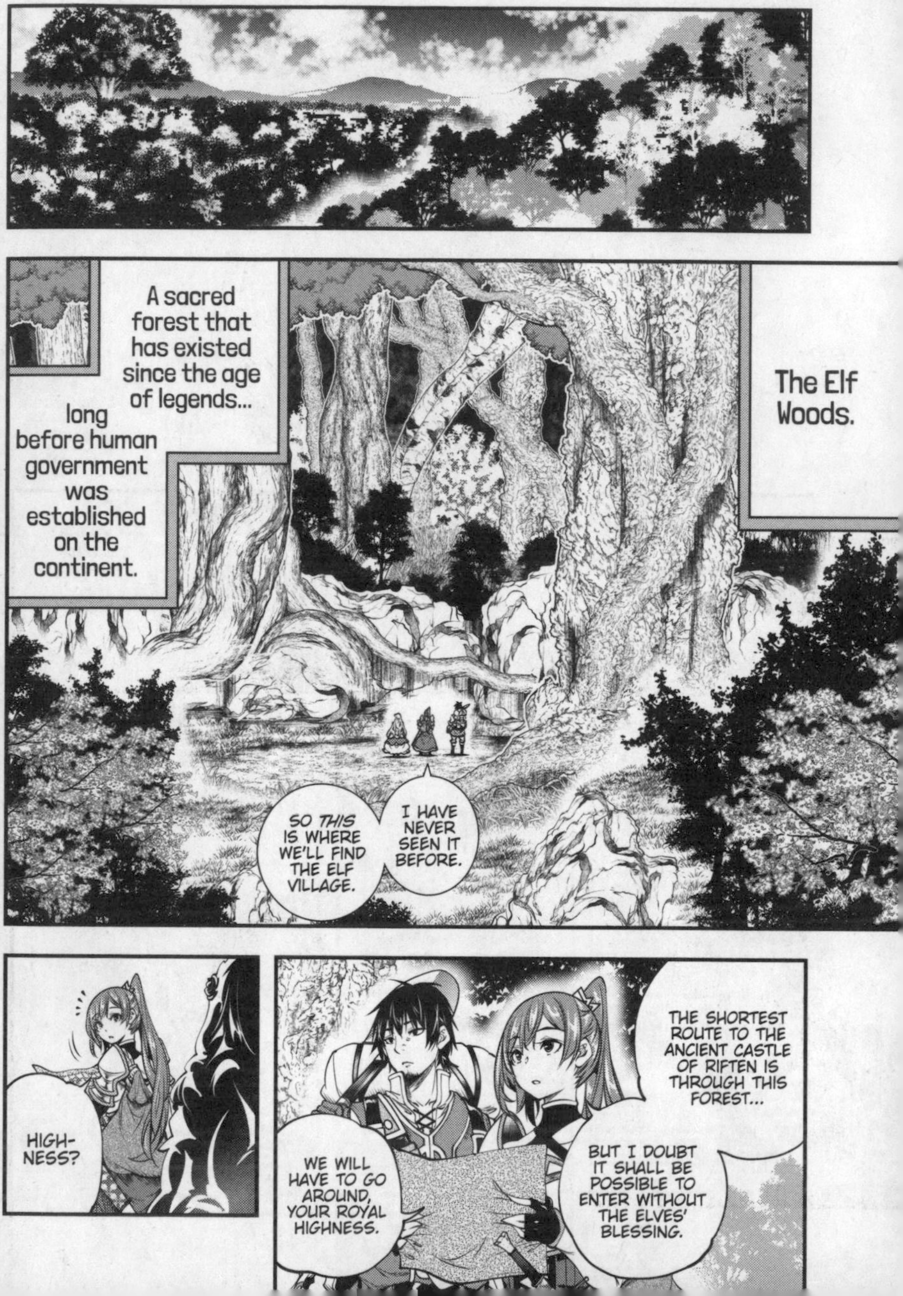
The Elf Woods.
A sacred forest that has existed since the age of legends...
long before human government was established on the continent.
I HAVE NEVER SEEN IT BEFORE.
SO *THIS* IS WHERE WE'LL FIND THE ELF VILLAGE.
THE SHORTEST ROUTE TO THE ANCIENT CASTLE OF RIFTEN IS THROUGH THIS FOREST...
BUT I DOUBT IT SHALL BE POSSIBLE TO ENTER WITHOUT THE ELVES' BLESSING.
WE WILL HAVE TO GO AROUND, YOUR ROYAL HIGHNESS.
HIGH-NESS?

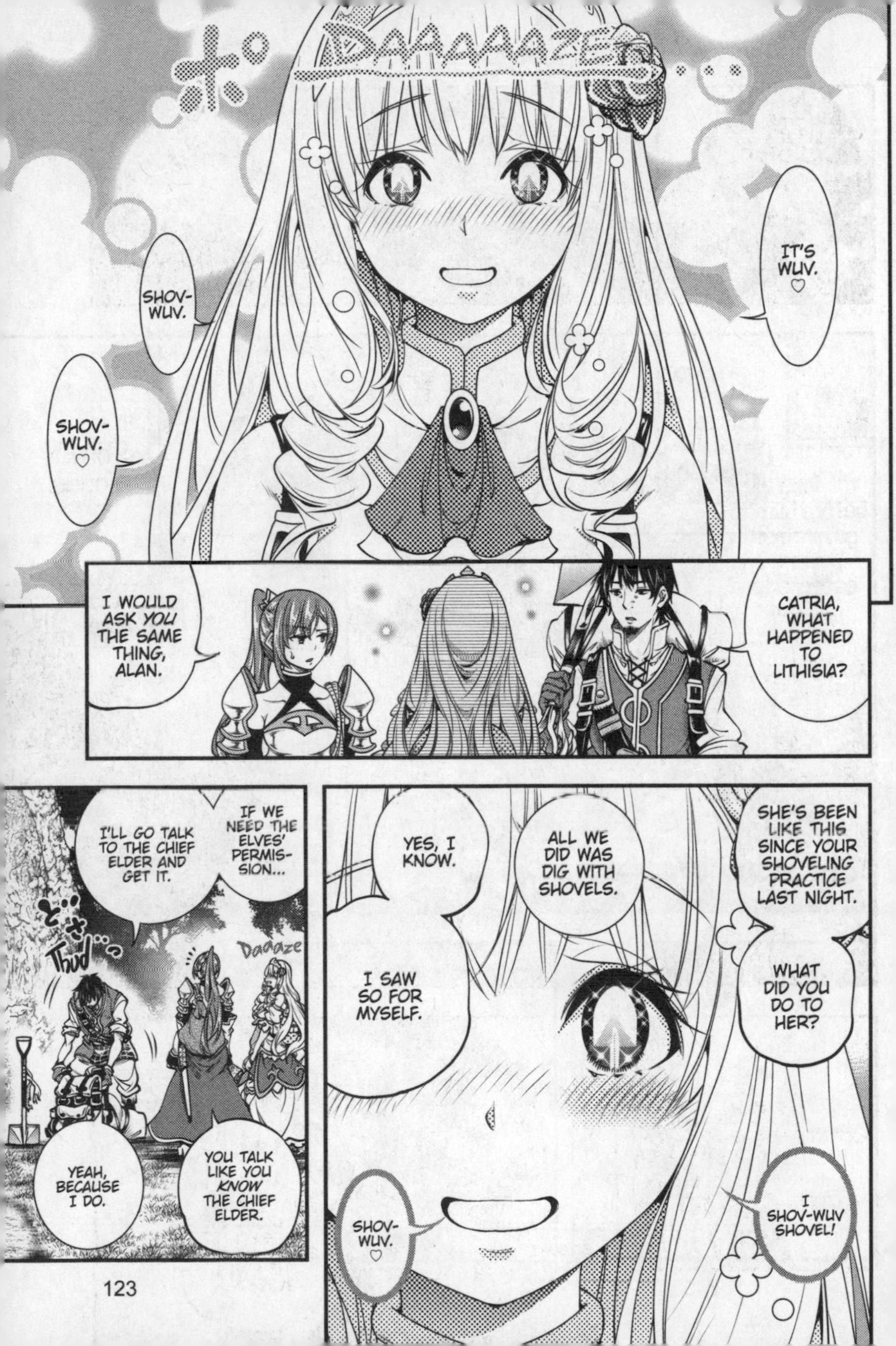
DAAAAAZE
IT'S WUV. ♡
SHOV-WUV.
SHOV-WUV. ♡
CATRIA, WHAT HAPPENED TO LITHISIA?
I WOULD ASK *YOU* THE SAME THING, ALAN.
SHE'S BEEN LIKE THIS SINCE YOUR SHOVELING PRACTICE LAST NIGHT.
ALL WE DID WAS DIG WITH SHOVELS.
YES, I KNOW.
WHAT DID YOU DO TO HER?
I SAW SO FOR MYSELF.
I SHOV-WUV SHOVEL!
SHOV-WUV. ♡
IF WE NEED THE ELVES' PERMISSION...
I'LL GO TALK TO THE CHIEF ELDER AND GET IT.
Thud
Daaaze
YOU TALK LIKE YOU *KNOW* THE CHIEF ELDER.
YEAH, BECAUSE I DO.

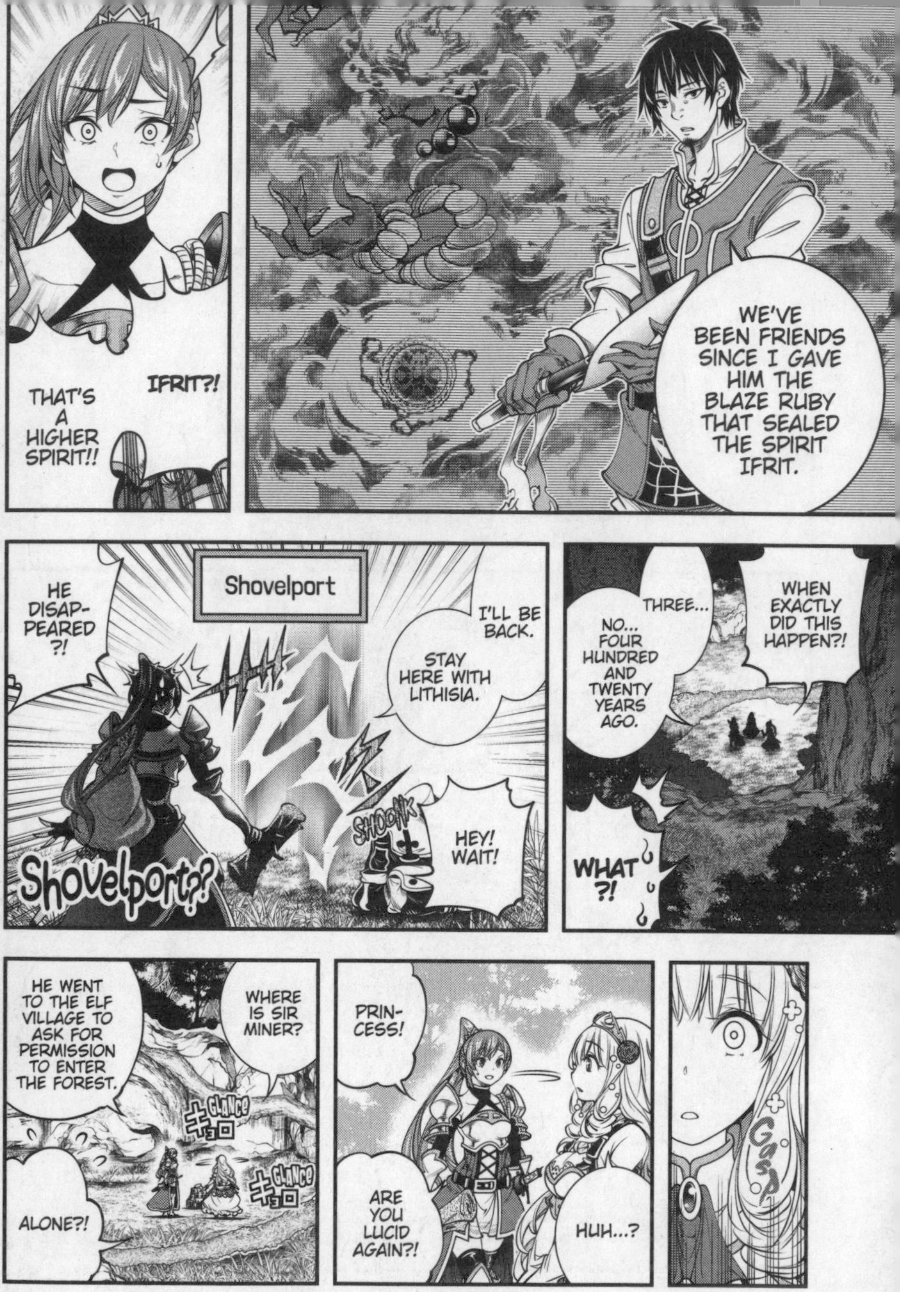
WE'VE BEEN FRIENDS SINCE I GAVE HIM THE BLAZE RUBY THAT SEALED THE SPIRIT IFRIT.
IFRIT?!
THAT'S A HIGHER SPIRIT!!
WHEN EXACTLY DID THIS HAPPEN?!
THREE...
NO... FOUR HUNDRED AND TWENTY YEARS AGO.
WHAT ?!
I'LL BE BACK.
STAY HERE WITH LITHISIA.
Shovelport
HE DISAP-PEARED ?!
HEY! WAIT!
SHOONK
Shovelport?!
GASP
PRIN-CESS!
ARE YOU LUCID AGAIN?!
HUH...?
WHERE IS SIR MINER?
HE WENT TO THE ELF VILLAGE TO ASK FOR PERMISSION TO ENTER THE FOREST.
GLANCE
GLANCE
ALONE?!

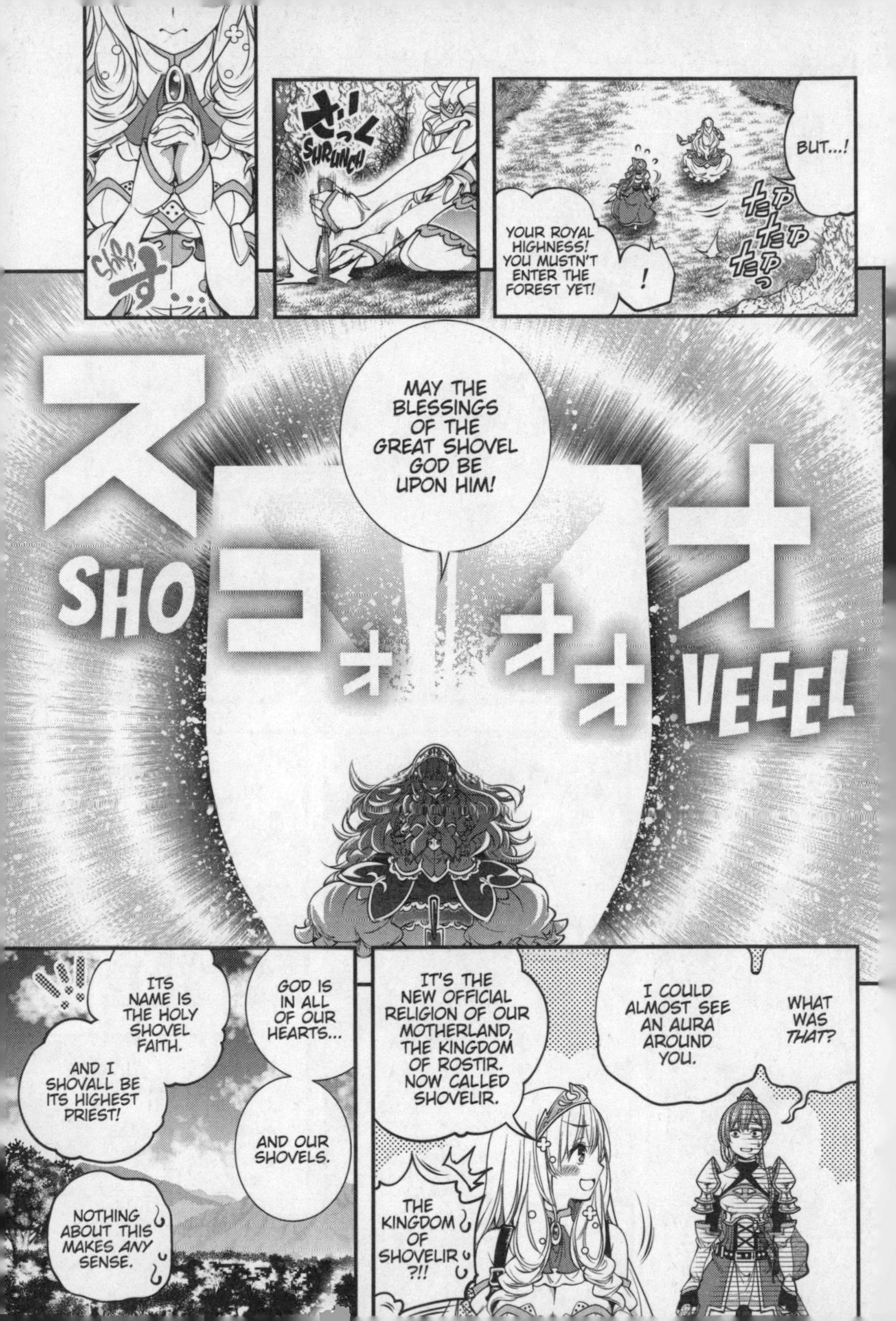
BUT...!
たったったっ
YOUR ROYAL HIGHNESS! YOU MUSTN'T ENTER THE FOREST YET!
!
ざっく
SHRUNCH
すっ
SHF
MAY THE BLESSINGS OF THE GREAT SHOVEL GOD BE UPON HIM!
スコォーォォオ
SHOVEEEL
WHAT WAS THAT?
I COULD ALMOST SEE AN AURA AROUND YOU.
IT'S THE NEW OFFICIAL RELIGION OF OUR MOTHERLAND, THE KINGDOM OF ROSTIR. NOW CALLED SHOVELIR.
THE KINGDOM OF SHOVELIR ?!!
GOD IS IN ALL OF OUR HEARTS...
AND OUR SHOVELS.
ITS NAME IS THE HOLY SHOVEL FAITH.
AND I SHOVALL BE ITS HIGHEST PRIEST!
NOTHING ABOUT THIS MAKES ANY SENSE.

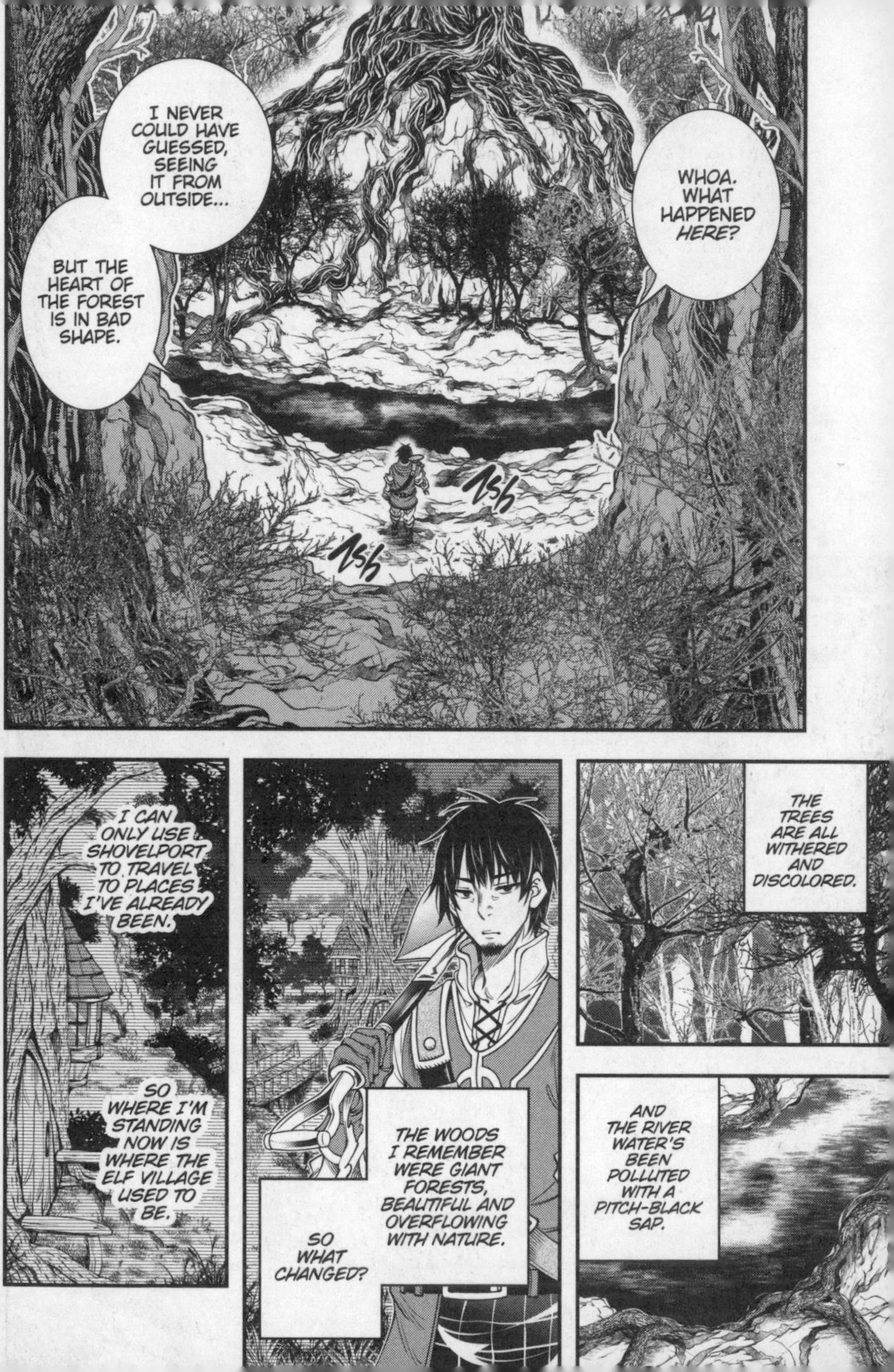
WHOA. WHAT HAPPENED HERE?
I NEVER COULD HAVE GUESSED, SEEING IT FROM OUTSIDE...
BUT THE HEART OF THE FOREST IS IN BAD SHAPE.
THE TREES ARE ALL WITHERED AND DISCOLORED.
AND THE RIVER WATER'S BEEN POLLUTED WITH A PITCH-BLACK SAP.
THE WOODS I REMEMBER WERE GIANT FORESTS, BEAUTIFUL AND OVERFLOWING WITH NATURE.
SO WHAT CHANGED?
I CAN ONLY USE SHOVELPORT TO TRAVEL TO PLACES I'VE ALREADY BEEN.
SO WHERE I'M STANDING NOW IS WHERE THE ELF VILLAGE USED TO BE.

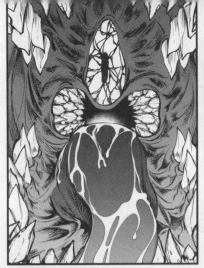

I HOPE THE ELVES ARE ALL RIGHT.

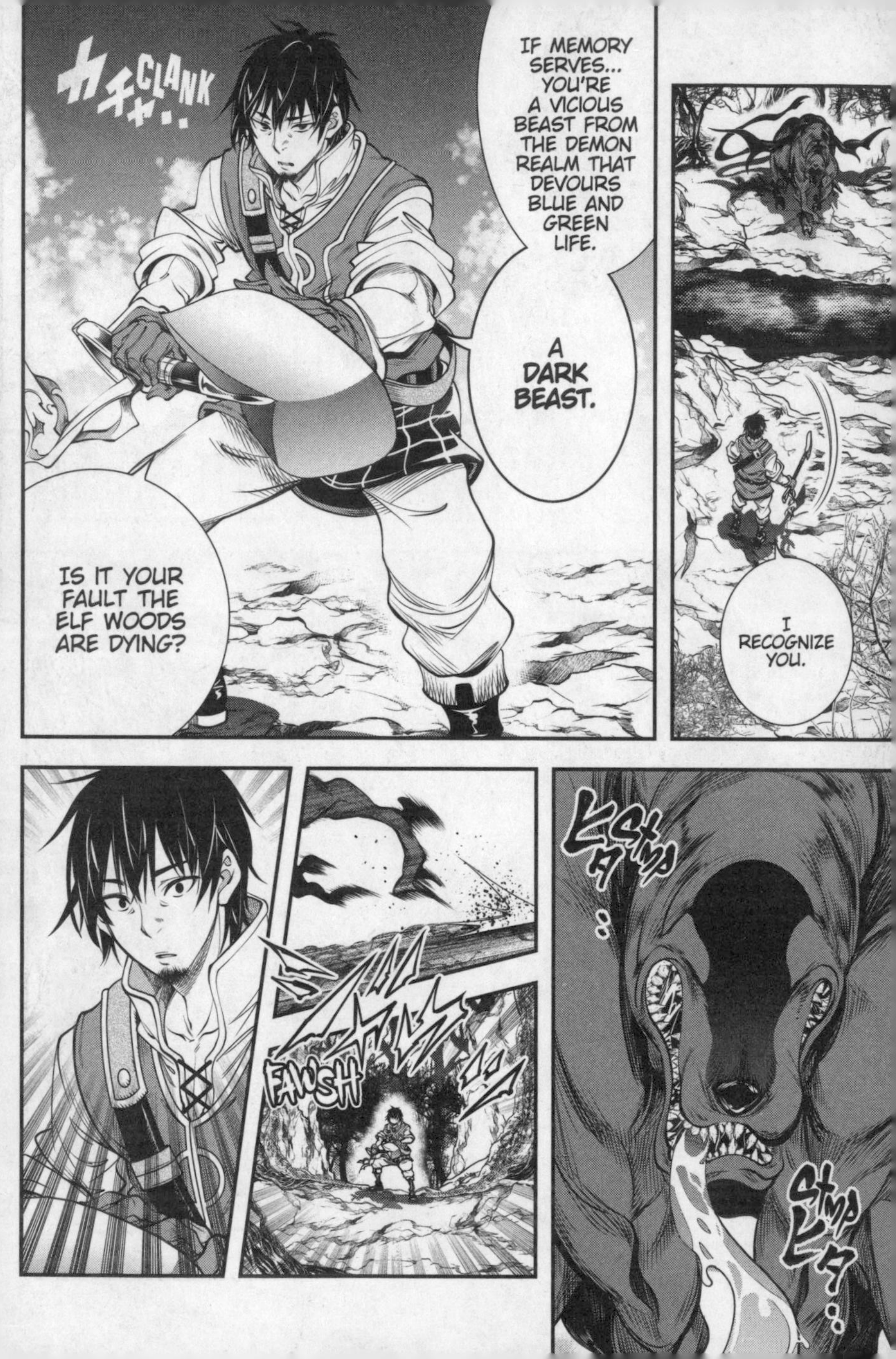
I RECOGNIZE YOU.
カチャ..
CLANK
IF MEMORY SERVES... YOU'RE A VICIOUS BEAST FROM THE DEMON REALM THAT DEVOURS BLUE AND GREEN LIFE.
A DARK BEAST.
IS IT YOUR FAULT THE ELF WOODS ARE DYING?
ヒタ
STMP
STMP
ヒタ
FWOSH

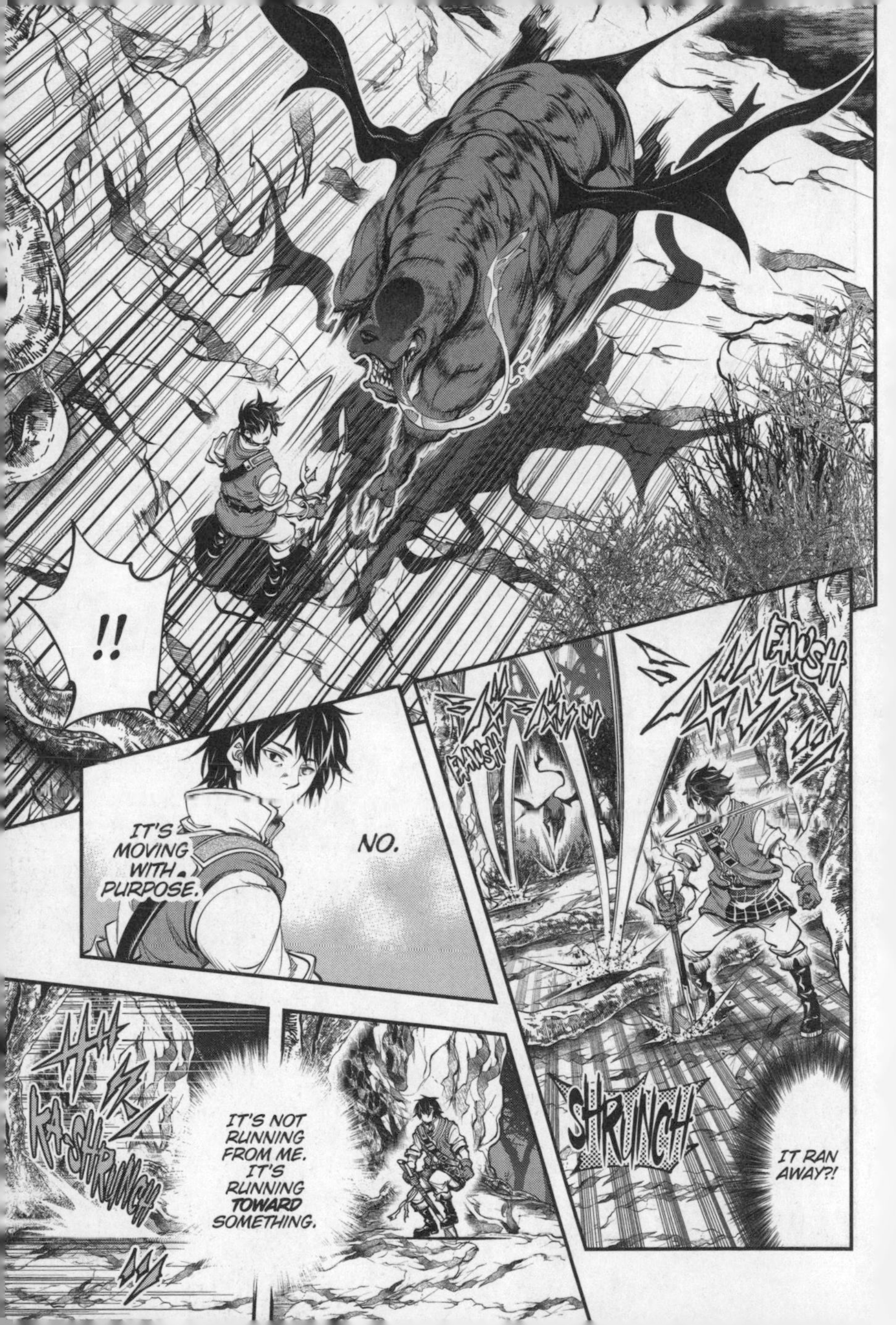
!!
SHRUNCH
IT RAN AWAY?!
NO.
IT'S MOVING WITH PURPOSE.
IT'S NOT RUNNING FROM ME. IT'S RUNNING **TOWARD** SOMETHING.
KA-SHRUNCH

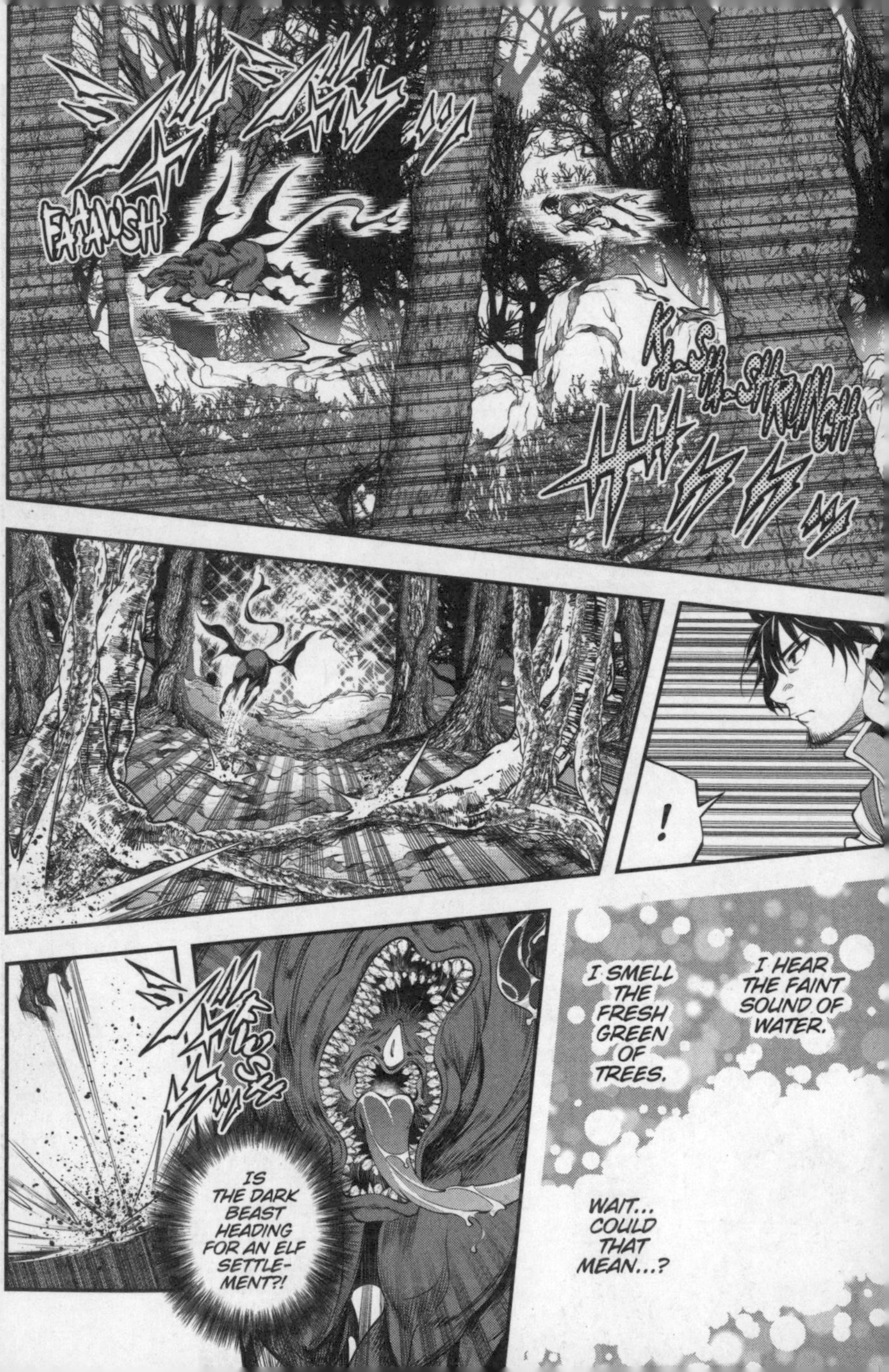
KA-SHA-SHRUNCH
FAAWSH
!
I HEAR THE FAINT SOUND OF WATER.
I SMELL THE FRESH GREEN OF TREES.
WAIT... COULD THAT MEAN...?
IS THE DARK BEAST HEADING FOR AN ELF SETTLE-MENT?!

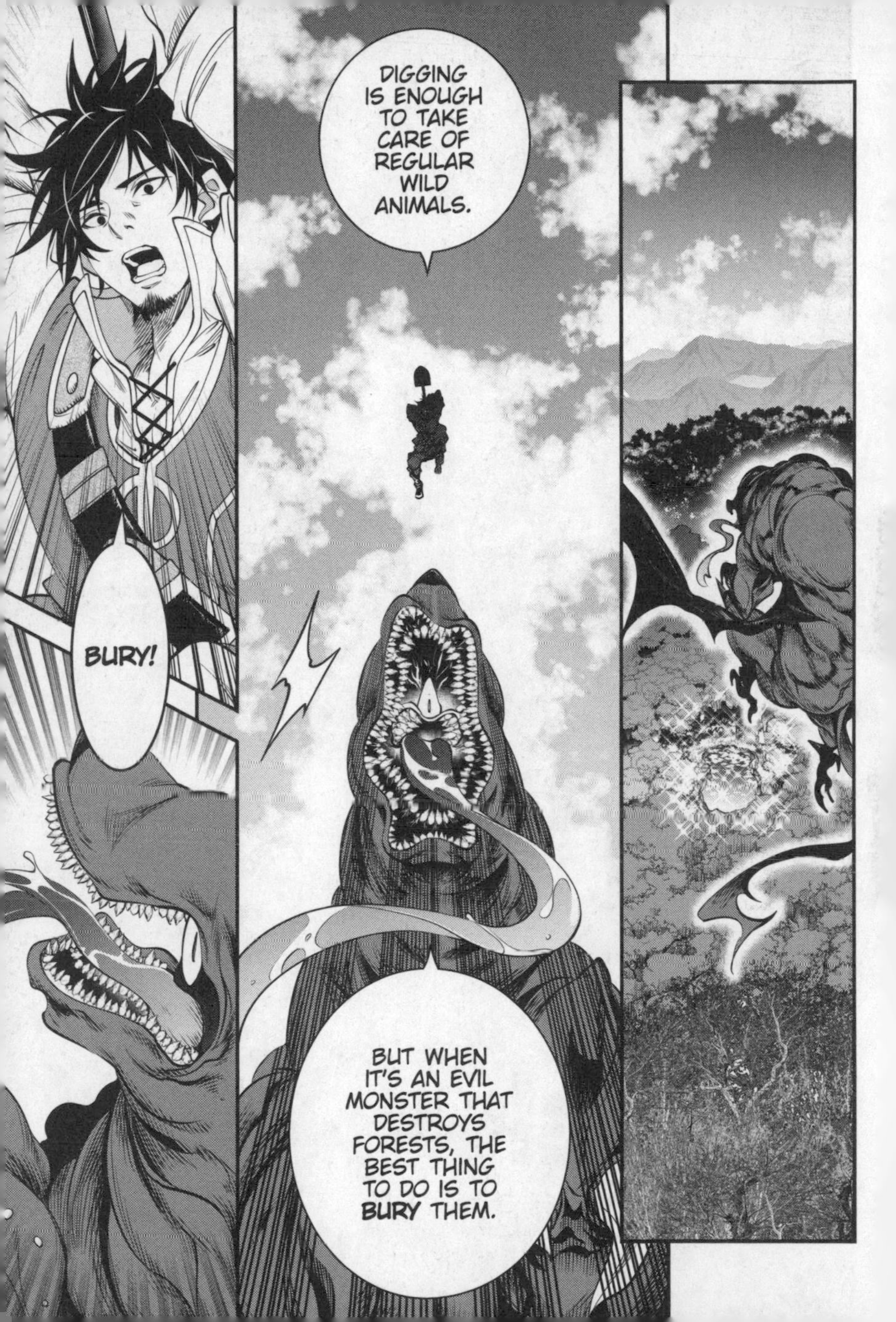
DIGGING IS ENOUGH TO TAKE CARE OF REGULAR WILD ANIMALS.
BUT WHEN IT'S AN EVIL MONSTER THAT DESTROYS FORESTS, THE BEST THING TO DO IS TO **BURY** THEM.
BURY!

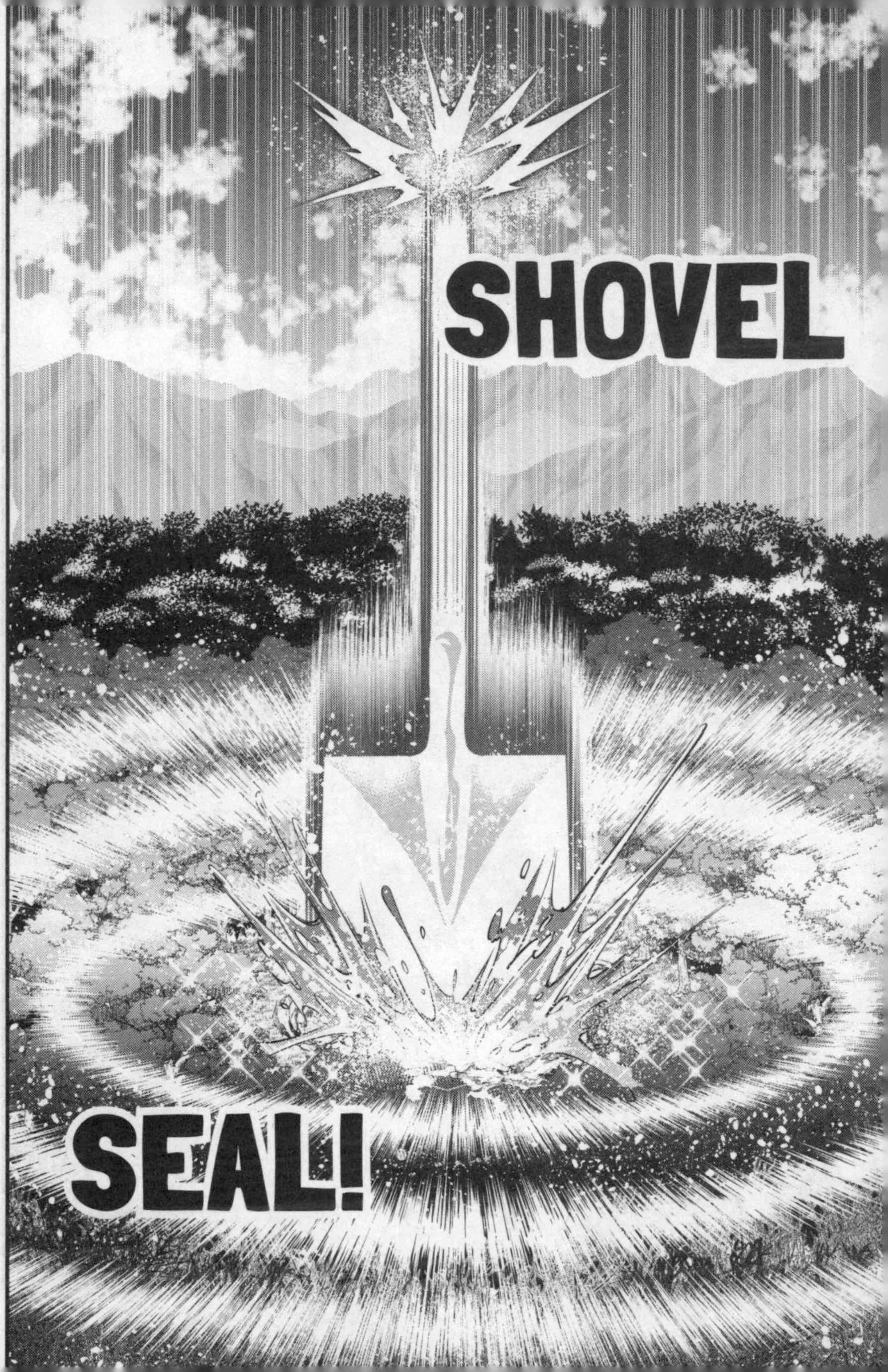
SHOVEL
SEAL!

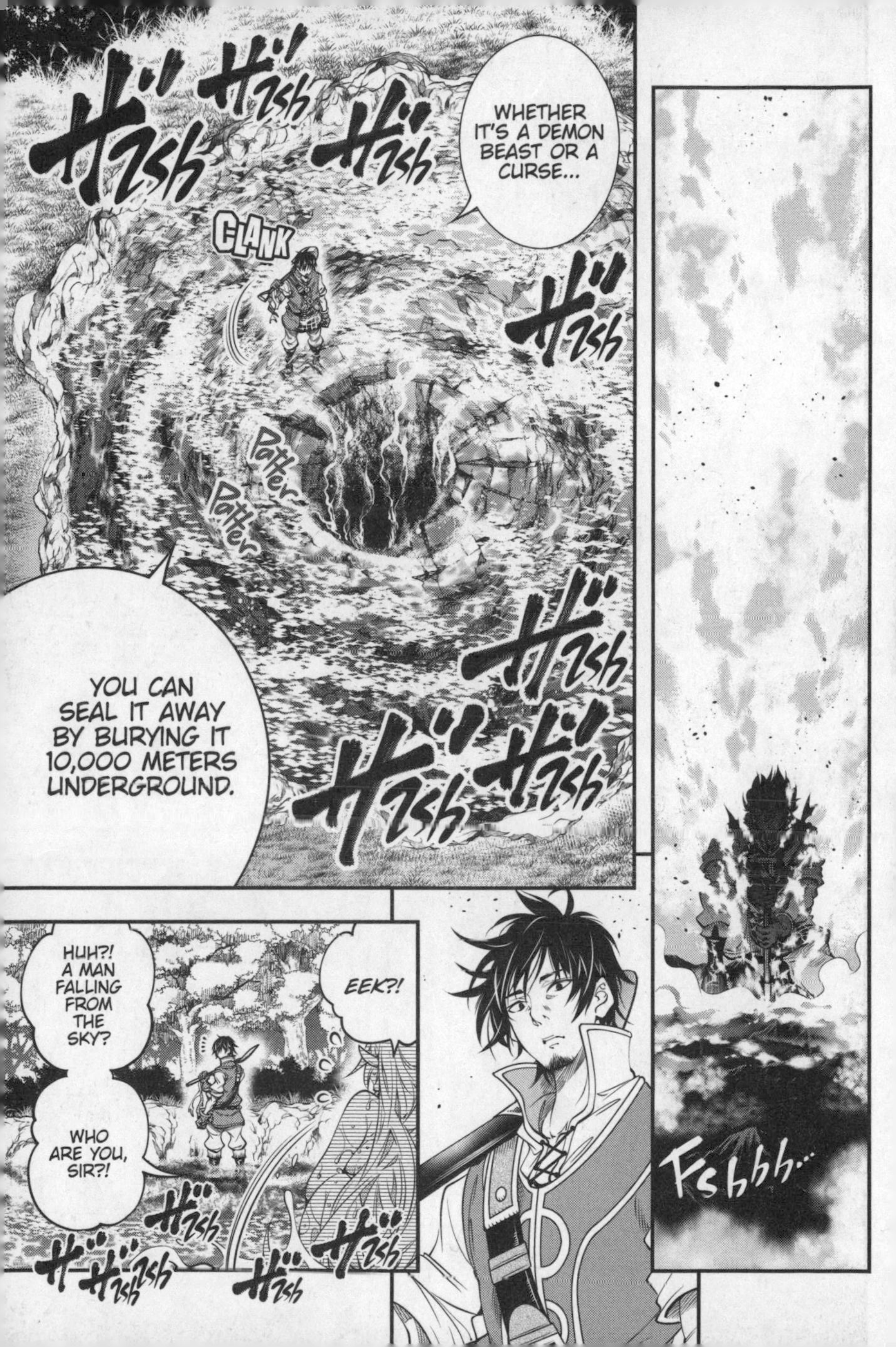
Fshhh...
CLANK
WHETHER IT'S A DEMON BEAST OR A CURSE...
Patter
Patter
Patter
YOU CAN SEAL IT AWAY BY BURYING IT 10,000 METERS UNDERGROUND.
EEK?!
HUH?! A MAN FALLING FROM THE SKY?
WHO ARE YOU, SIR?!

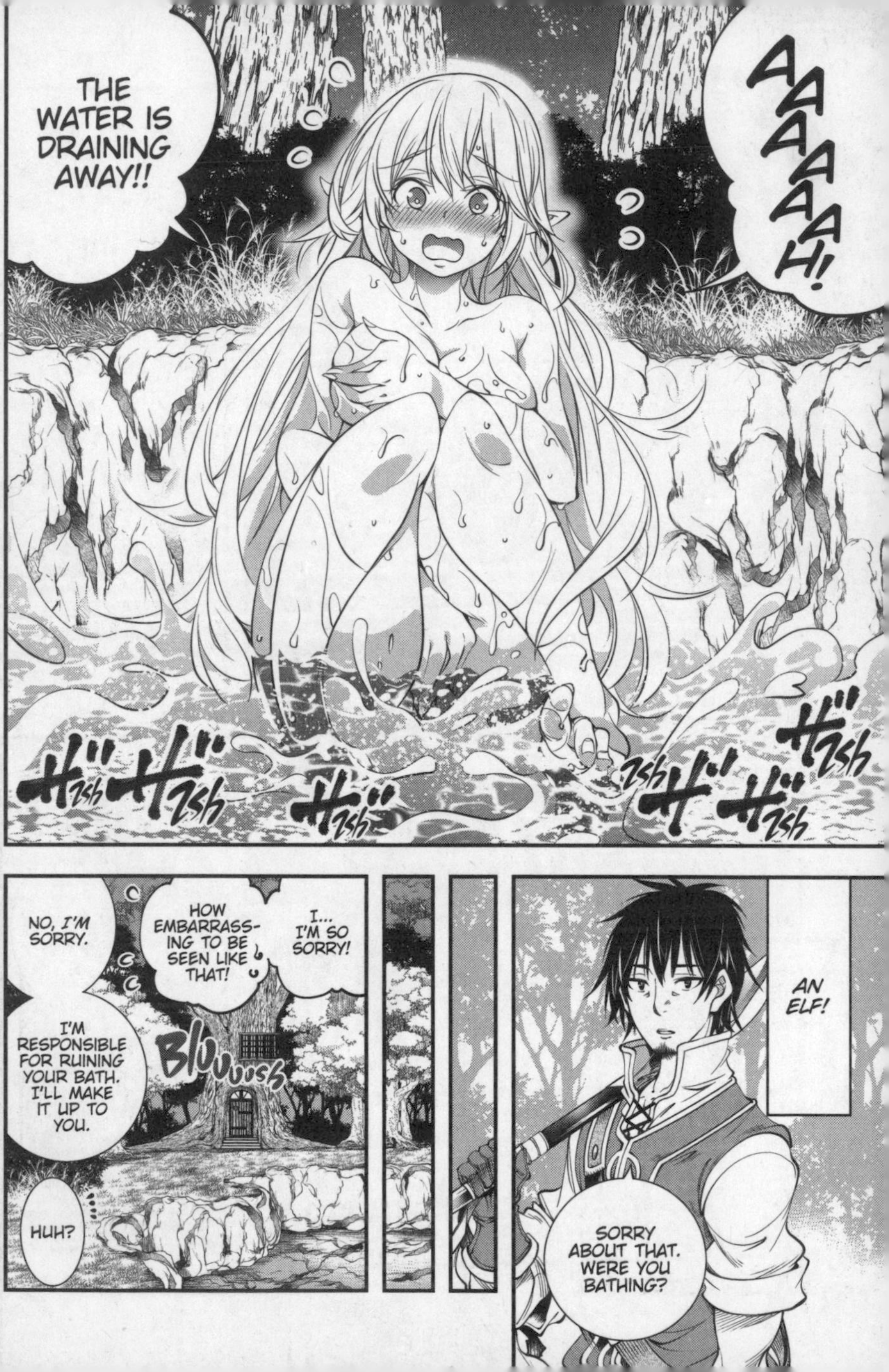
AAAAAAH!
THE WATER IS DRAINING AWAY!!
AN ELF!
SORRY ABOUT THAT. WERE YOU BATHING?
I... I'M SO SORRY!
HOW EMBARRASSING TO BE SEEN LIKE THAT!
NO, I'M SORRY.
I'M RESPONSIBLE FOR RUINING YOUR BATH. I'LL MAKE IT UP TO YOU.
BLUUUUSH
......
HUH?

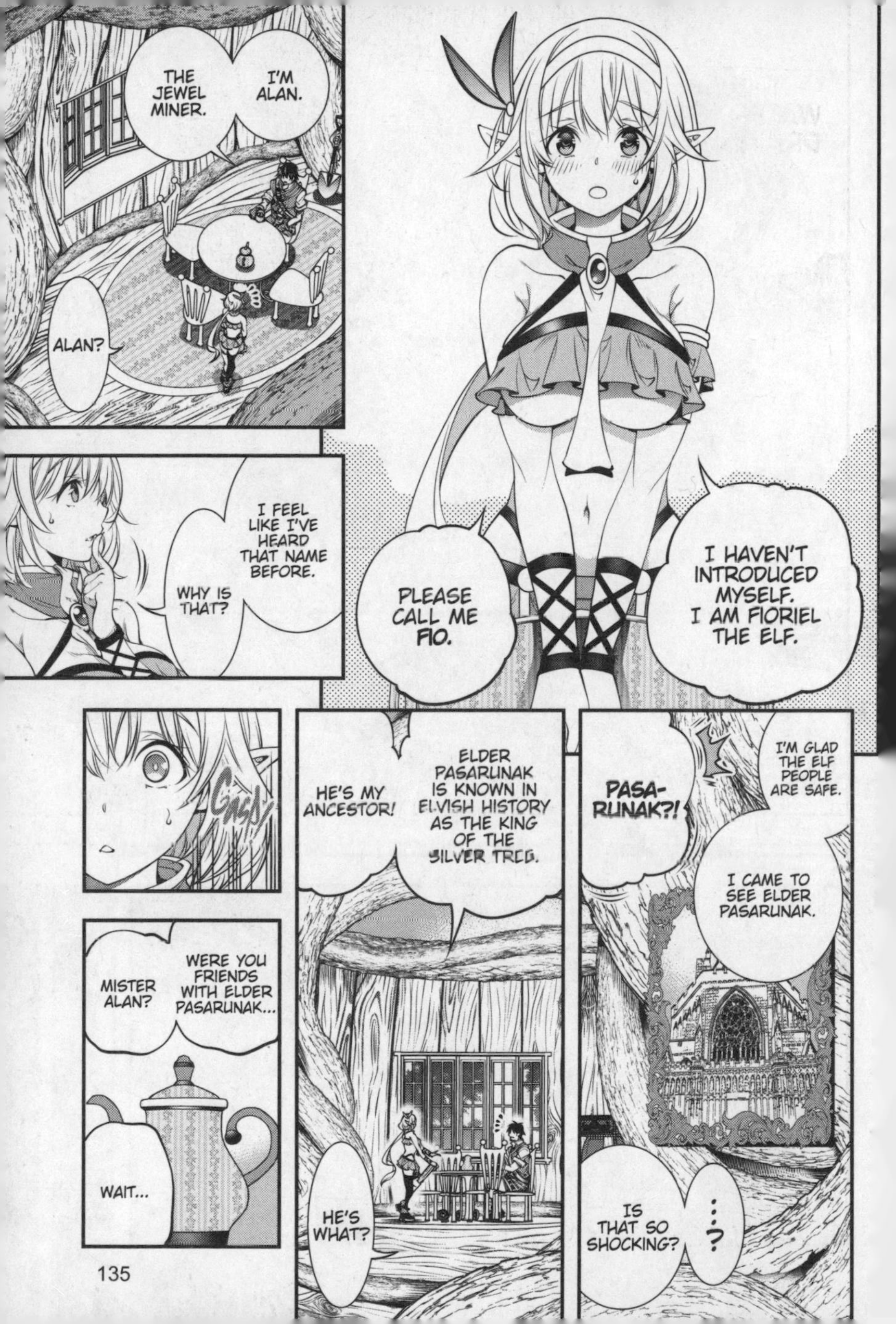
I HAVEN'T INTRODUCED MYSELF. I AM FIORIEL THE ELF.
PLEASE CALL ME FIO.
I'M ALAN.
THE JEWEL MINER.
ALAN?
I FEEL LIKE I'VE HEARD THAT NAME BEFORE.
WHY IS THAT?
I'M GLAD THE ELF PEOPLE ARE SAFE.
I CAME TO SEE ELDER PASARUNAK.
PASA-RUNAK?!
...?
IS THAT SO SHOCKING?
ELDER PASARUNAK IS KNOWN IN ELVISH HISTORY AS THE KING OF THE SILVER TREE.
HE'S MY ANCESTOR!
HE'S WHAT?
GASP!
WERE YOU FRIENDS WITH ELDER PASARUNAK...
MISTER ALAN?
WAIT...

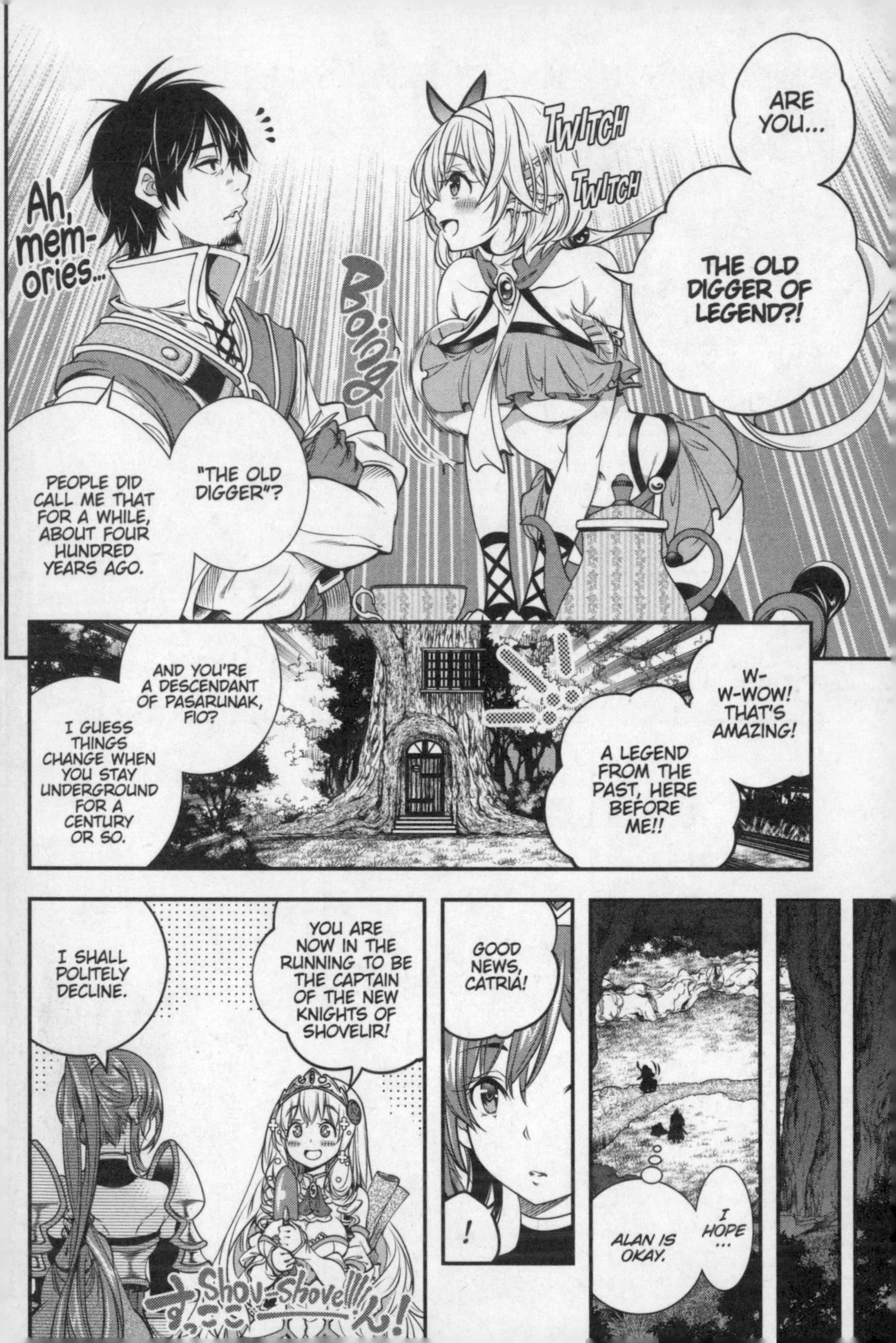
ARE YOU...
THE OLD DIGGER OF LEGEND?!
TWITCH
TWITCH
Boing
Ah, mem-ories...
"THE OLD DIGGER"?
PEOPLE DID CALL ME THAT FOR A WHILE, ABOUT FOUR HUNDRED YEARS AGO.
W-W-WOW! THAT'S AMAZING!
A LEGEND FROM THE PAST, HERE BEFORE ME!!
AND YOU'RE A DESCENDANT OF PASARUNAK, FIO?
I GUESS THINGS CHANGE WHEN YOU STAY UNDERGROUND FOR A CENTURY OR SO.
I HOPE...
ALAN IS OKAY.
GOOD NEWS, CATRIA!
!
YOU ARE NOW IN THE RUNNING TO BE THE CAPTAIN OF THE NEW KNIGHTS OF SHOVELIR!
I SHALL POLITELY DECLINE.
Shov Shove!!!!

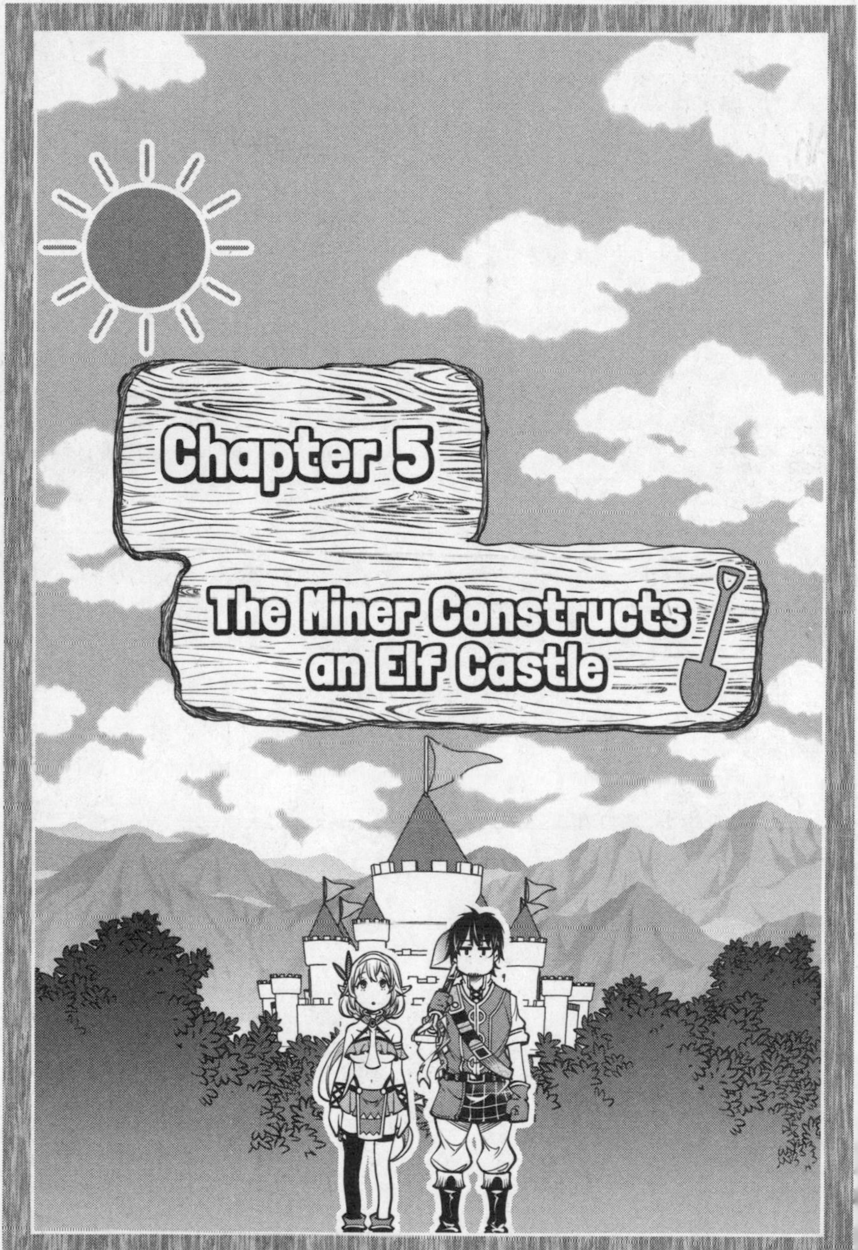
Chapter 5
The Miner Constructs an Elf Castle

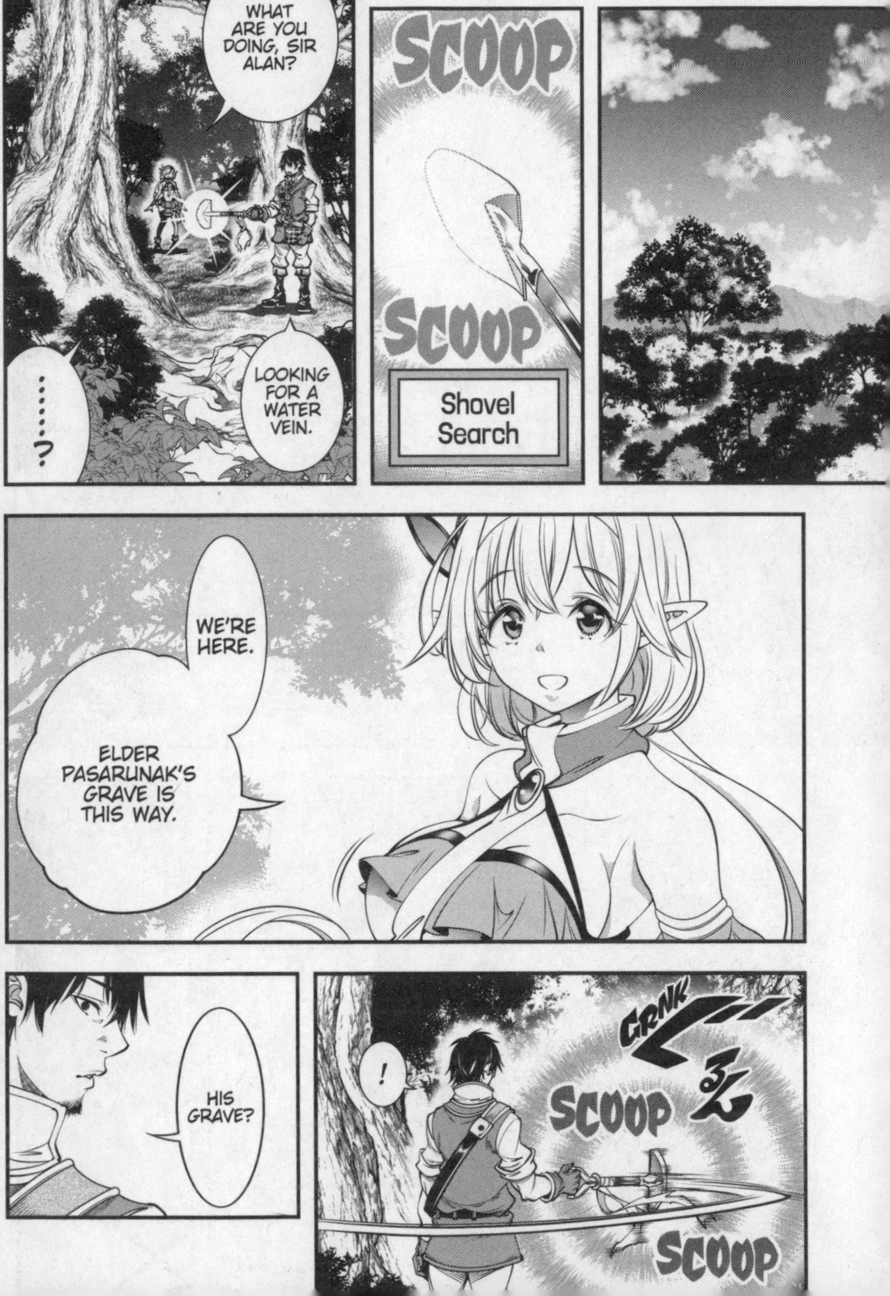
SCOOP
SCOOP
Shovel Search
WHAT ARE YOU DOING, SIR ALAN?
LOOKING FOR A WATER VEIN.
……?
WE'RE HERE.
ELDER PASARUNAK'S GRAVE IS THIS WAY.
GRNK
!
SCOOP
SCOOP
HIS GRAVE?

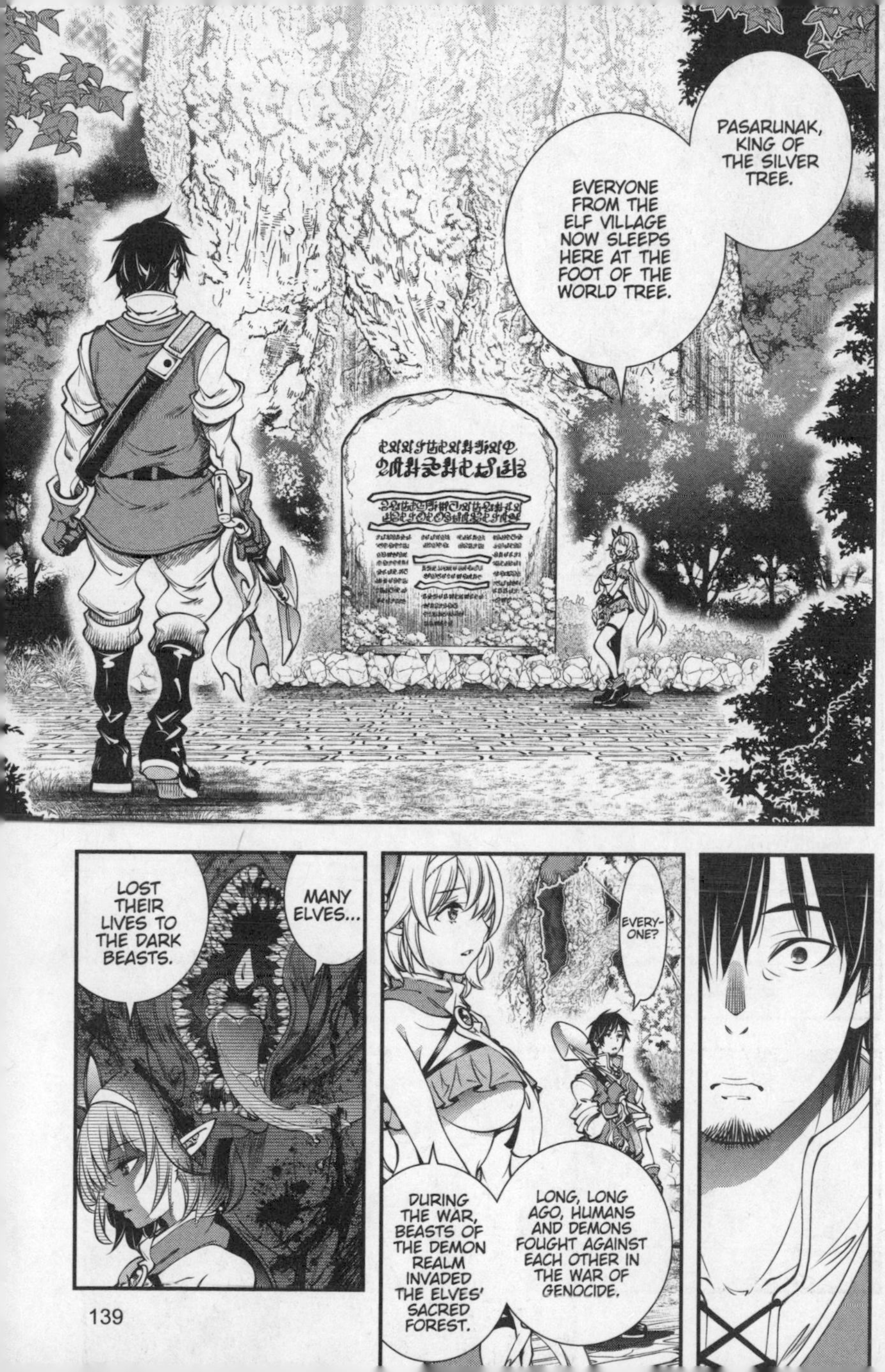
PASARUNAK, KING OF THE SILVER TREE.
EVERYONE FROM THE ELF VILLAGE NOW SLEEPS HERE AT THE FOOT OF THE WORLD TREE.
EVERY-ONE?
LONG, LONG AGO, HUMANS AND DEMONS FOUGHT AGAINST EACH OTHER IN THE WAR OF GENOCIDE.
DURING THE WAR, BEASTS OF THE DEMON REALM INVADED THE ELVES' SACRED FOREST.
MANY ELVES...
LOST THEIR LIVES TO THE DARK BEASTS.

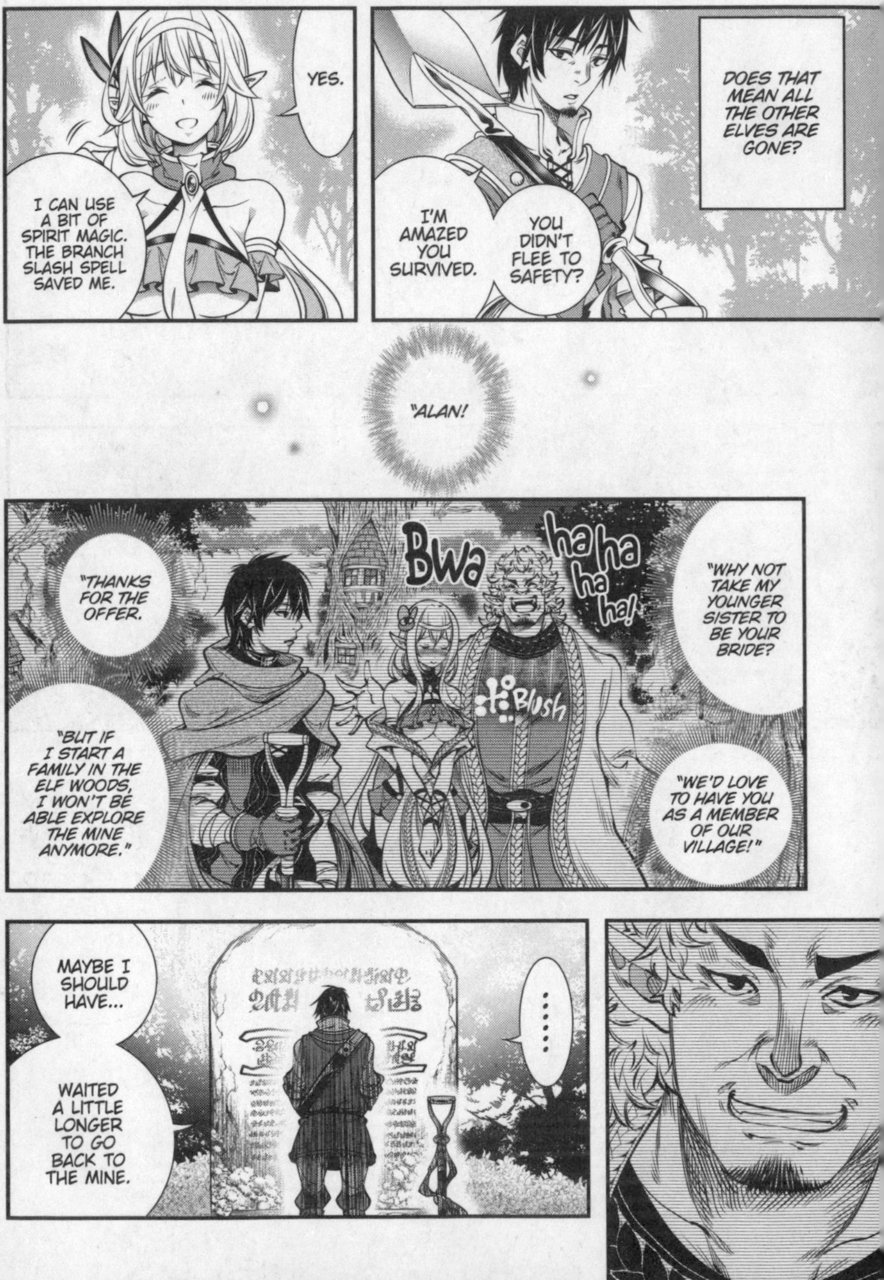
DOES THAT MEAN ALL THE OTHER ELVES ARE GONE?
YOU DIDN'T FLEE TO SAFETY?
I'M AMAZED YOU SURVIVED.
YES.
I CAN USE A BIT OF SPIRIT MAGIC. THE BRANCH SLASH SPELL SAVED ME.
"ALAN!
"WHY NOT TAKE MY YOUNGER SISTER TO BE YOUR BRIDE?
Bwa ha ha ha ha!
"WE'D LOVE TO HAVE YOU AS A MEMBER OF OUR VILLAGE!"
Blush
"THANKS FOR THE OFFER.
"BUT IF I START A FAMILY IN THE ELF WOODS, I WON'T BE ABLE EXPLORE THE MINE ANYMORE."
......
MAYBE I SHOULD HAVE...
WAITED A LITTLE LONGER TO GO BACK TO THE MINE.

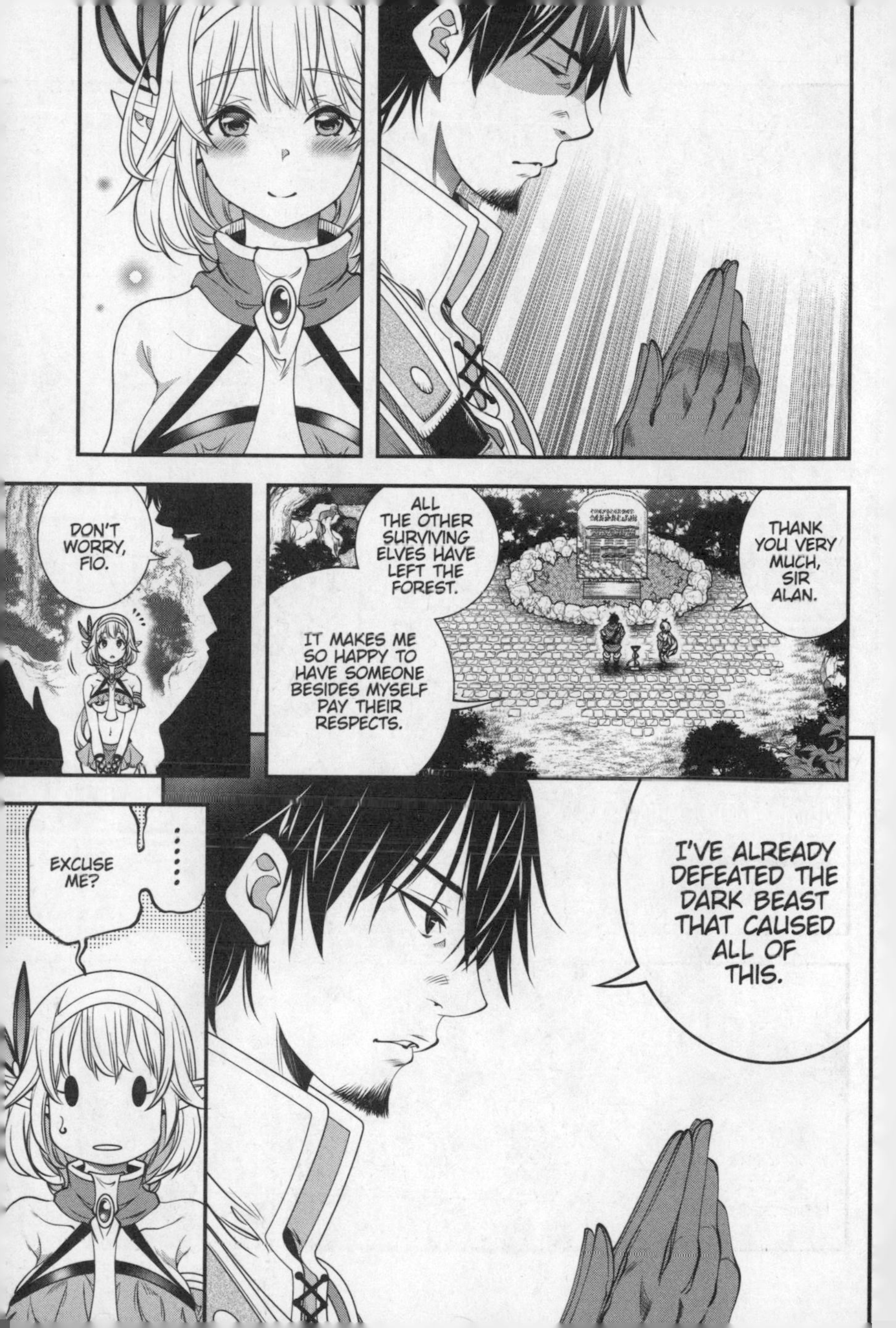
THANK YOU VERY MUCH, SIR ALAN.
ALL THE OTHER SURVIVING ELVES HAVE LEFT THE FOREST.
IT MAKES ME SO HAPPY TO HAVE SOMEONE BESIDES MYSELF PAY THEIR RESPECTS.
DON'T WORRY, FIO.
I'VE ALREADY DEFEATED THE DARK BEAST THAT CAUSED ALL OF THIS.
......
EXCUSE ME?

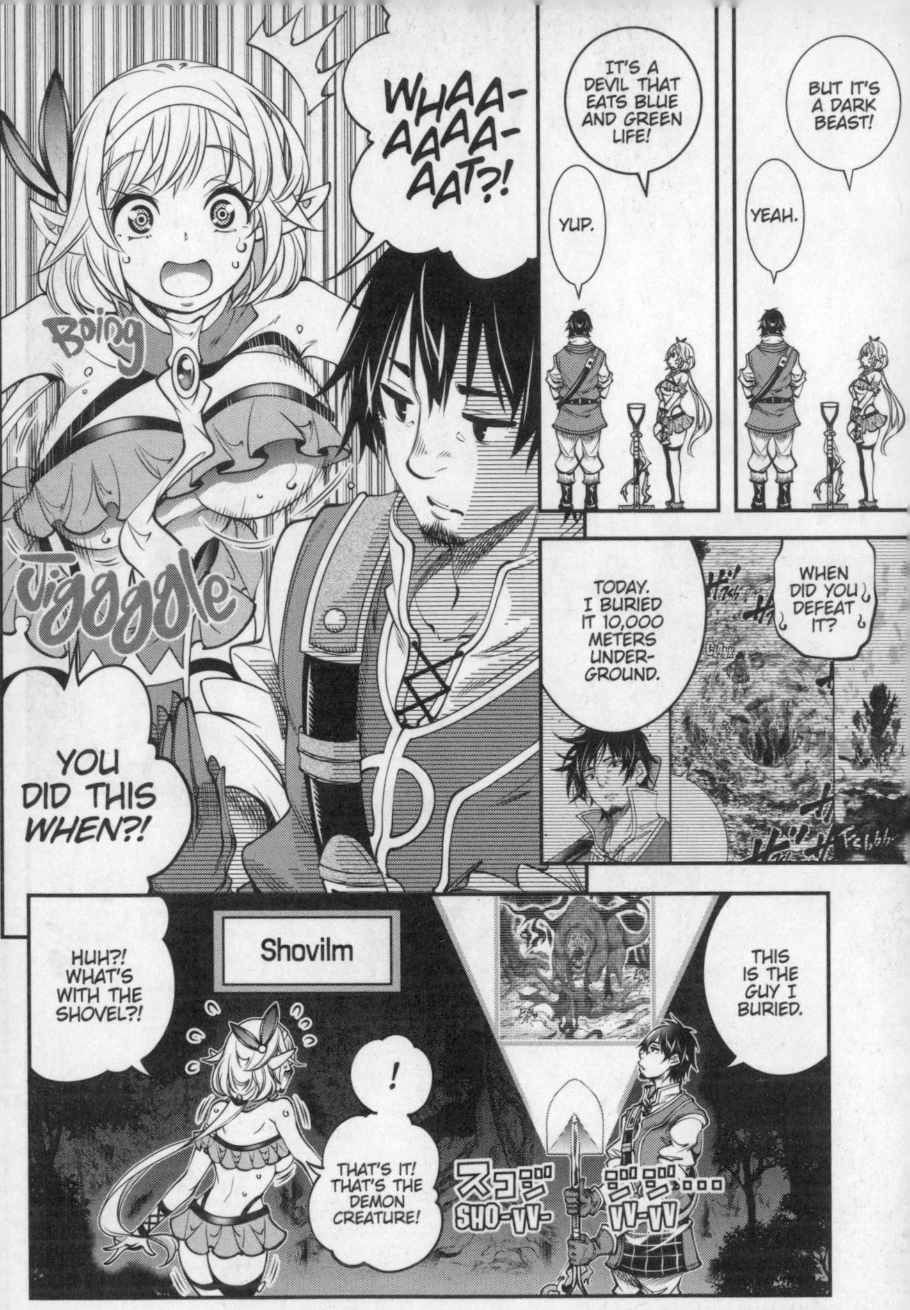
BUT IT'S A DARK BEAST!
YEAH.
IT'S A DEVIL THAT EATS BLUE AND GREEN LIFE!
YUP.
WHEN DID YOU DEFEAT IT?
TODAY. I BURIED IT 10,000 METERS UNDERGROUND.
WHAAA-AAAA-AAT?!
Boing
Jigggle
YOU DID THIS WHEN?!
THIS IS THE GUY I BURIED.
Shovilm
!
THAT'S IT! THAT'S THE DEMON CREATURE!
SHO-VV-
VV-VV
HUH?! WHAT'S WITH THE SHOVEL?!

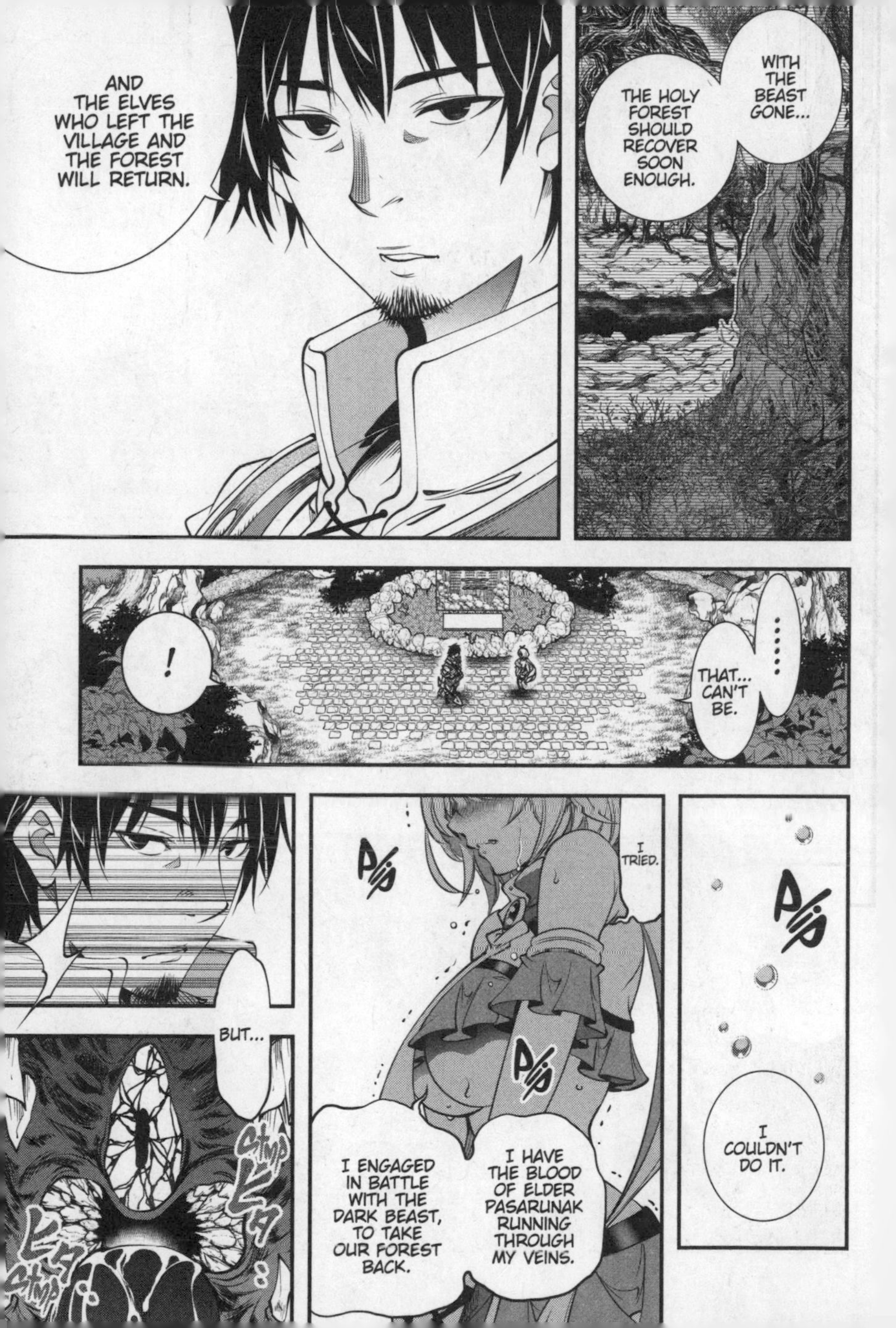
WITH THE BEAST GONE...
THE HOLY FOREST SHOULD RECOVER SOON ENOUGH.
AND THE ELVES WHO LEFT THE VILLAGE AND THE FOREST WILL RETURN.
......
THAT... CAN'T BE.
!
Plip
I COULDN'T DO IT.
I TRIED.
Plip
Plip
I HAVE THE BLOOD OF ELDER PASARUNAK RUNNING THROUGH MY VEINS.
I ENGAGED IN BATTLE WITH THE DARK BEAST, TO TAKE OUR FOREST BACK.
BUT...
Stmp
Stmp

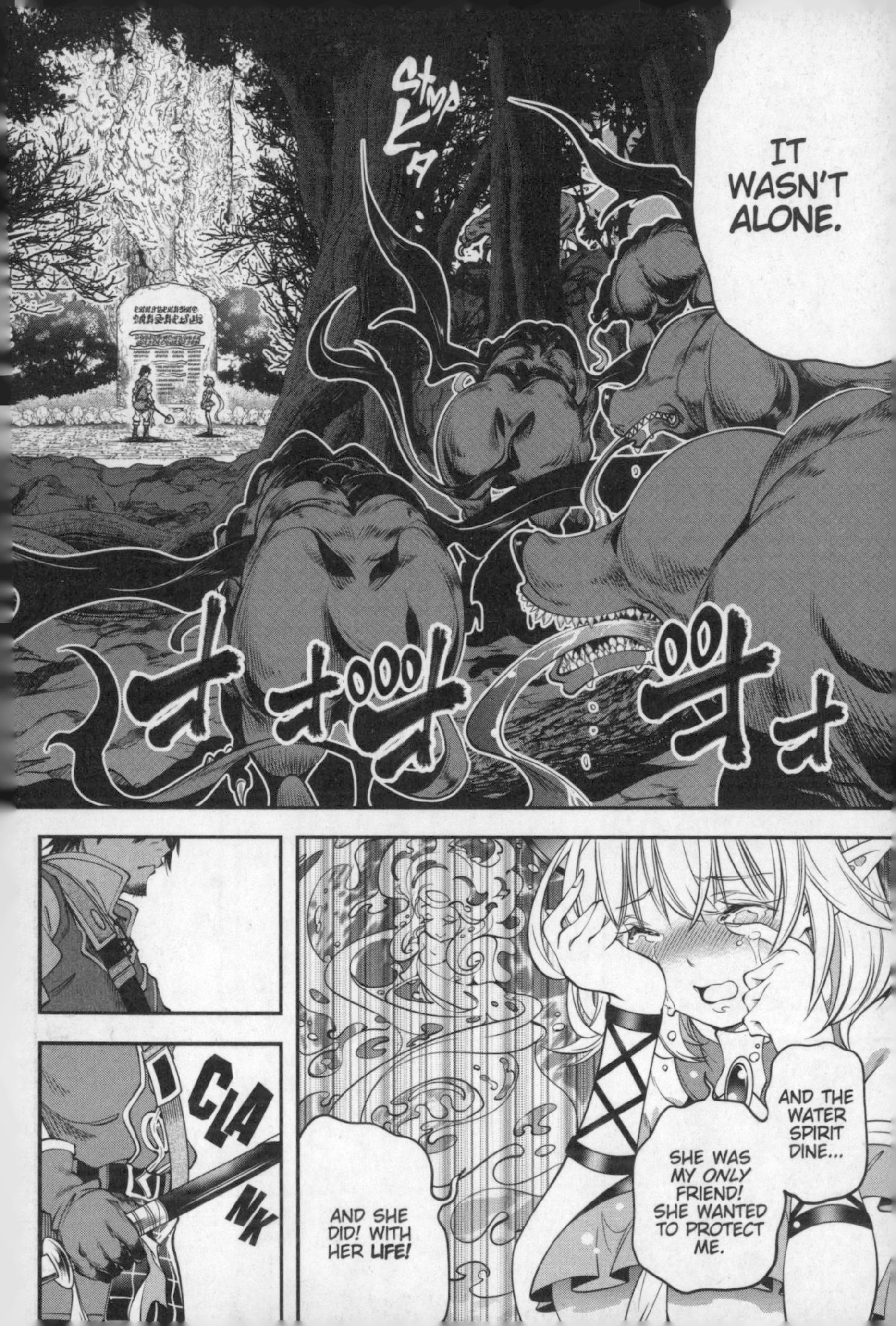
Stmp
IT WASN'T ALONE.
OOO!
OO!
AND THE WATER SPIRIT DINE...
SHE WAS MY *ONLY* FRIEND! SHE WANTED TO PROTECT ME.
AND SHE DID! WITH HER **LIFE!**
CLANK

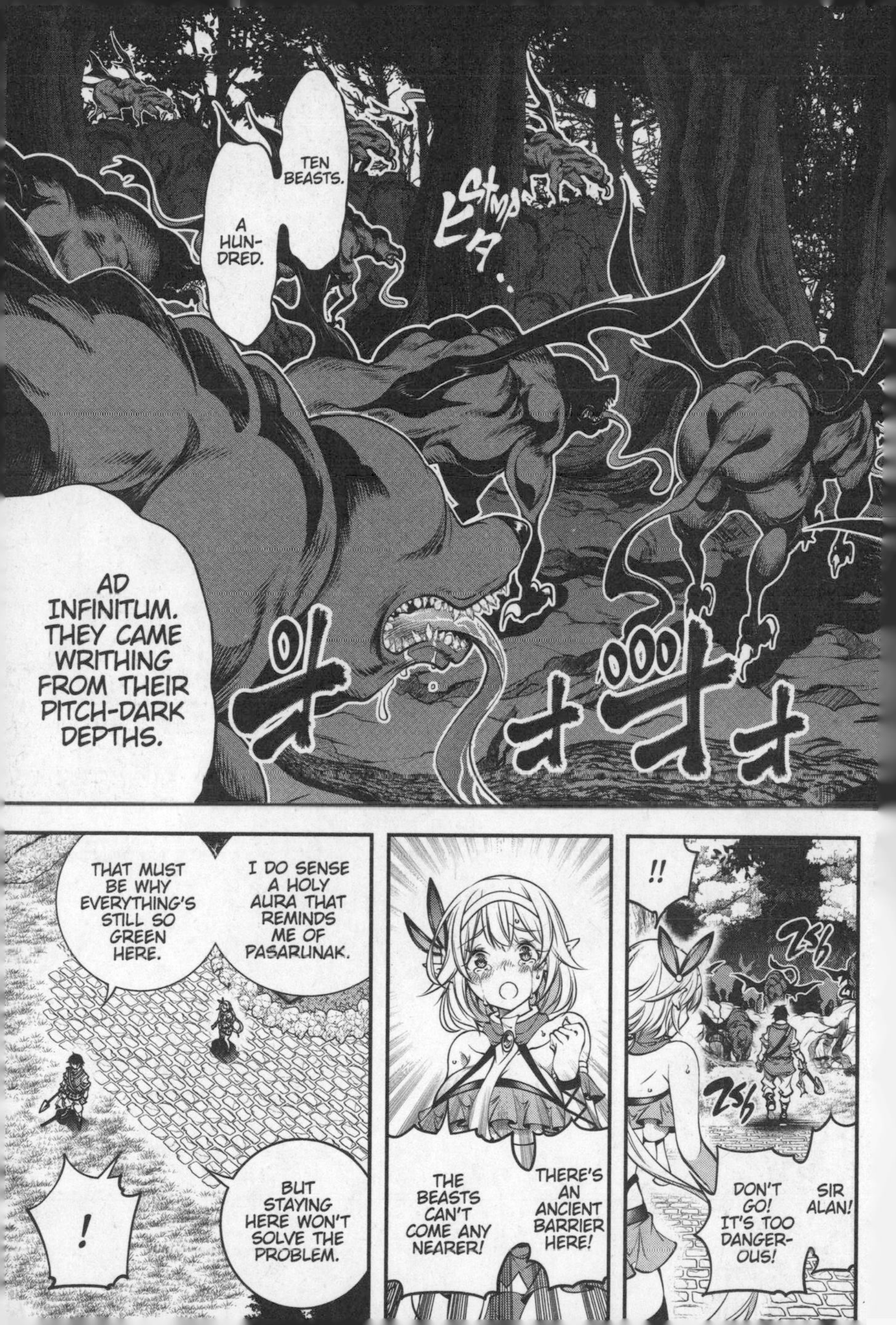
TEN BEASTS.
A HUN-DRED.
STMP
AD INFINITUM. THEY CAME WRITHING FROM THEIR PITCH-DARK DEPTHS.
!!
ZSH
ZSH
SIR ALAN!
DON'T GO! IT'S TOO DANGER-OUS!
THERE'S AN ANCIENT BARRIER HERE!
THE BEASTS CAN'T COME ANY NEARER!
I DO SENSE A HOLY AURA THAT REMINDS ME OF PASARUNAK.
THAT MUST BE WHY EVERYTHING'S STILL SO GREEN HERE.
BUT STAYING HERE WON'T SOLVE THE PROBLEM.
!

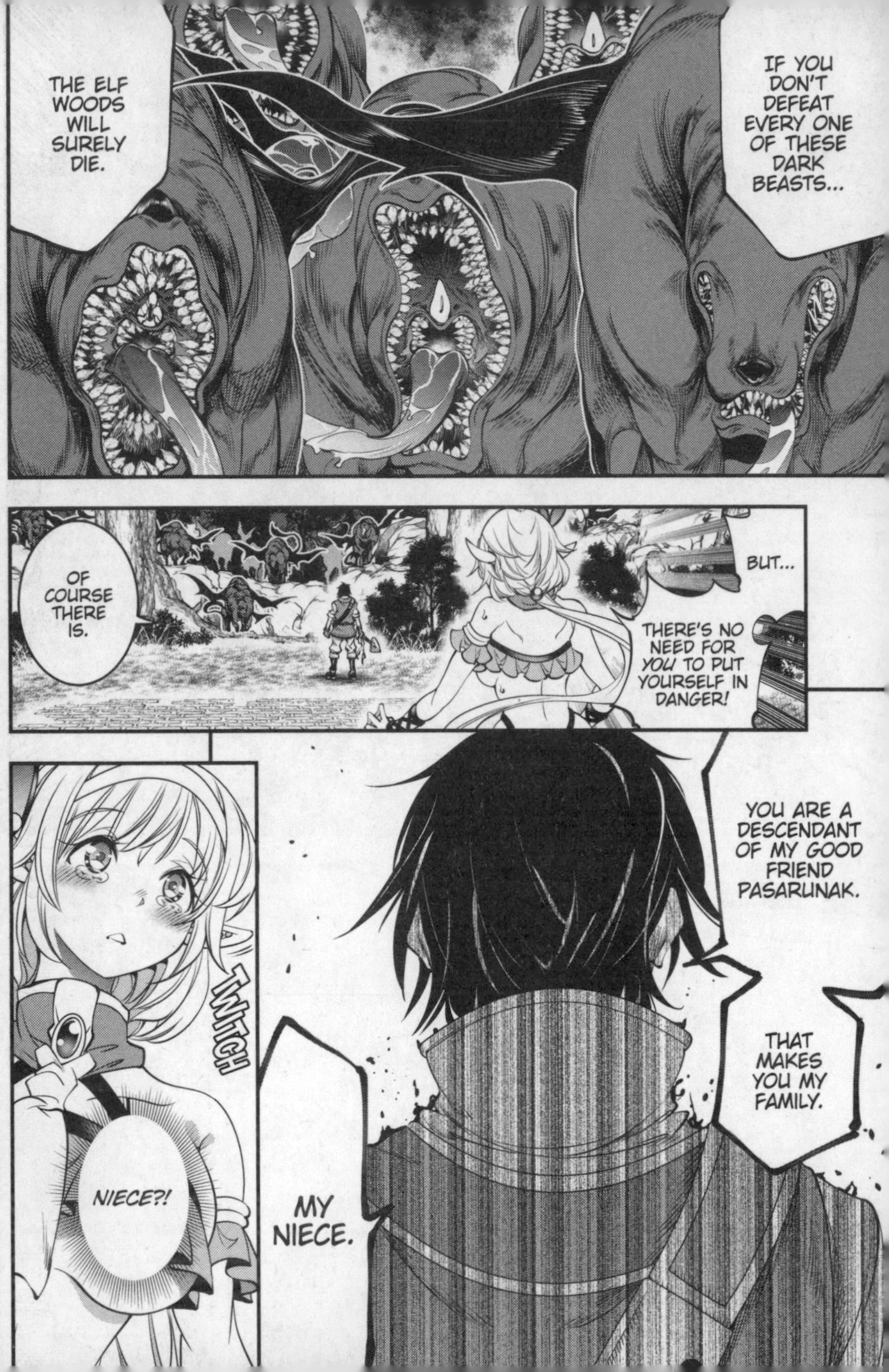
IF YOU DON'T DEFEAT EVERY ONE OF THESE DARK BEASTS...
THE ELF WOODS WILL SURELY DIE.
BUT...
THERE'S NO NEED FOR *YOU* TO PUT YOURSELF IN DANGER!
OF COURSE THERE IS.
YOU ARE A DESCENDANT OF MY GOOD FRIEND PASARUNAK.
THAT MAKES YOU MY FAMILY.
MY NIECE.
TWITCH
NIECE?!

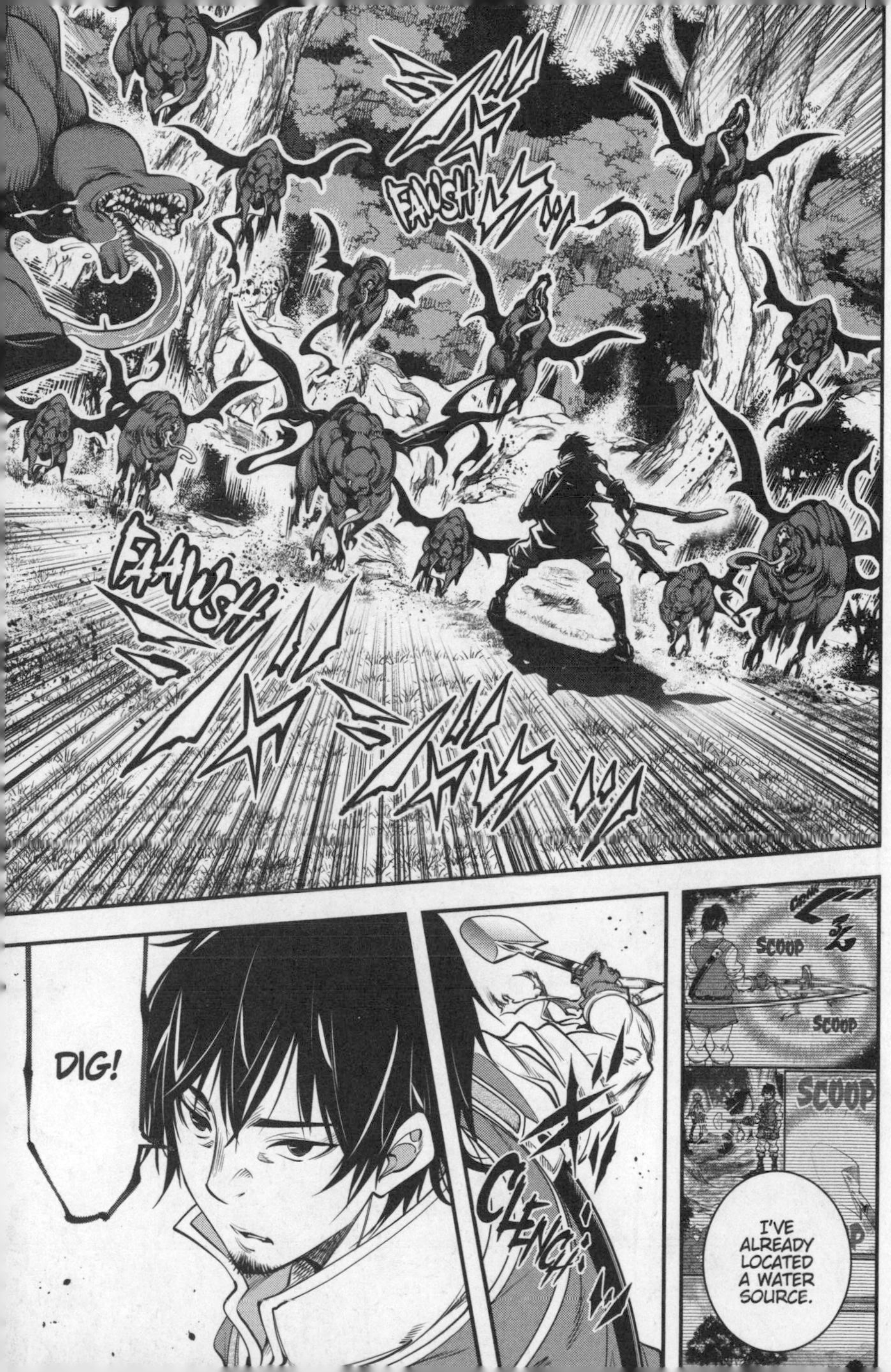
FWOSH
FWOSH
SCOOP
SCOOP
SCOOP
I'VE ALREADY LOCATED A WATER SOURCE.
CLENCH!
DIG!

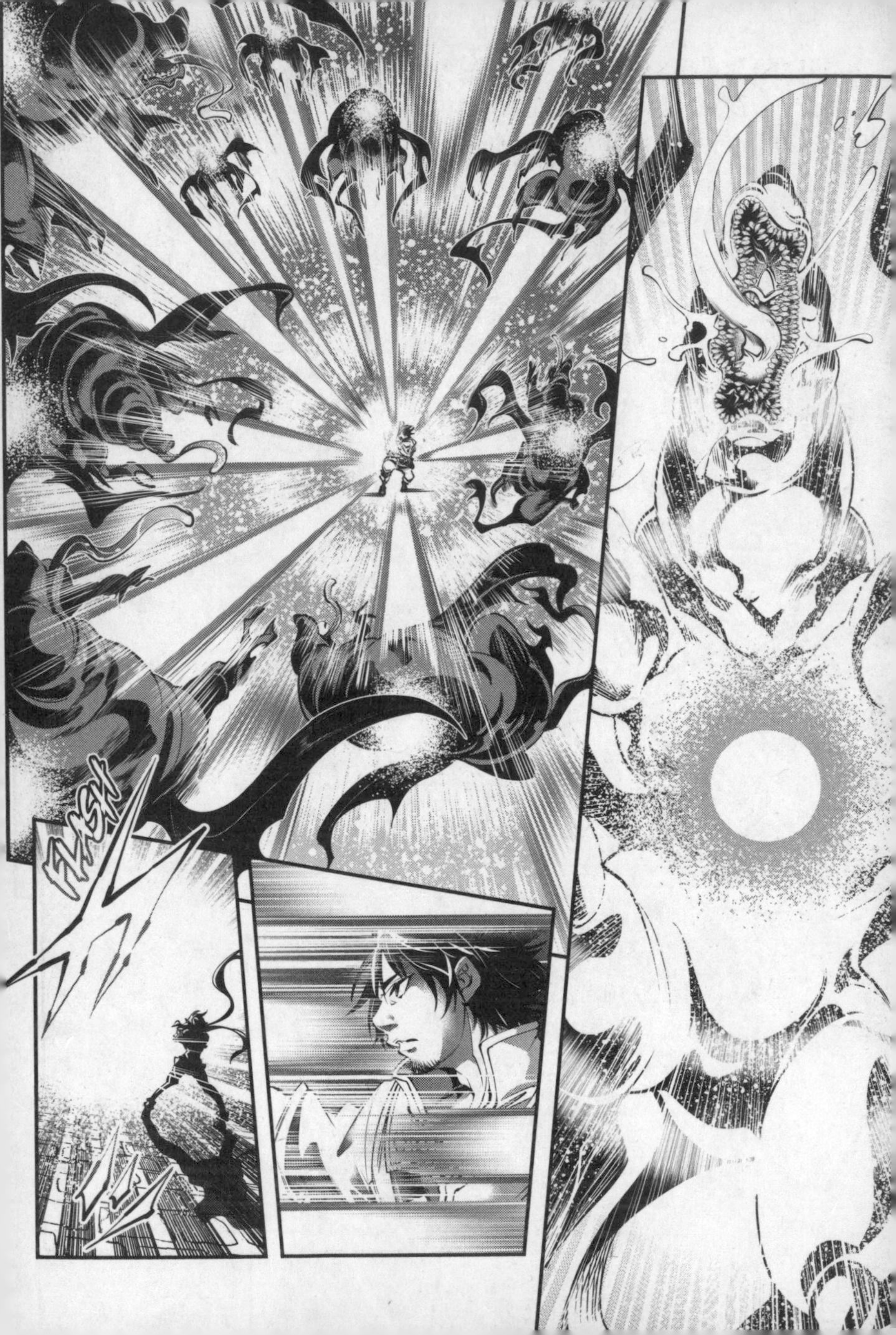
FLASH

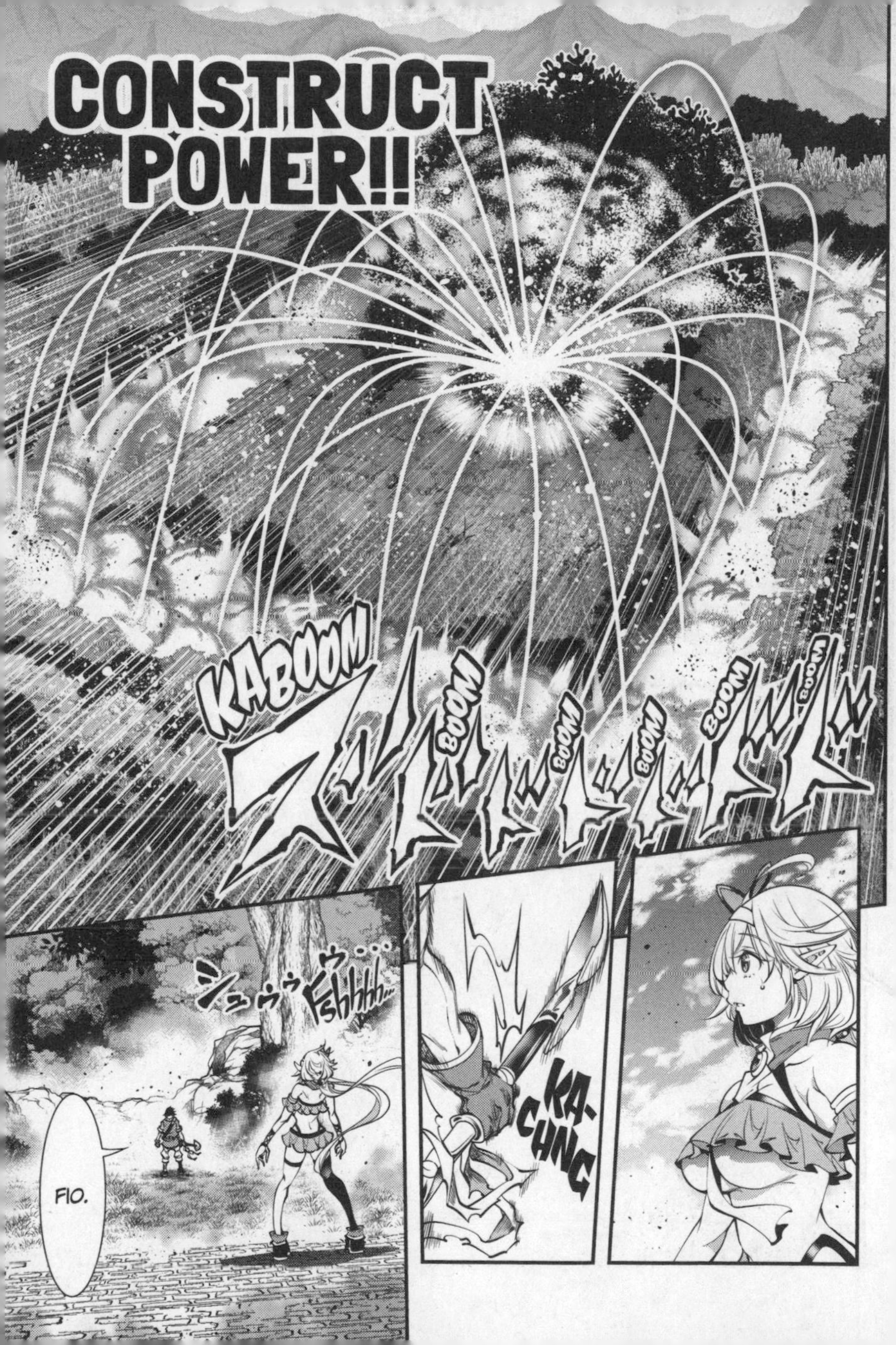
CONSTRUCT POWER!!
KABOOM
BOOM
BOOM
BOOM
BOOM
BOOM
KA-CHNG
Fshhhh...
FIO.

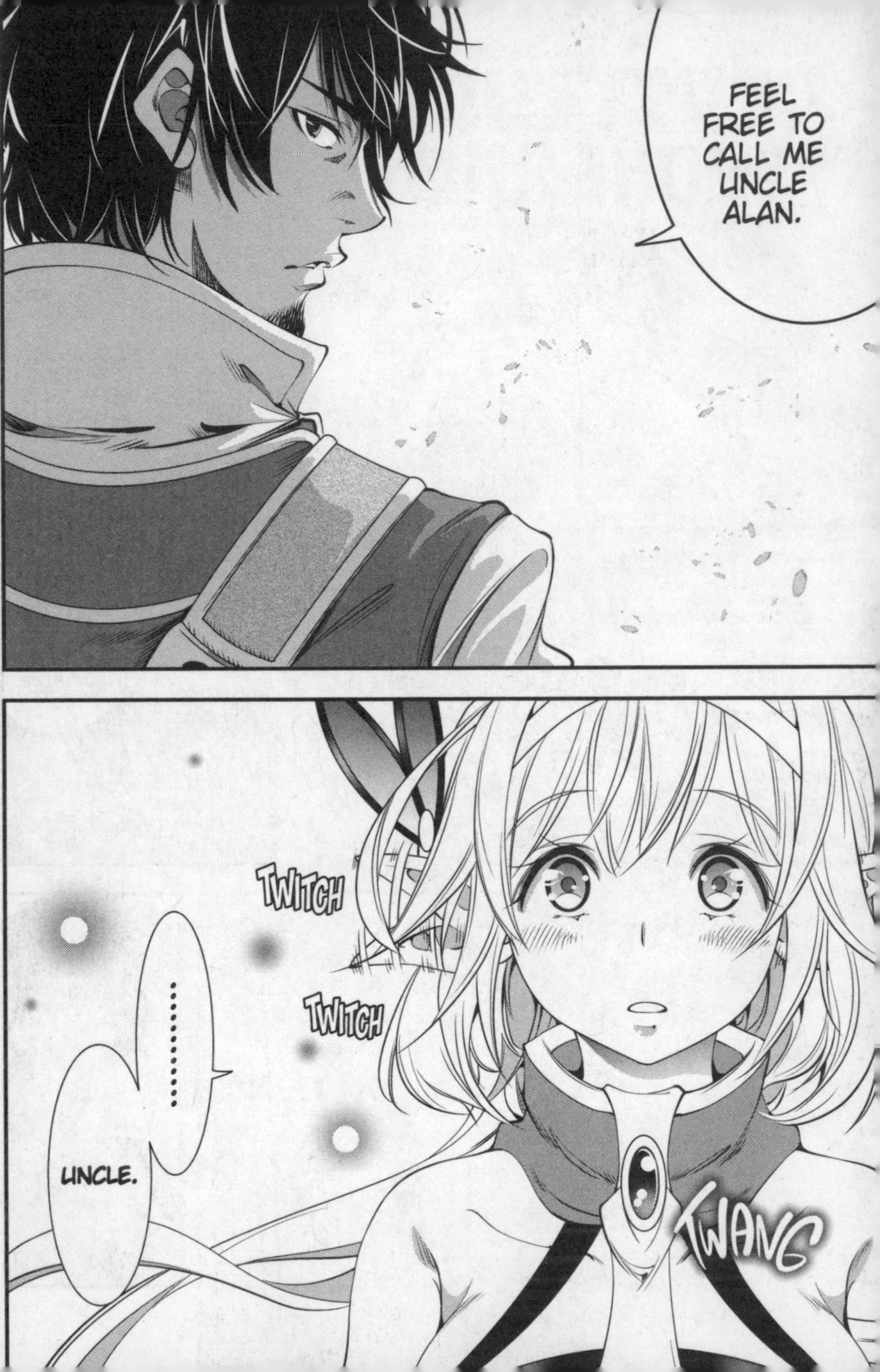
FEEL FREE TO CALL ME UNCLE ALAN.
TWITCH
TWITCH
TWANG
......
UNCLE.

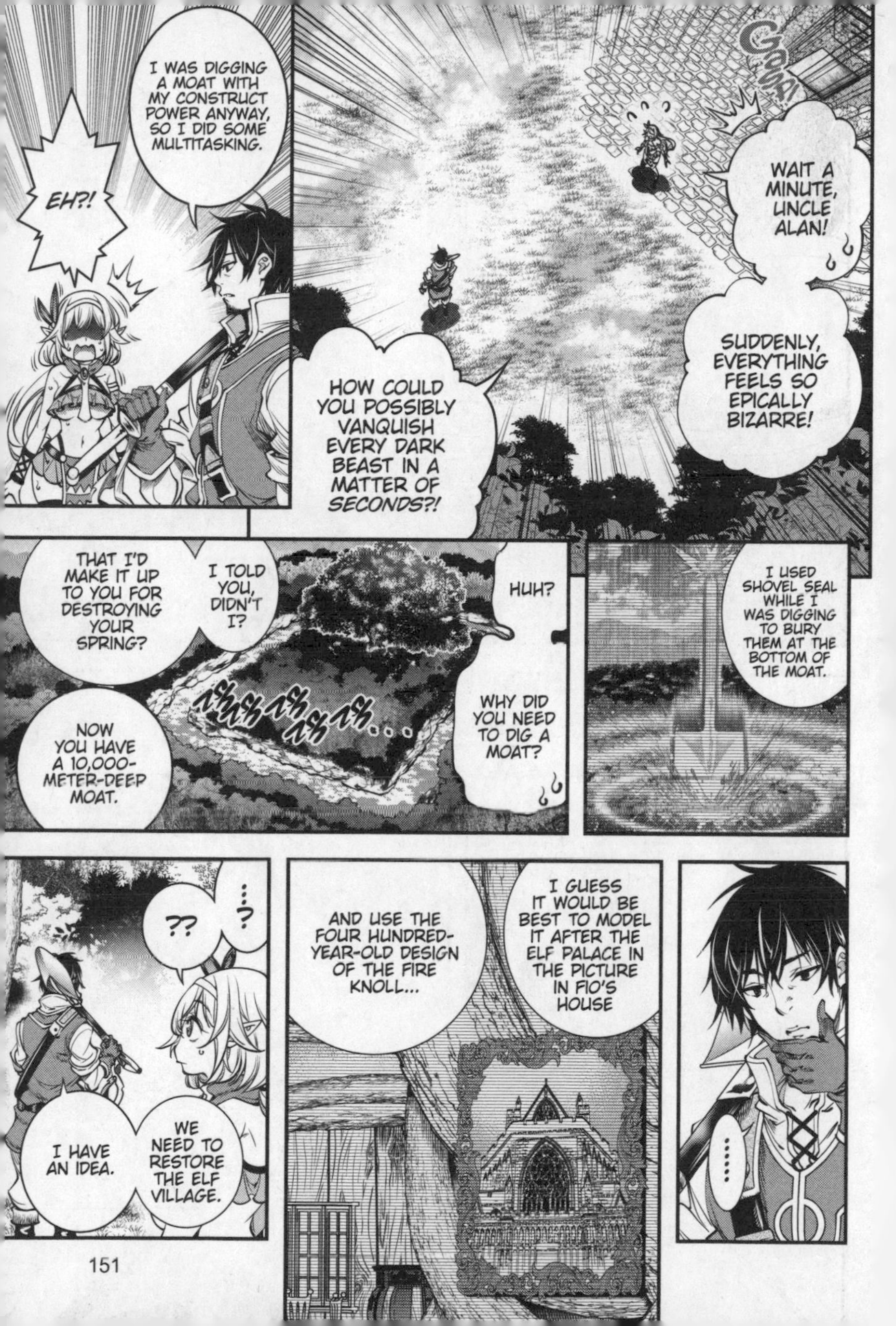
GASA!
WAIT A MINUTE, UNCLE ALAN!
SUDDENLY, EVERYTHING FEELS SO EPICALLY BIZARRE!
HOW COULD YOU POSSIBLY VANQUISH EVERY DARK BEAST IN A MATTER OF SECONDS?!
I WAS DIGGING A MOAT WITH MY CONSTRUCT POWER ANYWAY, SO I DID SOME MULTITASKING.
EH?!
I USED SHOVEL SEAL WHILE I WAS DIGGING TO BURY THEM AT THE BOTTOM OF THE MOAT.
HUH?
WHY DID YOU NEED TO DIG A MOAT?
I TOLD YOU, DIDN'T I?
THAT I'D MAKE IT UP TO YOU FOR DESTROYING YOUR SPRING?
NOW YOU HAVE A 10,000-METER-DEEP MOAT.
......
I GUESS IT WOULD BE BEST TO MODEL IT AFTER THE ELF PALACE IN THE PICTURE IN FIO'S HOUSE
AND USE THE FOUR HUNDRED-YEAR-OLD DESIGN OF THE FIRE KNOLL...
...?
??
WE NEED TO RESTORE THE ELF VILLAGE.
I HAVE AN IDEA.

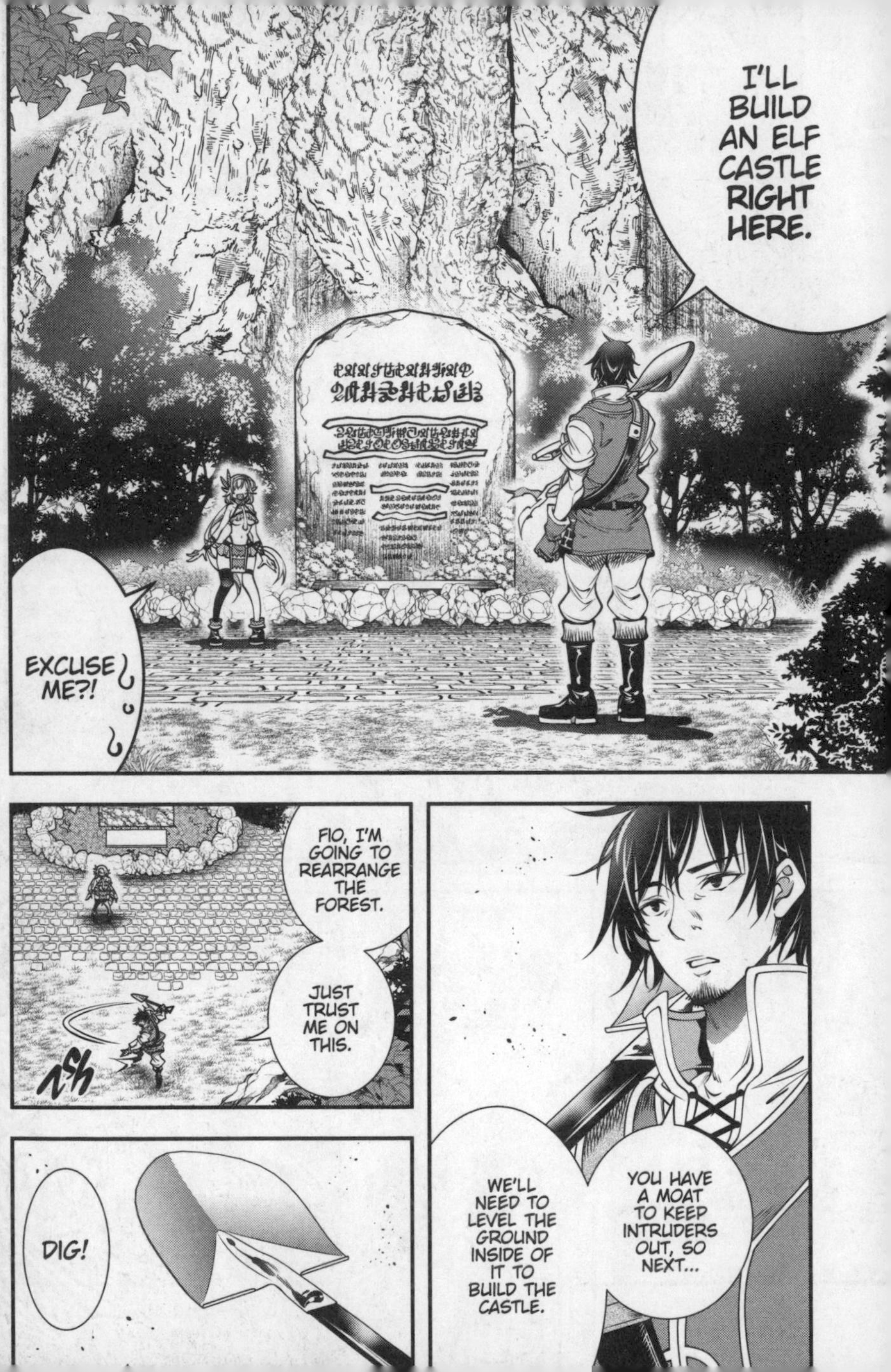
I'LL BUILD AN ELF CASTLE RIGHT HERE.
EXCUSE ME?!
YOU HAVE A MOAT TO KEEP INTRUDERS OUT, SO NEXT...
WE'LL NEED TO LEVEL THE GROUND INSIDE OF IT TO BUILD THE CASTLE.
FIO, I'M GOING TO REARRANGE THE FOREST.
JUST TRUST ME ON THIS.
DIG!

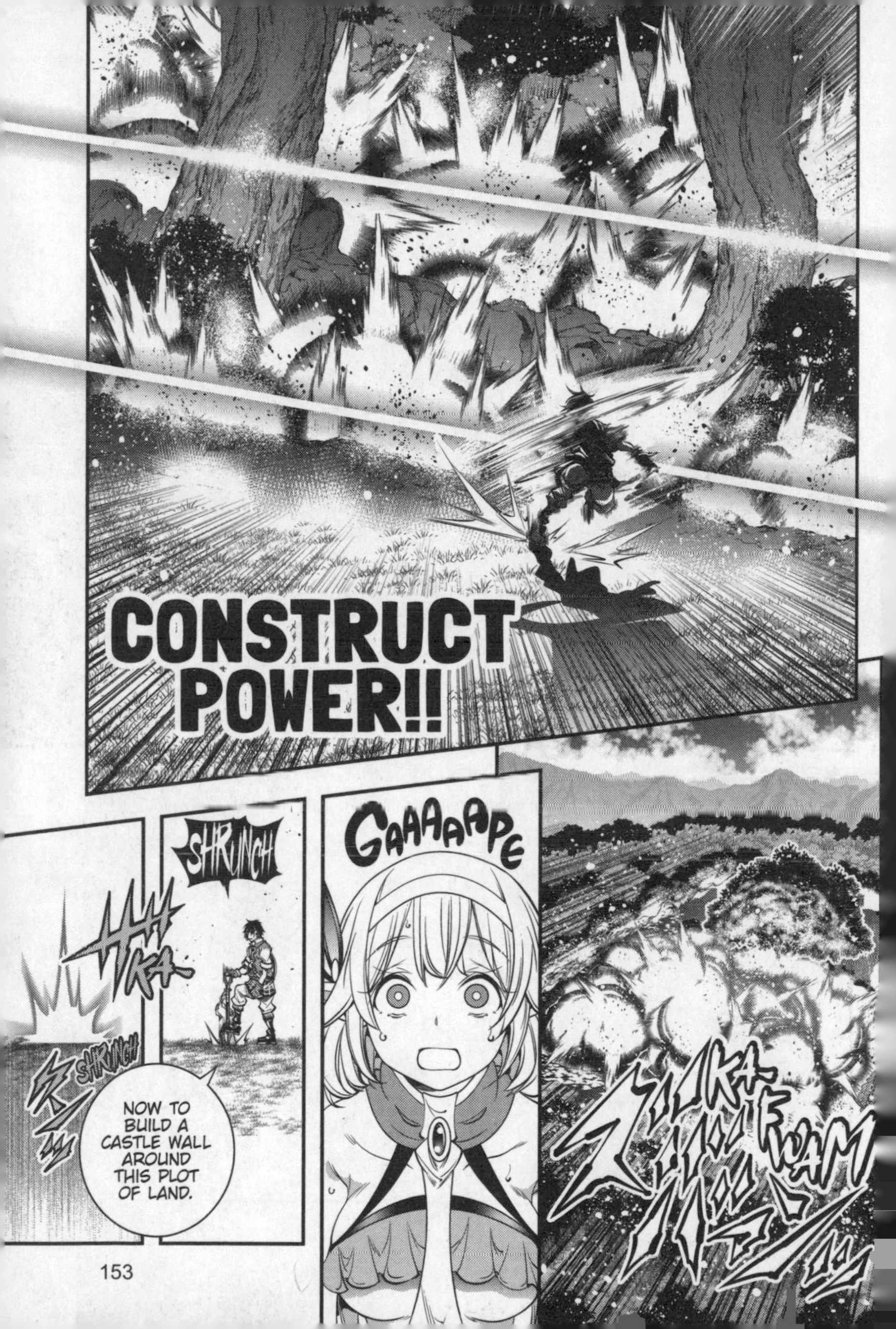
CONSTRUCT POWER!!
FWAM
GAAAAAPE
SHRUNCH
KA-
SHRINCH
NOW TO BUILD A CASTLE WALL AROUND THIS PLOT OF LAND.

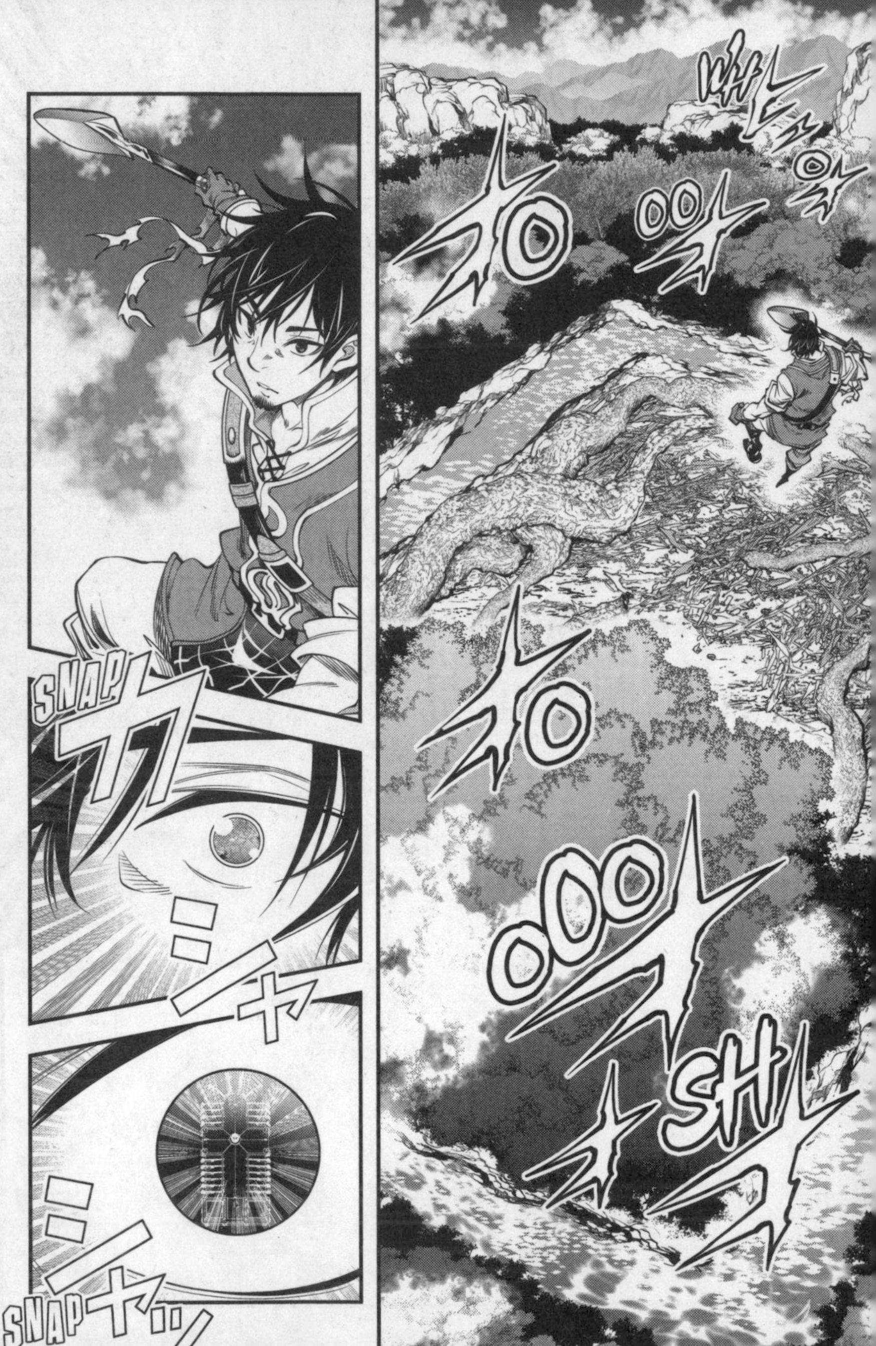
WHOOOOOOOOSH
SNAP
SNAP

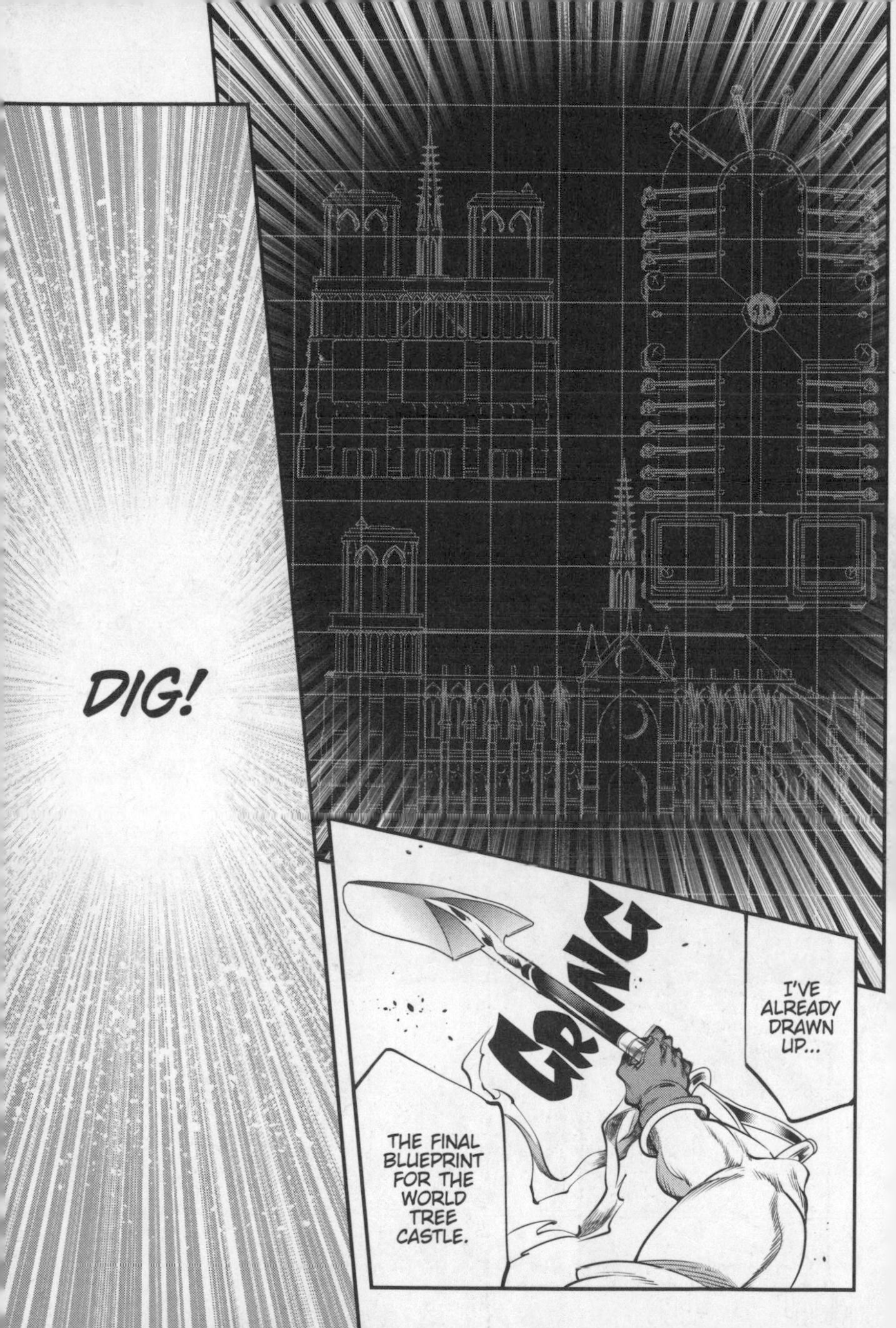
I'VE ALREADY DRAWN UP...
GRING
THE FINAL BLUEPRINT FOR THE WORLD TREE CASTLE.
DIG!

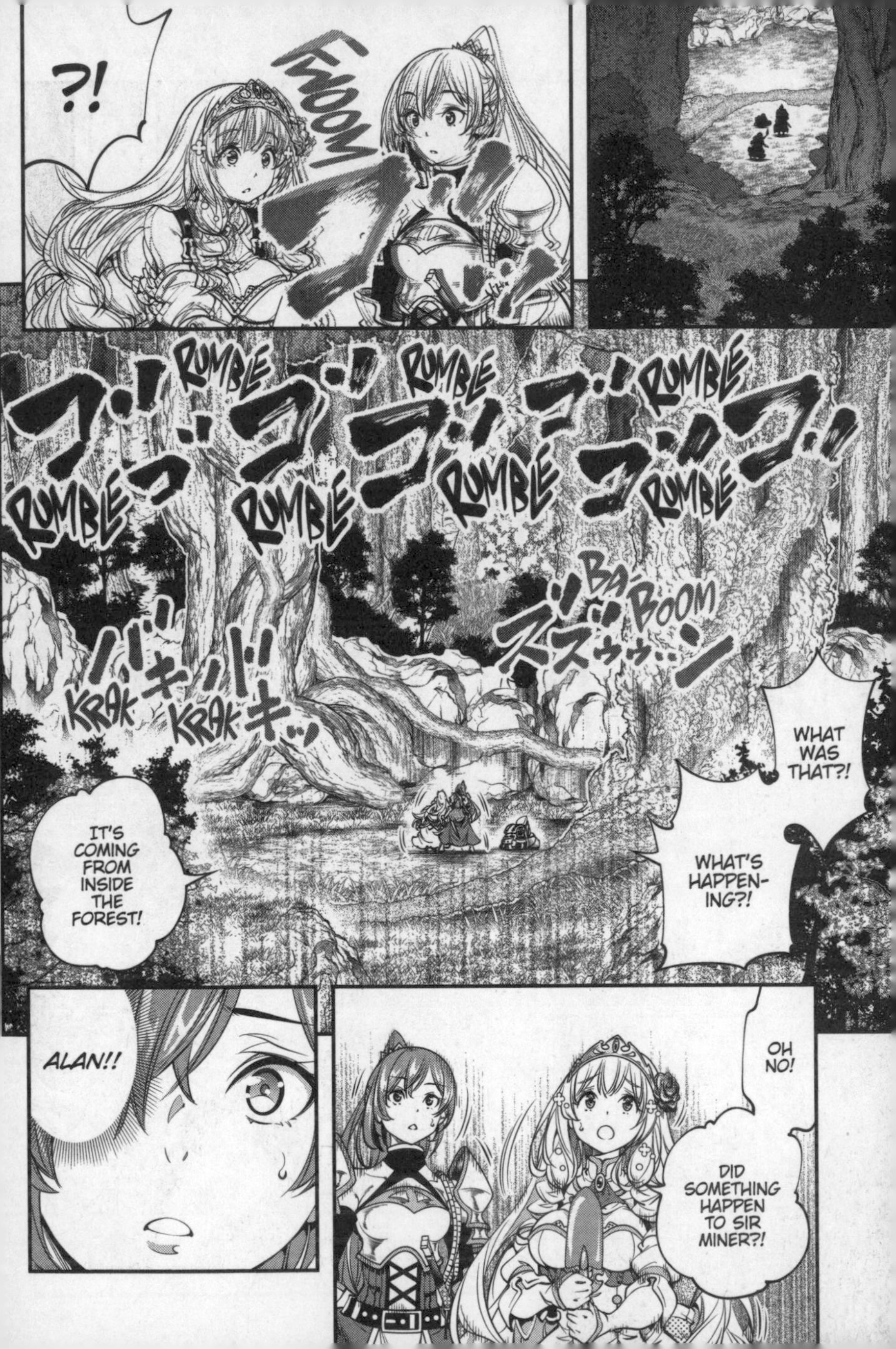
?!
FWOOM!
RUMBLE RUMBLE RUMBLE RUMBLE
RUMBLE RUMBLE RUMBLE RUMBLE
BA-BOOM
KRAK KRAK
WHAT WAS THAT?!
WHAT'S HAPPEN-ING?!
IT'S COMING FROM INSIDE THE FOREST!
OH NO!
DID SOMETHING HAPPEN TO SIR MINER?!
ALAN!!

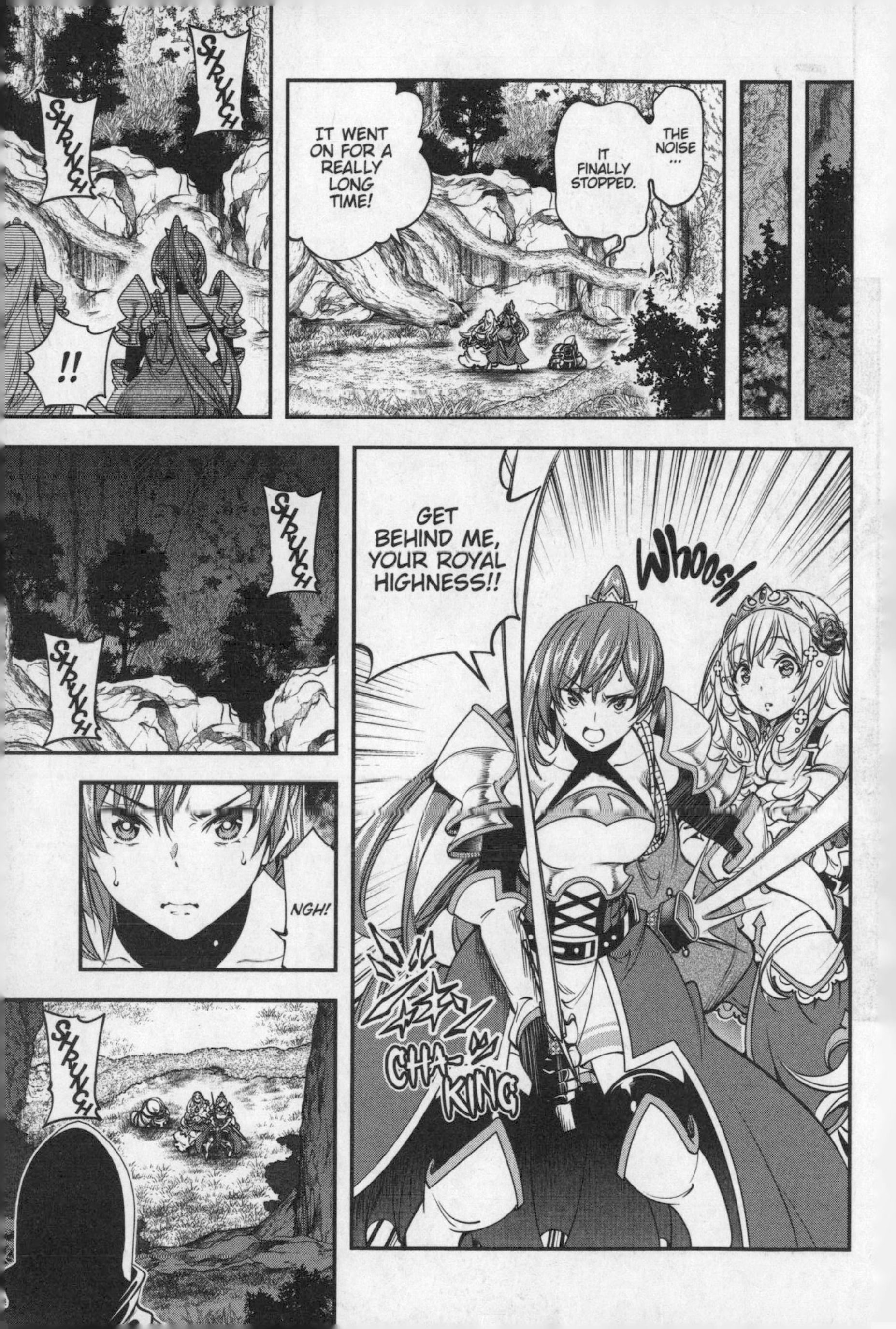
THE NOISE...
IT FINALLY STOPPED.
IT WENT ON FOR A REALLY LONG TIME!
SHRUNCH
SHRUNCH
!!
GET BEHIND ME, YOUR ROYAL HIGHNESS!!
Whoosh
CHA-KING
SHRUNCH
SHRUNCH
NGH!
SHRUNCH

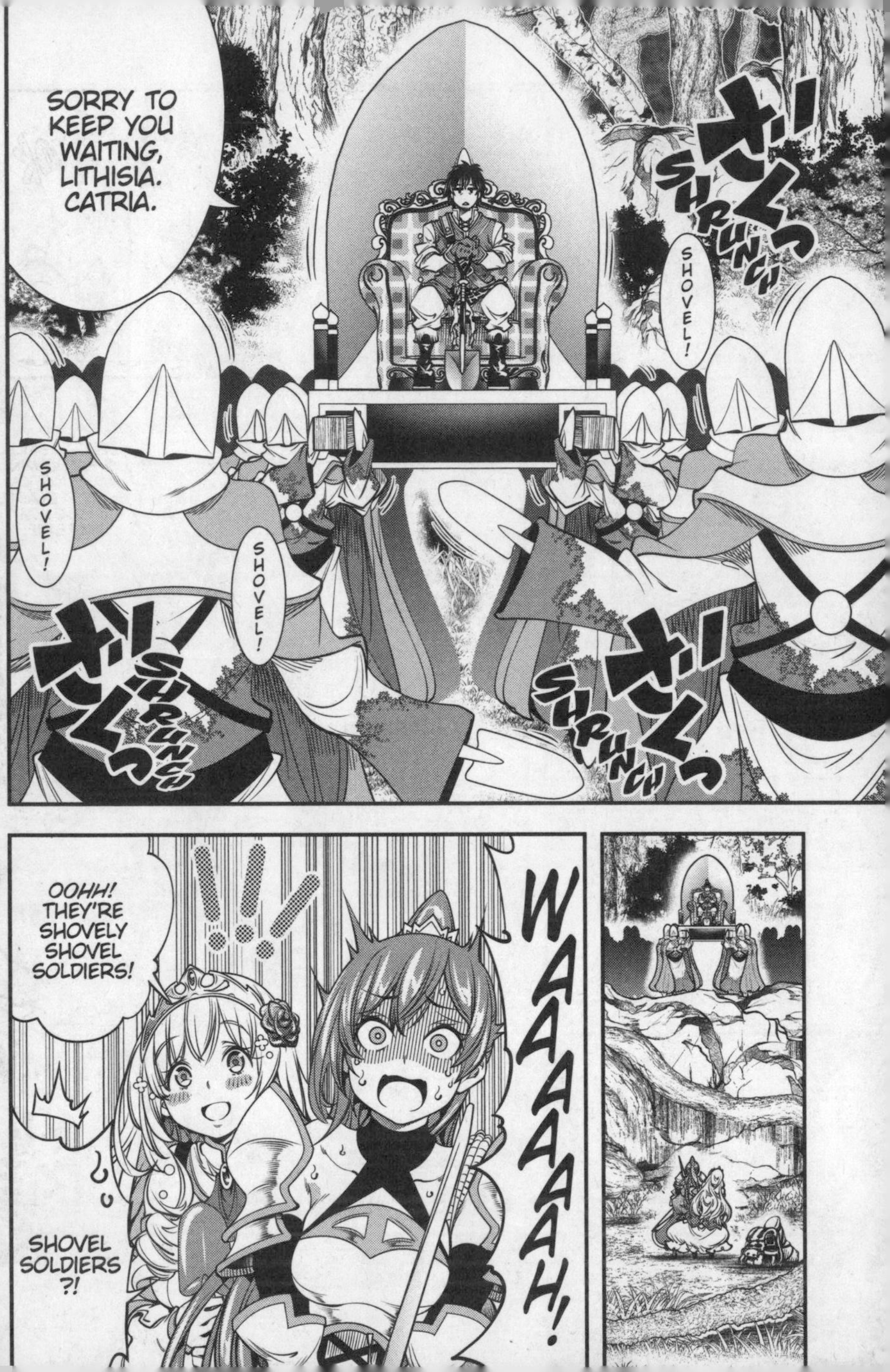
ざくっ
SHRUNCH
SHOVEL!
SORRY TO KEEP YOU WAITING, LITHISIA. CATRIA.
SHOVEL!
SHOVEL!
ざくっ
SHRUNCH
ざくっ
SHRUNCH
WAAAAAAH!
!!!
OOHH! THEY'RE SHOVELY SHOVEL SOLDIERS!
SHOVEL SOLDIERS?!

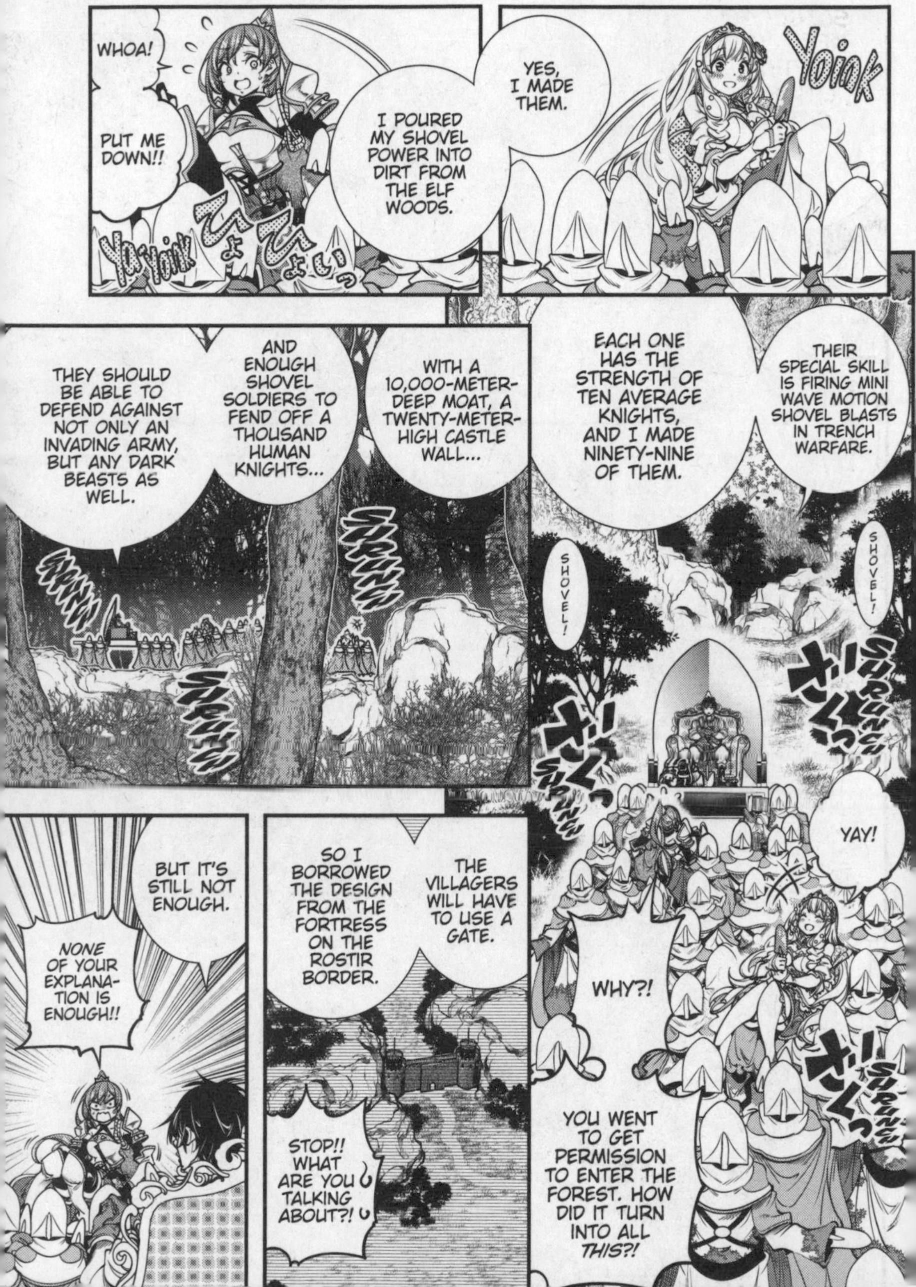

Yoink
YES, I MADE THEM.
I POURED MY SHOVEL POWER INTO DIRT FROM THE ELF WOODS.
WHOA!
PUT ME DOWN!!
Ya-Yoink
THEIR SPECIAL SKILL IS FIRING MINI WAVE MOTION SHOVEL BLASTS IN TRENCH WARFARE.
EACH ONE HAS THE STRENGTH OF TEN AVERAGE KNIGHTS, AND I MADE NINETY-NINE OF THEM.
SHOVEL!
SHOVEL!
SHRUNCH
SHRUNCH
YAY!
WHY?!
SHRUNCH
YOU WENT TO GET PERMISSION TO ENTER THE FOREST. HOW DID IT TURN INTO ALL *THIS*?!
WITH A 10,000-METER-DEEP MOAT, A TWENTY-METER-HIGH CASTLE WALL...
AND ENOUGH SHOVEL SOLDIERS TO FEND OFF A THOUSAND HUMAN KNIGHTS...
THEY SHOULD BE ABLE TO DEFEND AGAINST NOT ONLY AN INVADING ARMY, BUT ANY DARK BEASTS AS WELL.
SHRUNCH
SHRUNCH
SHRUNCH
THE VILLAGERS WILL HAVE TO USE A GATE.
SO I BORROWED THE DESIGN FROM THE FORTRESS ON THE ROSTIR BORDER.
STOP!! WHAT ARE YOU TALKING ABOUT?!
BUT IT'S STILL NOT ENOUGH.
NONE OF YOUR EXPLANATION IS ENOUGH!!

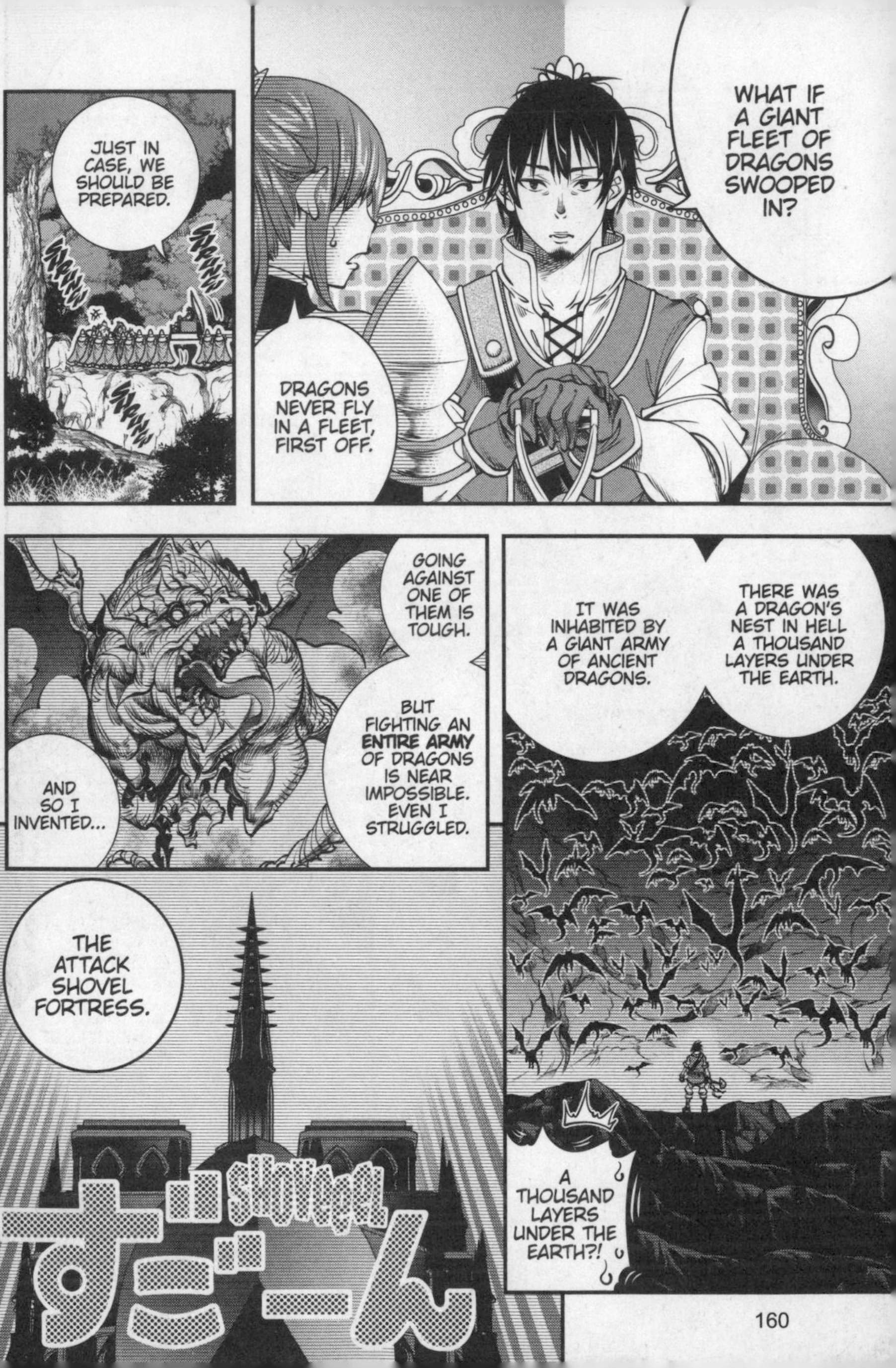
WHAT IF A GIANT FLEET OF DRAGONS SWOOPED IN?
DRAGONS NEVER FLY IN A FLEET, FIRST OFF.
JUST IN CASE, WE SHOULD BE PREPARED.
THERE WAS A DRAGON'S NEST IN HELL A THOUSAND LAYERS UNDER THE EARTH.
IT WAS INHABITED BY A GIANT ARMY OF ANCIENT DRAGONS.
A THOUSAND LAYERS UNDER THE EARTH?!
GOING AGAINST ONE OF THEM IS TOUGH.
BUT FIGHTING AN **ENTIRE ARMY** OF DRAGONS IS NEAR IMPOSSIBLE. EVEN I STRUGGLED.
AND SO I INVENTED...
THE ATTACK SHOVEL FORTRESS.
SHING!!

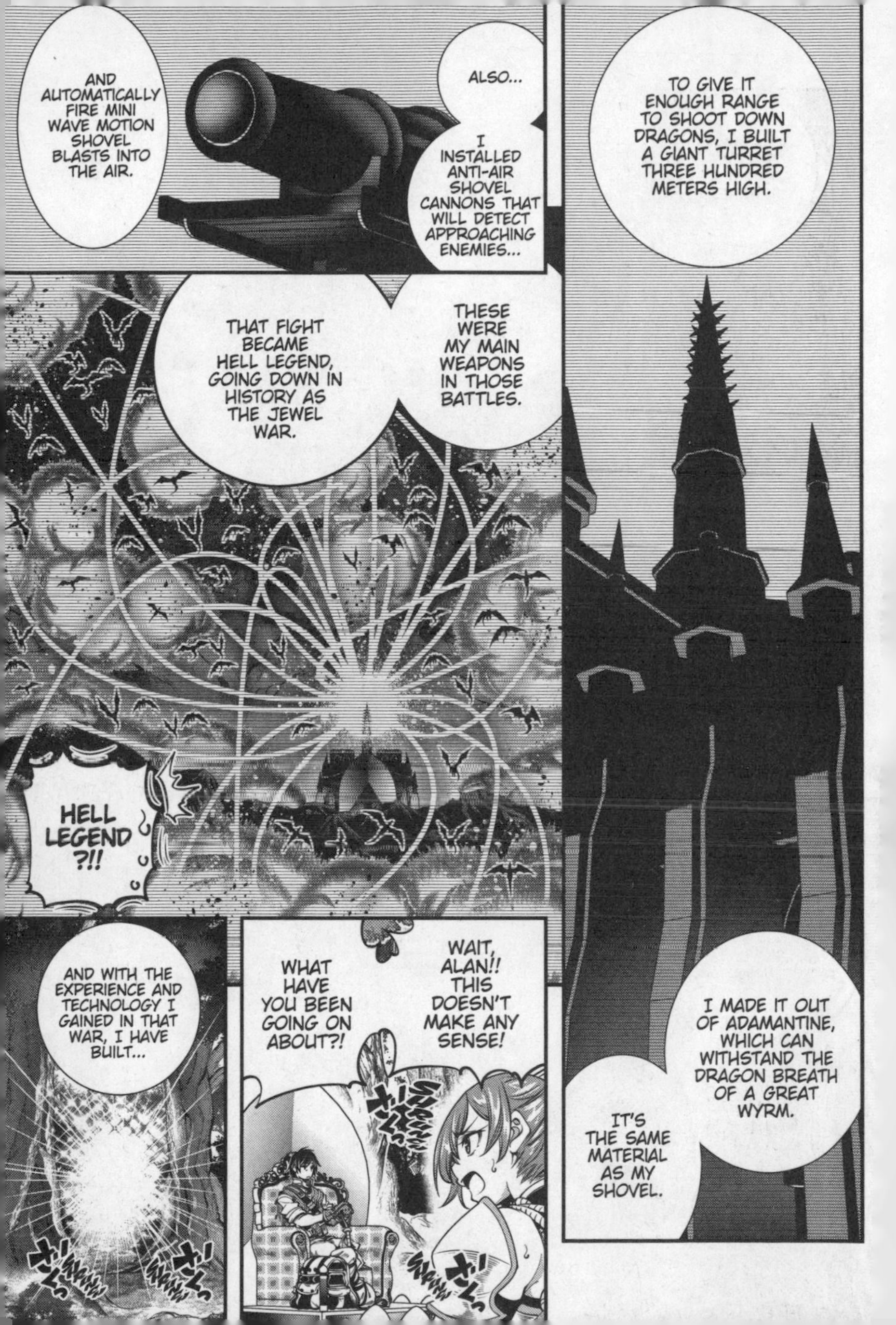
TO GIVE IT ENOUGH RANGE TO SHOOT DOWN DRAGONS, I BUILT A GIANT TURRET THREE HUNDRED METERS HIGH.
I MADE IT OUT OF ADAMANTINE, WHICH CAN WITHSTAND THE DRAGON BREATH OF A GREAT WYRM.
IT'S THE SAME MATERIAL AS MY SHOVEL.
ALSO...
I INSTALLED ANTI-AIR SHOVEL CANNONS THAT WILL DETECT APPROACHING ENEMIES...
AND AUTOMATICALLY FIRE MINI WAVE MOTION SHOVEL BLASTS INTO THE AIR.
THESE WERE MY MAIN WEAPONS IN THOSE BATTLES.
THAT FIGHT BECAME HELL LEGEND, GOING DOWN IN HISTORY AS THE JEWEL WAR.
HELL LEGEND ?!!
WAIT, ALAN!! THIS DOESN'T MAKE ANY SENSE!
WHAT HAVE YOU BEEN GOING ON ABOUT?!
AND WITH THE EXPERIENCE AND TECHNOLOGY I GAINED IN THAT WAR, I HAVE BUILT...

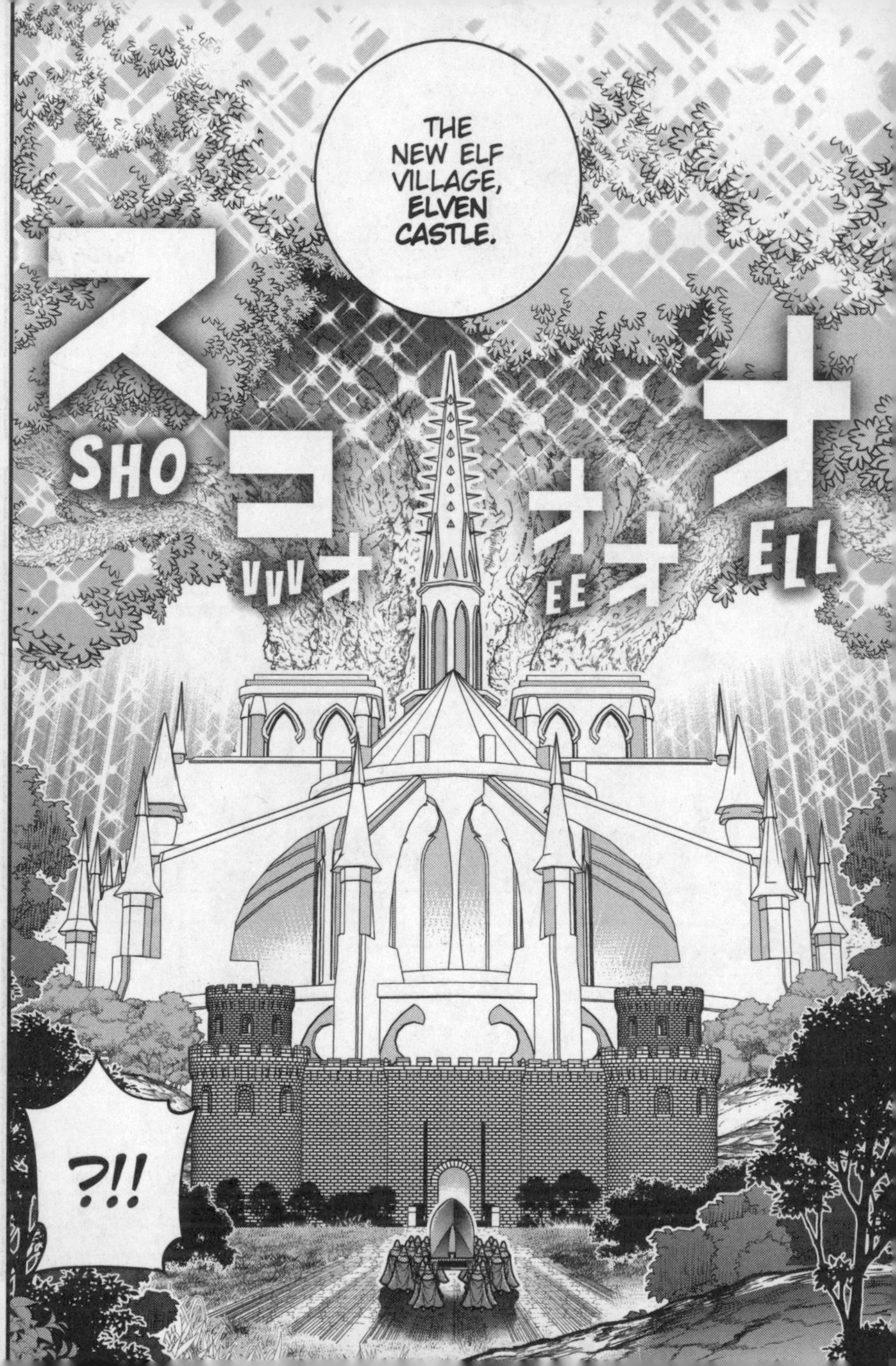
THE NEW ELF VILLAGE, ELVEN CASTLE.
スコォォォ
SHO VVV EE ELL
?!!

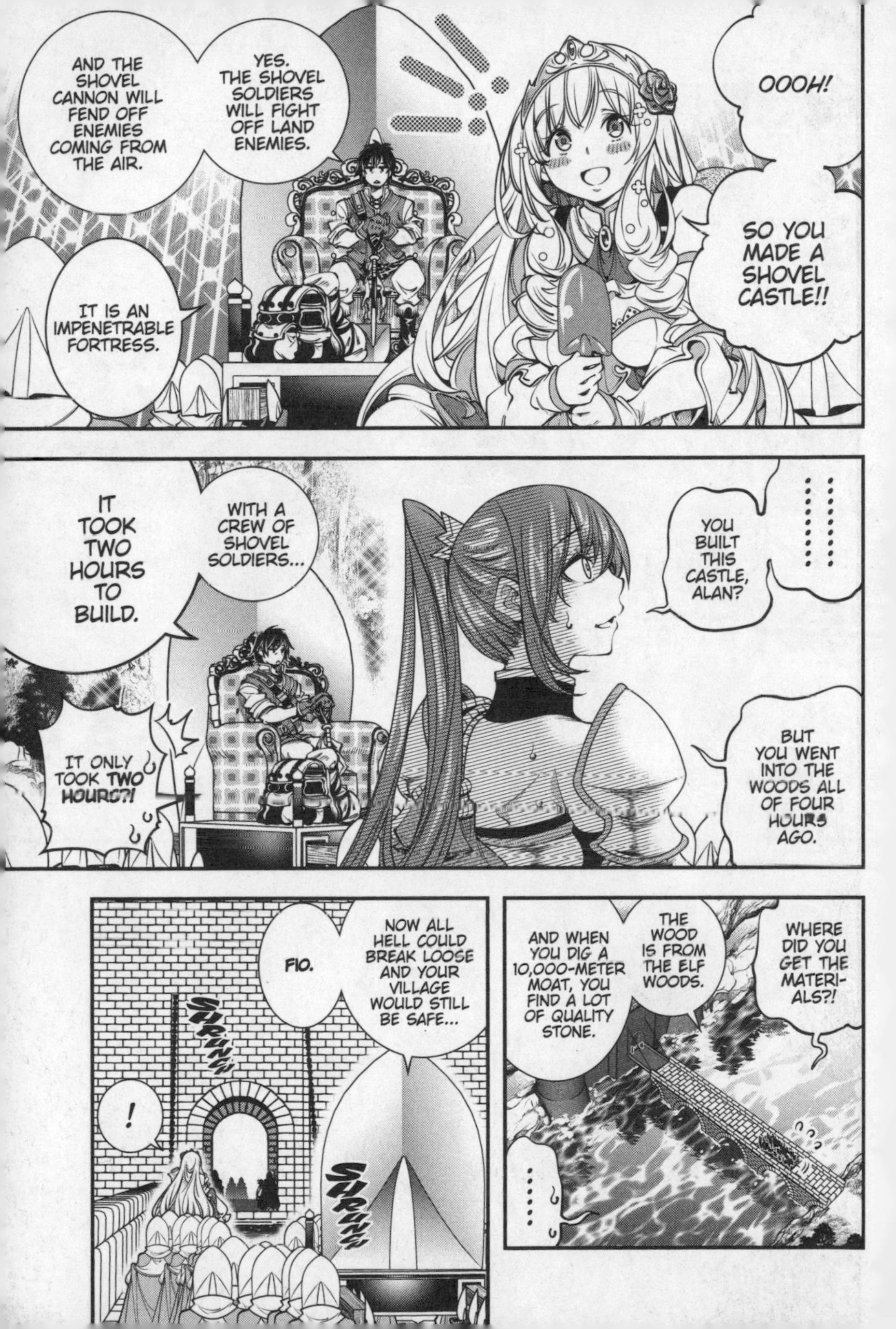
OOOH!
SO YOU MADE A SHOVEL CASTLE!!
YES. THE SHOVEL SOLDIERS WILL FIGHT OFF LAND ENEMIES.
AND THE SHOVEL CANNON WILL FEND OFF ENEMIES COMING FROM THE AIR.
IT IS AN IMPENETRABLE FORTRESS.
......
YOU BUILT THIS CASTLE, ALAN?
BUT YOU WENT INTO THE WOODS ALL OF FOUR HOURS AGO.
WITH A CREW OF SHOVEL SOLDIERS...
IT TOOK TWO HOURS TO BUILD.
IT ONLY TOOK TWO HOURS?!
WHERE DID YOU GET THE MATERI-ALS?!
THE WOOD IS FROM THE ELF WOODS.
AND WHEN YOU DIG A 10,000-METER MOAT, YOU FIND A LOT OF QUALITY STONE.
......
NOW ALL HELL COULD BREAK LOOSE AND YOUR VILLAGE WOULD STILL BE SAFE...
FIO.
!

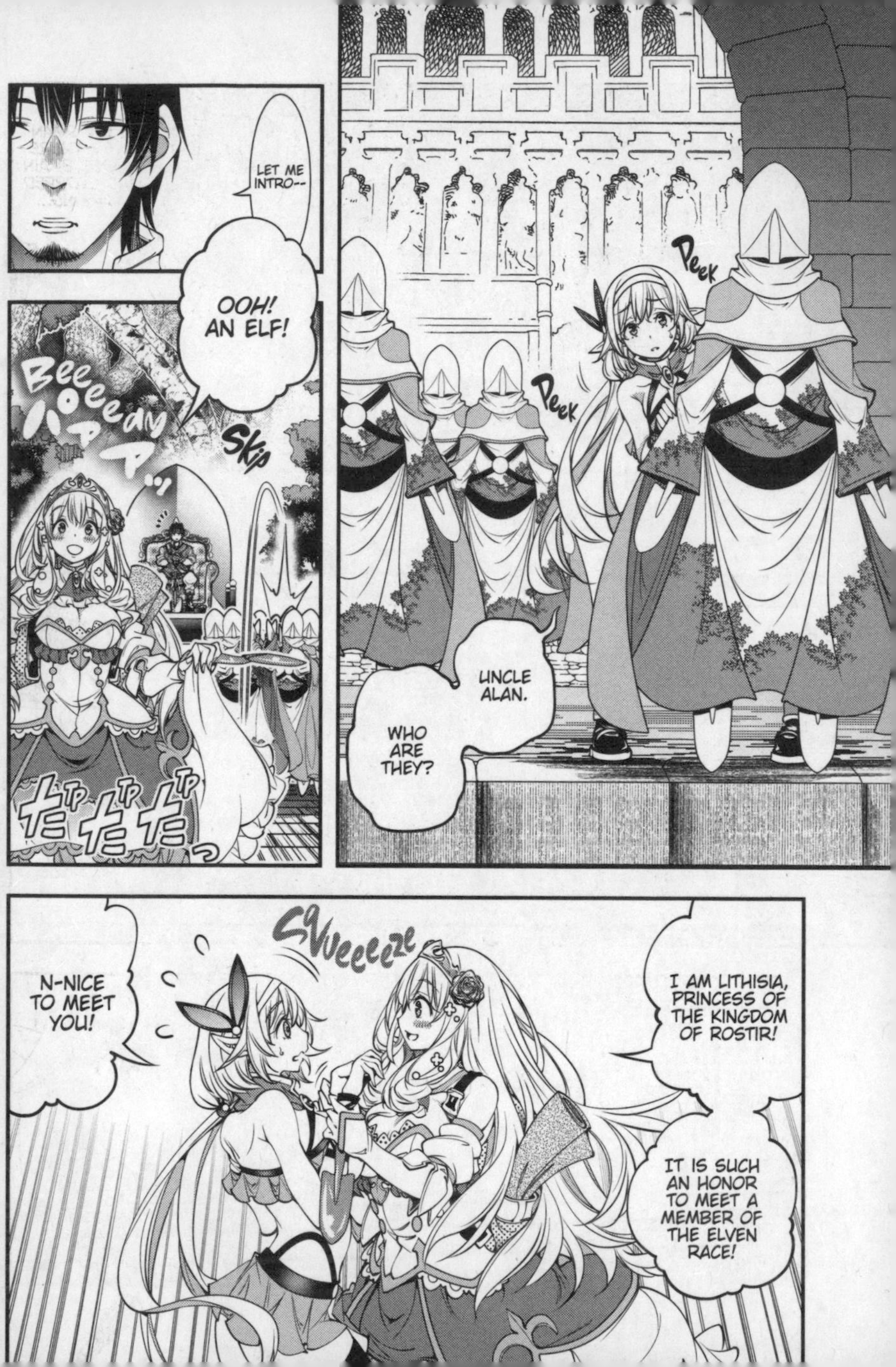
Peek
Peek
UNCLE ALAN.
WHO ARE THEY?
LET ME INTRO--
OOH! AN ELF!
Skip
Tp Tp Tp
I AM LITHISIA, PRINCESS OF THE KINGDOM OF ROSTIR!
IT IS SUCH AN HONOR TO MEET A MEMBER OF THE ELVEN RACE!
Squeeeeze
N-NICE TO MEET YOU!

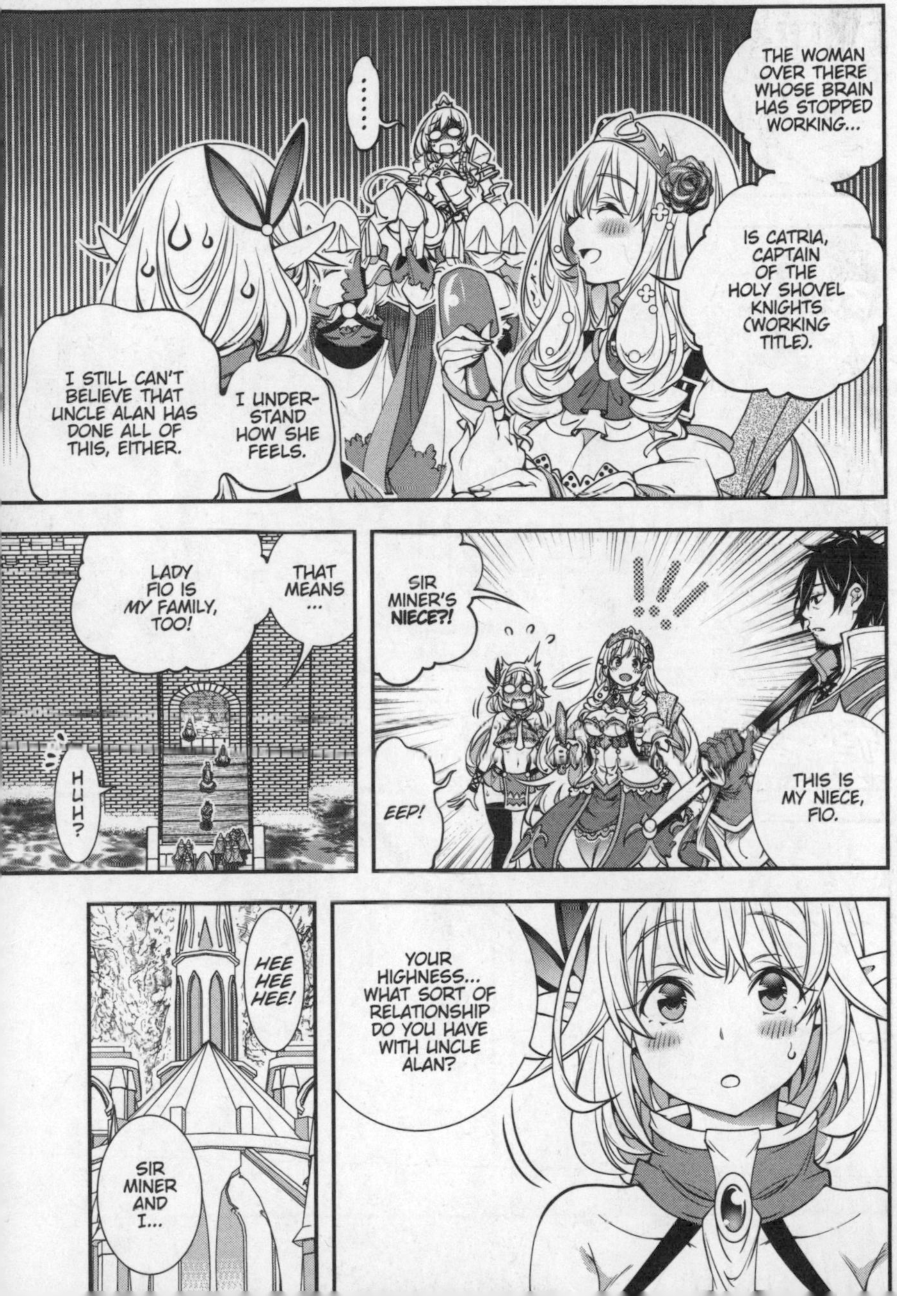
THE WOMAN OVER THERE WHOSE BRAIN HAS STOPPED WORKING...
IS CATRIA, CAPTAIN OF THE HOLY SHOVEL KNIGHTS (WORKING TITLE).
......
I UNDER-STAND HOW SHE FEELS.
I STILL CAN'T BELIEVE THAT UNCLE ALAN HAS DONE ALL OF THIS, EITHER.
THIS IS MY NIECE, FIO.
!!
SIR MINER'S **NIECE?!**
EEP!
THAT MEANS ...
LADY FIO IS *MY* FAMILY, TOO!
HUH?
YOUR HIGHNESS... WHAT SORT OF RELATIONSHIP DO YOU HAVE WITH UNCLE ALAN?
HEE HEE HEE!
SIR MINER AND I...

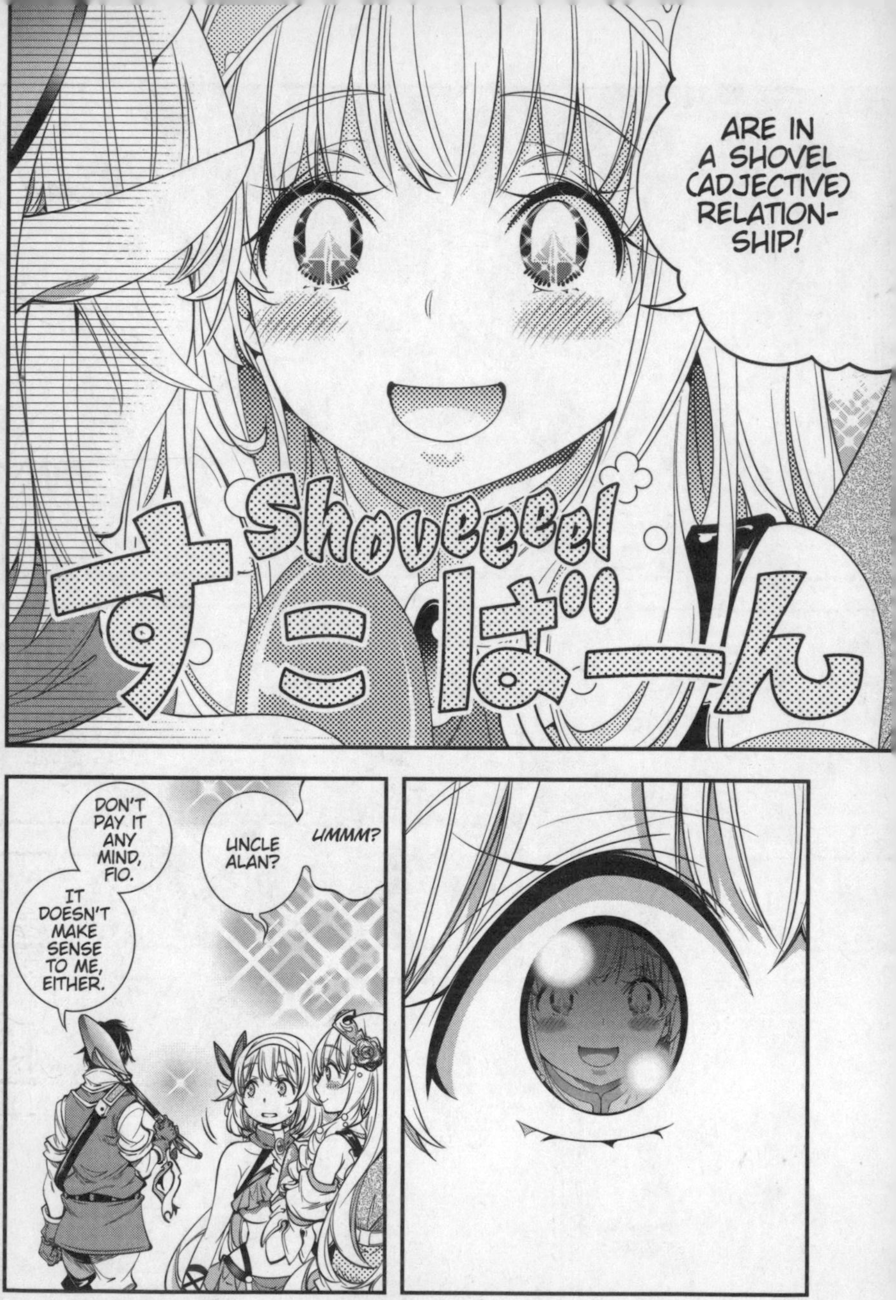
ARE IN A SHOVEL (ADJECTIVE) RELATION-SHIP!
Shoveeeel
すこばーん
UMMM?
UNCLE ALAN?
DON'T PAY IT ANY MIND, FIO.
IT DOESN'T MAKE SENSE TO ME, EITHER.

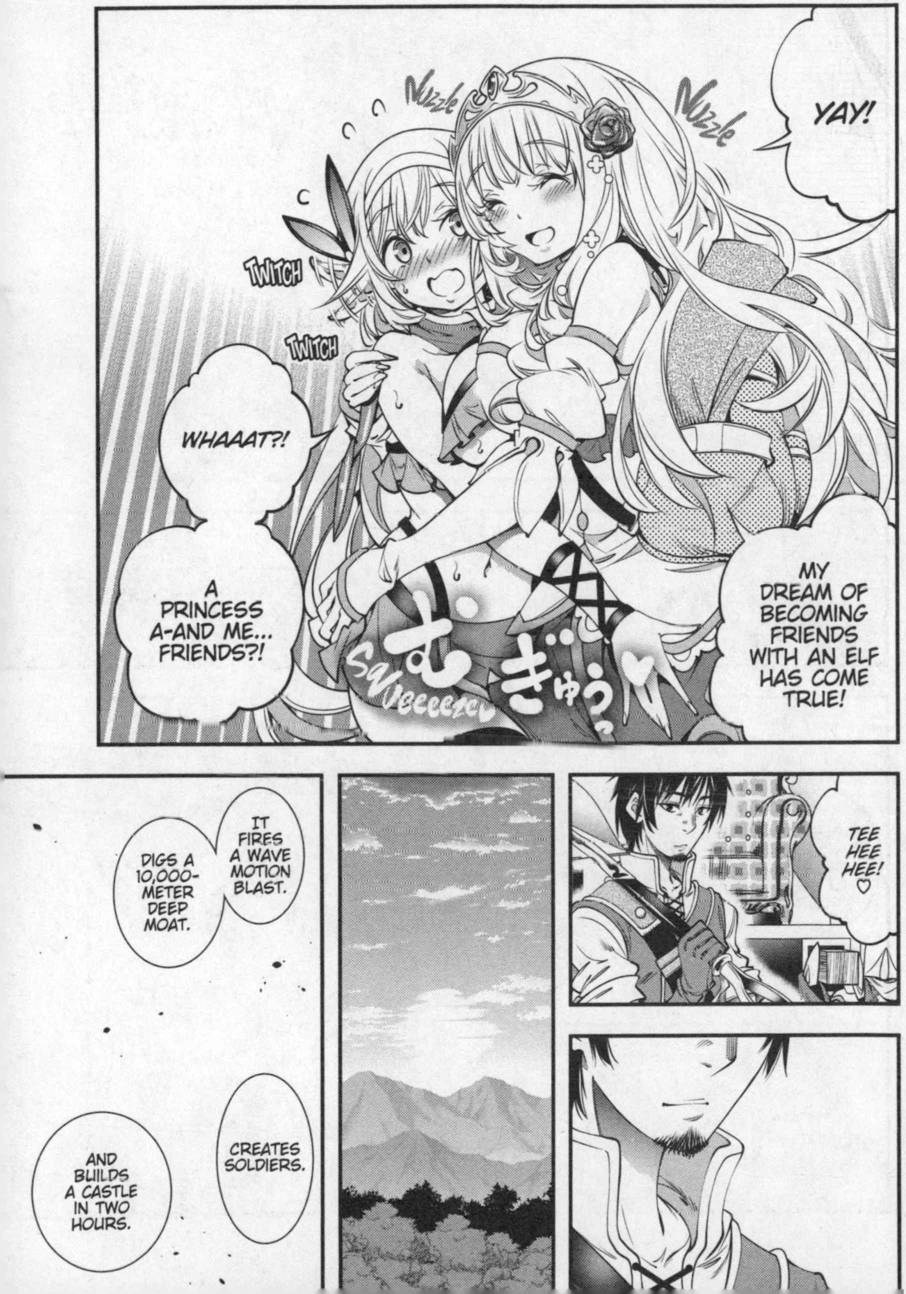
YAY!
NUZZLE
NUZZLE
MY DREAM OF BECOMING FRIENDS WITH AN ELF HAS COME TRUE!
TWITCH
TWITCH
WHAAAT?!
A PRINCESS A-AND ME... FRIENDS?!
むぎゅう
TEE HEE HEE! ♡
IT FIRES A WAVE MOTION BLAST.
DIGS A 10,000-METER DEEP MOAT.
CREATES SOLDIERS.
AND BUILDS A CASTLE IN TWO HOURS.

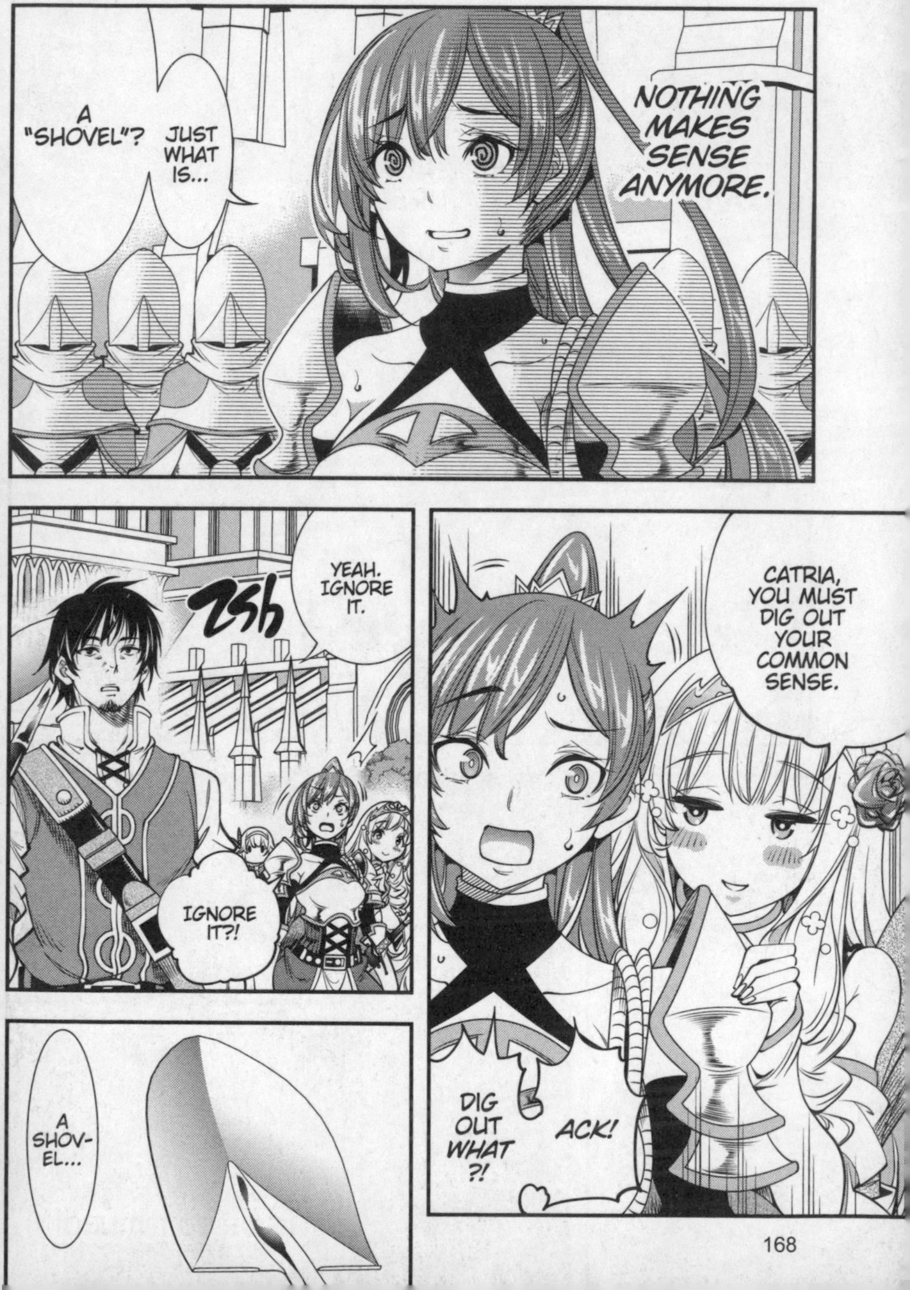
NOTHING MAKES SENSE ANYMORE.
JUST WHAT IS...
A "SHOVEL"?
CATRIA, YOU MUST DIG OUT YOUR COMMON SENSE.
ACK!
DIG OUT WHAT?!
YEAH. IGNORE IT.
IGNORE IT?!
A SHOVEL...

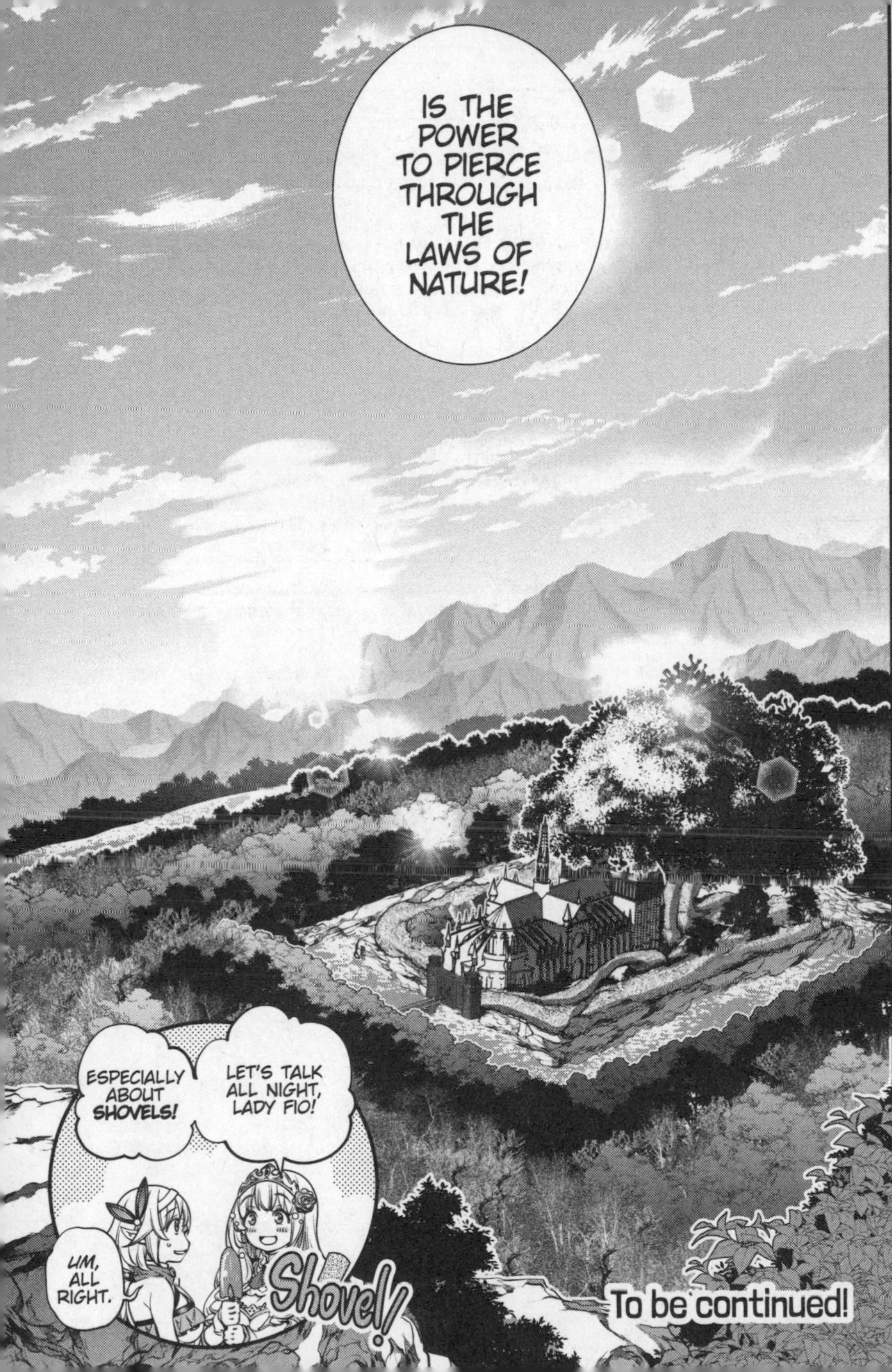
IS THE POWER TO PIERCE THROUGH THE LAWS OF NATURE!
LET'S TALK ALL NIGHT, LADY FIO!
ESPECIALLY ABOUT SHOVELS!
Shovel!
UM, ALL RIGHT.
To be continued!

In Regards to the Release of *The Invincible Shovel* manga, Volume 1:

Hello! I'm Yasohachi Tsuchise, the author of the novel this manga was based on. The bandit boss was so cute (non sequitur opinion)! In the novel's afterword, I explained what I was thinking when I wrote the novel, so I'm going to follow in that vein and explain what I was thinking when I had it made into a manga.

But actually, I have doubts as to whether or not little old me actually accomplished anything. I'm sure those of you who have read this volume are already aware of Fukuhara-sensei's epic artistic skills, and epic storyboarding skills, and epic character skills! The shovelanga power is too shoveltastic!

Even just looking at the characters, the boss is adorable, Alan is awesome, Lithisia is cutesy-crazy, Fio is twitchy-twitchy-fio-fio, Catria is so damn sho-lovable. I'm especially eager to see the boss make another appearance. What do you mean he's not in the novel? So if I put him in the next novel you'll have no choice but to draw him? *Heh heh heh.* In that case, I'll put him in the next... Oops, sorry, I've gotten off track.

Back to our original topic, if the novel's author is able to contribute anything other than the original text, I would say it's this: a heart that believes a shovel can be classic fantasy.

Personally, as a prerequisite to this belief, I think one needs to maintain a logic that is difficult for humankind to comprehend, a deep-rooted ideology that proactively affirms contradictions. And so I put this ideology into practice as much as possible while sharing said ideology. You may also call it proselytizing.

Specifically, I obsessed to death over things that most people wouldn't care about. I discussed the souls of the characters in shovelistic terms, and I proclaimed my shovelistic ideology to Fukuhara-sensei while sending him twenty-year-old adult manga for reference. Wait, what is this guy even doing? Thinking back on it, I should get a sanity check. All I can do is apologize to Fukuhara-sensei. I am deeply, truly sorry.

So, if you were to ask me what all of this insanity has accomplished, I can answer with certainty that I have absolutely no doubt that I was a nuisance. I can't say that I helped at all. Nevertheless, regardless of any hand I may or may not have had in it, this first volume of manga has been published and has become the greatest shovel manga in the universe. It's funny, it's tear-jerking, it's naughty, and it's entertaining. This manga can shoot for the stars! As a fan, I look forward to every new installment. I hope you'll stick with it.

And one last thing...

I again want to congratulate Fukuhara-sensei on the release of Volume 1, and express my thanks for drawing the best manga. And to all you readers, I hope that you will continue to enjoy shovels, and to shovel (verb) along with Alan and the shovely girls.

This has been Yasohachi Tsuchise! Shovel (greeting)!

Yasohachi Tsuchise

Novel by: **Yasohachi Tsuchise**   Character Designs by: **Hagure Yuuki**

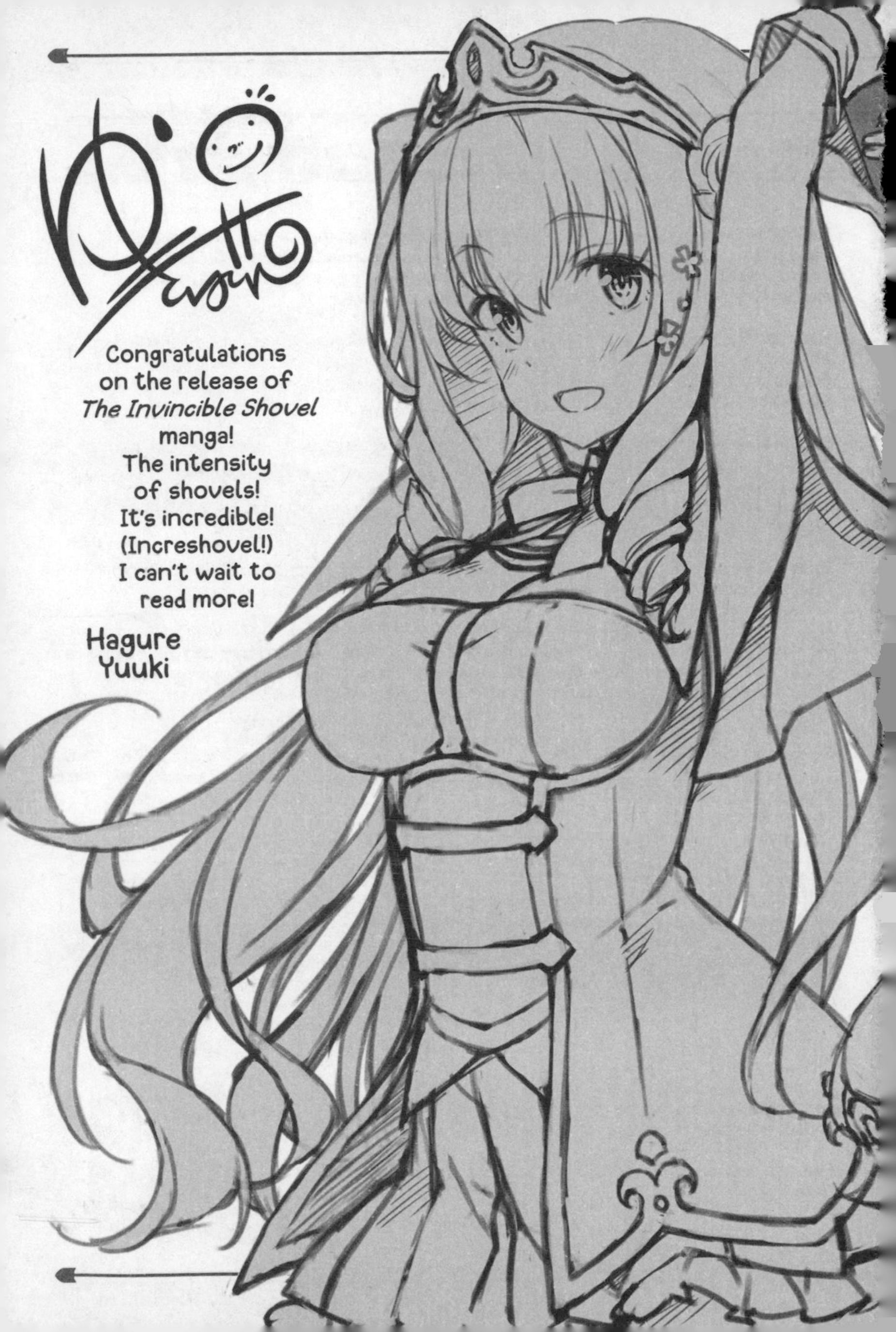
Congratulations on the release of *The Invincible Shovel* manga!
The intensity of shovels!
It's incredible!
(Increshovel!)
I can't wait to read more!
Hagure Yuuki

SEVEN SEAS ENTERTAINMENT PRESENTS

THE INVINCIBLE SHOVEL

Vol. 1

art by **RENJI FUKUHARA** / story by **YASOHACHI TSUCHISE** / character design by **HAGURE YUUKI**

TRANSLATION
Alethea & Athena Nibley

ADAPTATION
Jamal Joseph Jr.

LETTERING
Arbash M.

COVER DESIGN
Nicky Lim

EDITOR
Peter Adrian Behravesh
Shannon Fay

PREPRESS TECHNICIAN
annon Rasmussen-Silverstein

PRODUCTION ASSOCIATE
Christa Miesner

PRODUCTION MANAGER
Lissa Pattillo

MANAGING EDITOR
Julie Davis

ASSOCIATE PUBLISHER
Adam Arnold

PUBLISHER
Jason DeAngelis

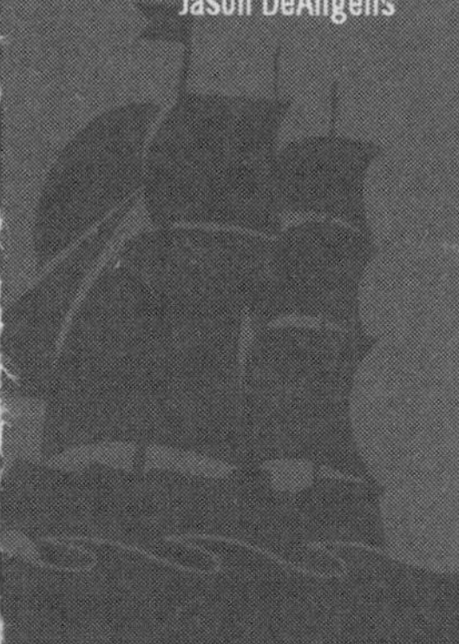

SCOOP MUSO 「SCOOP HADOHO!」
(｀・ω・´)♂〓〓〓〓★(ﾟДﾟ ;;;).:∴DOGOoo Vol.1

First published in Japan in 2020 by KADOKAWA CORPORATION, Tokyo.
English translation rights arranged with KADOKAWA CORPORATION, Tokyo.

Seven Seas press and purchase enquiries can be sent to Marketing Manager Lianne Sentar at press@gomanga.com. Information regarding the distribution and purchase of digital editions is available from Digital Manager CK Russell at digital@gomanga.com.

ISBN: 978-1-64827-428-2
Printed in Canada
First Printing: July 2021
10 9 8 7 6 5 4 3 2 1

READING DIRECTIONS

This book reads from ***right to left***, Japanese style. If this is your first time reading manga, you start reading from the top right panel on each page and take it from there. If you get lost, just follow the numbered diagram here. It may seem backwards at first, but you'll get the hang of it! Have fun!!

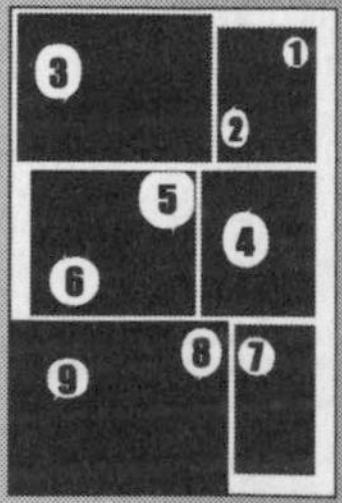

1
2
3
4
5
6
7
8
9

Follow us online: www.SevenSeasEntertainment.com